GOTHAM CENTRAL

BOOK THREE: ON THE FREAK BEA

THE PENGU
POISON IVY

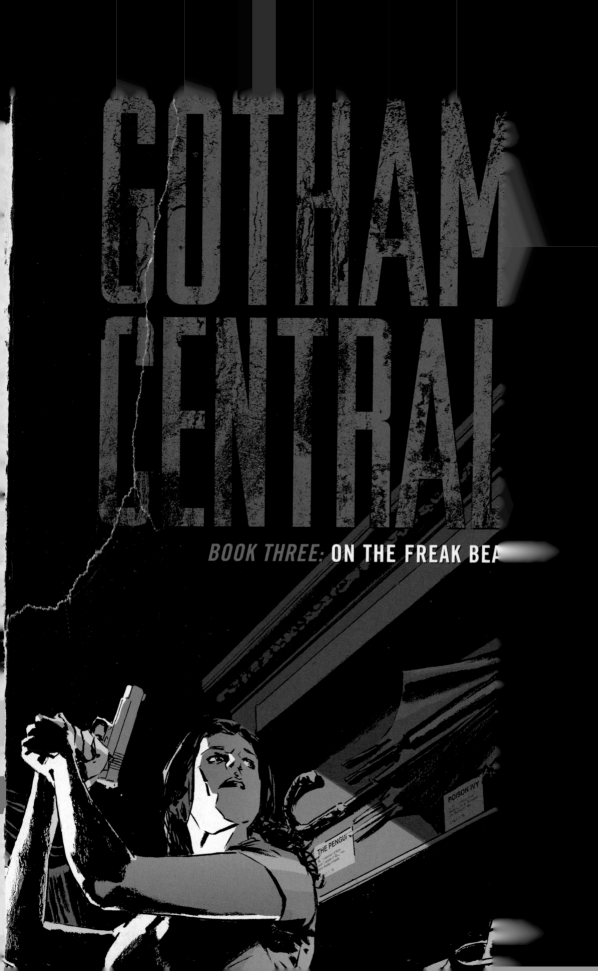

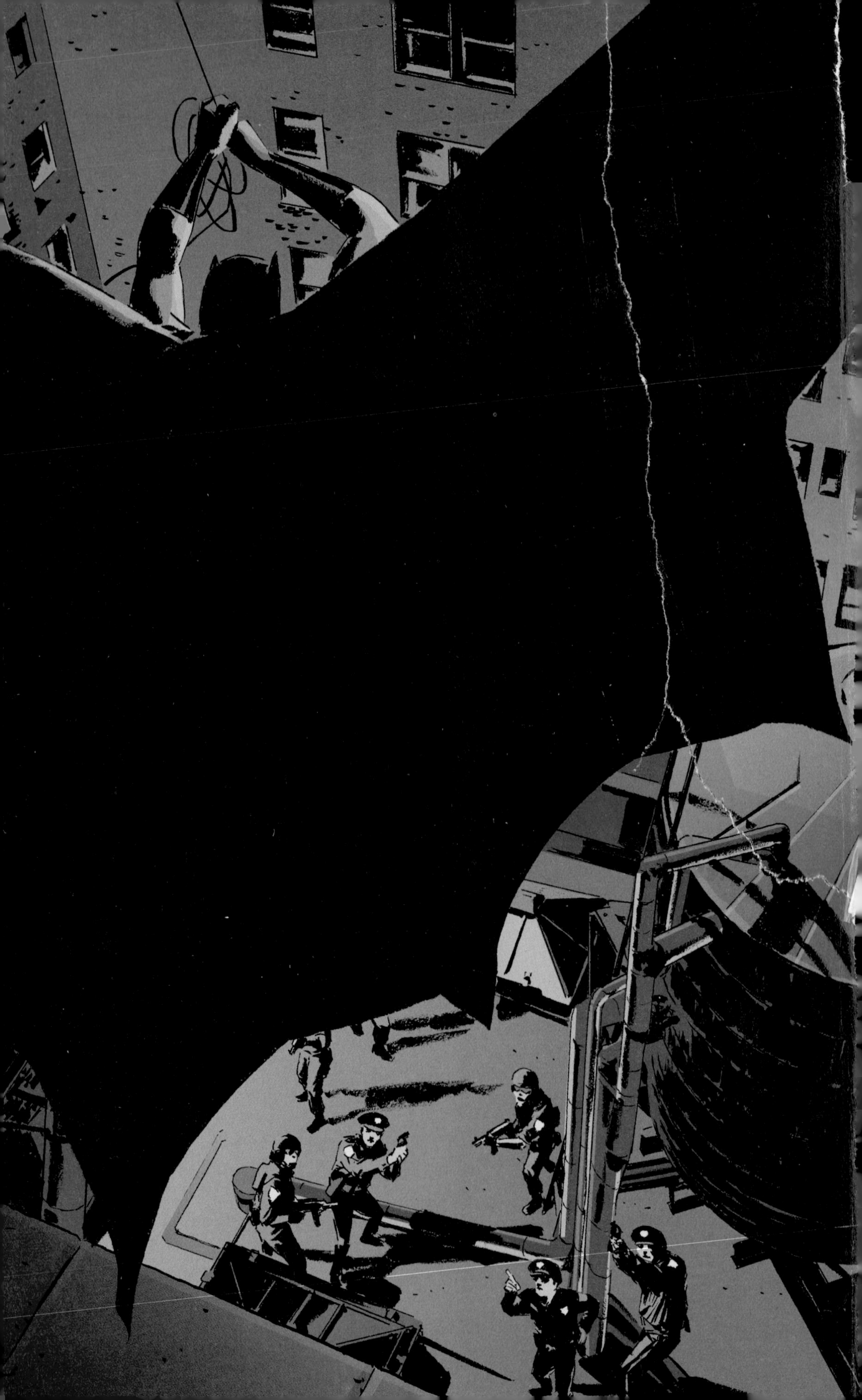

GOTHAM CENTRAL

BOOK THREE: **ON THE FREAK BEAT**

Written by
GREG RUCKA & ED BRUBAKER

Pencils by
MICHAEL LARK
STEFANO GAUDIANO
JASON ALEXANDER

Inks by
STEFANO GAUDIANO
JASON ALEXANDER
KANO
GARY AMARO

Batman created
*by **BOB KANE***

Colors by
LEE LOUGHRIDGE

Letters by
CLEM ROBINS

Covers by
MICHAEL LARK (#23-30)
and

FIRST SHIFT

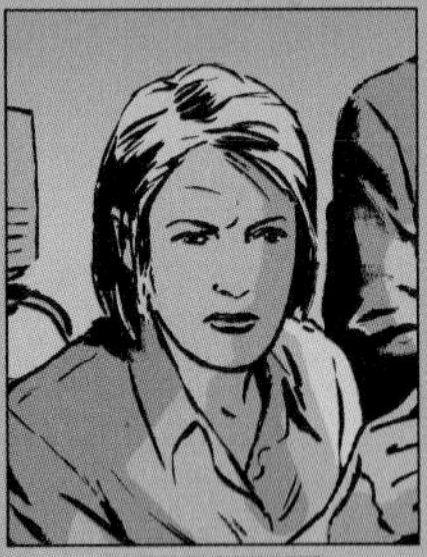
DETECTIVE JOELY BARTLETT
Partner of Vincent Del Arrazio.

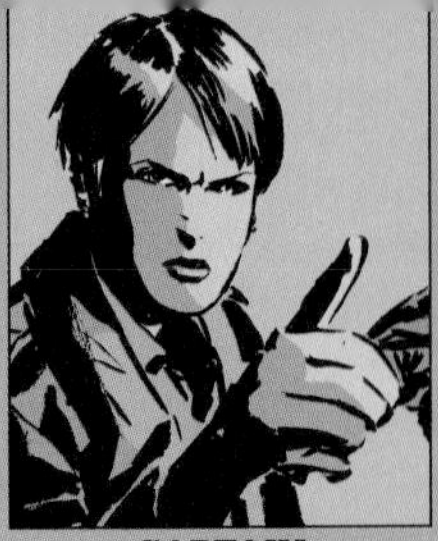
CAPTAIN MAGGIE SAWYER
First shift commander; formerly head of Metropolis Special Crimes Unit.

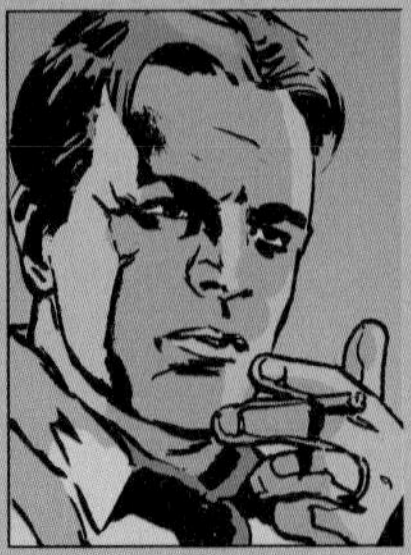
SGT. VINCENT DEL ARRAZIO
First shift second-in-command; partner of Joely Bartlett.

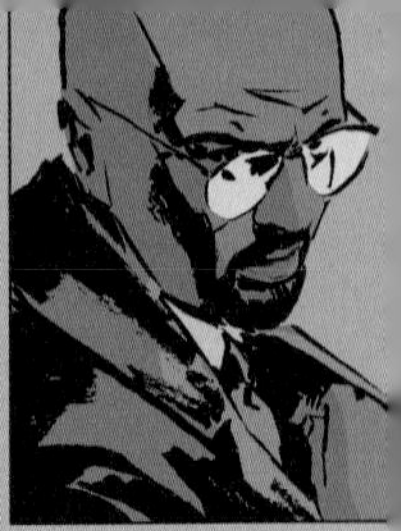
DETECTIVE CRISPUS ALLEN
Partner of Renee Montoya.

GOTHAM CITY POLICE DEPARTMENT MAJOR CRIMES UNIT

SECOND SHIFT

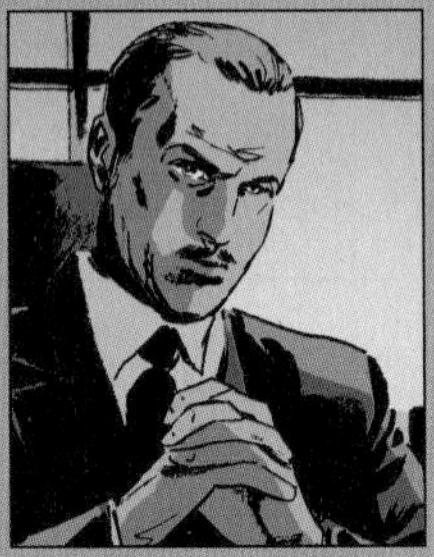
LT. DAVID CORNWELL
Second shift commander.

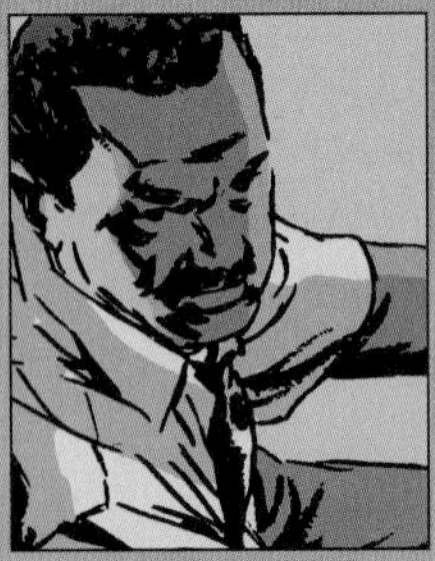
SGT. JACKSON "SARGE" DAVIES
Second shift co-second-in-command; partner of Crowe.

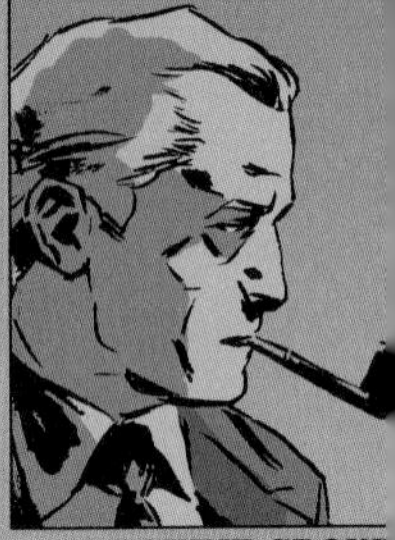
DETECTIVE CROWE
Partner of Sarge Davies.

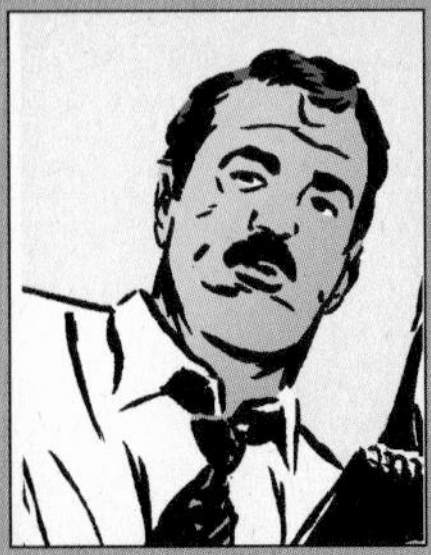
DETECTIVE JOSH AZEVEDA
Partner of Trey Hartley.

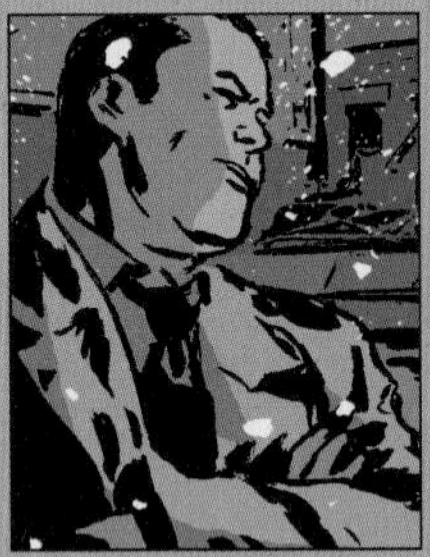
DETECTIVE NATE PATTON
Partner of Romy Chandler.

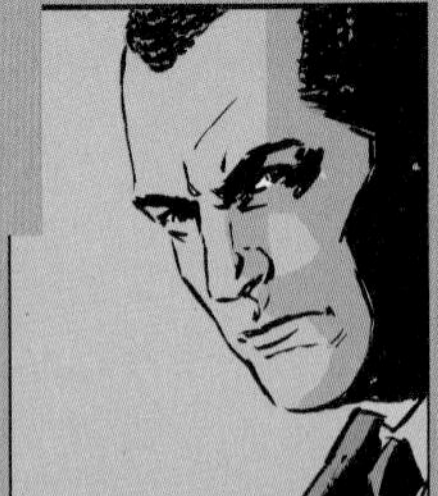
LT. RON PROBSON
Second shift co-second-in-command.

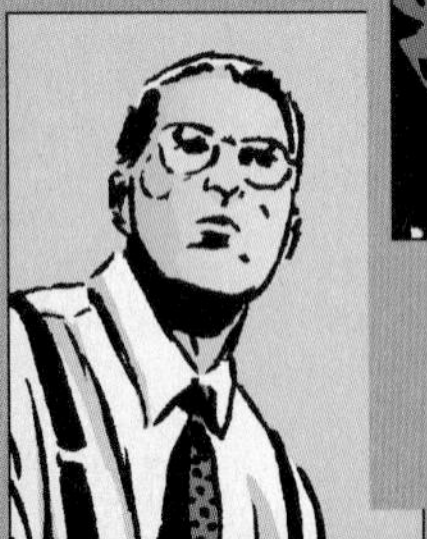
DETECTIVE TREY HARTLEY
Partner of Josh Azeveda.

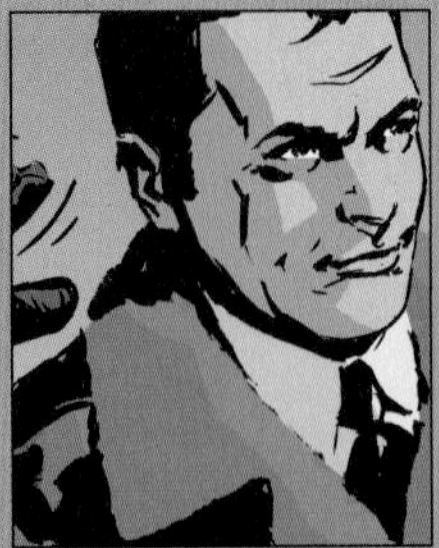
DETECTIVE MARCUS DRIVER
Last MCU officer to be selected by former Commissioner James W. Gordon.

DETECTIVE ERIC COHEN
Partner of Andi Kasinsky.

DETECTIVE ANDI KASINSKY
Partner of Eric Cohen.

DETECTIVE 2ND GRADE RENEE MONTOYA
Partner of Crispus Allen.

DETECTIVE TOMMY BURKE
Partner of Dagmar Procjnow.

DETECTIVE JOSEPHINE "JOSIE MAC" MACDONALD
Has the distinction of being the first MCU officer selected after Jim Gordon's retirement.

DETECTIVE DAGMAR PROCJNOW
Partner of Tommy Burke.

DETECTIVE ROMY CHANDLER
Partner of Nate Patton.

NORA FIELDS
City coroner.

STACY
Receptionist; only person permitted to operate the Bat-Signal.

POLICE SUPPORT

COMMISSIONER MICHAEL AKINS
Former commissioner for Gateway City, replaced James W. Gordon.

JIM CORRIGAN
GCPD crime scene investigator.

JAMES W. GORDON
Former Gotham City police commissioner, and 20-year veteran of the force. Currently teaches criminology at Gotham University.

DAN DIDIO SVP-EXECUTIVE EDITOR
MATT IDELSON EDITOR-ORIGINAL SERIES
NACHIE CASTRO ASSISTANT EDITOR-ORIGINAL SERIES
BOB HARRAS GROUP EDITOR-COLLECTED EDITIONS
ANTON KAWASAKI EDITOR
ROBBIN BROSTERMAN DESIGN DIRECTOR-BOOKS

DC COMICS
DIANE NELSON PRESIDENT
DAN DIDIO AND JIM LEE CO-PUBLISHERS
GEOFF JOHNS CHIEF CREATIVE OFFICER
PATRICK CALDON EVP-FINANCE AND ADMINISTRATION
JOHN ROOD EVP-SALES, MARKETING AND BUSINESS DEVELOPMENT
AMY GENKINS SVP-BUSINESS AND LEGAL AFFAIRS
STEVE ROTTERDAM SVP-SALES AND MARKETING
JOHN CUNNINGHAM VP-MARKETING
TERRI CUNNINGHAM VP-MANAGING EDITOR
ALISON GILL VP-MANUFACTURING
DAVID HYDE VP-PUBLICITY
SUE POHJA VP-BOOK TRADE SALES
ALYSSE SOLL VP-ADVERTISING AND CUSTOM PUBLISHING
BOB WAYNE VP-SALES
MARK CHIARELLO ART DIRECTOR

Cover by Cliff Chiang. Publication design by Brainchild Studios/NYC.

GOTHAM CENTRAL BOOK THREE: ON THE FREAK BEAT
Published by DC Comics. Cover and compilation copyright © 2010 DC Comics.
All Rights Reserved. Originally published in single magazine form in GOTHAM
CENTRAL 23-31. Copyright © 2004, 2005 DC Comics. All Rights Reserved. All
characters, their distinctive likenesses and related elements featured in this
publication are trademarks of DC Comics. The stories, characters and incidents
featured in this publication are entirely fictional. DC Comics does not read or
accept unsolicited submissions of ideas, stories or artwork.

DC Comics, 1700 Broadway, New York, NY 10019
A Warner Bros. Entertainment Company
Printed by RR Donnelley, Roanoke, VA, USA 5/12/10.
HC ISBN: 978-1-4012-2754-8
SC ISBN: 978-1-4012-2765-4

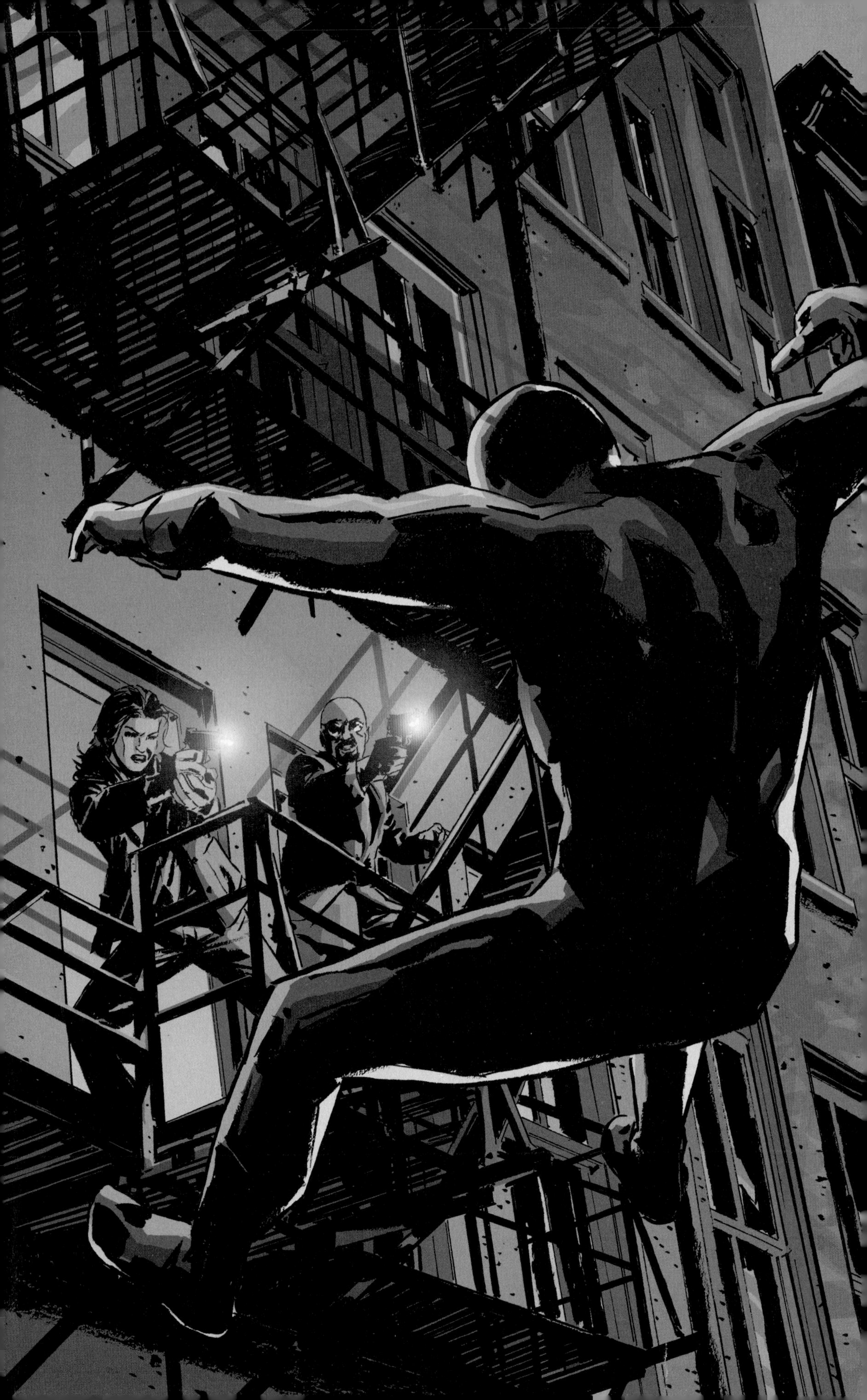

CORRIGAN

Written by
GREG RUCKA

Art by
MICHAEL LARK & STEFANO GAUDIANO

Colors by
LEE LOUGHRIDGE

Letters by
CLEM ROBINS

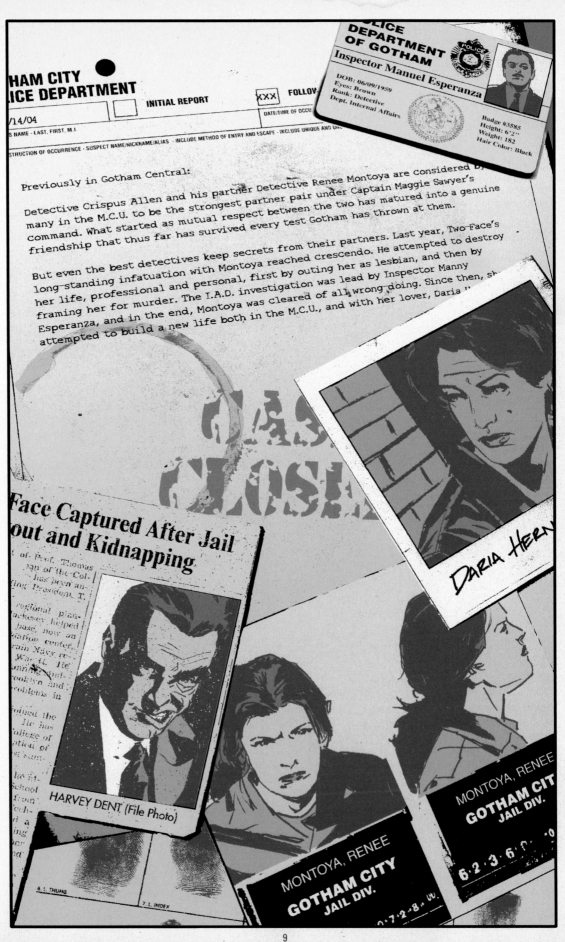

GOTHAM CITY
POLICE DEPARTMENT

INITIAL REPORT   XXX   FOLLOW-

/14/04   DATE/TIME OF OCCU

S NAME - LAST, FIRST, M.I.

STRUCTION OF OCCURRENCE - SUSPECT NAME/NICKNAME/ALIAS - INCLUDE METHOD OF ENTRY AND ESCAPE - INCLUDE UNIQUE AND UN

POLICE
DEPARTMENT
OF GOTHAM

Inspector Manuel Esperanza

DOB: 06/09/1959
Eyes: Brown
Rank: Detective
Dept. Internal Affairs

Badge #3585
Height: 6'2"
Weight: 182
Hair Color: Black

Previously in Gotham Central:

Detective Crispus Allen and his partner Detective Renee Montoya are considered by many in the M.C.U. to be the strongest partner pair under Captain Maggie Sawyer's command. What started as mutual respect between the two has matured into a genuine friendship that thus far has survived every test Gotham has thrown at them.

But even the best detectives keep secrets from their partners. Last year, Two-Face's long-standing infatuation with Montoya reached crescendo. He attempted to destroy her life, professional and personal, first by outing her as lesbian, and then by framing her for murder. The I.A.D. investigation was lead by Inspector Manny Esperanza, and in the end, Montoya was cleared of all wrong doing. Since then, sh attempted to build a new life both in the M.C.U., and with her lover, Daria H

CAS
CLOSE

DARIA HERN

Face Captured After Jail
out and Kidnapping

HARVEY DENT (File Photo)

MONTOYA, RENEE
GOTHAM CITY
JAIL DIV.

MONTOYA, RENEE
GOTHAM CIT
JAIL DIV.

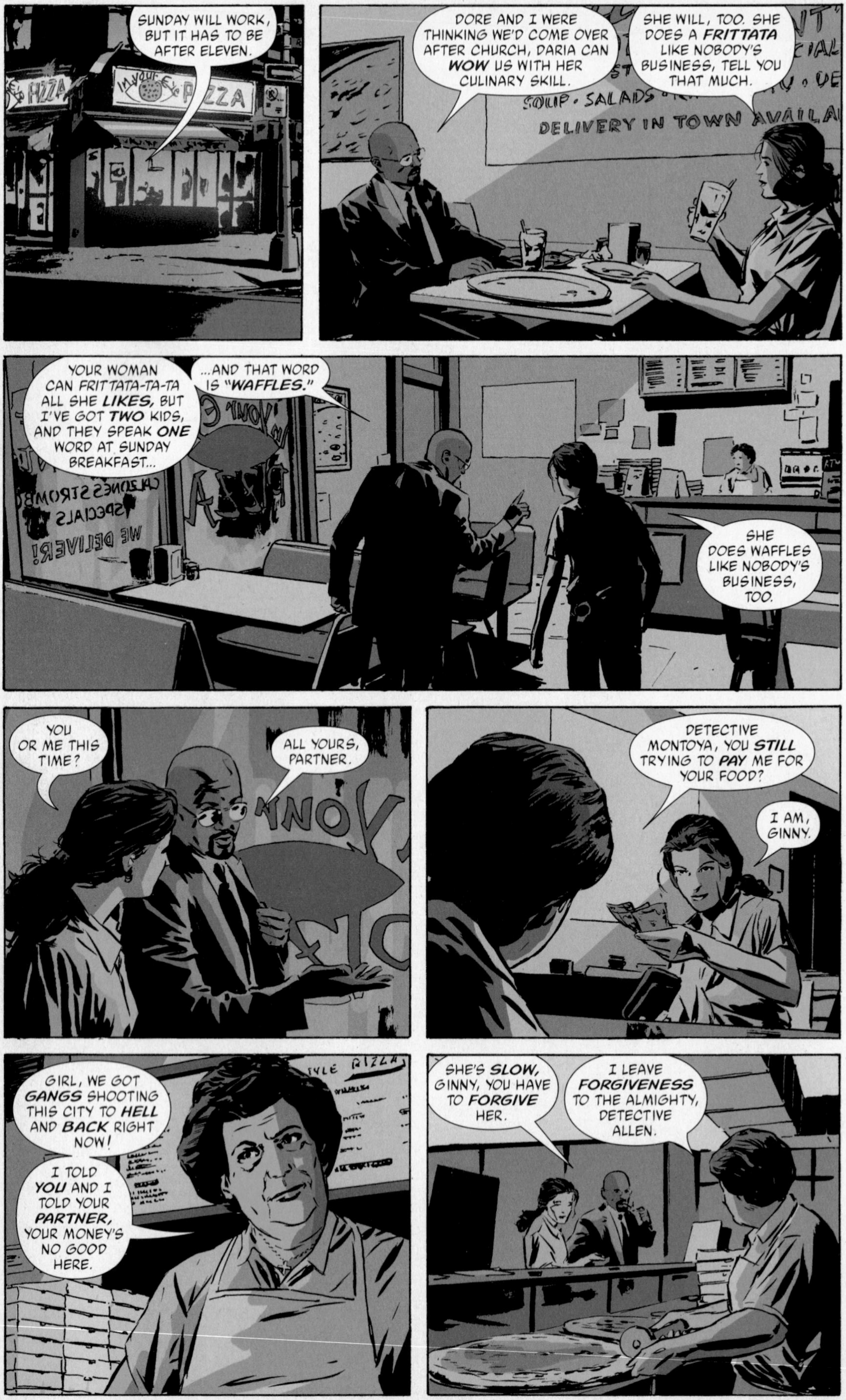
SUNDAY WILL WORK, BUT IT HAS TO BE AFTER ELEVEN.
DORE AND I WERE THINKING WE'D COME OVER AFTER CHURCH, DARIA CAN WOW US WITH HER CULINARY SKILL.
SHE WILL, TOO. SHE DOES A FRITTATA LIKE NOBODY'S BUSINESS, TELL YOU THAT MUCH.
YOUR WOMAN CAN FRITTATA-TA-TA ALL SHE LIKES, BUT I'VE GOT TWO KIDS, AND THEY SPEAK ONE WORD AT SUNDAY BREAKFAST...
...AND THAT WORD IS "WAFFLES."
SHE DOES WAFFLES LIKE NOBODY'S BUSINESS, TOO.
YOU OR ME THIS TIME?
ALL YOURS, PARTNER.
DETECTIVE MONTOYA, YOU STILL TRYING TO PAY ME FOR YOUR FOOD?
I AM, GINNY.
GIRL, WE GOT GANGS SHOOTING THIS CITY TO HELL AND BACK RIGHT NOW!
I TOLD YOU AND I TOLD YOUR PARTNER, YOUR MONEY'S NO GOOD HERE.
SHE'S SLOW, GINNY, YOU HAVE TO FORGIVE HER.
I LEAVE FORGIVENESS TO THE ALMIGHTY, DETECTIVE ALLEN.

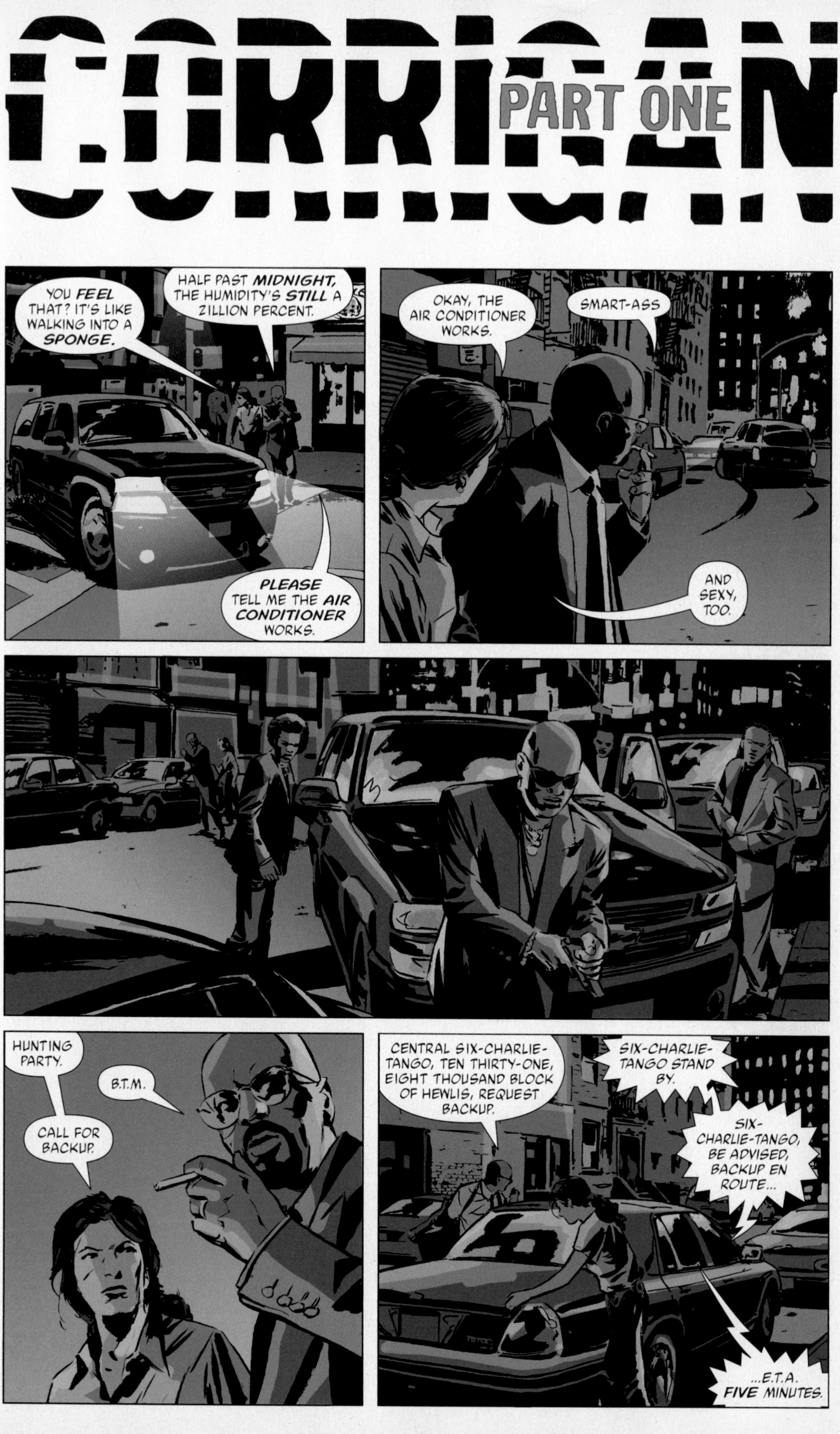
CORRIGAN
PART ONE
YOU FEEL THAT? IT'S LIKE WALKING INTO A SPONGE.
HALF PAST MIDNIGHT, THE HUMIDITY'S STILL A ZILLION PERCENT.
PLEASE TELL ME THE AIR CONDITIONER WORKS.
OKAY, THE AIR CONDITIONER WORKS.
SMART-ASS
AND SEXY, TOO.
HUNTING PARTY.
B.T.M.
CALL FOR BACKUP.
CENTRAL SIX-CHARLIE-TANGO, TEN THIRTY-ONE, EIGHT THOUSAND BLOCK OF HEWLIS, REQUEST BACKUP.
SIX-CHARLIE-TANGO STAND BY.
SIX-CHARLIE-TANGO, BE ADVISED, BACKUP EN ROUTE...
...E.T.A. FIVE MINUTES.

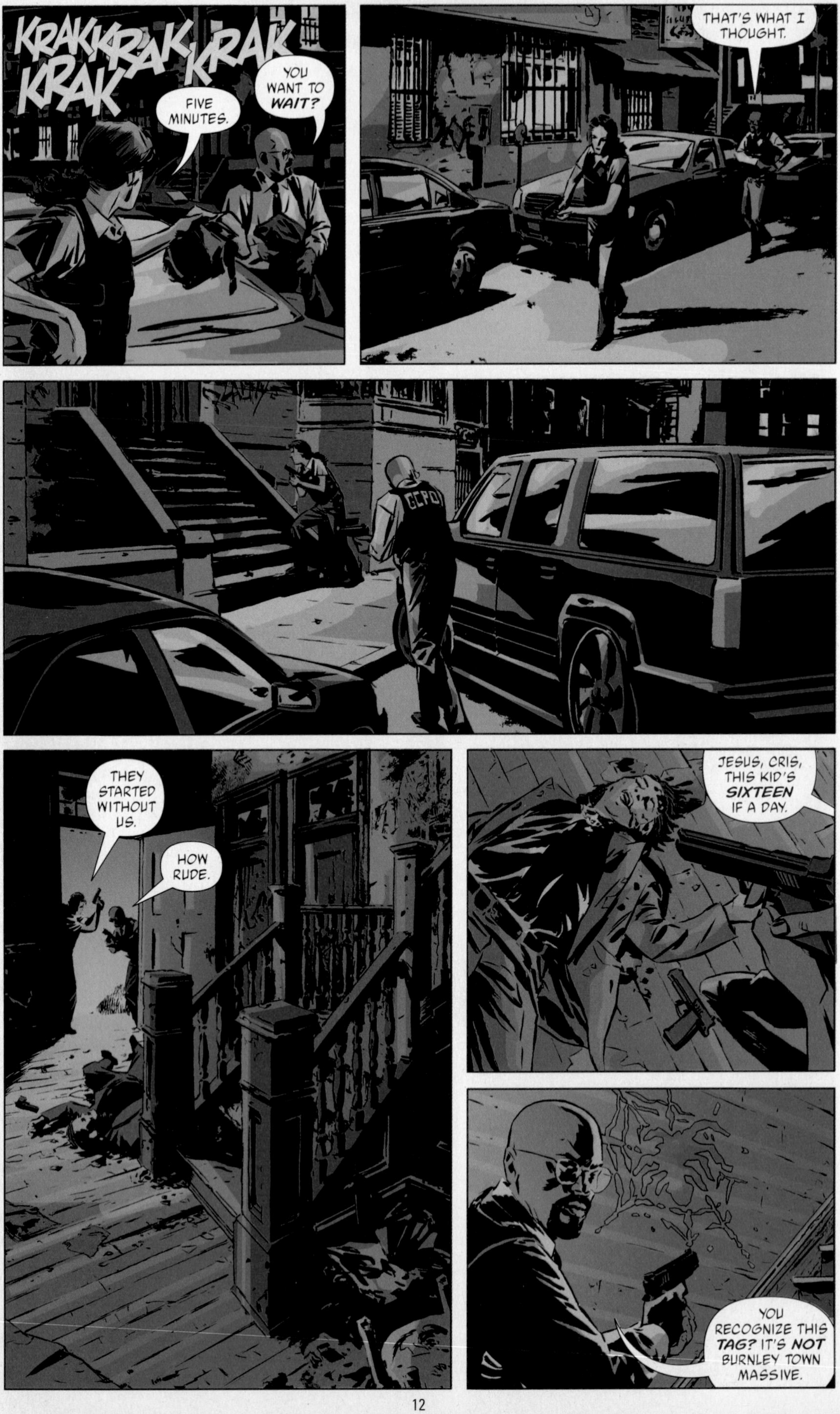
KRAKKRAKKRAK KRAK KRAK
YOU WANT TO WAIT?
FIVE MINUTES.
THAT'S WHAT I THOUGHT.
THEY STARTED WITHOUT US.
HOW RUDE.
JESUS, CRIS, THIS KID'S SIXTEEN IF A DAY.
YOU RECOGNIZE THIS TAG? IT'S NOT BURNLEY TOWN MASSIVE.

KRAK KRAK
KRAK KRAK

CHAK CHAK CHAK
CHAK CHAK

HNNN

MUH-MUH-
FUHNNNN

MAN, CAN'T *SEE* HIM!

KEEP LOOKING! HE AROUND HERE SOMEWHERE!

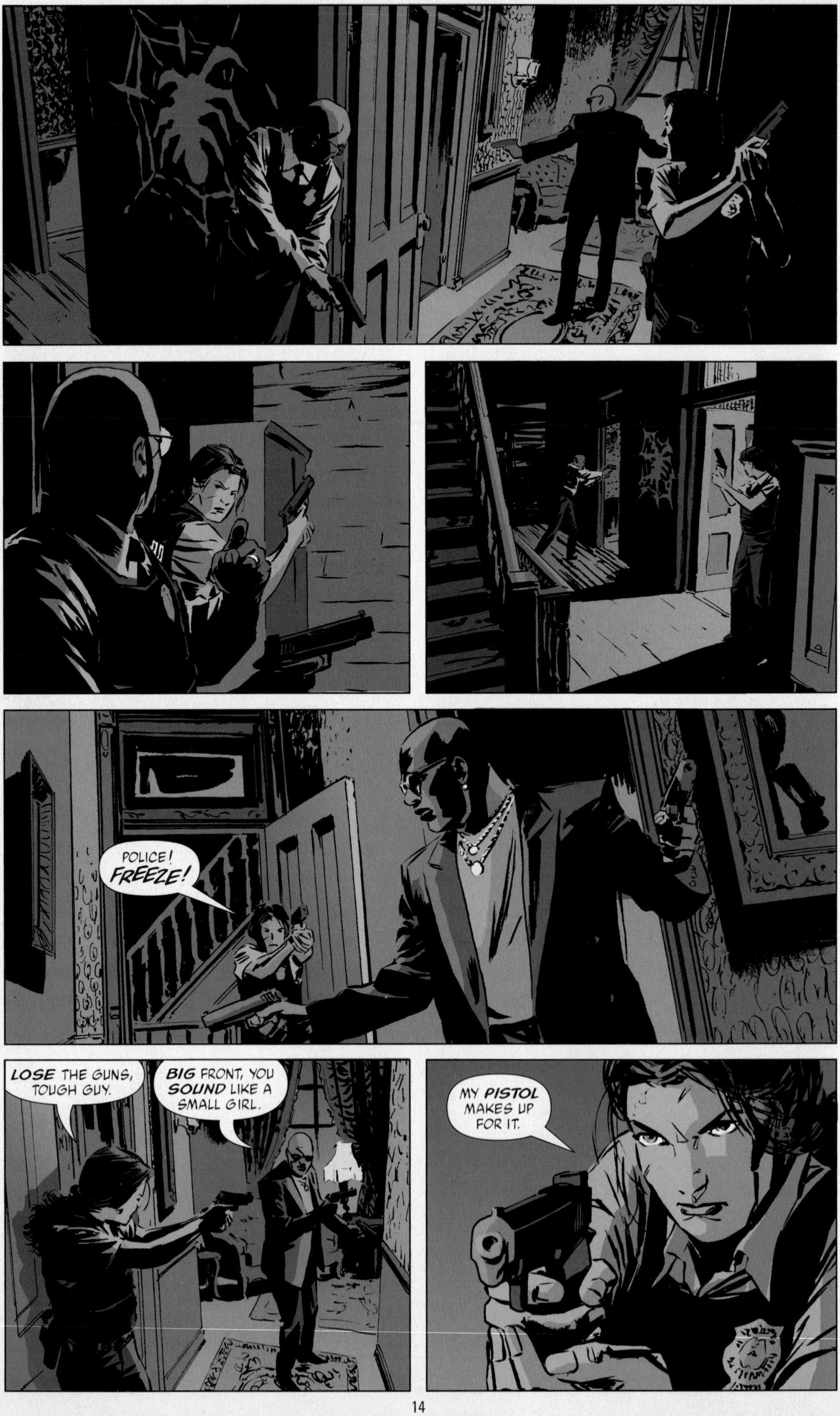
POLICE! FREEZE!
LOSE THE GUNS, TOUGH GUY.
BIG FRONT, YOU SOUND LIKE A SMALL GIRL.
MY PISTOL MAKES UP FOR IT.

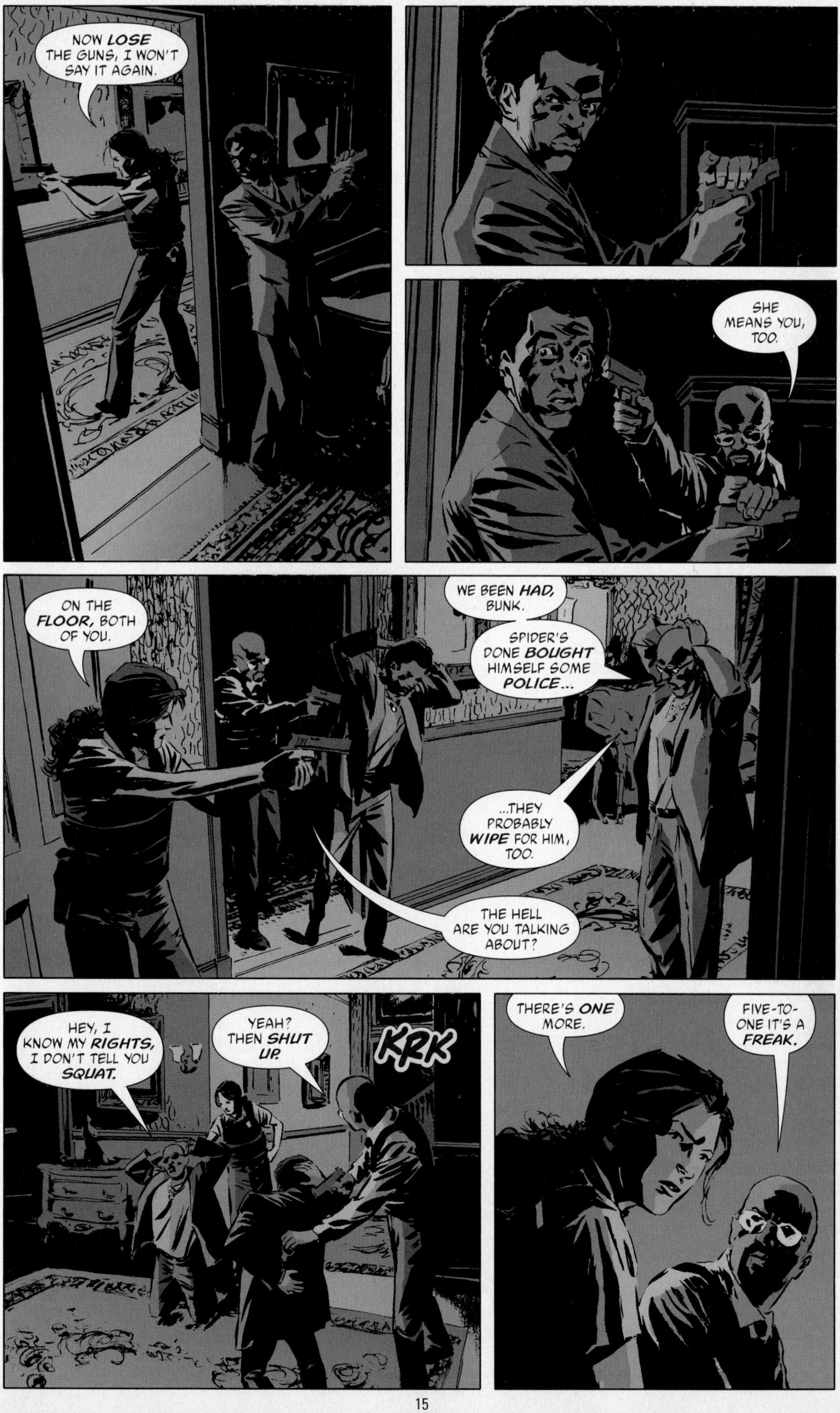
NOW LOSE THE GUNS, I WON'T SAY IT AGAIN.
SHE MEANS YOU, TOO.
ON THE FLOOR, BOTH OF YOU.
WE BEEN HAD, BUNK.
SPIDER'S DONE BOUGHT HIMSELF SOME POLICE...
...THEY PROBABLY WIPE FOR HIM, TOO.
THE HELL ARE YOU TALKING ABOUT?
HEY, I KNOW MY RIGHTS, I DON'T TELL YOU SQUAT.
YEAH? THEN SHUT UP.
KRK
THERE'S ONE MORE.
FIVE-TO-ONE IT'S A FREAK.

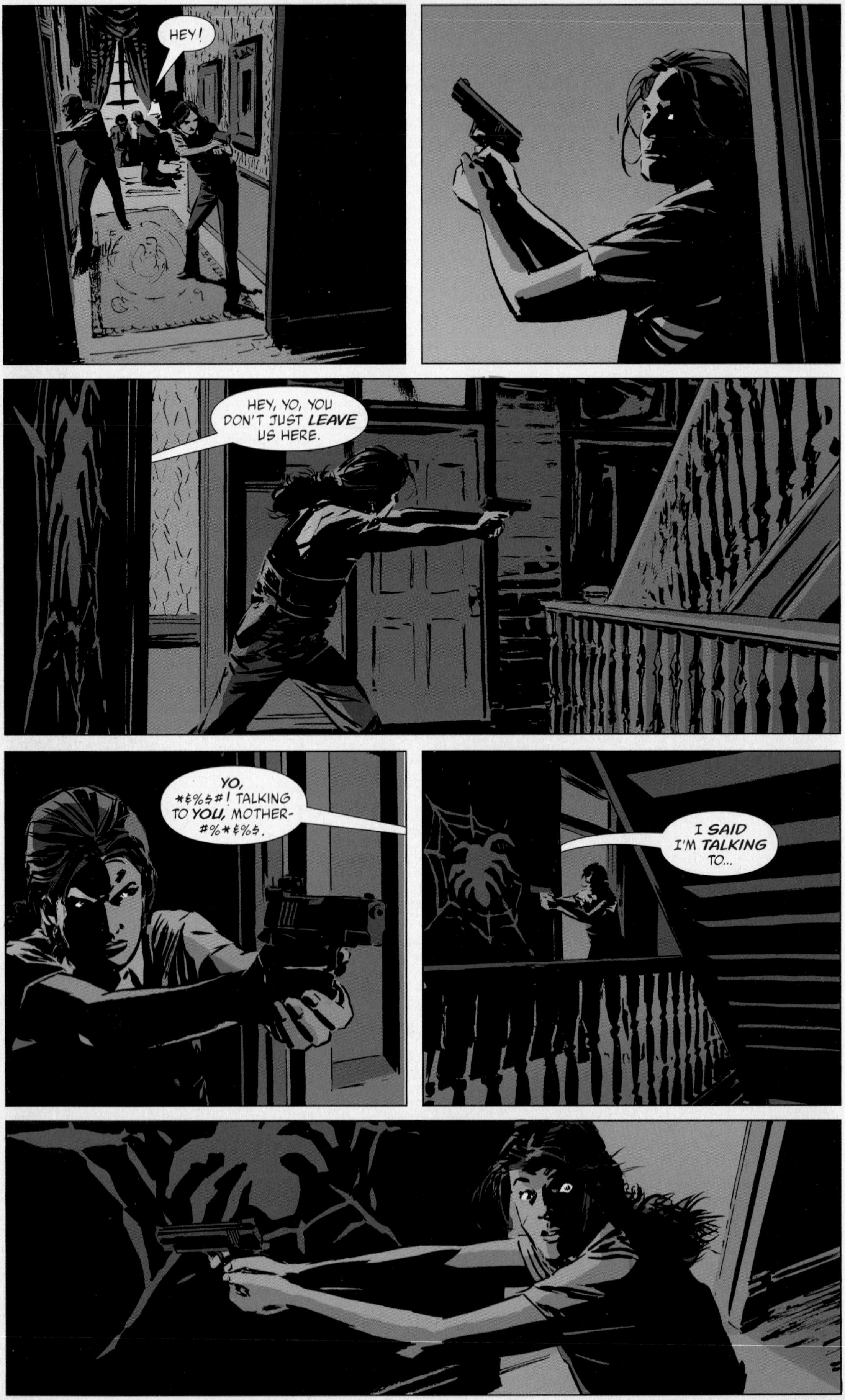
HEY!
HEY, YO, YOU DON'T JUST LEAVE US HERE.
YO, *&%$#! TALKING TO YOU, MOTHER-#%*&%$.
I SAID I'M TALKING TO...

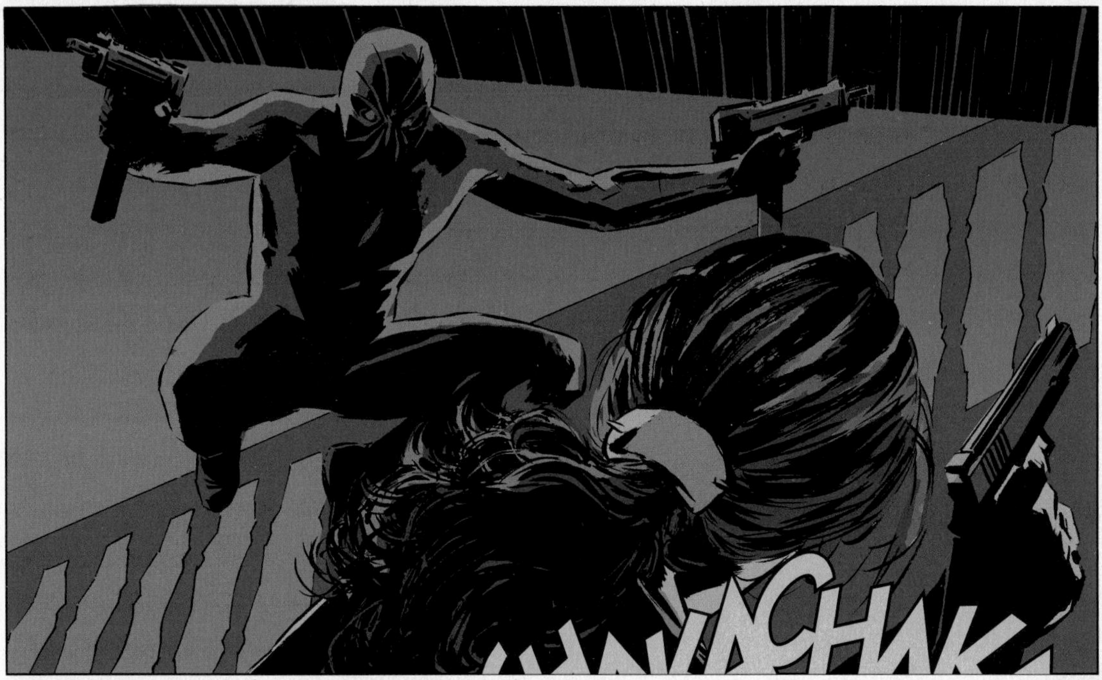

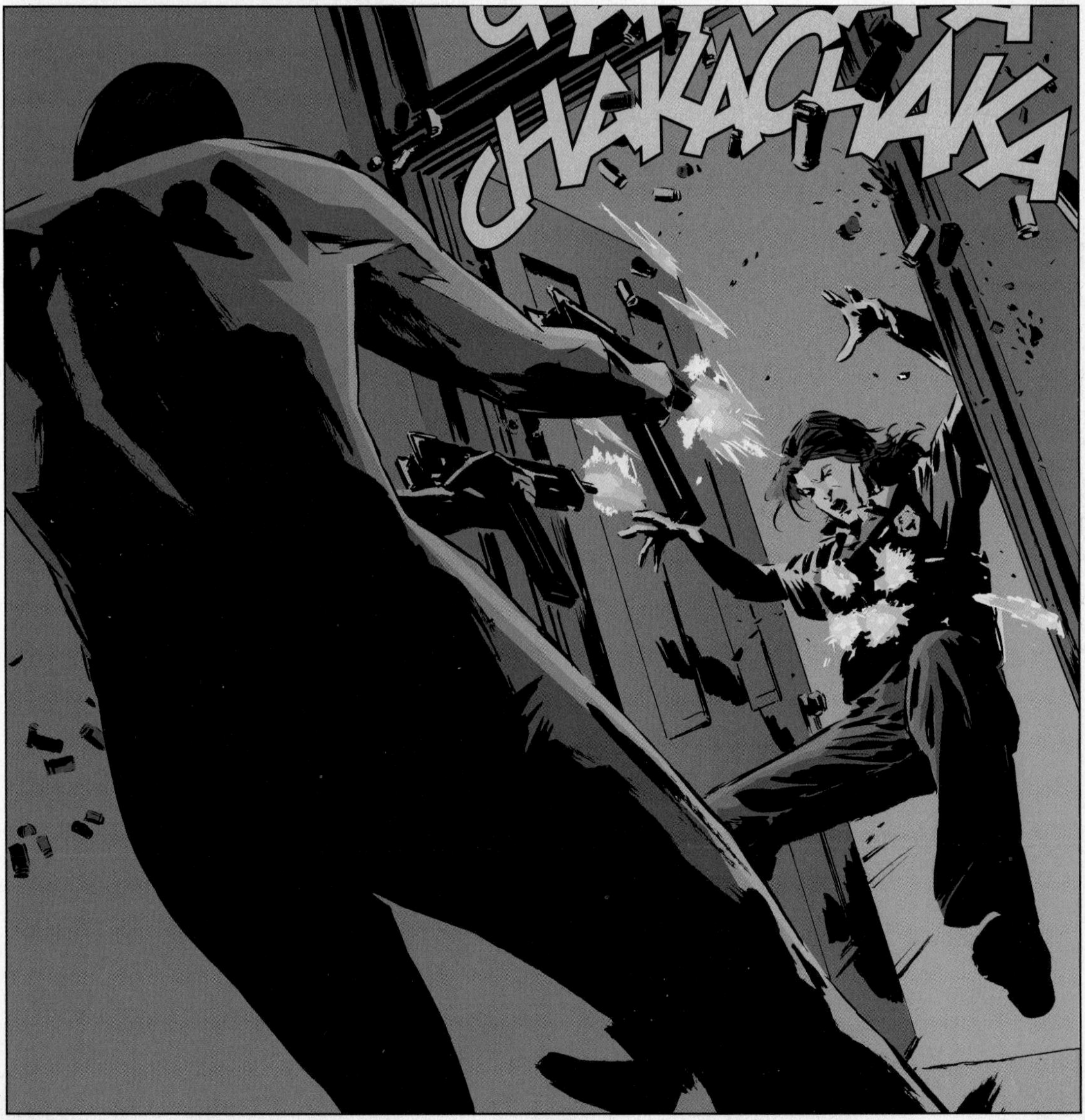
CHAKACHAKA
CHAKACHAKA

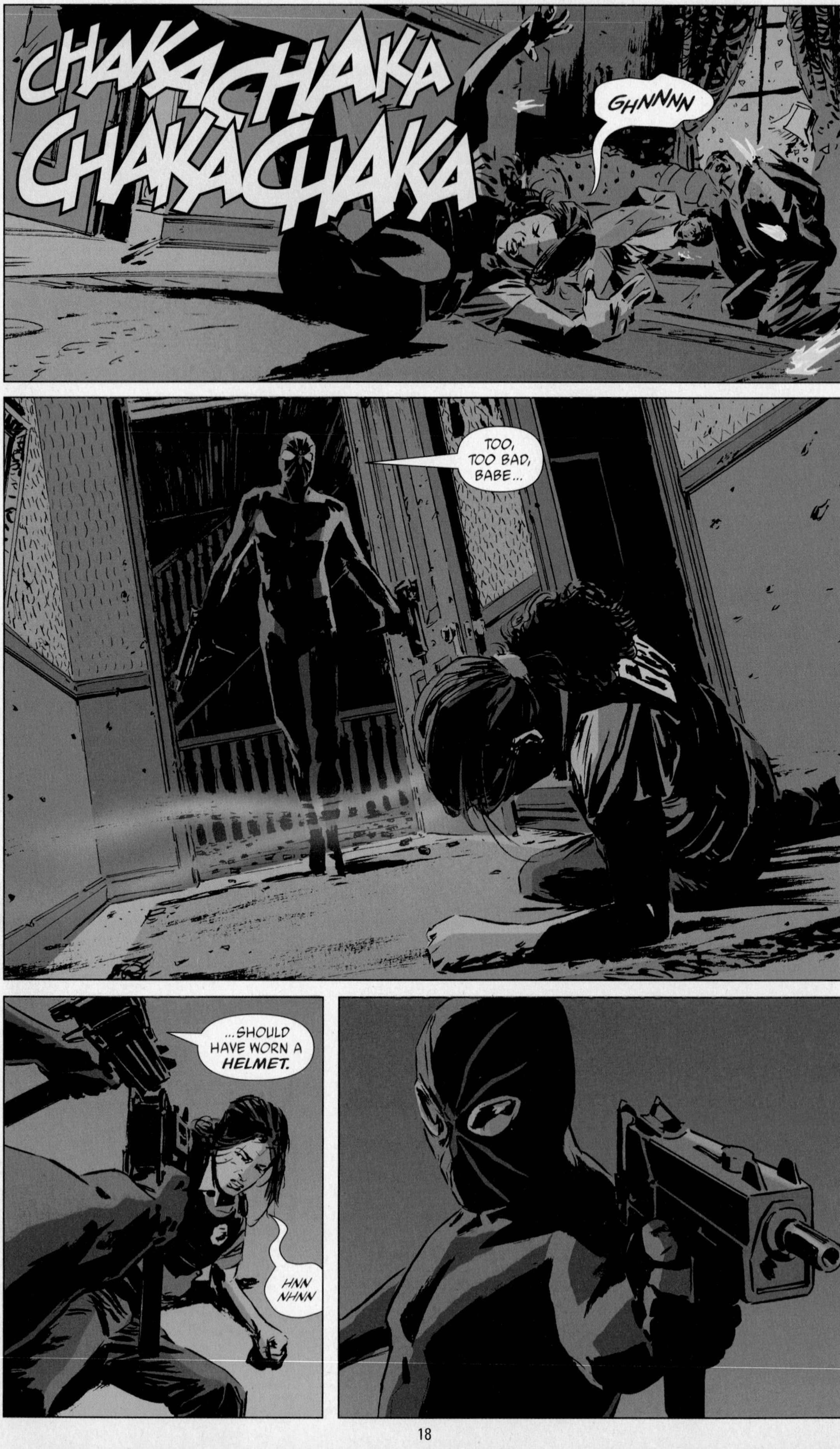
CHAKACHAKA
CHAKACHAKA
GHNNNN
TOO, TOO BAD, BABE...
...SHOULD HAVE WORN A HELMET.
HNN NHNN

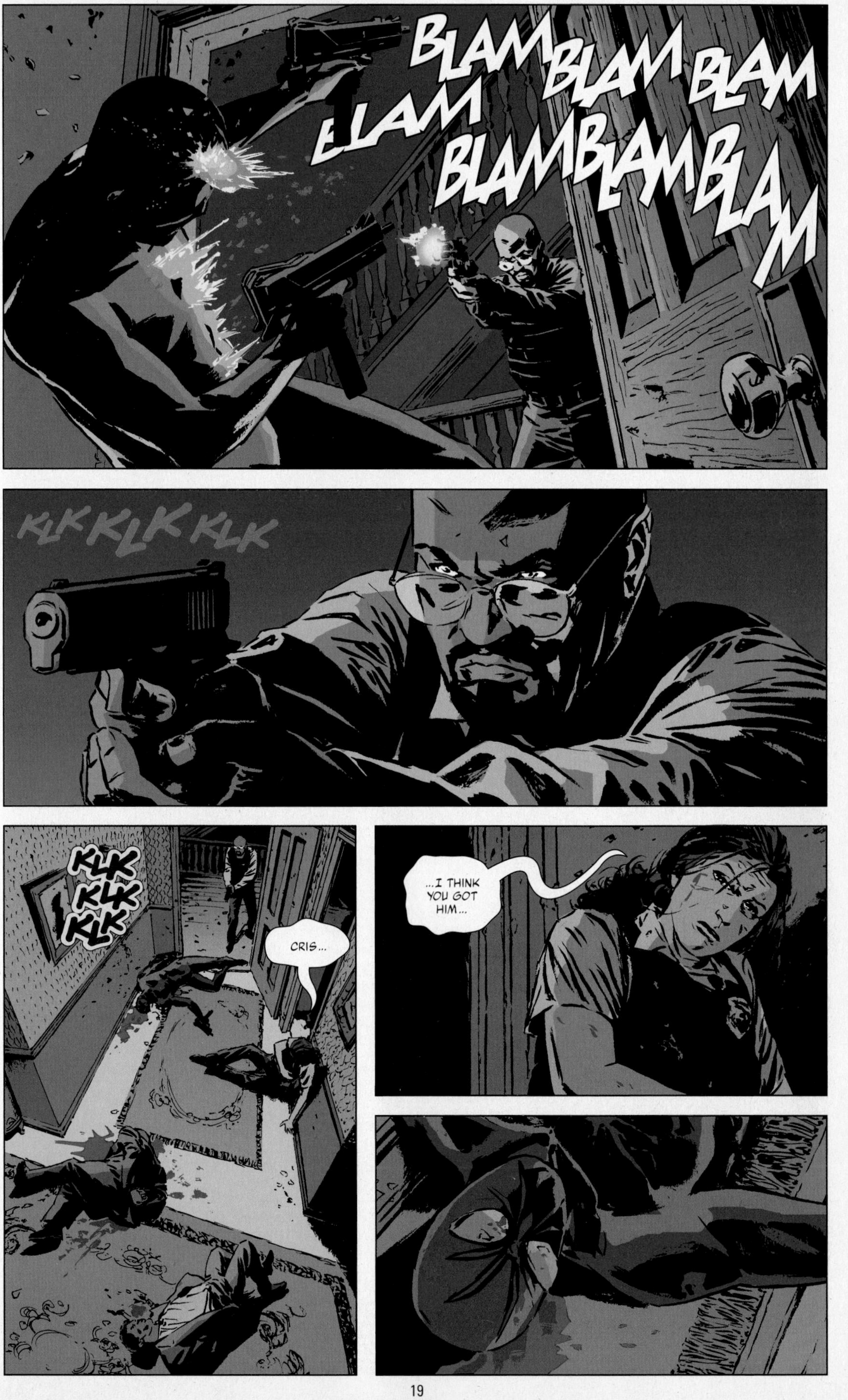
BLAM BLAM BLAM
BLAM
BLAM BLAM BLAM
KLK KLK KLK
KLK KLK KLK
CRIS...
...I THINK YOU GOT HIM...

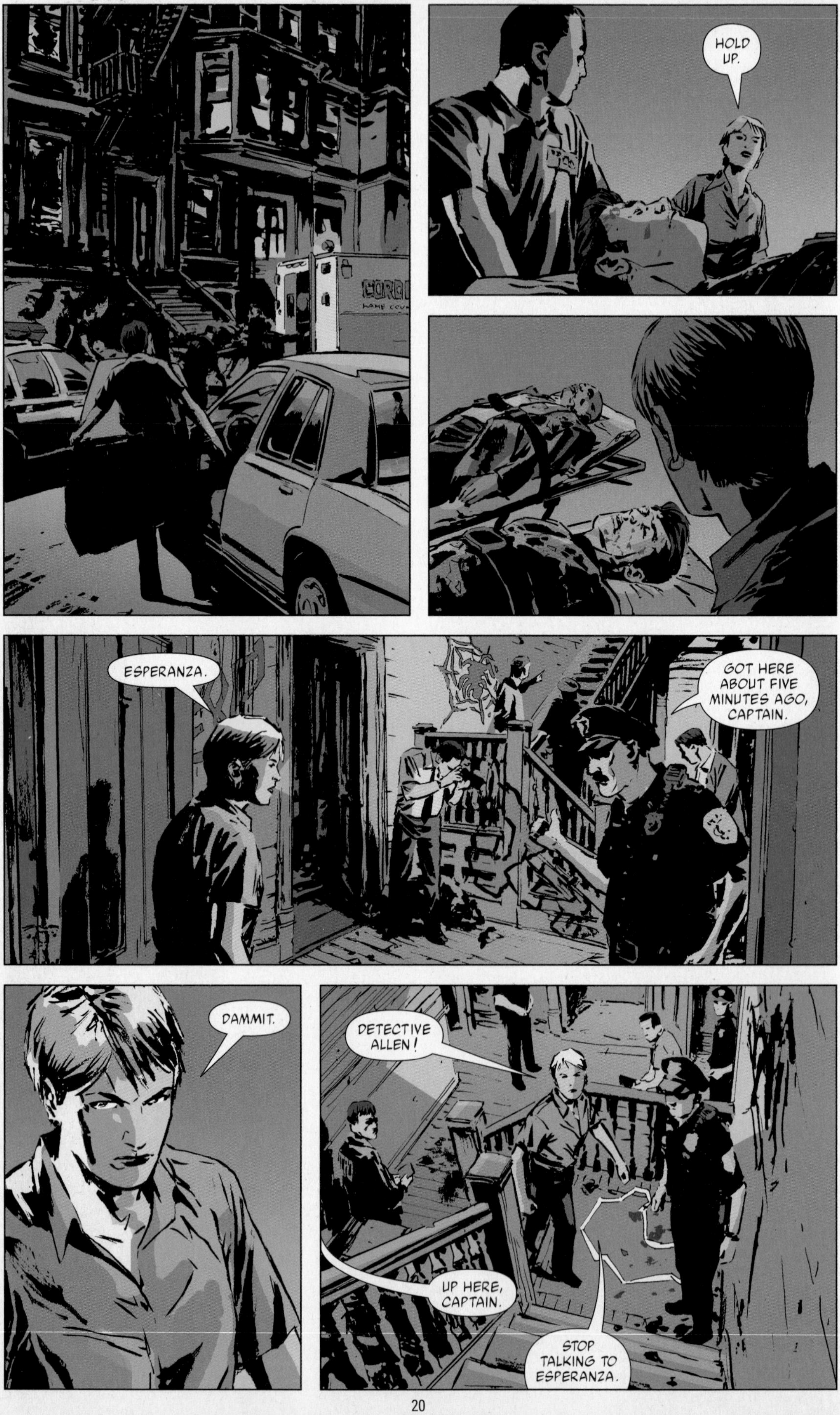
HOLD UP.
ESPERANZA.
GOT HERE ABOUT FIVE MINUTES AGO, CAPTAIN.
DAMMIT.
DETECTIVE ALLEN!
UP HERE, CAPTAIN.
STOP TALKING TO ESPERANZA.

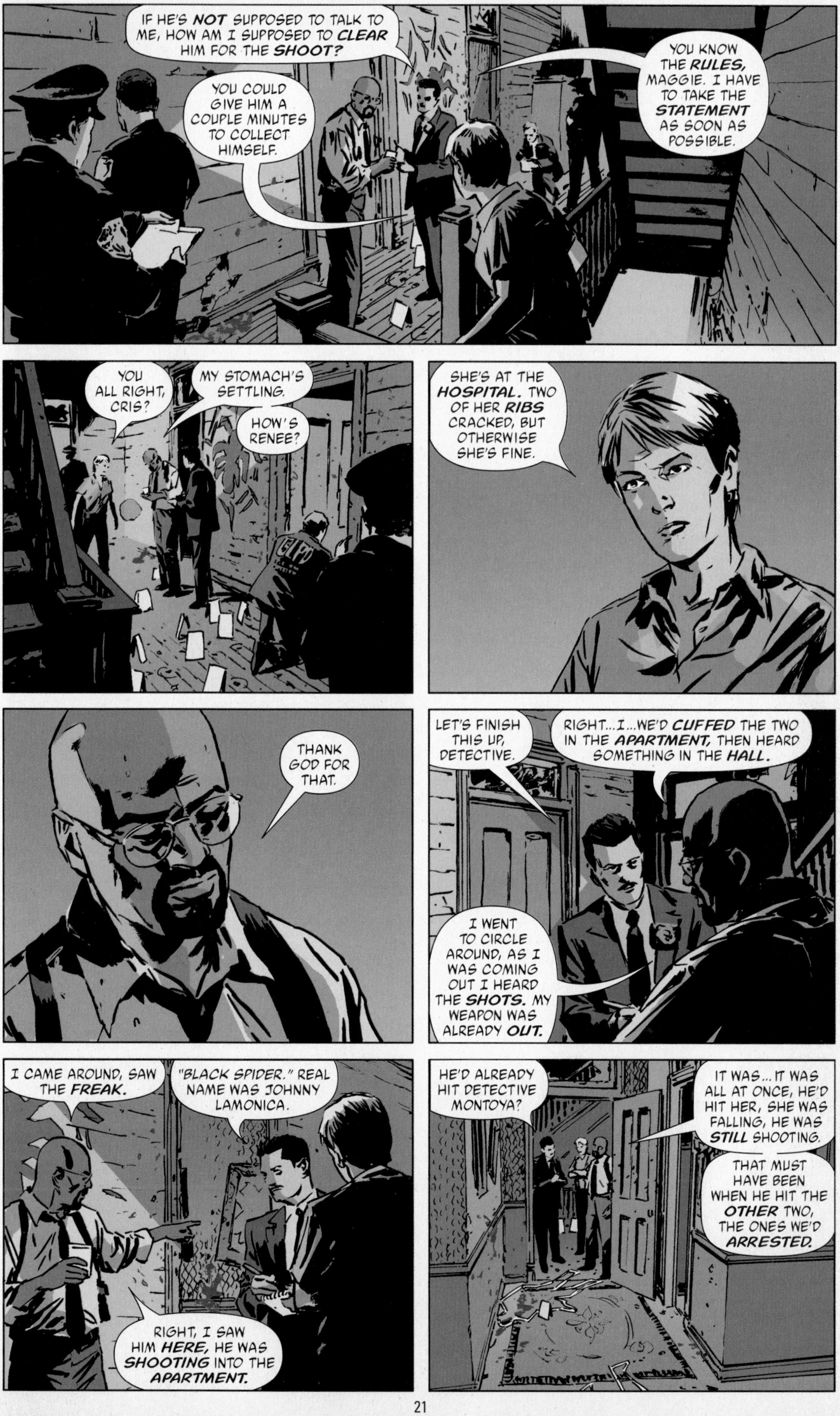
IF HE'S NOT SUPPOSED TO TALK TO ME, HOW AM I SUPPOSED TO CLEAR HIM FOR THE SHOOT?
YOU COULD GIVE HIM A COUPLE MINUTES TO COLLECT HIMSELF.
YOU KNOW THE RULES, MAGGIE. I HAVE TO TAKE THE STATEMENT AS SOON AS POSSIBLE.
YOU ALL RIGHT, CRIS?
MY STOMACH'S SETTLING.
HOW'S RENEE?
SHE'S AT THE HOSPITAL. TWO OF HER RIBS CRACKED, BUT OTHERWISE SHE'S FINE.
THANK GOD FOR THAT.
LET'S FINISH THIS UP, DETECTIVE.
RIGHT...I...WE'D CUFFED THE TWO IN THE APARTMENT, THEN HEARD SOMETHING IN THE HALL.
I WENT TO CIRCLE AROUND, AS I WAS COMING OUT I HEARD THE SHOTS. MY WEAPON WAS ALREADY OUT.
I CAME AROUND, SAW THE FREAK.
"BLACK SPIDER." REAL NAME WAS JOHNNY LAMONICA.
RIGHT, I SAW HIM HERE, HE WAS SHOOTING INTO THE APARTMENT.
HE'D ALREADY HIT DETECTIVE MONTOYA?
IT WAS... IT WAS ALL AT ONCE, HE'D HIT HER, SHE WAS FALLING, HE WAS STILL SHOOTING.
THAT MUST HAVE BEEN WHEN HE HIT THE OTHER TWO, THE ONES WE'D ARRESTED.

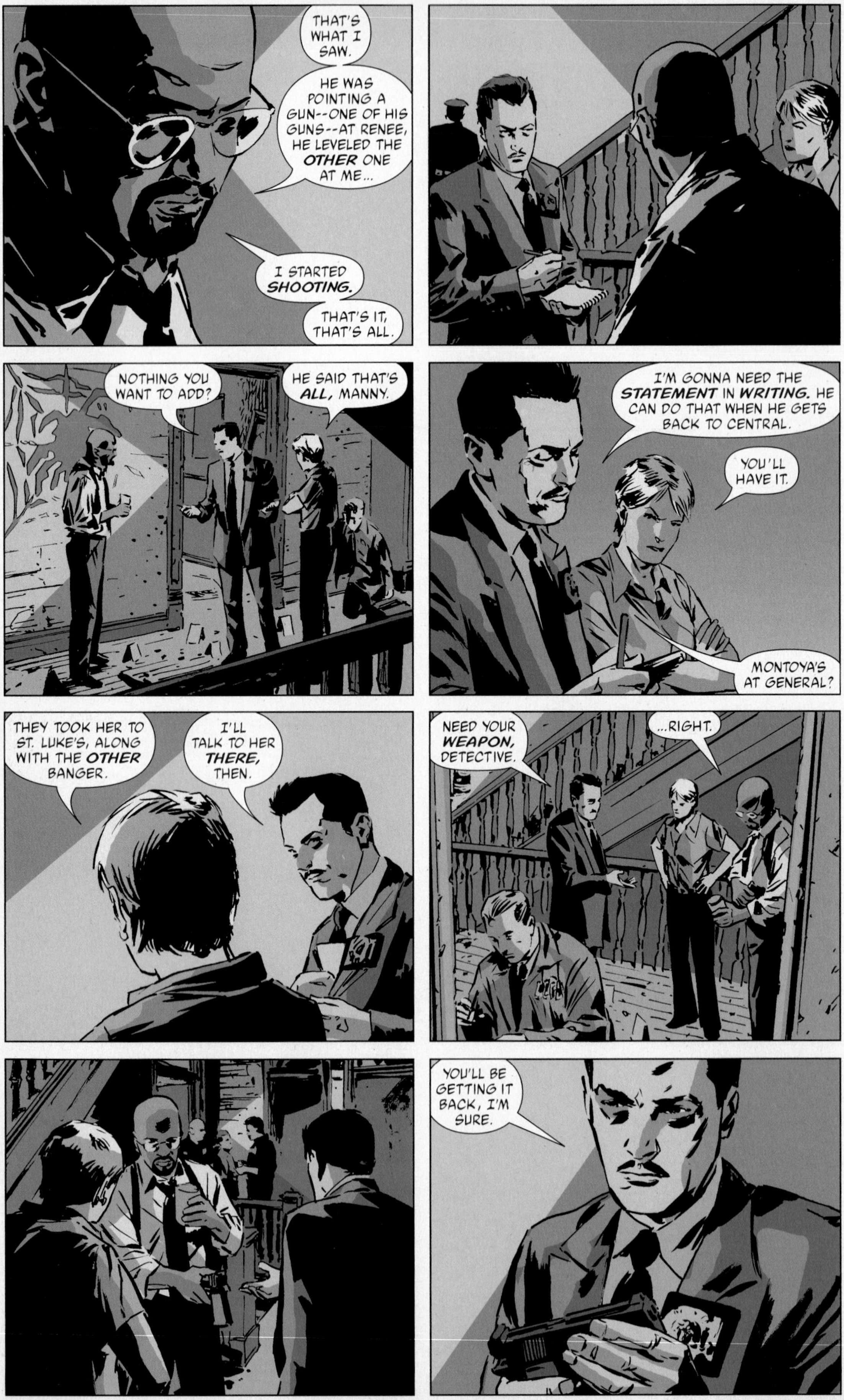
THAT'S WHAT I SAW.
HE WAS POINTING A GUN--ONE OF HIS GUNS--AT RENEE, HE LEVELED THE **OTHER** ONE AT ME...
I STARTED **SHOOTING.**
THAT'S IT, THAT'S ALL.
NOTHING YOU WANT TO ADD?
HE SAID THAT'S **ALL,** MANNY.
I'M GONNA NEED THE **STATEMENT** IN **WRITING.** HE CAN DO THAT WHEN HE GETS BACK TO CENTRAL.
YOU'LL HAVE IT.
MONTOYA'S AT GENERAL?
THEY TOOK HER TO ST. LUKE'S, ALONG WITH THE **OTHER** BANGER.
I'LL TALK TO HER **THERE,** THEN.
NEED YOUR **WEAPON,** DETECTIVE.
...RIGHT.
YOU'LL BE GETTING IT BACK, I'M SURE.

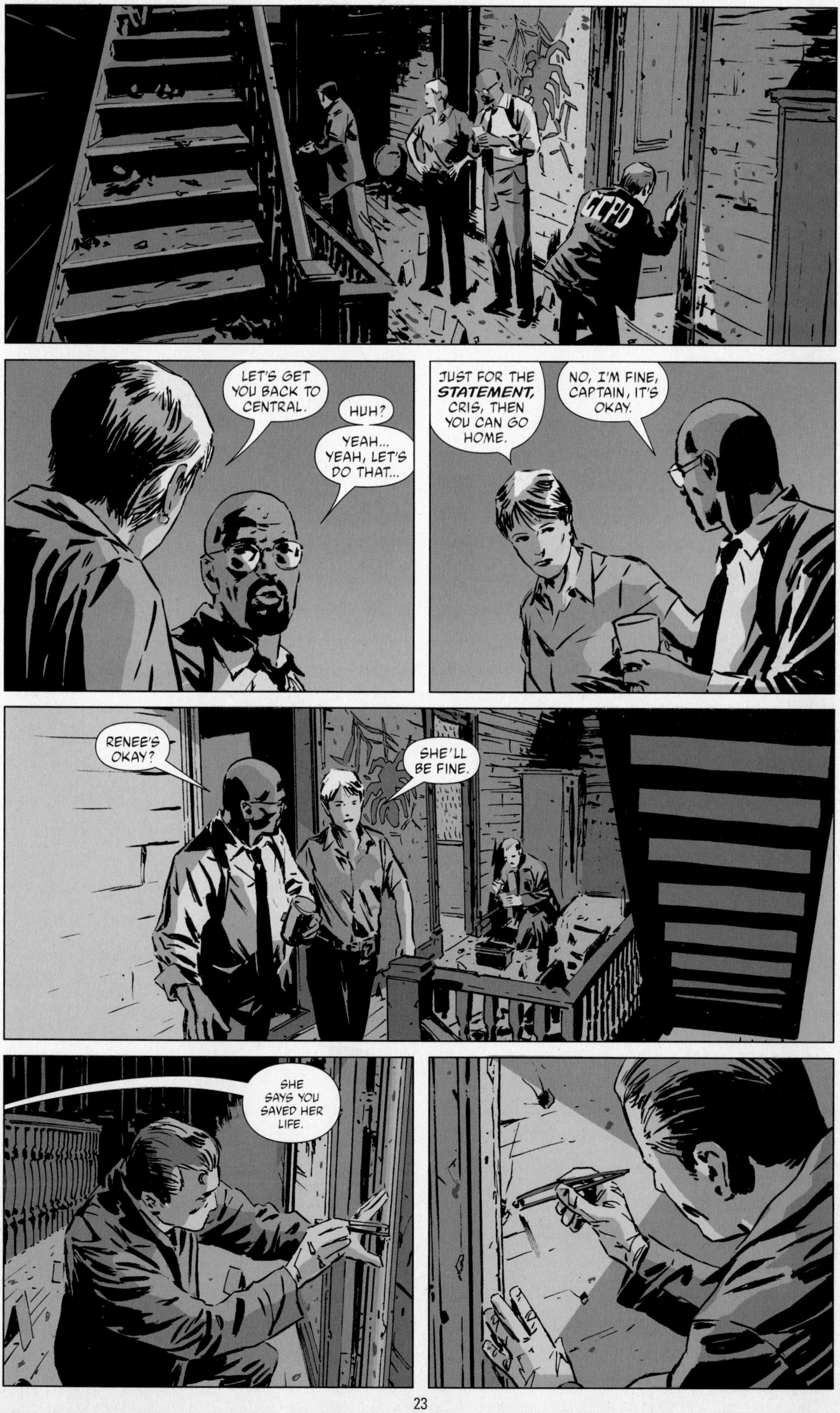
GCPD
LET'S GET YOU BACK TO CENTRAL.
HUH?
YEAH... YEAH, LET'S DO THAT...
JUST FOR THE STATEMENT, CRIS, THEN YOU CAN GO HOME.
NO, I'M FINE, CAPTAIN, IT'S OKAY.
RENEE'S OKAY?
SHE'LL BE FINE.
SHE SAYS YOU SAVED HER LIFE.

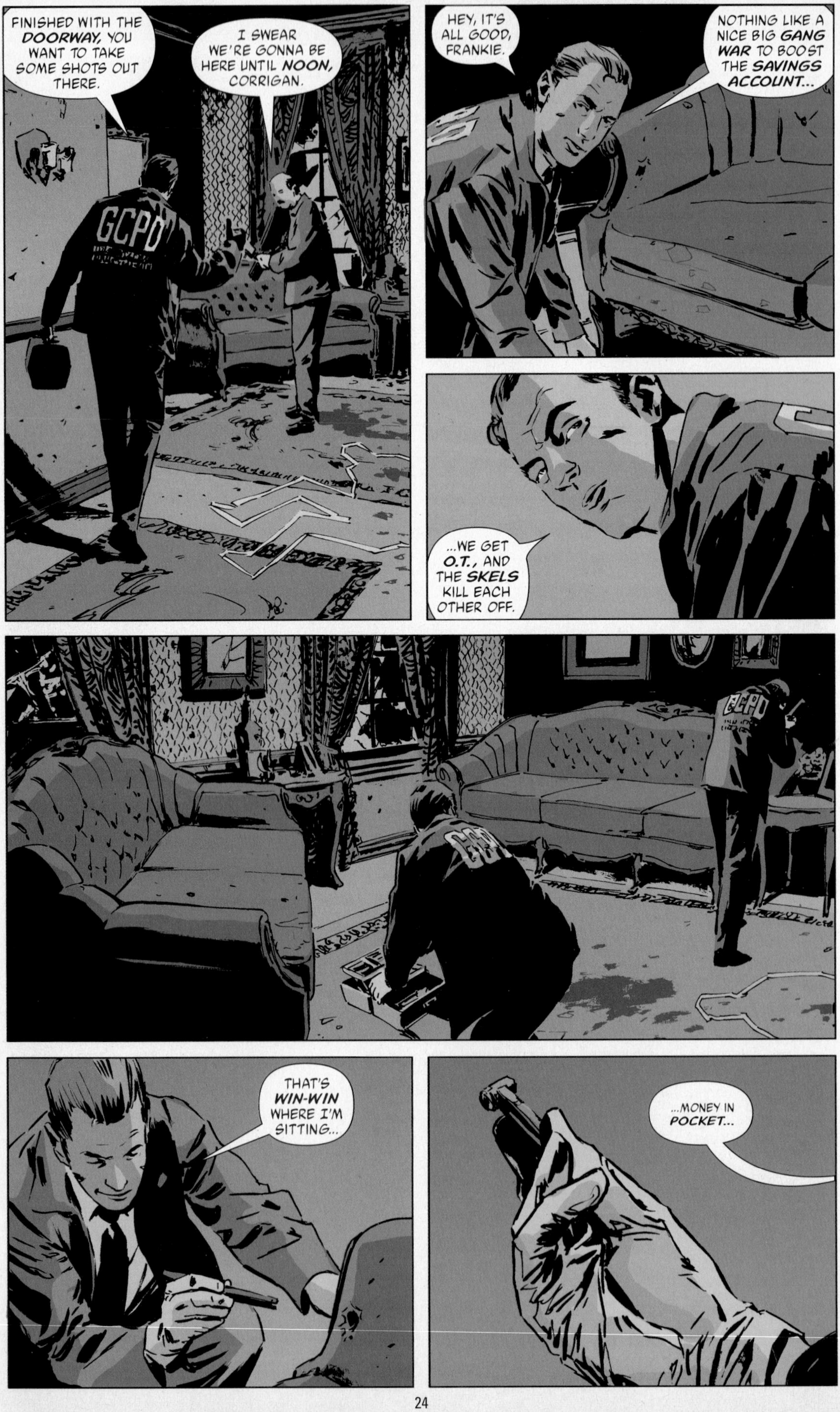
FINISHED WITH THE DOORWAY, YOU WANT TO TAKE SOME SHOTS OUT THERE.
I SWEAR WE'RE GONNA BE HERE UNTIL NOON, CORRIGAN.
HEY, IT'S ALL GOOD, FRANKIE.
NOTHING LIKE A NICE BIG GANG WAR TO BOOST THE SAVINGS ACCOUNT...
...WE GET O.T., AND THE SKELS KILL EACH OTHER OFF.
GCPD
THAT'S WIN-WIN WHERE I'M SITTING...
...MONEY IN POCKET...

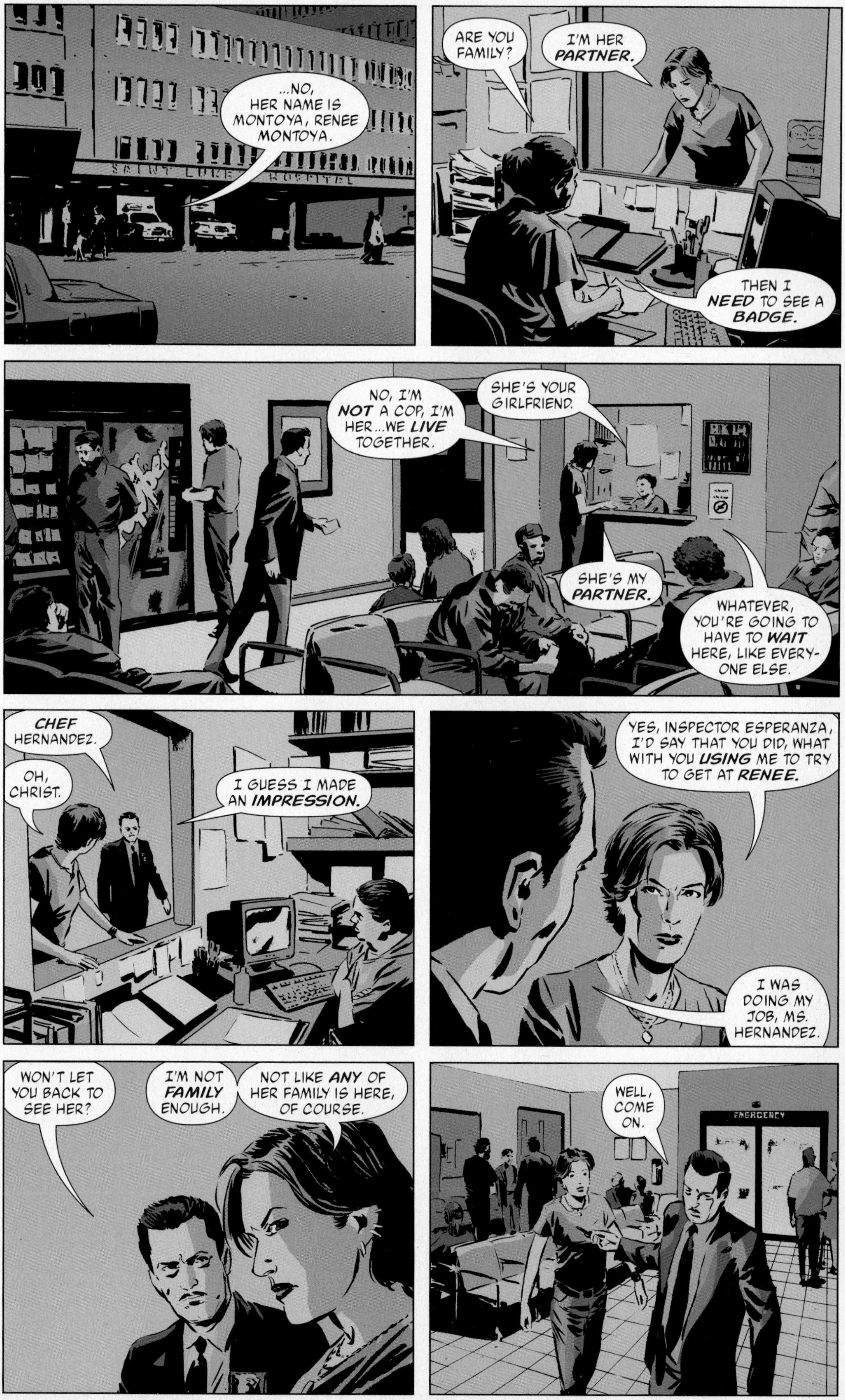

...NO, HER NAME IS MONTOYA, RENEE MONTOYA.
ARE YOU FAMILY?
I'M HER PARTNER.
THEN I NEED TO SEE A BADGE.
NO, I'M NOT A COP, I'M HER...WE LIVE TOGETHER.
SHE'S YOUR GIRLFRIEND.
SHE'S MY PARTNER.
WHATEVER, YOU'RE GOING TO HAVE TO WAIT HERE, LIKE EVERY-ONE ELSE.
CHEF HERNANDEZ.
OH, CHRIST.
I GUESS I MADE AN IMPRESSION.
YES, INSPECTOR ESPERANZA, I'D SAY THAT YOU DID, WHAT WITH YOU USING ME TO TRY TO GET AT RENEE.
I WAS DOING MY JOB, MS. HERNANDEZ.
WON'T LET YOU BACK TO SEE HER?
I'M NOT FAMILY ENOUGH.
NOT LIKE ANY OF HER FAMILY IS HERE, OF COURSE.
WELL, COME ON.
EMERGENCY

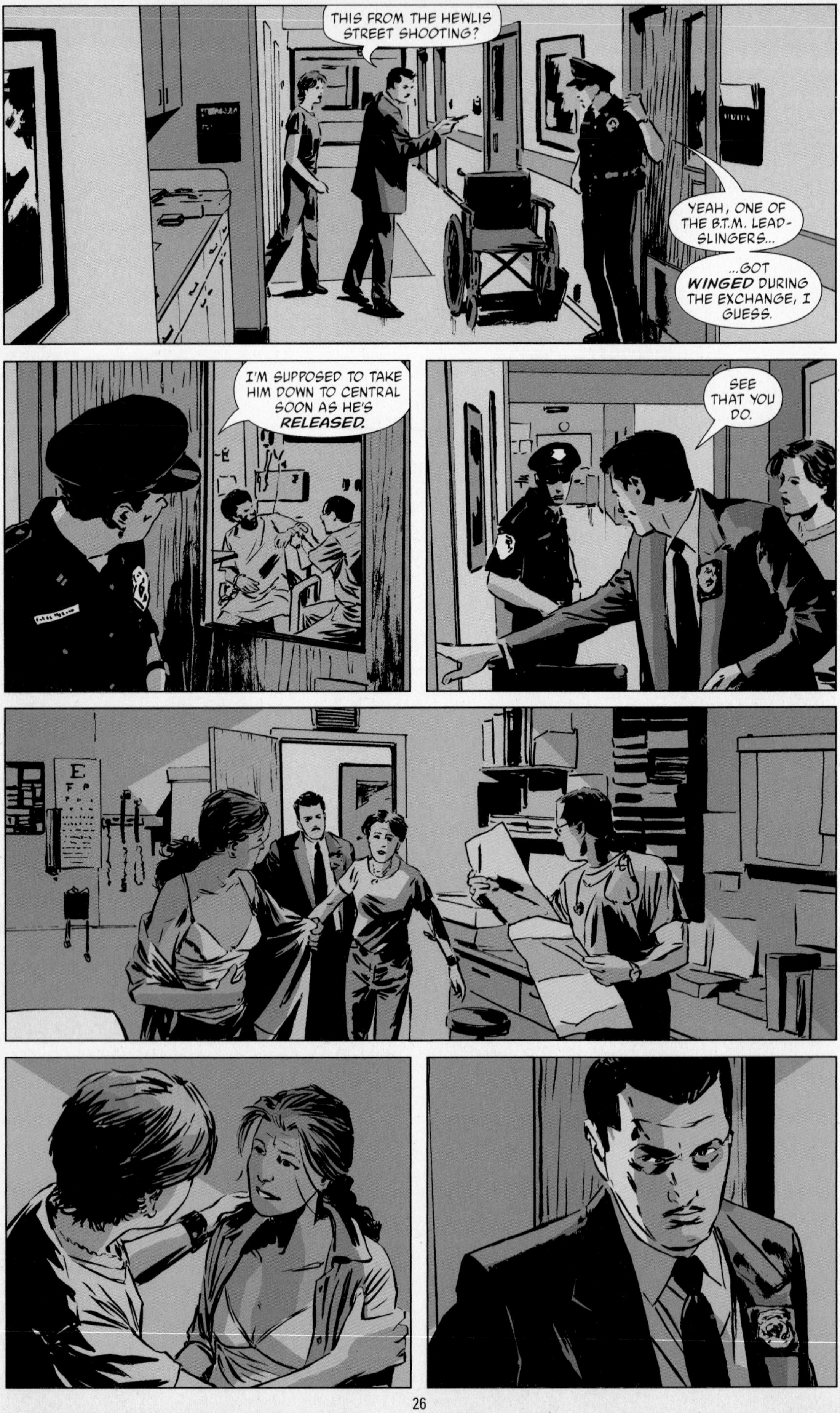
THIS FROM THE HEWLIS STREET SHOOTING?
YEAH, ONE OF THE B.T.M. LEAD-SLINGERS...
...GOT **WINGED** DURING THE EXCHANGE, I GUESS.
I'M SUPPOSED TO TAKE HIM DOWN TO CENTRAL SOON AS HE'S **RELEASED.**
SEE THAT YOU DO.

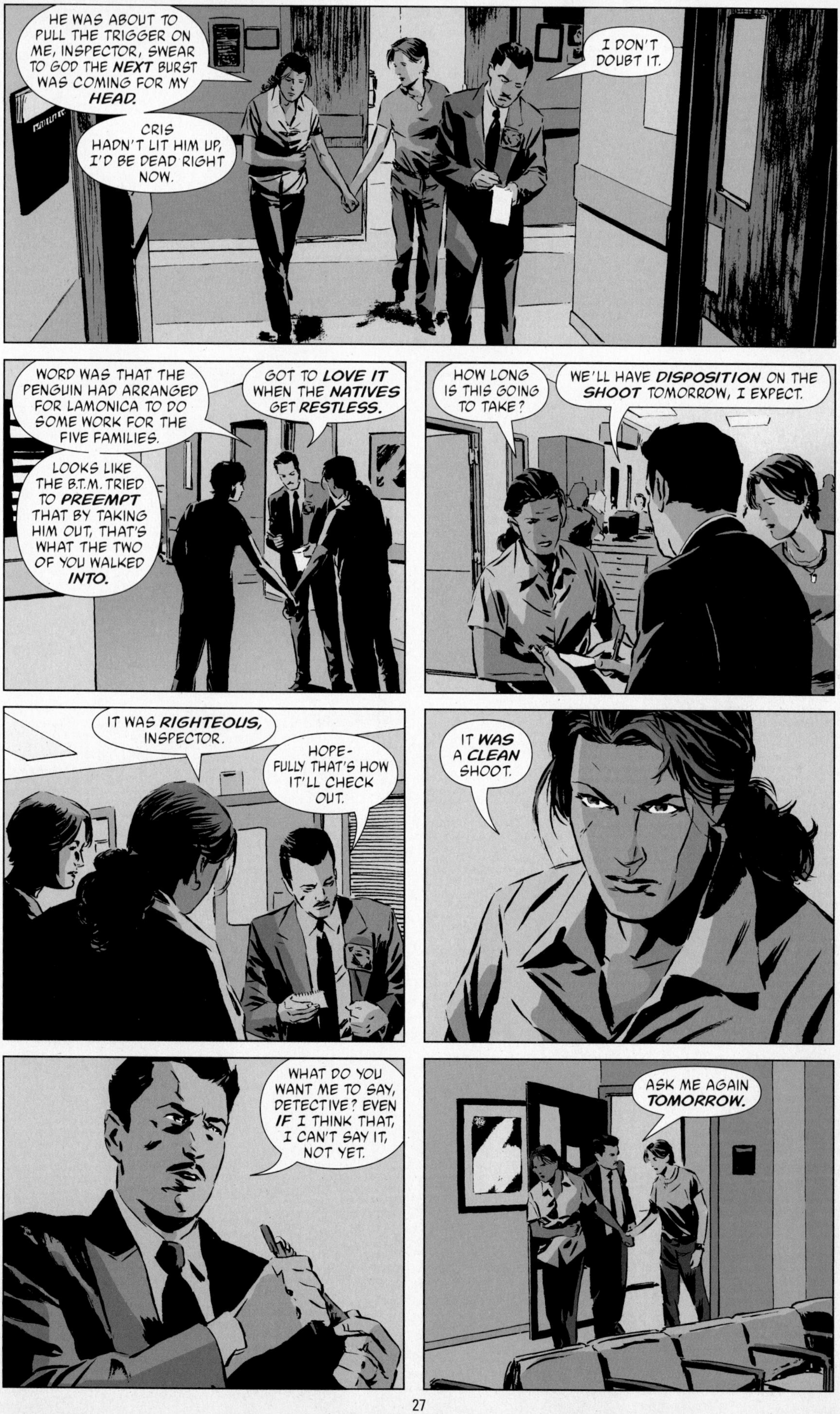
HE WAS ABOUT TO PULL THE TRIGGER ON ME, INSPECTOR, SWEAR TO GOD THE NEXT BURST WAS COMING FOR MY HEAD.
CRIS HADN'T LIT HIM UP, I'D BE DEAD RIGHT NOW.
I DON'T DOUBT IT.
WORD WAS THAT THE PENGUIN HAD ARRANGED FOR LAMONICA TO DO SOME WORK FOR THE FIVE FAMILIES.
LOOKS LIKE THE B.T.M. TRIED TO PREEMPT THAT BY TAKING HIM OUT, THAT'S WHAT THE TWO OF YOU WALKED INTO.
GOT TO LOVE IT WHEN THE NATIVES GET RESTLESS.
HOW LONG IS THIS GOING TO TAKE?
WE'LL HAVE DISPOSITION ON THE SHOOT TOMORROW, I EXPECT.
IT WAS RIGHTEOUS, INSPECTOR.
HOPE-FULLY THAT'S HOW IT'LL CHECK OUT.
IT WAS A CLEAN SHOOT.
WHAT DO YOU WANT ME TO SAY, DETECTIVE? EVEN IF I THINK THAT, I CAN'T SAY IT, NOT YET.
ASK ME AGAIN TOMORROW.

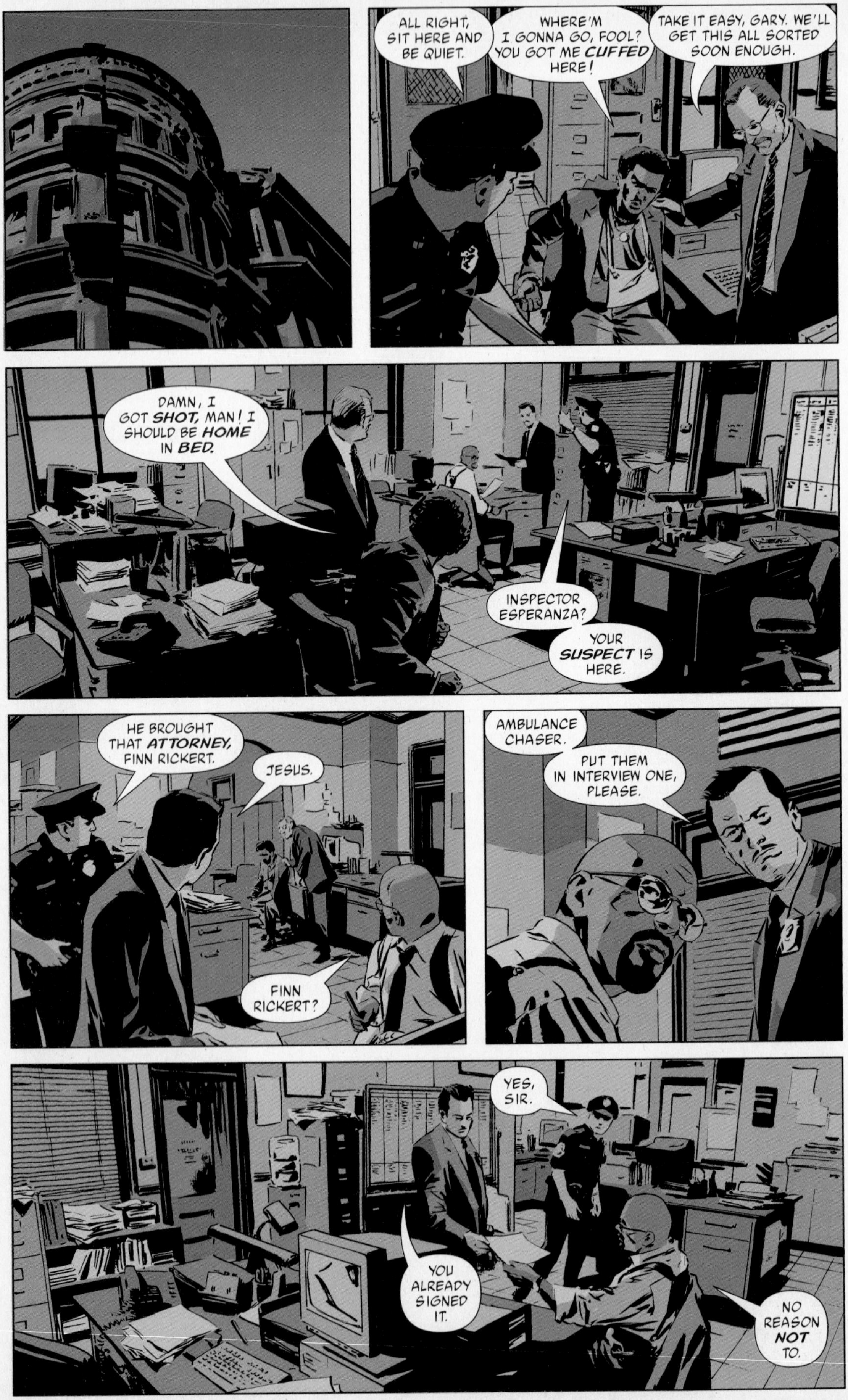
ALL RIGHT, SIT HERE AND BE QUIET.
WHERE'M I GONNA GO, FOOL? YOU GOT ME CUFFED HERE!
TAKE IT EASY, GARY. WE'LL GET THIS ALL SORTED SOON ENOUGH.
DAMN, I GOT SHOT, MAN! I SHOULD BE HOME IN BED.
INSPECTOR ESPERANZA?
YOUR SUSPECT IS HERE.
HE BROUGHT THAT ATTORNEY, FINN RICKERT.
JESUS.
FINN RICKERT?
AMBULANCE CHASER.
PUT THEM IN INTERVIEW ONE, PLEASE.
YES, SIR.
YOU ALREADY SIGNED IT.
NO REASON NOT TO.

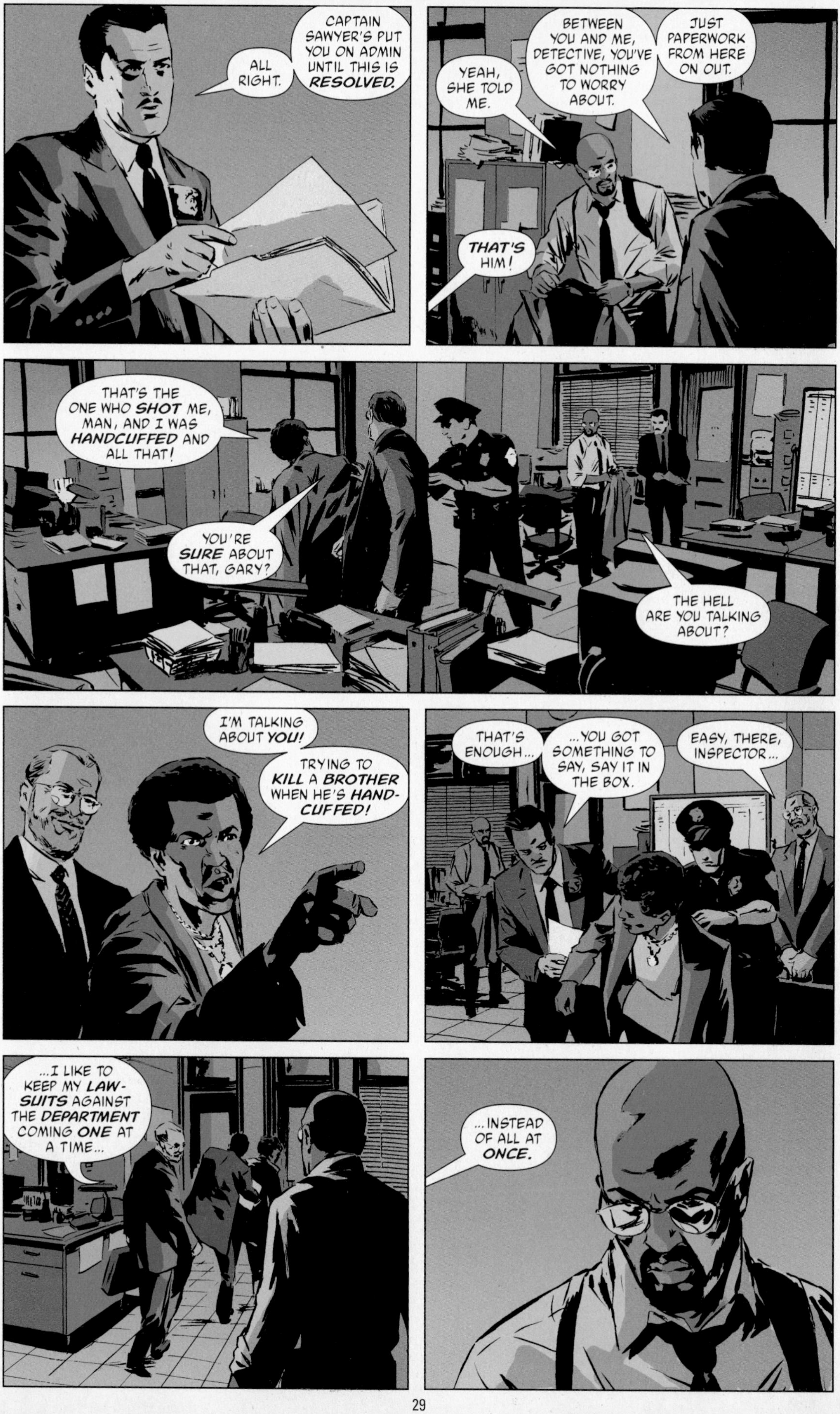
CAPTAIN SAWYER'S PUT YOU ON ADMIN UNTIL THIS IS RESOLVED.
ALL RIGHT.
BETWEEN YOU AND ME, DETECTIVE, YOU'VE GOT NOTHING TO WORRY ABOUT.
JUST PAPERWORK FROM HERE ON OUT.
YEAH, SHE TOLD ME.
THAT'S HIM!
THAT'S THE ONE WHO SHOT ME, MAN, AND I WAS HANDCUFFED AND ALL THAT!
YOU'RE SURE ABOUT THAT, GARY?
THE HELL ARE YOU TALKING ABOUT?
I'M TALKING ABOUT YOU!
TRYING TO KILL A BROTHER WHEN HE'S HAND-CUFFED!
THAT'S ENOUGH...
...YOU GOT SOMETHING TO SAY, SAY IT IN THE BOX.
EASY, THERE, INSPECTOR...
...I LIKE TO KEEP MY LAW-SUITS AGAINST THE DEPARTMENT COMING ONE AT A TIME...
...INSTEAD OF ALL AT ONCE.

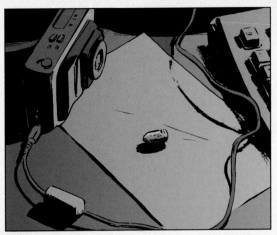

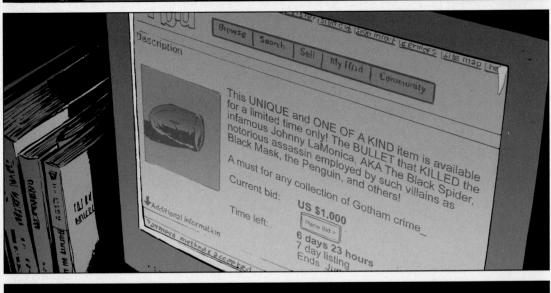

Browse
Search
Sell
Community
Description
This UNIQUE and ONE OF A KIND item is available for a limited time only! The BULLET that KILLED the infamous Johnny LaMonica, AKA The Black Spider, notorious assassin employed by such villains as Black Mask, the Penguin, and others!
A must for any collection of Gotham crime_
Current bid:
US $1,000
Time left:
Place Bid >
6 days 23 hours
7 day listing
Additional Information
COME TO PAPA.

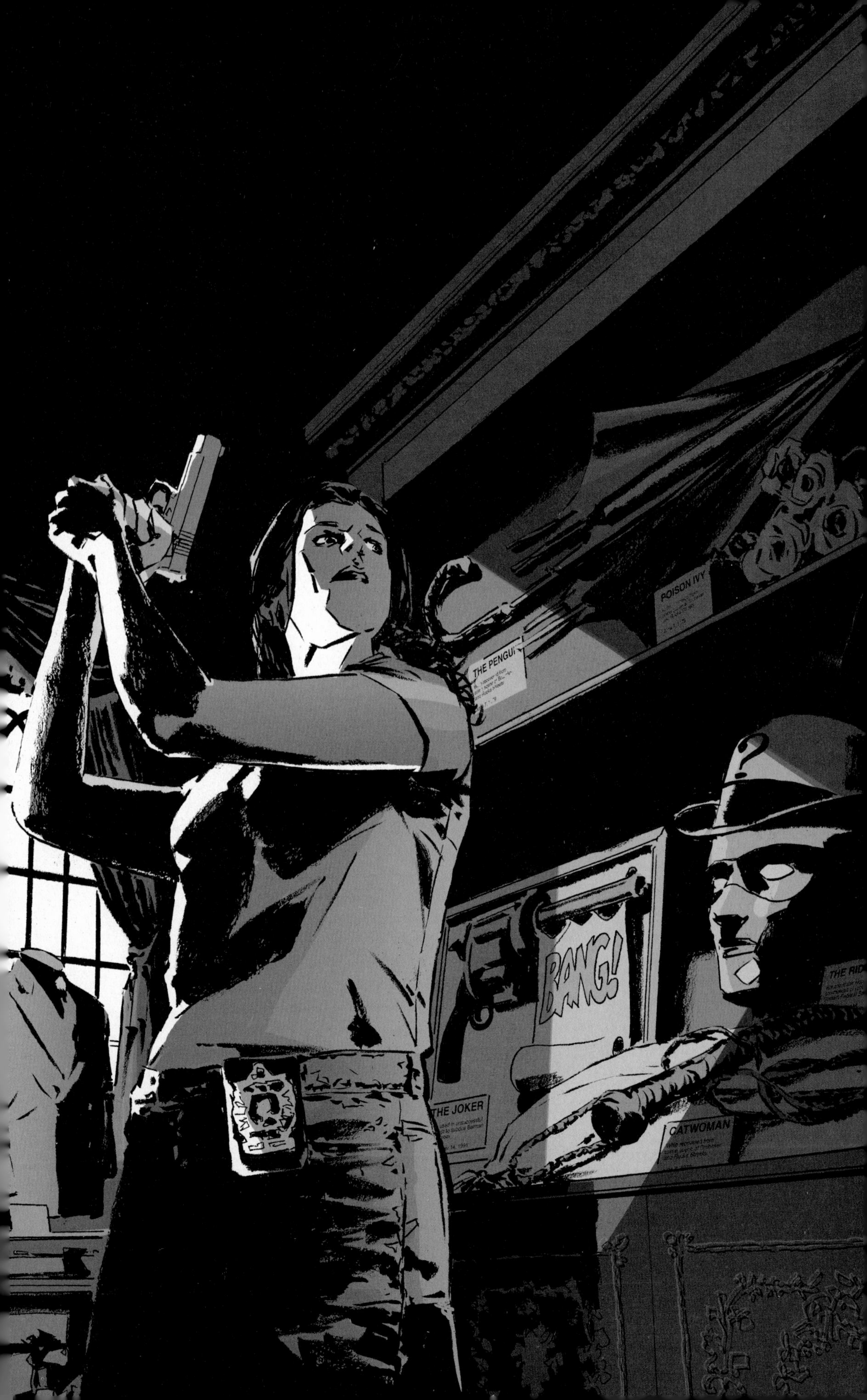
POISON IVY
THE PENGU
BANG!
THE RID
THE JOKER
CATWOMAN

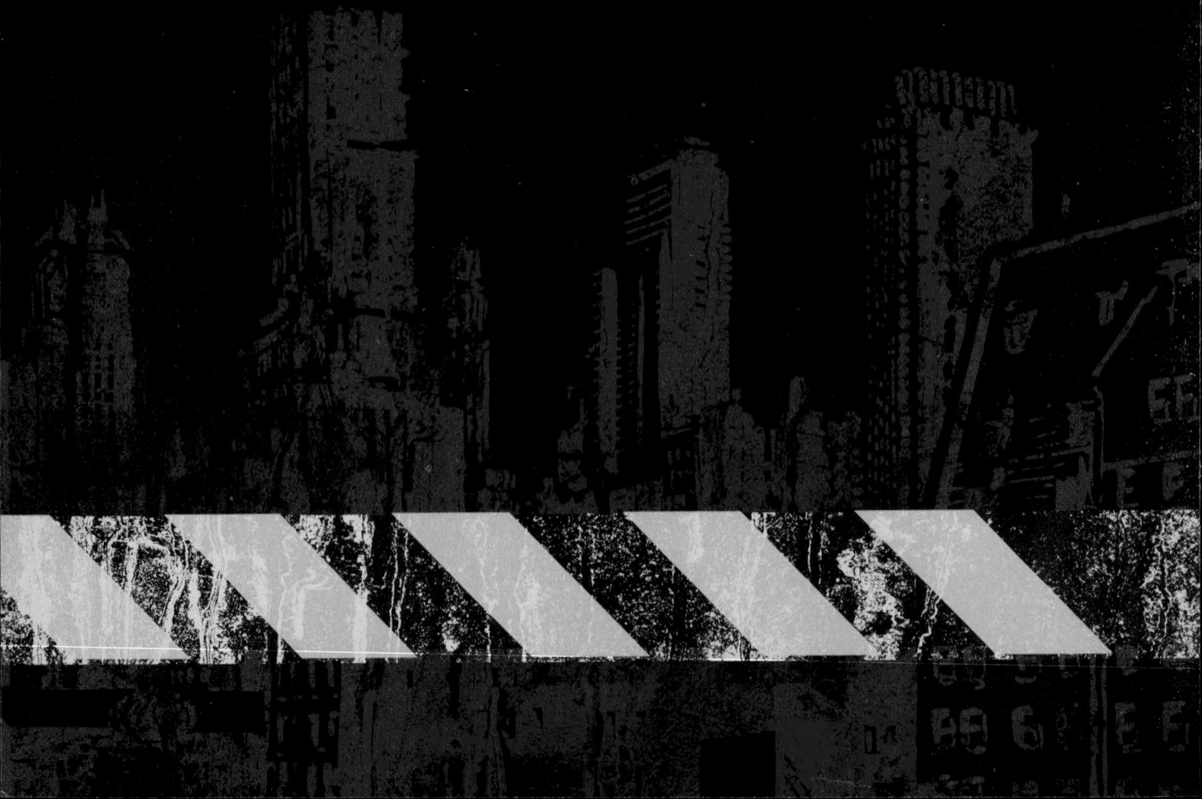

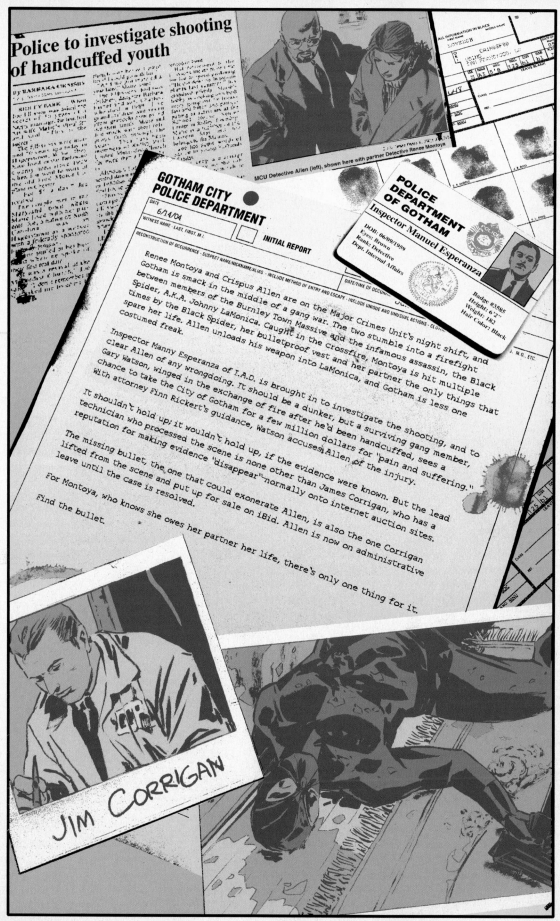

Police to investigate shooting
of handcuffed youth

MCU Detective Allen (left), shown here with partner Detective Renee Montoya

GOTHAM CITY POLICE DEPARTMENT

DATE 6/14/04

WITNESS NAME - LAST, FIRST, M.I.

INITIAL REPORT

RECONSTRUCTION OF OCCURRENCE - SUSPECT NAME/NICKNAME/ALIAS - INCLUDE METHOD OF ENTRY AND ESCAPE - INCLUDE UNIQUE AND UNUSUAL ACTIONS - CLOTHING

DATE/TIME OF OCCURRENCE

POLICE DEPARTMENT OF GOTHAM

Inspector Manuel Esperanza

DOB: 06/09/1959
Eyes: Brown
Rank: Detective
Dept.: Internal Affairs

Badge #3585
Height: 6'2"
Weight: 182
Hair Color: Black

Renee Montoya and Crispus Allen are on the Major Crimes Unit's night shift, and Gotham is smack in the middle of a gang war. The two stumble into a firefight between members of the Burnley Town Massive and the infamous assassin, the Black Spider, A.K.A. Johnny LaMonica. Caught in the crossfire, Montoya is hit multiple times by the Black Spider, her bulletproof vest and her partner the only things that spare her life. Allen unloads his weapon into LaMonica, and Gotham is less one costumed freak.

Inspector Manny Esperanza of I.A.D. is brought in to investigate the shooting, and to clear Allen of any wrongdoing. It should be a dunker, but a surviving gang member, Gary Watson, winged in the exchange of fire after he'd been handcuffed, sees a chance to take the City of Gotham for a few million dollars for "pain and suffering." With attorney Finn Rickert's guidance, Watson accuses Allen of the injury.

It shouldn't hold up; it wouldn't hold up, if the evidence were known. But the lead technician who processed the scene is none other than James Corrigan, who has a reputation for making evidence "disappear" normally onto internet auction sites.

The missing bullet, the one that could exonerate Allen, is also the one Corrigan lifted from the scene and put up for sale on iBid. Allen is now on administrative leave until the case is resolved.

For Montoya, who knows she owes her partner her life, there's only one thing for it.

Find the bullet.

JIM CORRIGAN

CORRIGAN PART TWO

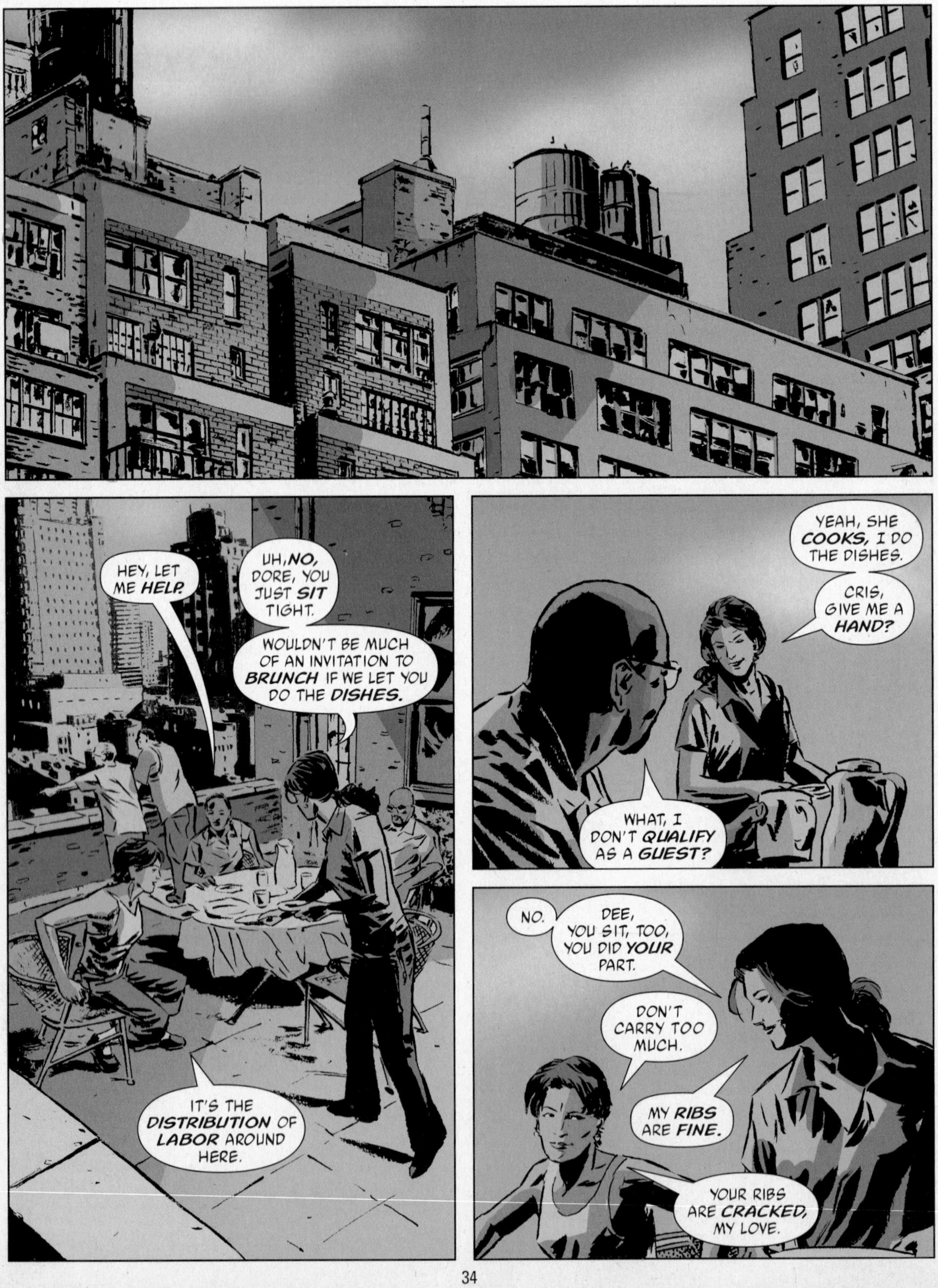
HEY, LET ME HELP.
UH, NO, DORE, YOU JUST SIT TIGHT.
WOULDN'T BE MUCH OF AN INVITATION TO BRUNCH IF WE LET YOU DO THE DISHES.
IT'S THE DISTRIBUTION OF LABOR AROUND HERE.
YEAH, SHE COOKS, I DO THE DISHES.
CRIS, GIVE ME A HAND?
WHAT, I DON'T QUALIFY AS A GUEST?
NO.
DEE, YOU SIT, TOO, YOU DID YOUR PART.
DON'T CARRY TOO MUCH.
MY RIBS ARE FINE.
YOUR RIBS ARE CRACKED, MY LOVE.

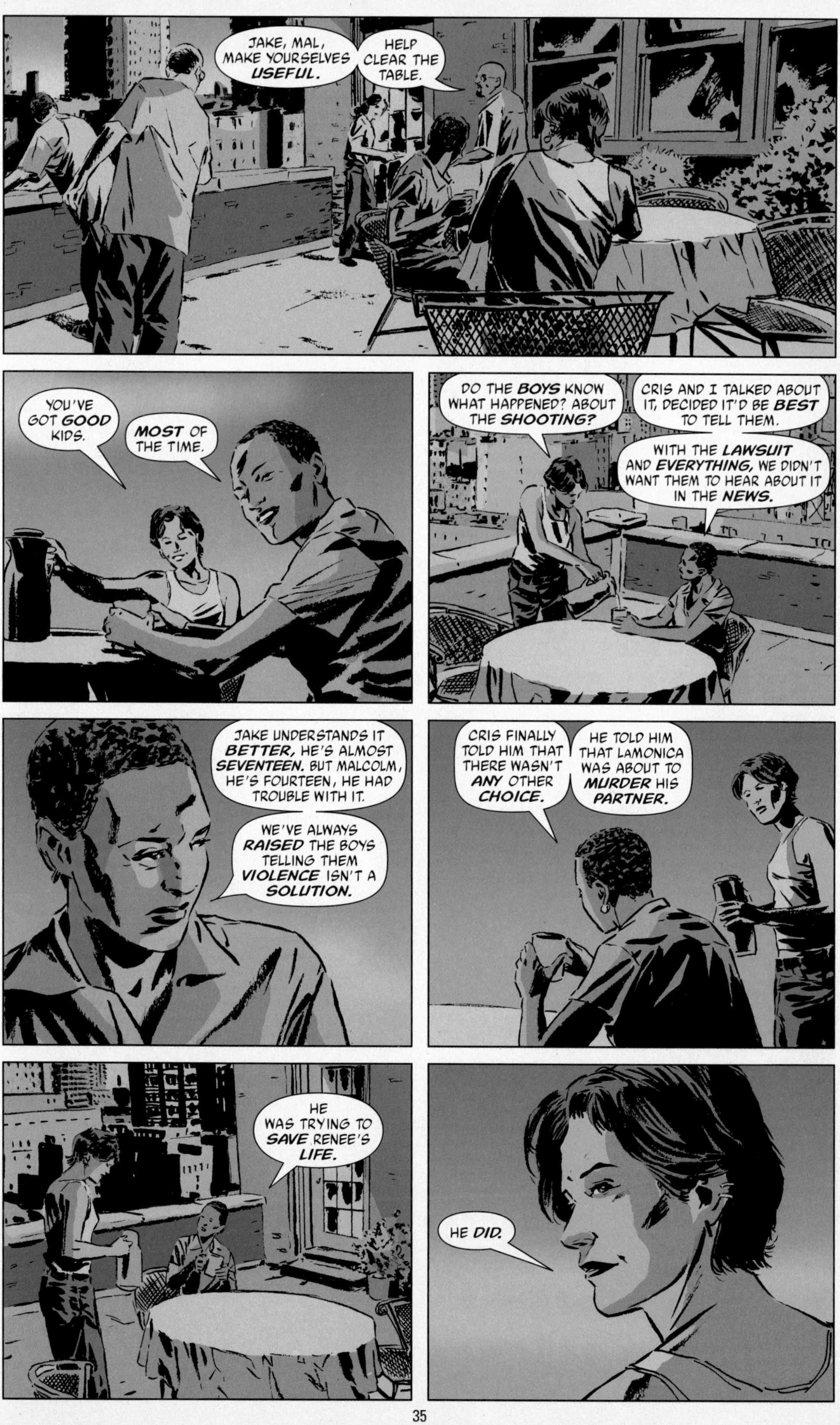
JAKE, MAL, MAKE YOURSELVES USEFUL.
HELP CLEAR THE TABLE.
YOU'VE GOT GOOD KIDS.
MOST OF THE TIME.
DO THE BOYS KNOW WHAT HAPPENED? ABOUT THE SHOOTING?
CRIS AND I TALKED ABOUT IT, DECIDED IT'D BE BEST TO TELL THEM.
WITH THE LAWSUIT AND EVERYTHING, WE DIDN'T WANT THEM TO HEAR ABOUT IT IN THE NEWS.
JAKE UNDERSTANDS IT BETTER, HE'S ALMOST SEVENTEEN. BUT MALCOLM, HE'S FOURTEEN, HE HAD TROUBLE WITH IT.
WE'VE ALWAYS RAISED THE BOYS TELLING THEM VIOLENCE ISN'T A SOLUTION.
CRIS FINALLY TOLD HIM THAT THERE WASN'T ANY OTHER CHOICE.
HE TOLD HIM THAT LAMONICA WAS ABOUT TO MURDER HIS PARTNER.
HE WAS TRYING TO SAVE RENEE'S LIFE.
HE DID.

THANKS, GUYS.

THERE'S A *VIDEO GAME* CONSOLE HOOKED UP TO THE TV, IF YOU WANT TO *SAVE* THE *EARTH* FROM AN ALIEN *INVASION* OR SOMETHING.

SICK!

CAN WE, DAD?

YOU MAY.

QUIETLY.

VIDEO GAMES?

THEY'RE DEE'S, I SWEAR.

SURE.

I TALKED TO *ESPERANZA* ON FRIDAY.

HE SAYS FINN RICKERT'S ALL SET TO *DEPOSE* YOU THIS WEEK.

HE SHOULDN'T HAVE TOLD YOU THAT.

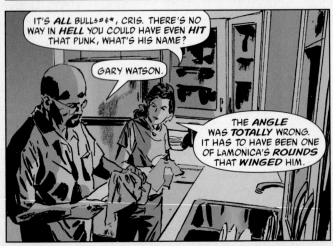

IT'S *ALL* BULL#%#*, CRIS. THERE'S NO WAY IN *HELL* YOU COULD HAVE EVEN *HIT* THAT PUNK, WHAT'S HIS NAME?

GARY WATSON.

THE *ANGLE* WAS *TOTALLY* WRONG. IT HAS TO HAVE BEEN ONE OF LAMONICA'S *ROUNDS* THAT *WINGED* HIM.

YEAH.

THAT'S WHAT *I* KEEP SAYING, TOO.

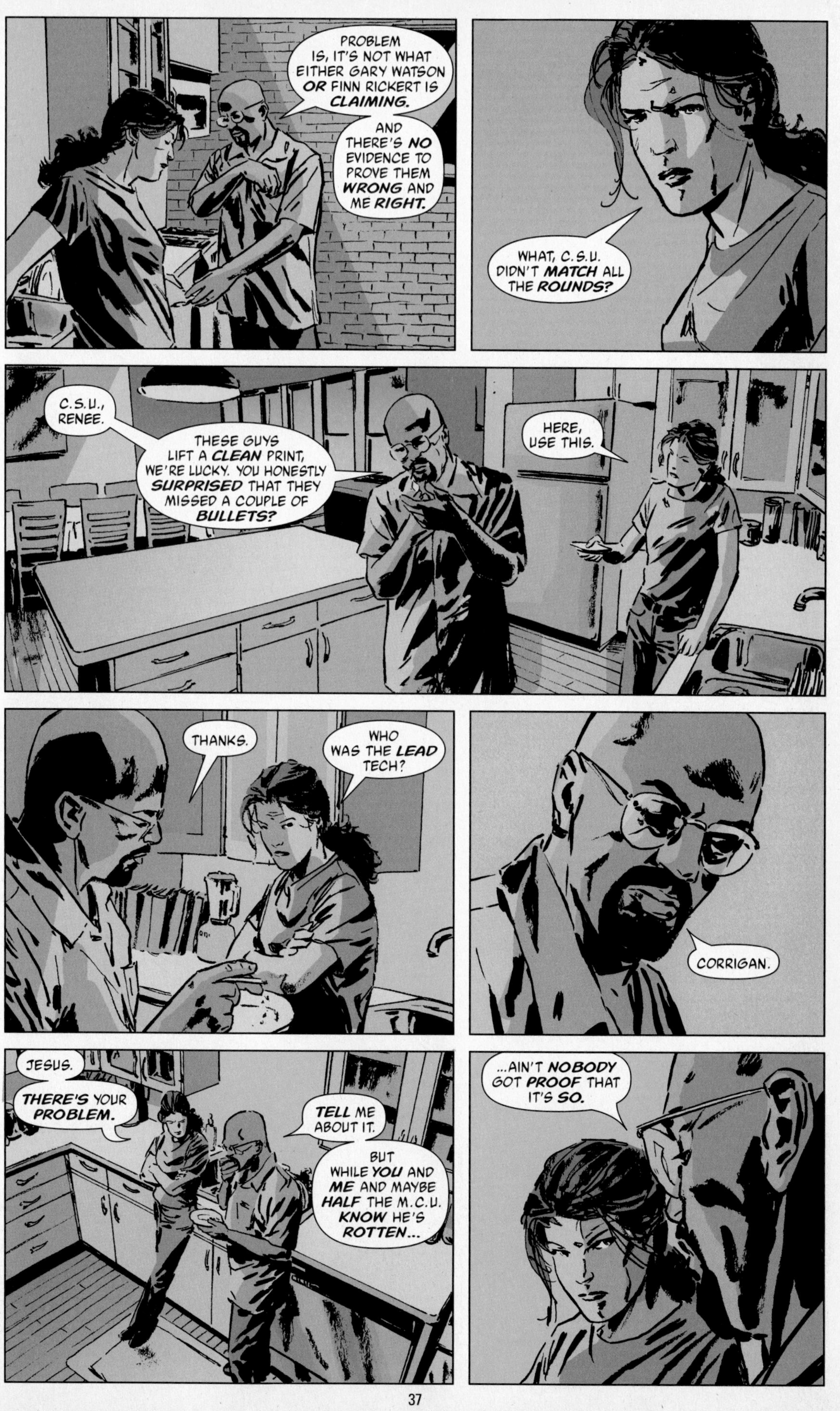

PROBLEM IS, IT'S NOT WHAT EITHER GARY WATSON **OR** FINN RICKERT IS **CLAIMING.**
AND THERE'S **NO** EVIDENCE TO PROVE THEM **WRONG** AND ME **RIGHT.**
WHAT, C.S.U. DIDN'T **MATCH** ALL THE **ROUNDS?**
C.S.U., RENEE.
THESE GUYS LIFT A **CLEAN** PRINT, WE'RE LUCKY. YOU HONESTLY **SURPRISED** THAT THEY MISSED A COUPLE OF **BULLETS?**
HERE, USE THIS.
THANKS.
WHO WAS THE **LEAD** TECH?
CORRIGAN.
JESUS.
THERE'S YOUR **PROBLEM.**
TELL ME ABOUT IT.
BUT WHILE **YOU** AND **ME** AND MAYBE **HALF** THE M.C.U. **KNOW** HE'S **ROTTEN...**
...AIN'T **NOBODY** GOT **PROOF** THAT IT'S **SO.**

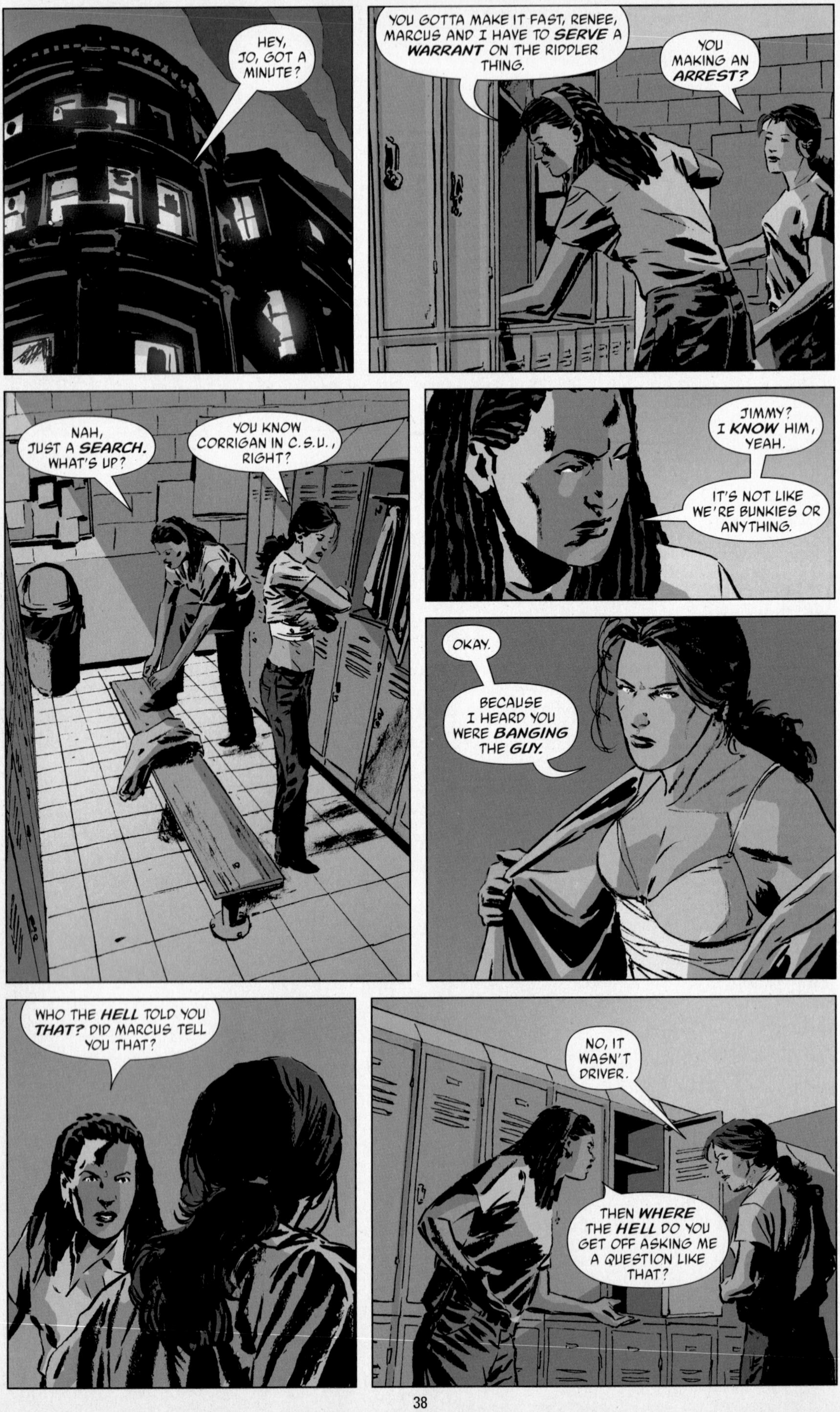
HEY, JO, GOT A MINUTE?
YOU GOTTA MAKE IT FAST, RENEE, MARCUS AND I HAVE TO SERVE A WARRANT ON THE RIDDLER THING.
YOU MAKING AN ARREST?
NAH, JUST A SEARCH. WHAT'S UP?
YOU KNOW CORRIGAN IN C.S.U., RIGHT?
JIMMY? I KNOW HIM, YEAH.
IT'S NOT LIKE WE'RE BUNKIES OR ANYTHING.
OKAY.
BECAUSE I HEARD YOU WERE BANGING THE GUY.
WHO THE HELL TOLD YOU THAT? DID MARCUS TELL YOU THAT?
NO, IT WASN'T DRIVER.
THEN WHERE THE HELL DO YOU GET OFF ASKING ME A QUESTION LIKE THAT?

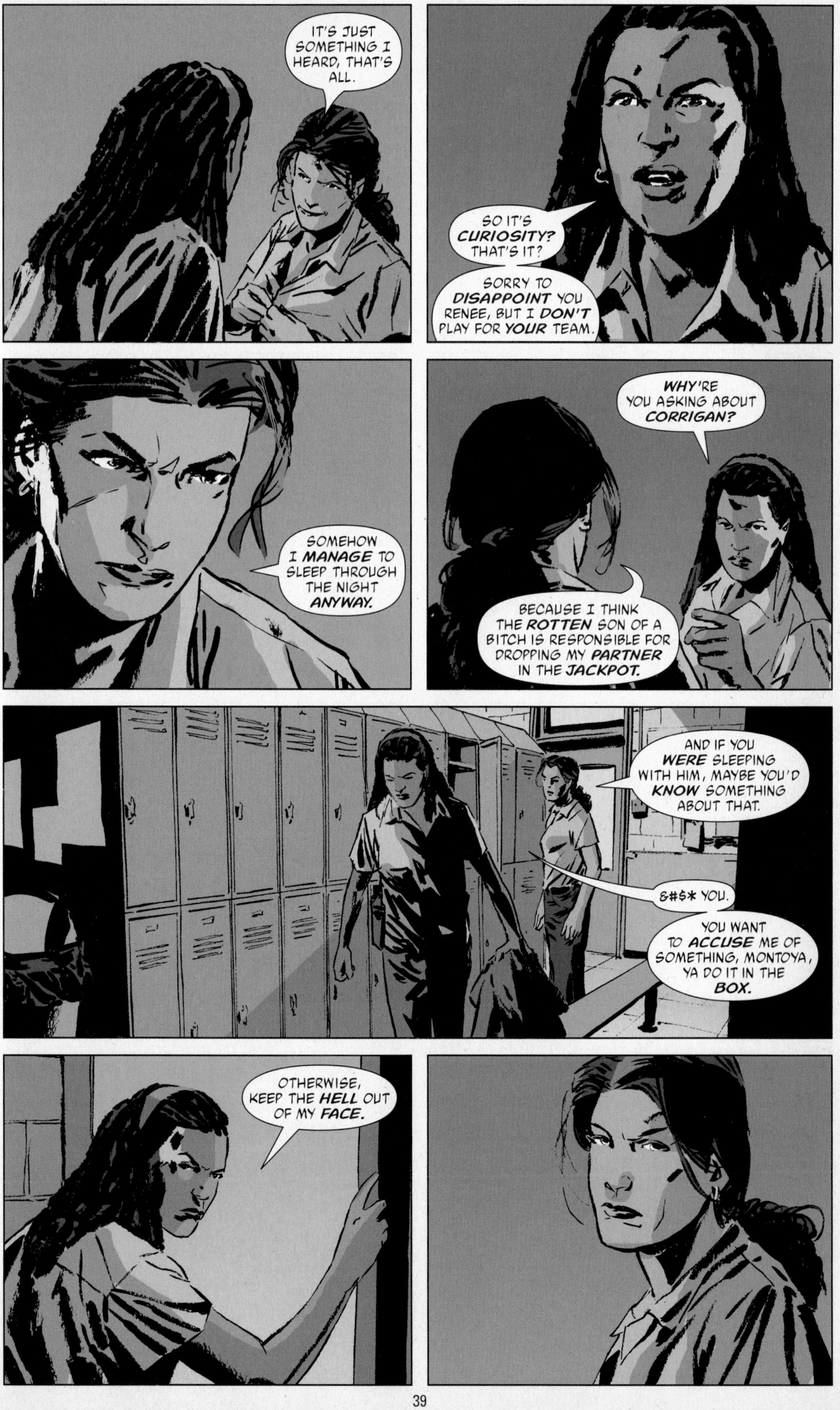
IT'S JUST SOMETHING I HEARD, THAT'S ALL.
SO IT'S CURIOSITY? THAT'S IT?
SORRY TO DISAPPOINT YOU RENEE, BUT I DON'T PLAY FOR YOUR TEAM.
SOMEHOW I MANAGE TO SLEEP THROUGH THE NIGHT ANYWAY.
WHY'RE YOU ASKING ABOUT CORRIGAN?
BECAUSE I THINK THE ROTTEN SON OF A BITCH IS RESPONSIBLE FOR DROPPING MY PARTNER IN THE JACKPOT.
AND IF YOU WERE SLEEPING WITH HIM, MAYBE YOU'D KNOW SOMETHING ABOUT THAT.
&#$* YOU.
YOU WANT TO ACCUSE ME OF SOMETHING, MONTOYA, YA DO IT IN THE BOX.
OTHERWISE, KEEP THE HELL OUT OF MY FACE.

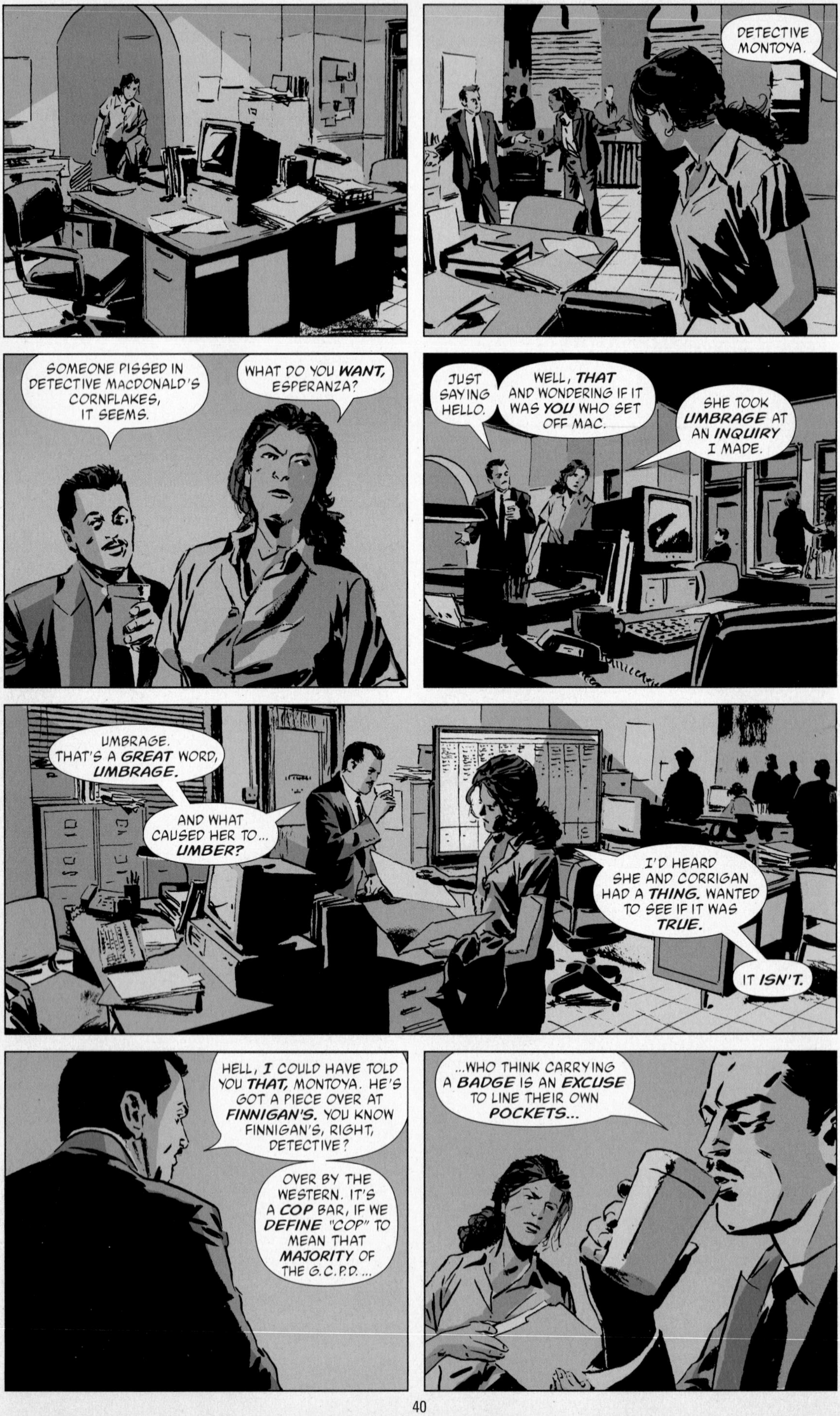
DETECTIVE MONTOYA.
SOMEONE PISSED IN DETECTIVE MACDONALD'S CORNFLAKES, IT SEEMS.
WHAT DO YOU *WANT*, ESPERANZA?
JUST SAYING HELLO.
WELL, *THAT* AND WONDERING IF IT WAS *YOU* WHO SET OFF MAC.
SHE TOOK *UMBRAGE* AT AN *INQUIRY* I MADE.
UMBRAGE. THAT'S A *GREAT* WORD, *UMBRAGE.*
AND WHAT CAUSED HER TO... *UMBER?*
I'D HEARD SHE AND CORRIGAN HAD A *THING.* WANTED TO SEE IF IT WAS *TRUE.*
IT *ISN'T.*
HELL, *I* COULD HAVE TOLD YOU *THAT,* MONTOYA. HE'S GOT A PIECE OVER AT *FINNIGAN'S.* YOU KNOW FINNIGAN'S, RIGHT, DETECTIVE?
OVER BY THE WESTERN. IT'S A *COP* BAR, IF WE *DEFINE* "COP" TO MEAN THAT *MAJORITY* OF THE G.C.P.D. ...
...WHO THINK CARRYING A *BADGE* IS AN *EXCUSE* TO LINE THEIR OWN *POCKETS...*

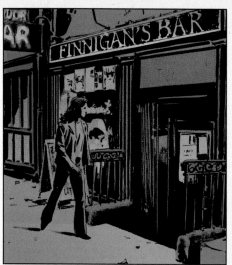

...SERIOUSLY CHERRY, YOU HAVE TO SEE THIS BABY, MADE TO PURR...

HEY, GINA! TWO MORE PITCHERS AND SOME PRETZELS!

...MAKING TIME-AND-A-*HALF* ON THIS IS A *GOLD MINE*...

...TAKE A LOOK AT THAT...

...SO *THAT* WAS ON TUESDAY, RIGHT? THEN ON WEDNESDAY, WE GET THE SAME CALL *AGAIN*...

--*DAMN DOMESTIC*, SO I STARTED USING MY *STICK* ON THEM *BOTH*...

SURE, I'M *ON DUTY*, BUT MY *SERGEANT* KNOWS I'M HERE.

--ABOUT HOW I'M NEVER HOME, SO I SHOW HER THE *BACK* OF MY *HAND*--

...NAH, NOT ANYMORE, BUT I'VE GOT A LITTLE S&W THAT I CARRY NOW AS A BACK-UP...

...NO, THE *OTHER* ONE, THE ONE IN *TRI-CORNER*, WITH THE *ORIENTAL* CHICKS...

--I.A.D. *BASTARD*, TOLD HIM HE WANTED TO HEAR MORE, TO CALL MY *UNION* REP!

...*HOT* LITTLE NUMBER, SO I TELL HER I *COULD* RIP THE *TICKET* BUT...

--HASN'T *PAID* UP YET, THINKING A *VISIT* MIGHT BE IN *ORDER*...

LOOKS LIKE SOME-BODY GOT LOST.

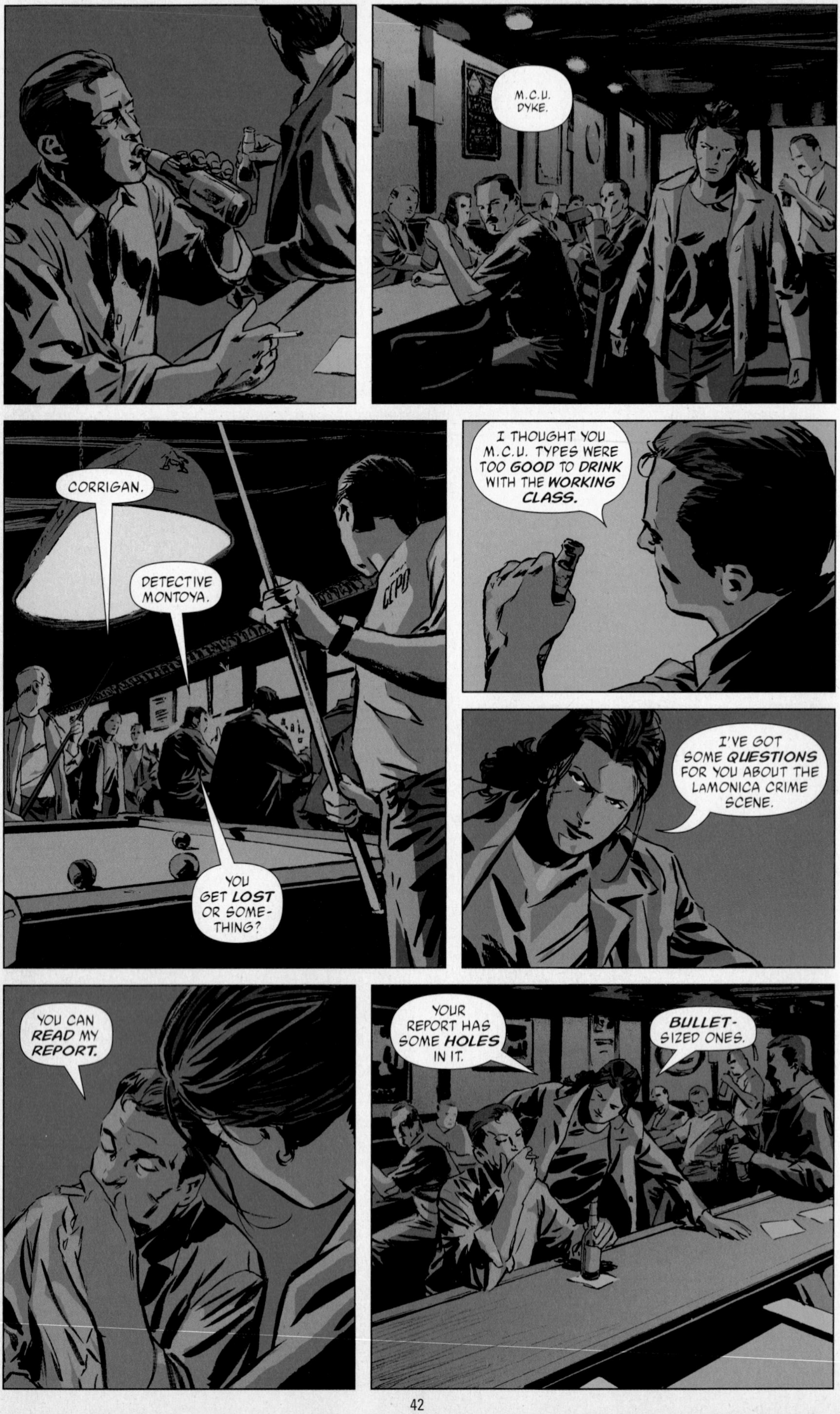
M.C.U. DYKE.
CORRIGAN.
DETECTIVE MONTOYA.
YOU GET LOST OR SOME-THING?
I THOUGHT YOU M.C.U. TYPES WERE TOO GOOD TO DRINK WITH THE WORKING CLASS.
I'VE GOT SOME QUESTIONS FOR YOU ABOUT THE LAMONICA CRIME SCENE.
YOU CAN READ MY REPORT.
YOUR REPORT HAS SOME HOLES IN IT.
BULLET-SIZED ONES.

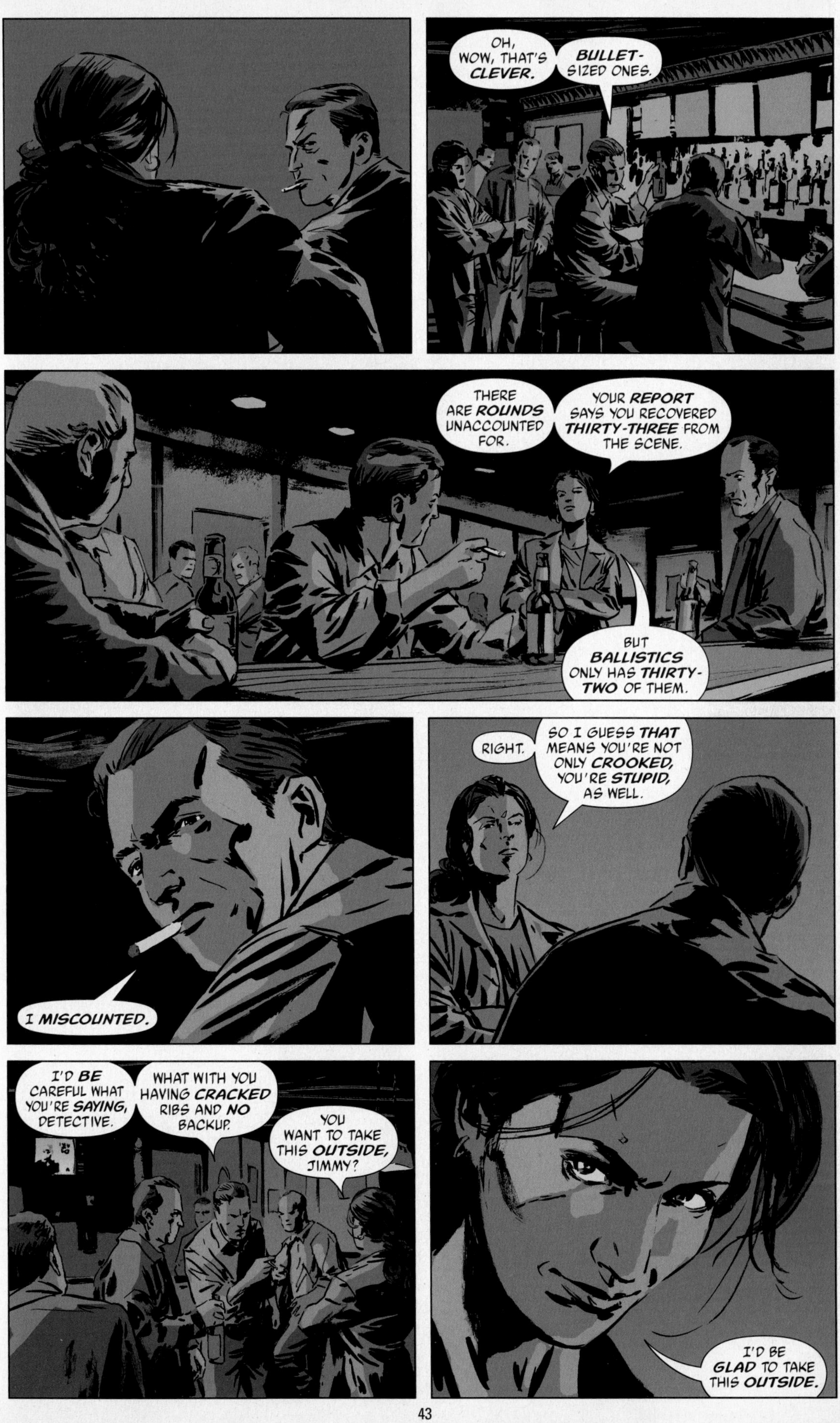
OH, WOW, THAT'S CLEVER.
BULLET-SIZED ONES.
THERE ARE ROUNDS UNACCOUNTED FOR.
YOUR REPORT SAYS YOU RECOVERED THIRTY-THREE FROM THE SCENE.
BUT BALLISTICS ONLY HAS THIRTY-TWO OF THEM.
I MISCOUNTED.
RIGHT.
SO I GUESS THAT MEANS YOU'RE NOT ONLY CROOKED, YOU'RE STUPID, AS WELL.
I'D BE CAREFUL WHAT YOU'RE SAYING, DETECTIVE.
WHAT WITH YOU HAVING CRACKED RIBS AND NO BACKUP.
YOU WANT TO TAKE THIS OUTSIDE, JIMMY?
I'D BE GLAD TO TAKE THIS OUTSIDE.

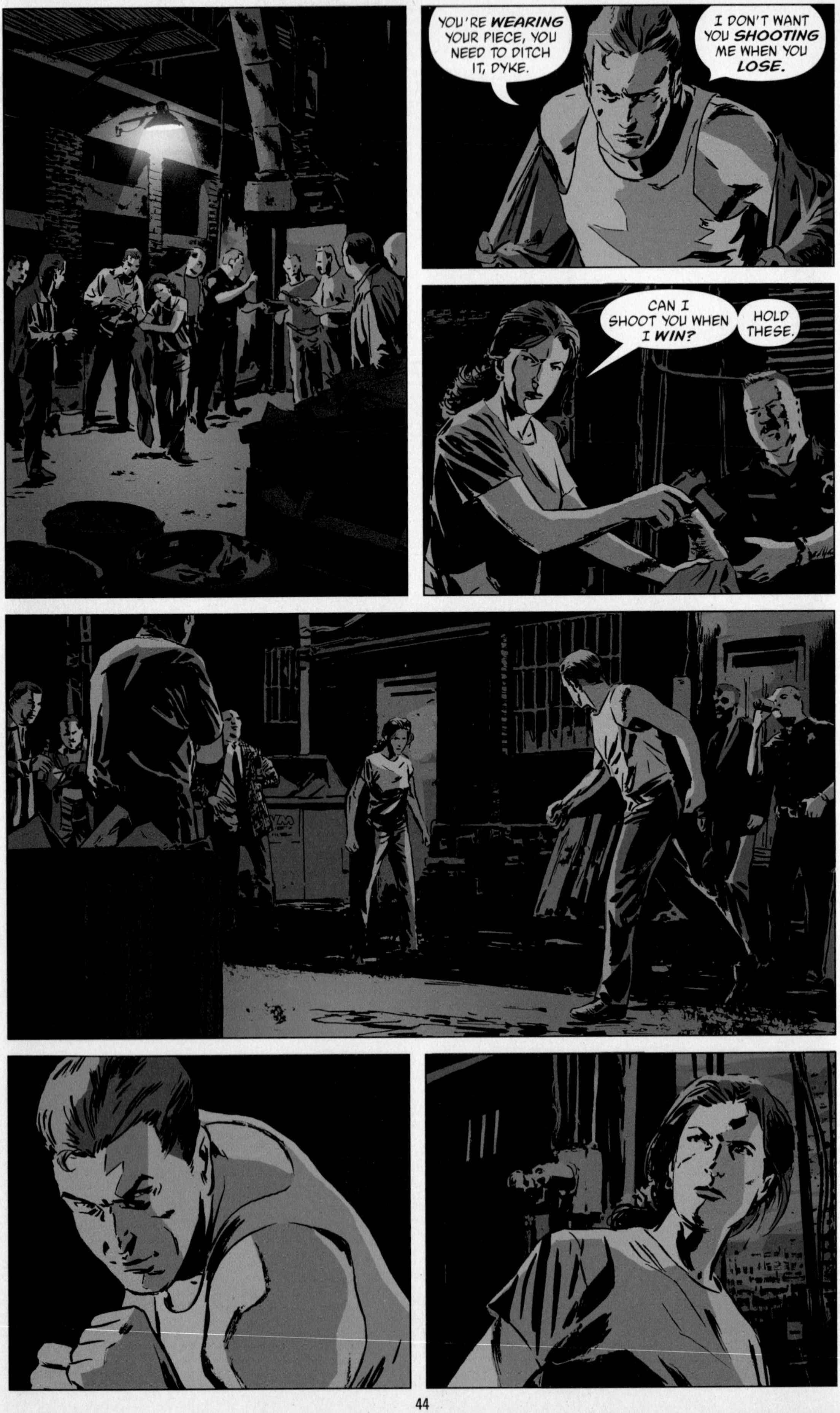
YOU'RE **WEARING** YOUR PIECE, YOU NEED TO DITCH IT, DYKE.
I DON'T WANT YOU **SHOOTING** ME WHEN YOU **LOSE.**
CAN I SHOOT YOU WHEN I **WIN?**
HOLD THESE.

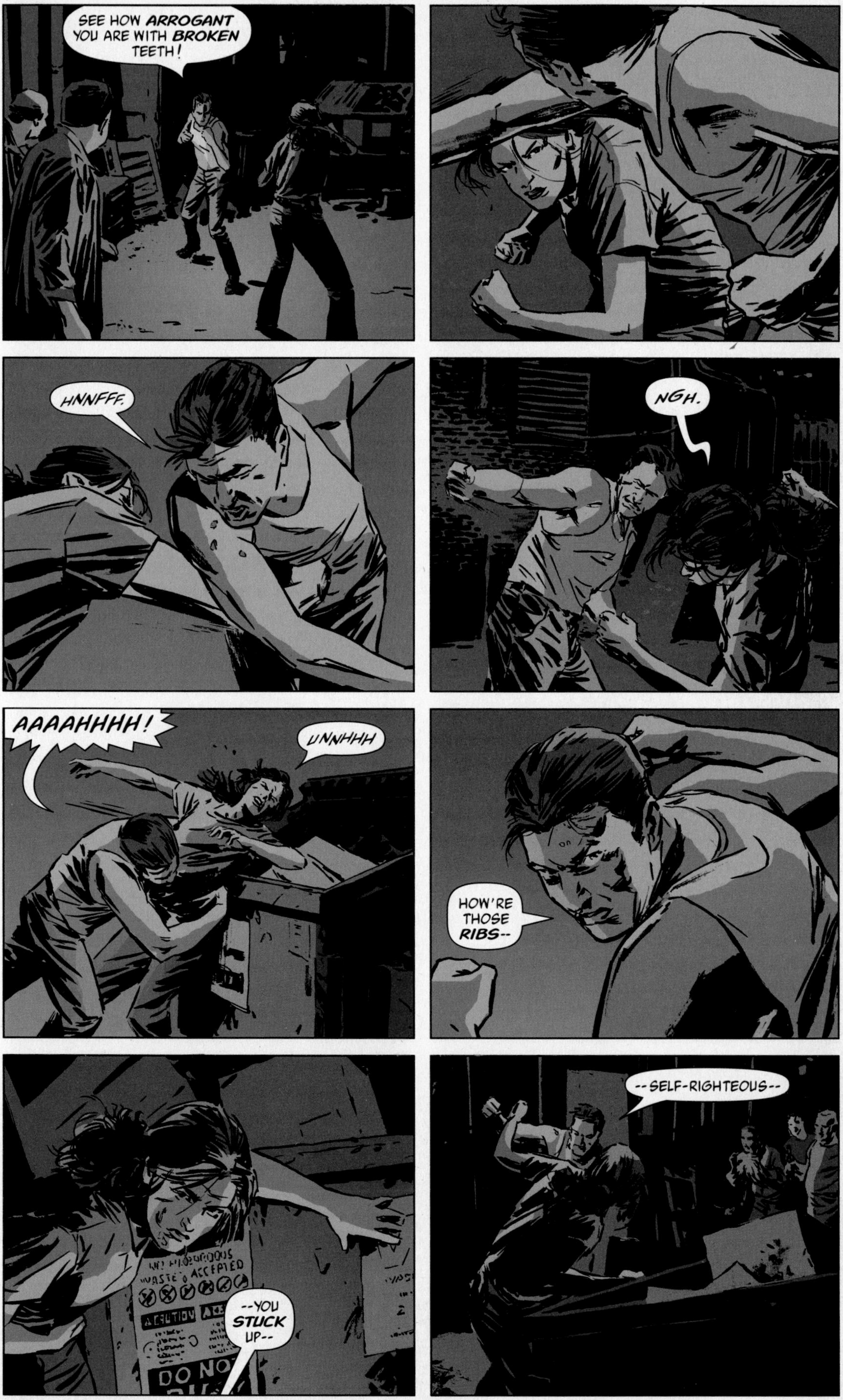
SEE HOW ARROGANT YOU ARE WITH BROKEN TEETH!
HNNFFF.
NGH.
AAAAHHHH!
UNNHHH
HOW'RE THOSE RIBS--
--YOU STUCK UP--
--SELF-RIGHTEOUS--

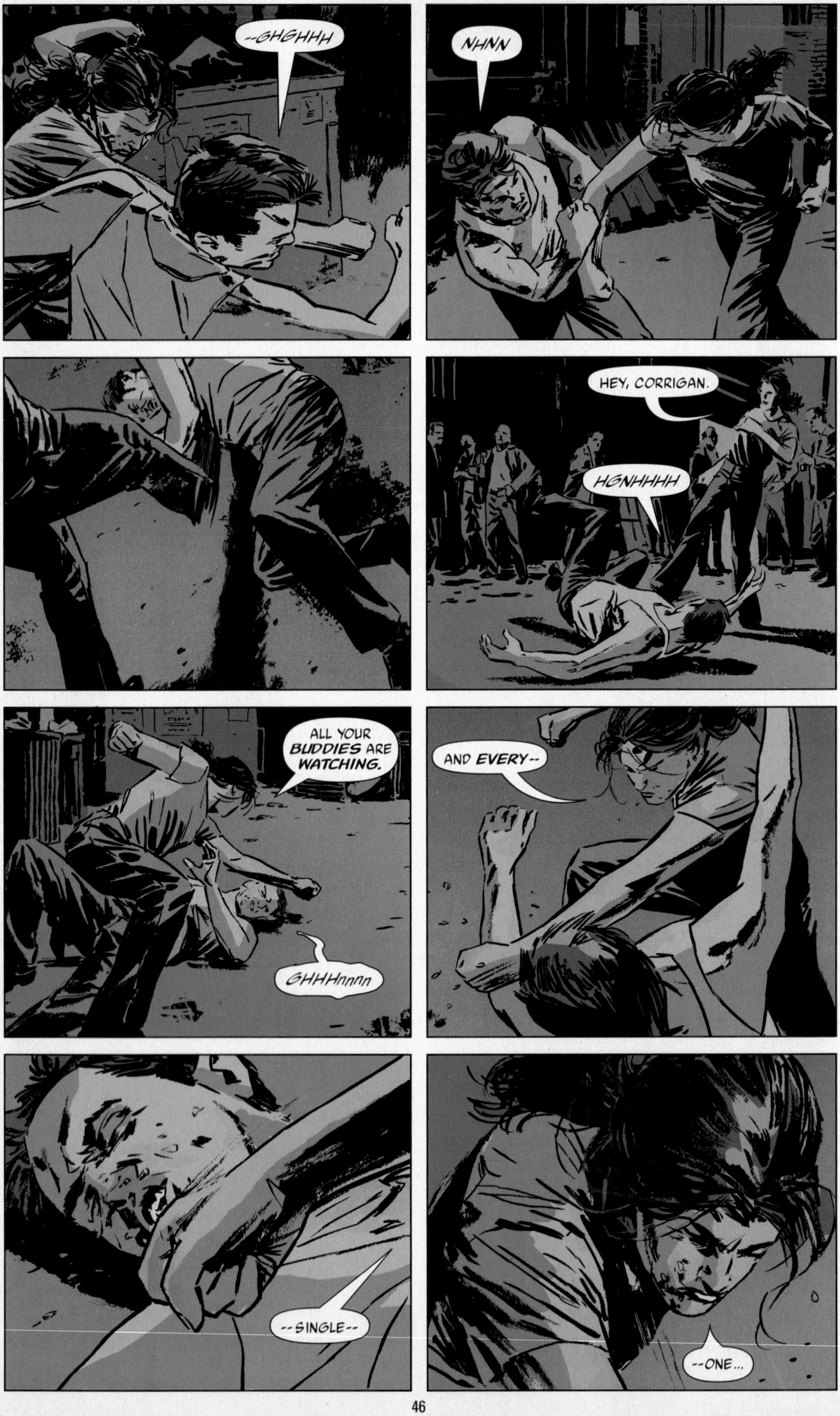
--GHGHHH
NHNN
HEY, CORRIGAN.
HGNHHHH
ALL YOUR BUDDIES ARE WATCHING.
GHHHnnnn
AND EVERY--
--SINGLE--
--ONE...

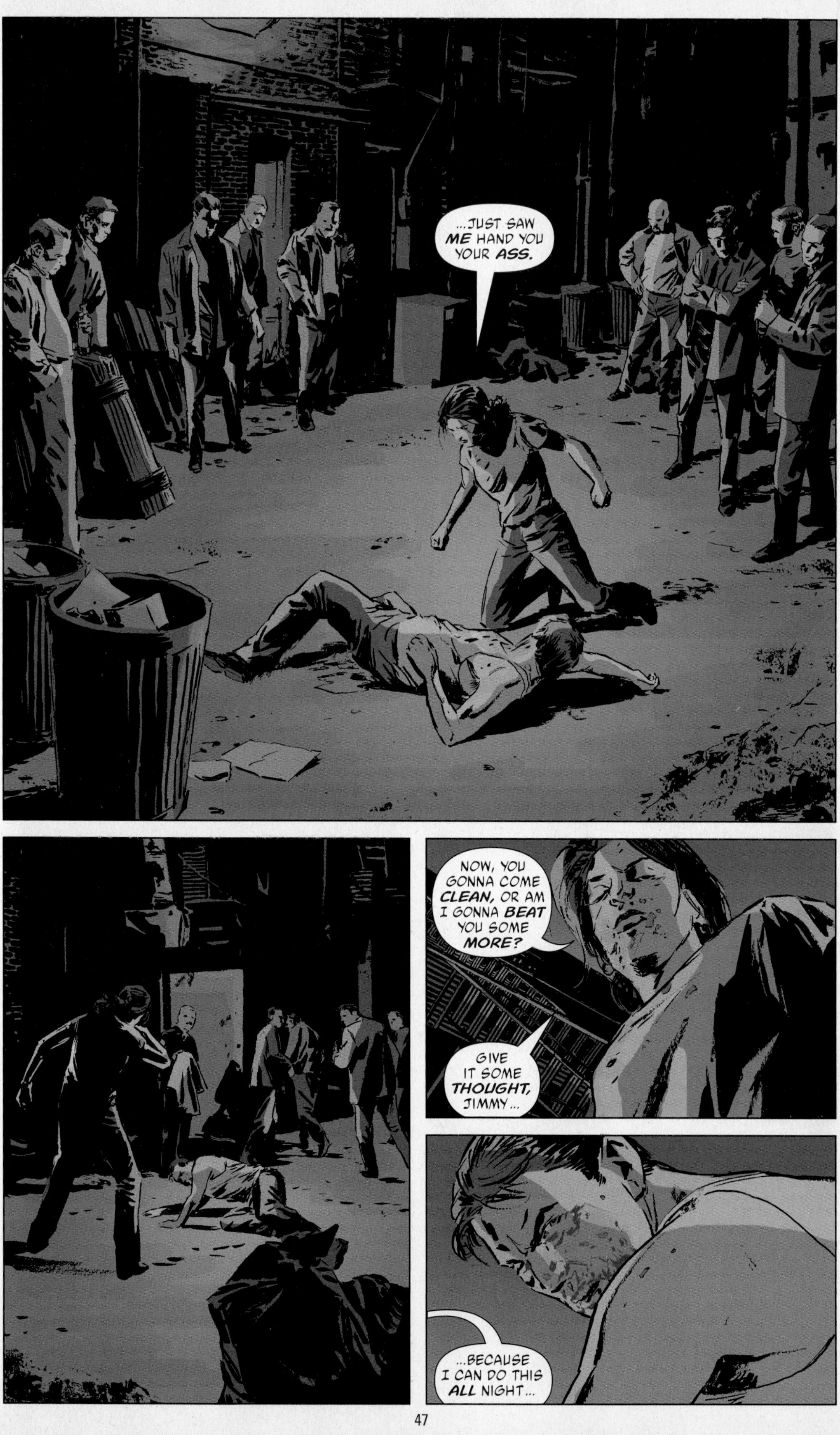
...JUST SAW ME HAND YOU YOUR ASS.
NOW, YOU GONNA COME CLEAN, OR AM I GONNA BEAT YOU SOME MORE?
GIVE IT SOME THOUGHT, JIMMY...
...BECAUSE I CAN DO THIS ALL NIGHT...

HE GIVE IT UP?

YOU **FOLLOW** ME?

DID HE GIVE IT **UP,** DETECTIVE?

HOW MUCH DID YOU **SEE?**

ENOUGH.

HE SOLD IT TO SOME **COLLECTOR** OUT IN THE '**BURBS** FOR ALMOST **TEN** GRAND.

NAME OF **JENNIFER GORDON-HEWITT.**

THEN I'LL VISIT MS. HEWITT IN THE **MORNING.**

LIKE HELL.

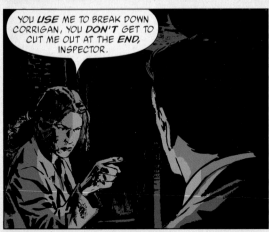

YOU **USE** ME TO BREAK DOWN CORRIGAN, YOU **DON'T** GET TO CUT ME OUT AT THE **END,** INSPECTOR.

I'LL MEET YOU AT **CENTRAL** IN THE **MORNING...**

...**WE** CAN TALK TO MS. HEWITT **TOGETHER.**

RENEE?

IT'S **OKAY.** GO BACK TO **SLEEP,** DEE.

DIDN'T MEAN TO **WAKE** YOU.

DID YOU GET INTO A **FIGHT?**

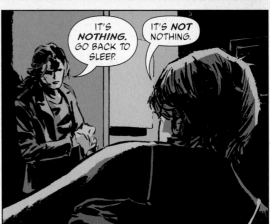

IT'S **NOTHING.** GO BACK TO SLEEP.

IT'S **NOT** NOTHING.

LET ME SEE.

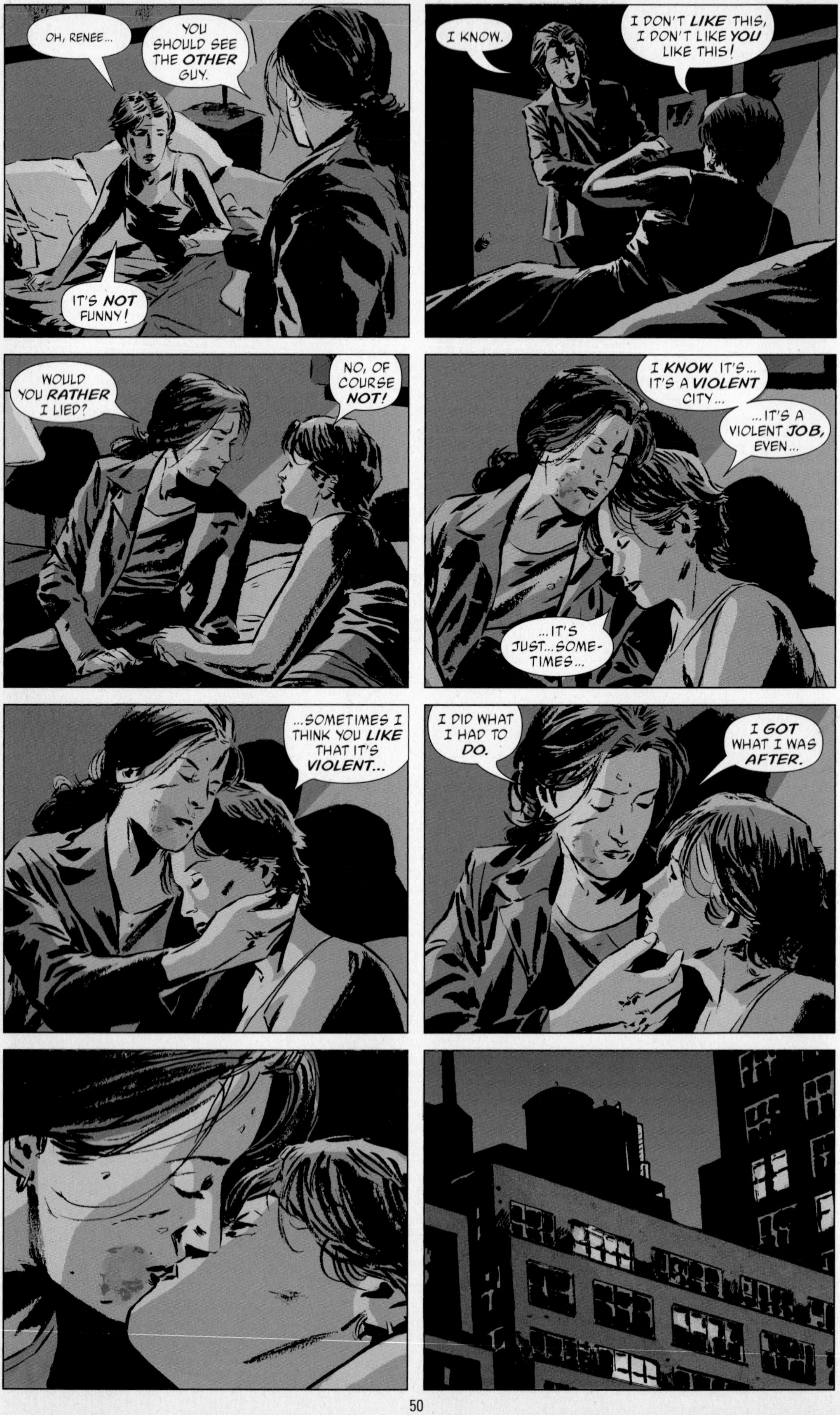
OH, RENEE...
YOU SHOULD SEE THE **OTHER** GUY.
IT'S **NOT** FUNNY!
I KNOW.
I DON'T **LIKE** THIS, I DON'T LIKE **YOU** LIKE THIS!
WOULD YOU **RATHER** I LIED?
NO, OF COURSE **NOT!**
I **KNOW** IT'S... IT'S A **VIOLENT** CITY...
...IT'S A VIOLENT **JOB,** EVEN...
...IT'S JUST...SOME-TIMES...
...SOMETIMES I THINK YOU **LIKE** THAT IT'S **VIOLENT...**
I DID WHAT I HAD TO **DO.**
I GOT WHAT I WAS **AFTER.**

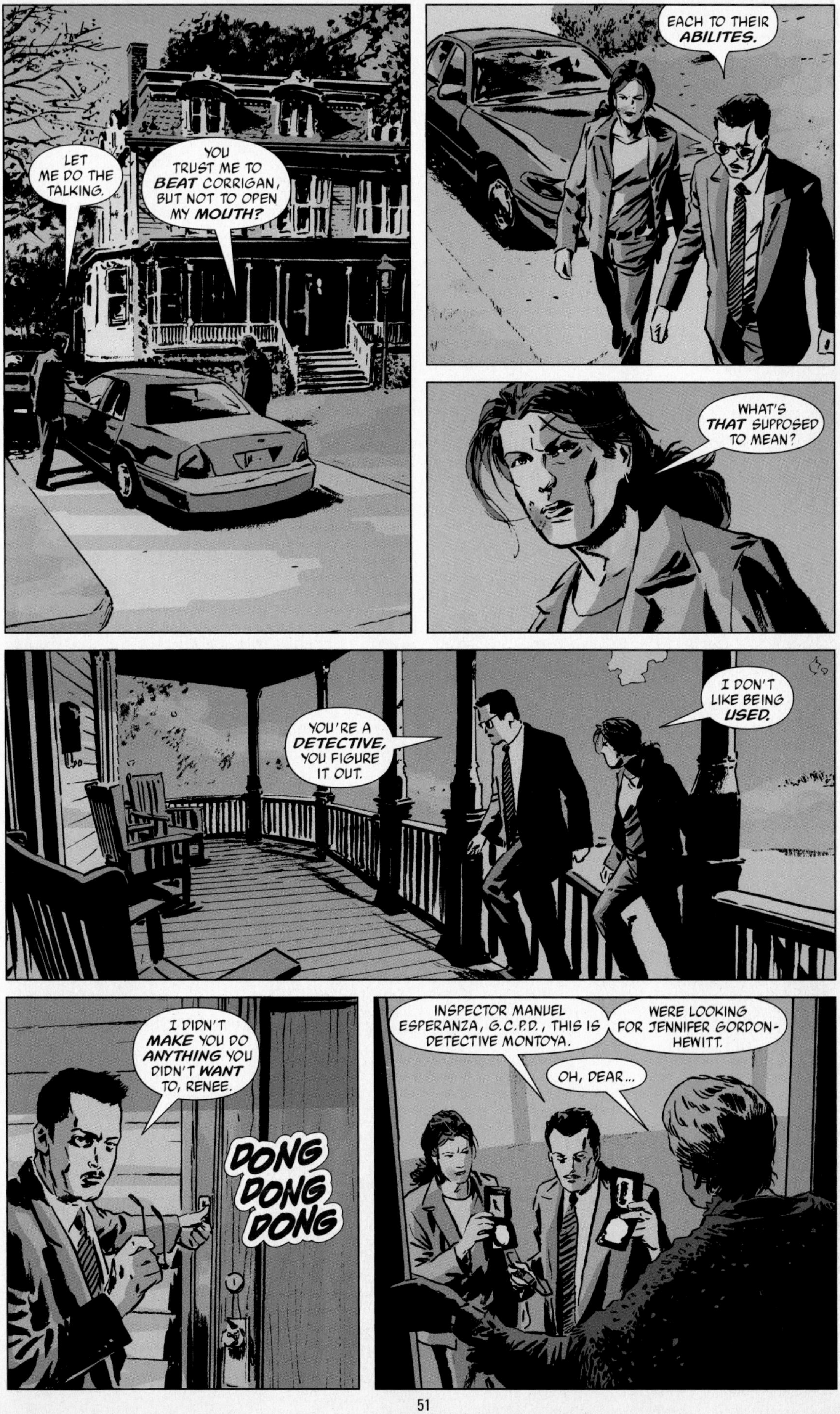
LET ME DO THE TALKING.
YOU TRUST ME TO BEAT CORRIGAN, BUT NOT TO OPEN MY MOUTH?
EACH TO THEIR ABILITES.
WHAT'S THAT SUPPOSED TO MEAN?
I DON'T LIKE BEING USED.
YOU'RE A DETECTIVE, YOU FIGURE IT OUT.
I DIDN'T MAKE YOU DO ANYTHING YOU DIDN'T WANT TO, RENEE.
DONG DONG DONG
INSPECTOR MANUEL ESPERANZA, G.C.P.D., THIS IS DETECTIVE MONTOYA.
WERE LOOKING FOR JENNIFER GORDON-HEWITT.
OH, DEAR...

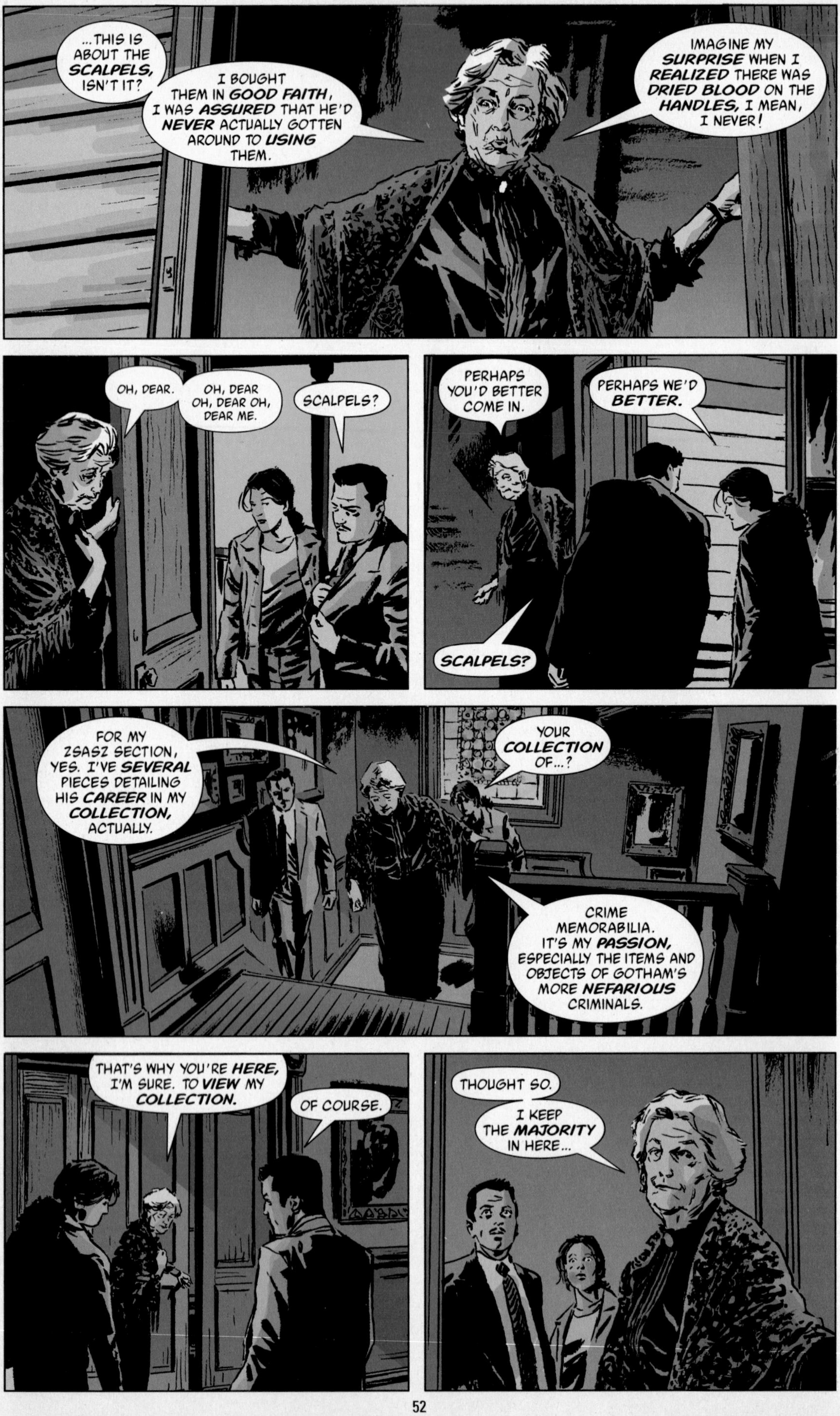
...THIS IS ABOUT THE SCALPELS, ISN'T IT?
I BOUGHT THEM IN GOOD FAITH, I WAS ASSURED THAT HE'D NEVER ACTUALLY GOTTEN AROUND TO USING THEM.
IMAGINE MY SURPRISE WHEN I REALIZED THERE WAS DRIED BLOOD ON THE HANDLES, I MEAN, I NEVER!
OH, DEAR.
OH, DEAR OH, DEAR OH, DEAR ME.
SCALPELS?
PERHAPS YOU'D BETTER COME IN.
PERHAPS WE'D BETTER.
SCALPELS?
FOR MY ZSASZ SECTION, YES. I'VE SEVERAL PIECES DETAILING HIS CAREER IN MY COLLECTION, ACTUALLY.
YOUR COLLECTION OF...?
CRIME MEMORABILIA. IT'S MY PASSION, ESPECIALLY THE ITEMS AND OBJECTS OF GOTHAM'S MORE NEFARIOUS CRIMINALS.
THAT'S WHY YOU'RE HERE, I'M SURE. TO VIEW MY COLLECTION.
OF COURSE.
THOUGHT SO.
I KEEP THE MAJORITY IN HERE...

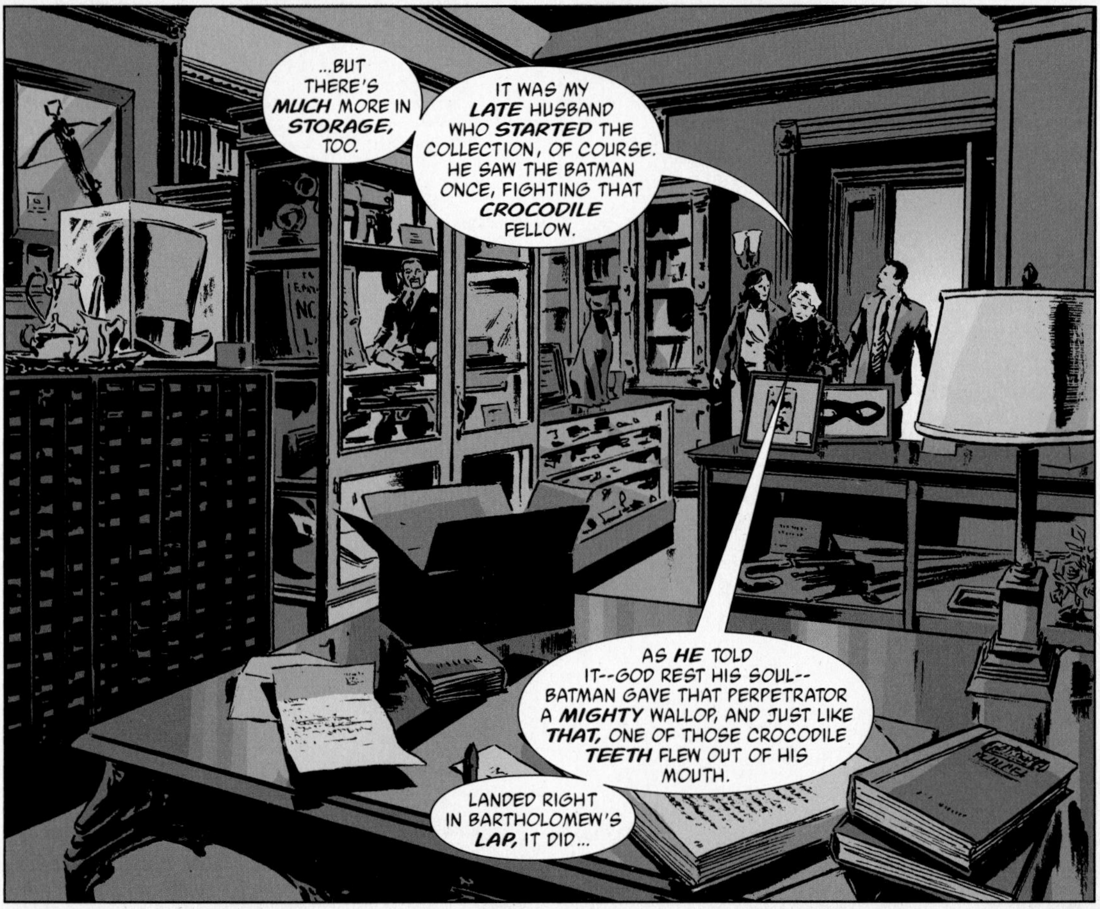
...BUT THERE'S MUCH MORE IN STORAGE, TOO.
IT WAS MY LATE HUSBAND WHO STARTED THE COLLECTION, OF COURSE. HE SAW THE BATMAN ONCE, FIGHTING THAT CROCODILE FELLOW.
AS HE TOLD IT--GOD REST HIS SOUL--BATMAN GAVE THAT PERPETRATOR A MIGHTY WALLOP, AND JUST LIKE THAT, ONE OF THOSE CROCODILE TEETH FLEW OUT OF HIS MOUTH.
LANDED RIGHT IN BARTHOLOMEW'S LAP, IT DID...

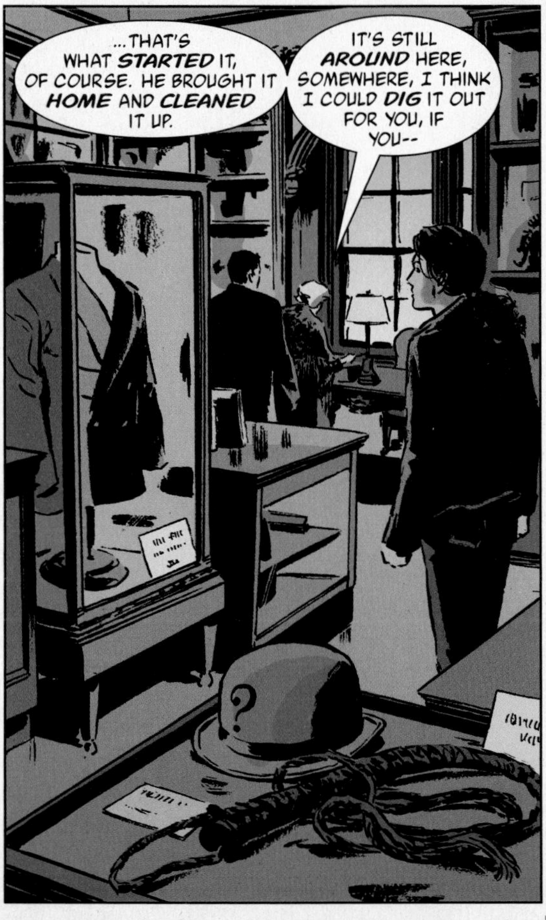
...THAT'S WHAT STARTED IT, OF COURSE. HE BROUGHT IT HOME AND CLEANED IT UP.
IT'S STILL AROUND HERE, SOMEWHERE, I THINK I COULD DIG IT OUT FOR YOU, IF YOU--

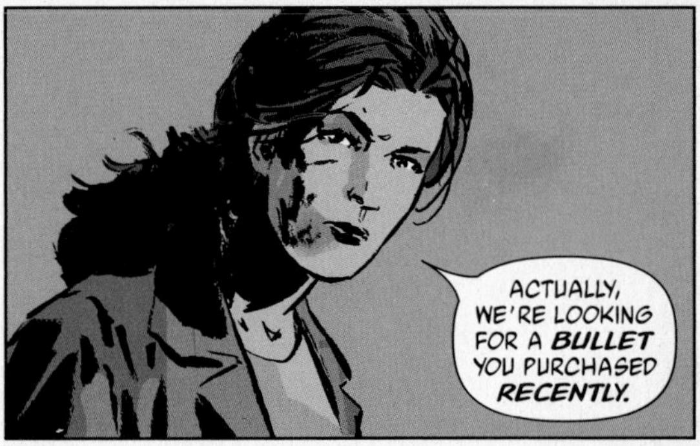
ACTUALLY, WE'RE LOOKING FOR A BULLET YOU PURCHASED RECENTLY.

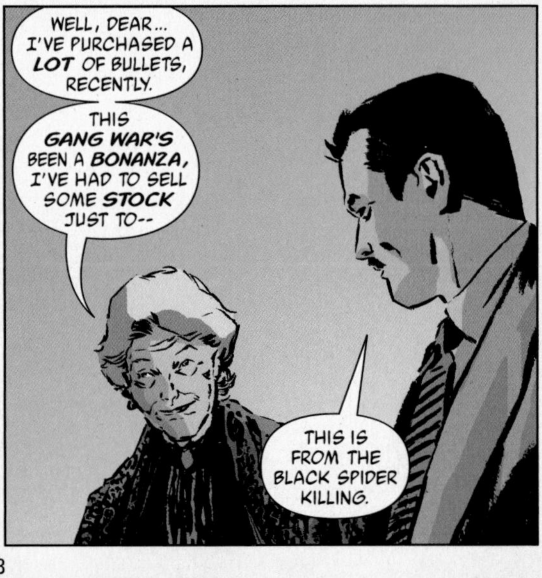
WELL, DEAR... I'VE PURCHASED A LOT OF BULLETS, RECENTLY.
THIS GANG WAR'S BEEN A BONANZA, I'VE HAD TO SELL SOME STOCK JUST TO--
THIS IS FROM THE BLACK SPIDER KILLING.

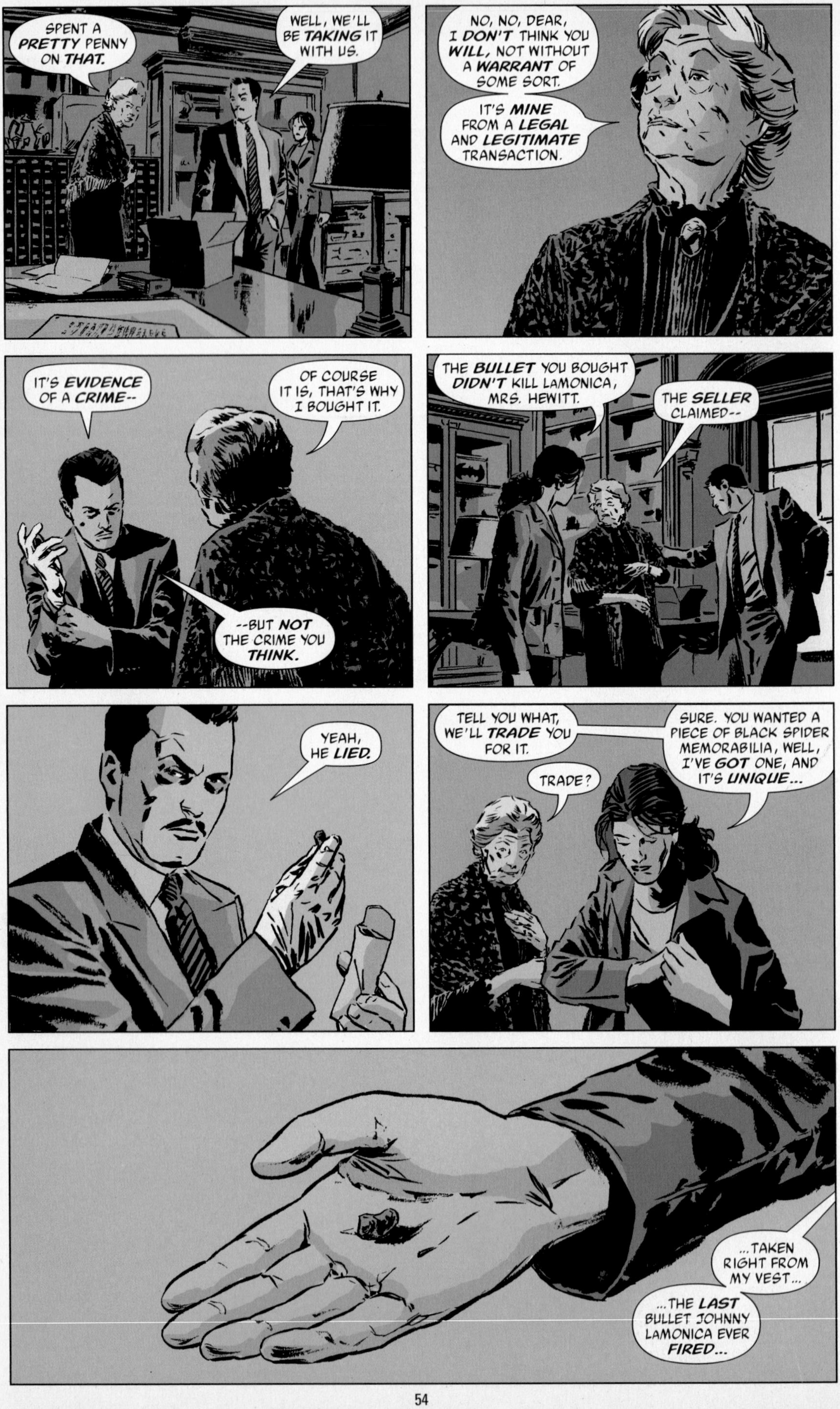
SPENT A PRETTY PENNY ON THAT.
WELL, WE'LL BE TAKING IT WITH US.
NO, NO, DEAR, I DON'T THINK YOU WILL, NOT WITHOUT A WARRANT OF SOME SORT.
IT'S MINE FROM A LEGAL AND LEGITIMATE TRANSACTION.
IT'S EVIDENCE OF A CRIME--
OF COURSE IT IS, THAT'S WHY I BOUGHT IT.
--BUT NOT THE CRIME YOU THINK.
THE BULLET YOU BOUGHT DIDN'T KILL LAMONICA, MRS. HEWITT.
THE SELLER CLAIMED--
YEAH, HE LIED.
TELL YOU WHAT, WE'LL TRADE YOU FOR IT.
TRADE?
SURE. YOU WANTED A PIECE OF BLACK SPIDER MEMORABILIA, WELL, I'VE GOT ONE, AND IT'S UNIQUE...
...TAKEN RIGHT FROM MY VEST...
...THE LAST BULLET JOHNNY LAMONICA EVER FIRED...

YOU'LL RUN THE **SLUG** DOWN TO THE **LAB** WHEN WE GET BACK.

YEAH, IF IT'S FROM ALLEN'S **GUN** LIKE WE FIGURE, THAT'LL BE THAT.

JUST KEEP IT AWAY FROM **CORRIGAN**, THAT'S ALL I **ASK**.

I SUSPECT CORRIGAN'S GONNA BE ON HIS **BEST** BEHAVIOR, EVEN **IF** THAT BOY'S ROTTEN TO THE **CORE**.

HE'S GONNA BE **UNTOUCHABLE**, NOW, YOU KNOW THAT.

ANYTHING YOU GET ON HIM, IT'S ALL FRUIT FROM THE **POISON** TREE.

I **KNOW**.

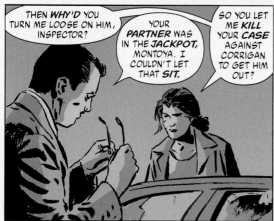

THEN **WHY'D** YOU TURN ME LOOSE ON HIM, INSPECTOR?

YOUR **PARTNER** WAS IN THE **JACKPOT**, MONTOYA. I COULDN'T LET THAT **SIT**.

SO YOU LET ME **KILL** YOUR **CASE** AGAINST CORRIGAN TO GET HIM OUT?

I DON'T **BELIEVE** YOU.

WHY'D YOU **DO** IT?

BECAUSE I **OWED** YOU ONE.

LET'S GIVE YOUR PARTNER THE **GOOD** NEWS.

THE END

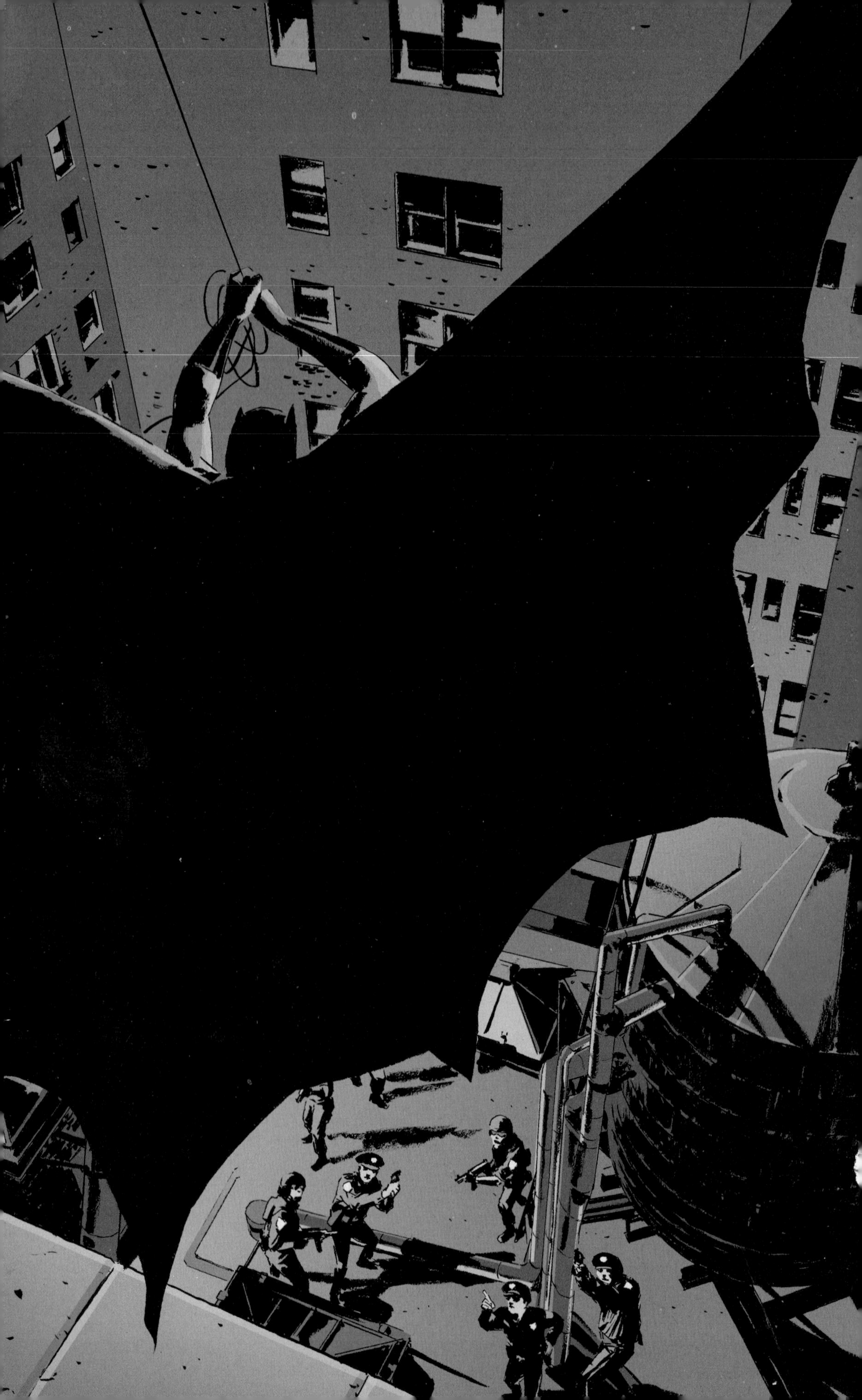

LIGHTS OUT

Written by
GREG RUCKA

Art by
MICHAEL LARK & STEFANO GAUDIANO

Colors by
LEE LOUGHRIDGE

Letters by
CLEM ROBINS

GOTHAM CITY
POLICE DEPARTMENT

HAM CITY
LICE DEPARTMENT

INITIAL REPORT

XXX FOLLOWUP REPORT

DATE/TIME OF OCCURRENCE June-October 2004

The apparent assassination of Gotham's top gang leaders led to all out war between the criminal factions of the city. As bodies began to drop faster and faster, the G.C.P.D. found itself stretched to its limits, its officers caught in the crossfire between the criminals and the Batman, who—to the eyes of the G.C.P.D. and Police Commissioner Michael Akins—seemed to view the police as his own private army.

This view was reinforced when Batman ignored police control of a hostage situation at the Louis H. Grieve Memorial High School, leading to the death of one student, and, later, commandeering control of the police band, in an attempt to issue direct orders to the G.C.P.D. The result was a disaster that left numerous officers wounded, and over two-dozen killed at the hands of Gotham's criminal element....

Mourners pay tribute to falle
Over 500 fill church to remember patrolman slain

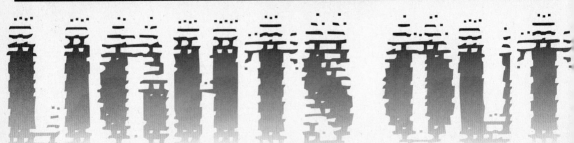

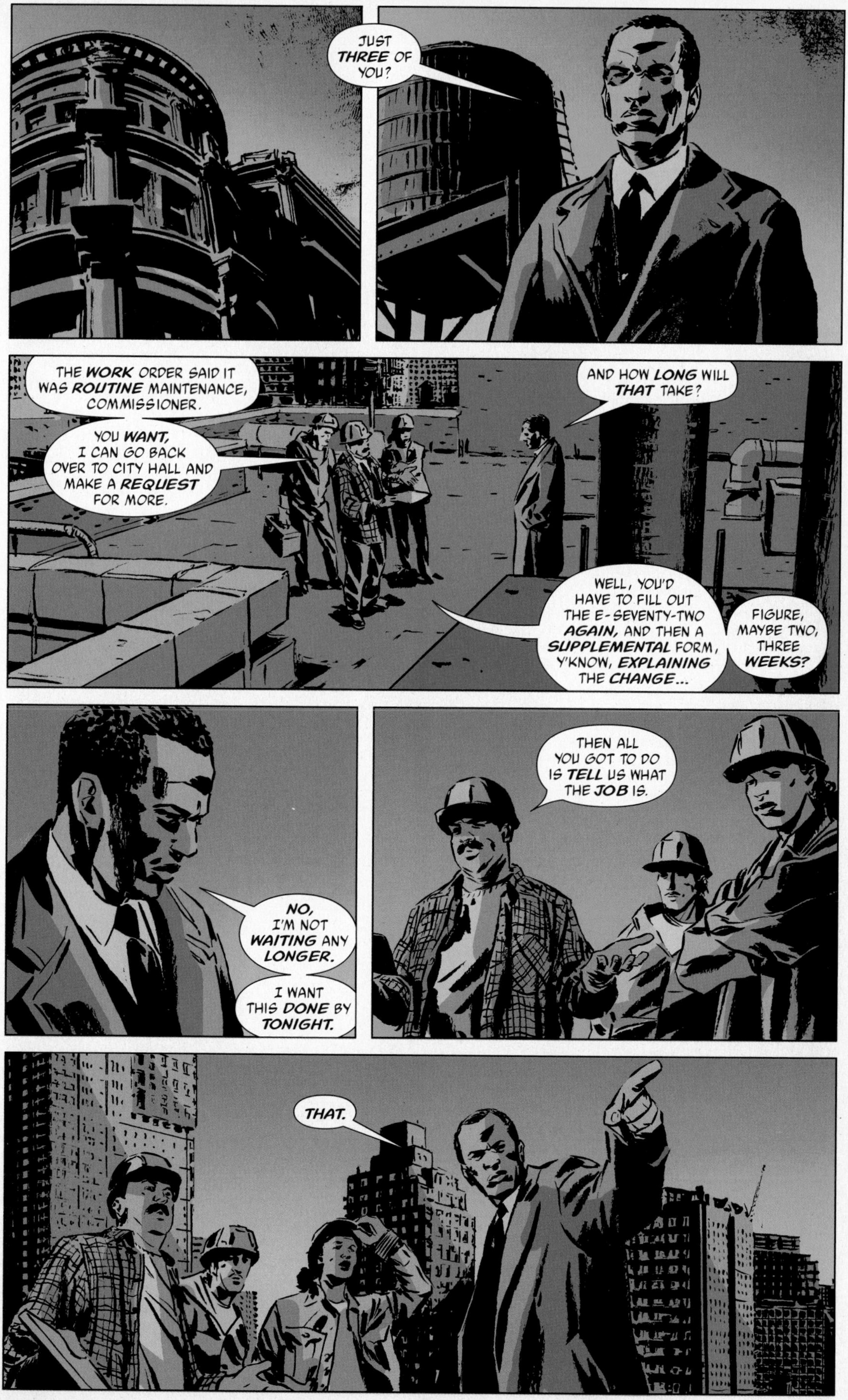

JUST THREE OF YOU?
THE WORK ORDER SAID IT WAS ROUTINE MAINTENANCE, COMMISSIONER.
YOU WANT, I CAN GO BACK OVER TO CITY HALL AND MAKE A REQUEST FOR MORE.
AND HOW LONG WILL THAT TAKE?
WELL, YOU'D HAVE TO FILL OUT THE E-SEVENTY-TWO AGAIN, AND THEN A SUPPLEMENTAL FORM, Y'KNOW, EXPLAINING THE CHANGE...
FIGURE, MAYBE TWO, THREE WEEKS?
NO, I'M NOT WAITING ANY LONGER.
I WANT THIS DONE BY TONIGHT.
THEN ALL YOU GOT TO DO IS TELL US WHAT THE JOB IS.
THAT.

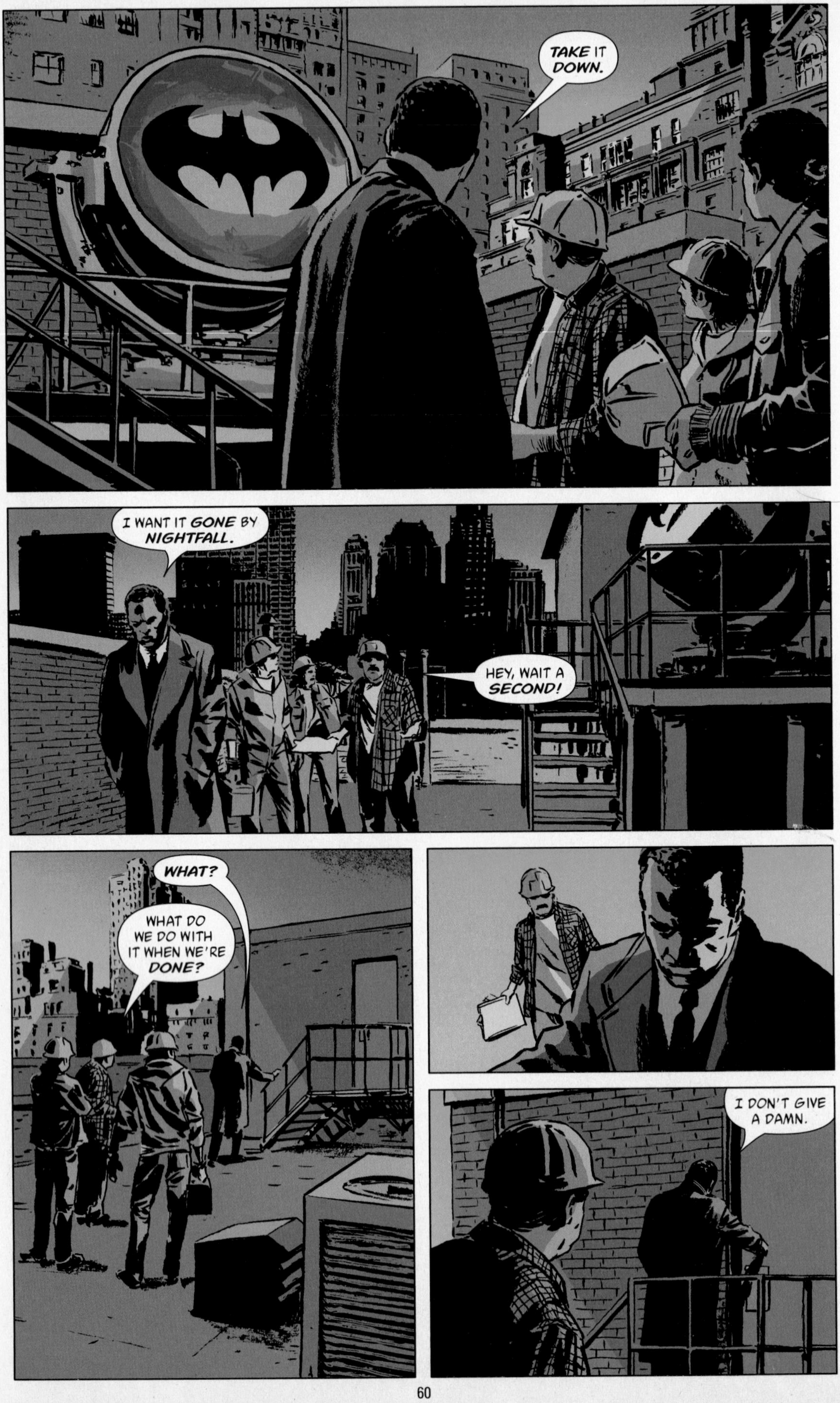
TAKE IT DOWN.
I WANT IT GONE BY NIGHTFALL.
HEY, WAIT A SECOND!
WHAT?
WHAT DO WE DO WITH IT WHEN WE'RE DONE?
I DON'T GIVE A DAMN.

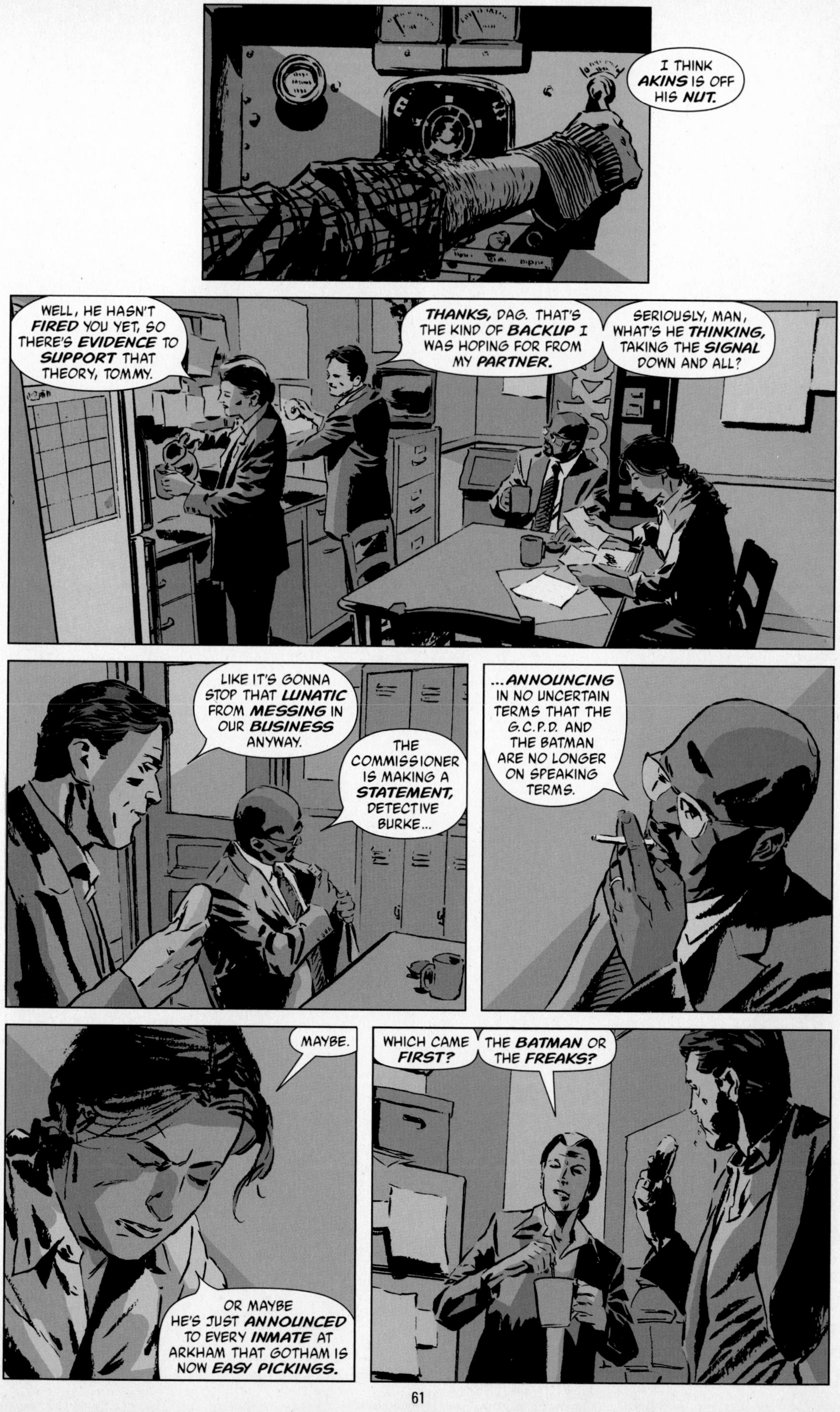
I THINK AKINS IS OFF HIS NUT.
WELL, HE HASN'T FIRED YOU YET, SO THERE'S EVIDENCE TO SUPPORT THAT THEORY, TOMMY.
THANKS, DAG. THAT'S THE KIND OF BACKUP I WAS HOPING FOR FROM MY PARTNER.
SERIOUSLY, MAN, WHAT'S HE THINKING, TAKING THE SIGNAL DOWN AND ALL?
LIKE IT'S GONNA STOP THAT LUNATIC FROM MESSING IN OUR BUSINESS ANYWAY.
THE COMMISSIONER IS MAKING A STATEMENT, DETECTIVE BURKE...
...ANNOUNCING IN NO UNCERTAIN TERMS THAT THE G.C.P.D. AND THE BATMAN ARE NO LONGER ON SPEAKING TERMS.
MAYBE.
OR MAYBE HE'S JUST ANNOUNCED TO EVERY INMATE AT ARKHAM THAT GOTHAM IS NOW EASY PICKINGS.
WHICH CAME FIRST?
THE BATMAN OR THE FREAKS?

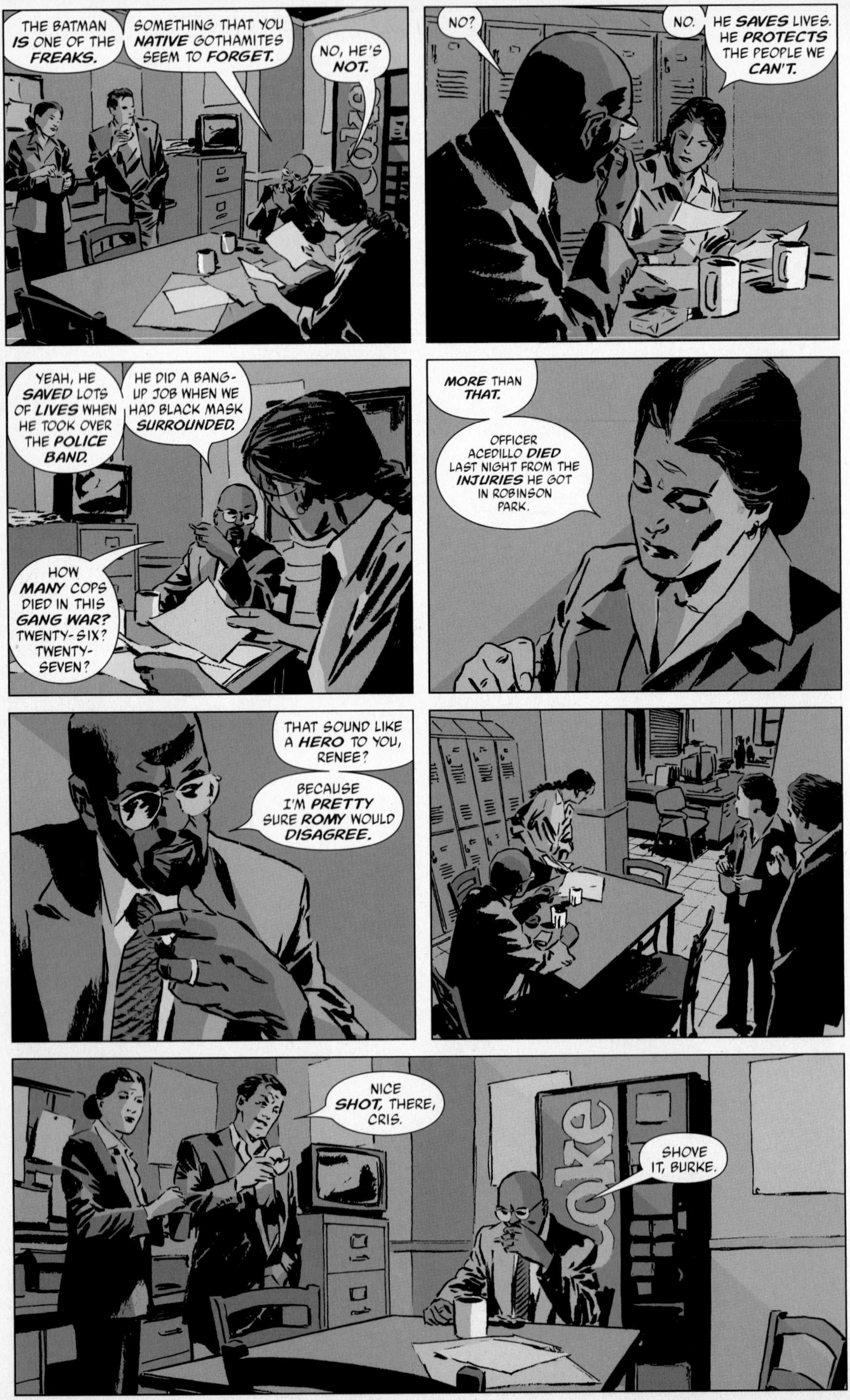
THE BATMAN IS ONE OF THE FREAKS.
SOMETHING THAT YOU NATIVE GOTHAMITES SEEM TO FORGET.
NO, HE'S NOT.
NO?
NO.
HE SAVES LIVES. HE PROTECTS THE PEOPLE WE CAN'T.
YEAH, HE SAVED LOTS OF LIVES WHEN HE TOOK OVER THE POLICE BAND.
HE DID A BANG-UP JOB WHEN WE HAD BLACK MASK SURROUNDED.
HOW MANY COPS DIED IN THIS GANG WAR? TWENTY-SIX? TWENTY-SEVEN?
MORE THAN THAT.
OFFICER ACEDILLO DIED LAST NIGHT FROM THE INJURIES HE GOT IN ROBINSON PARK.
THAT SOUND LIKE A HERO TO YOU, RENEE?
BECAUSE I'M PRETTY SURE ROMY WOULD DISAGREE.
NICE SHOT, THERE, CRIS.
SHOVE IT, BURKE.

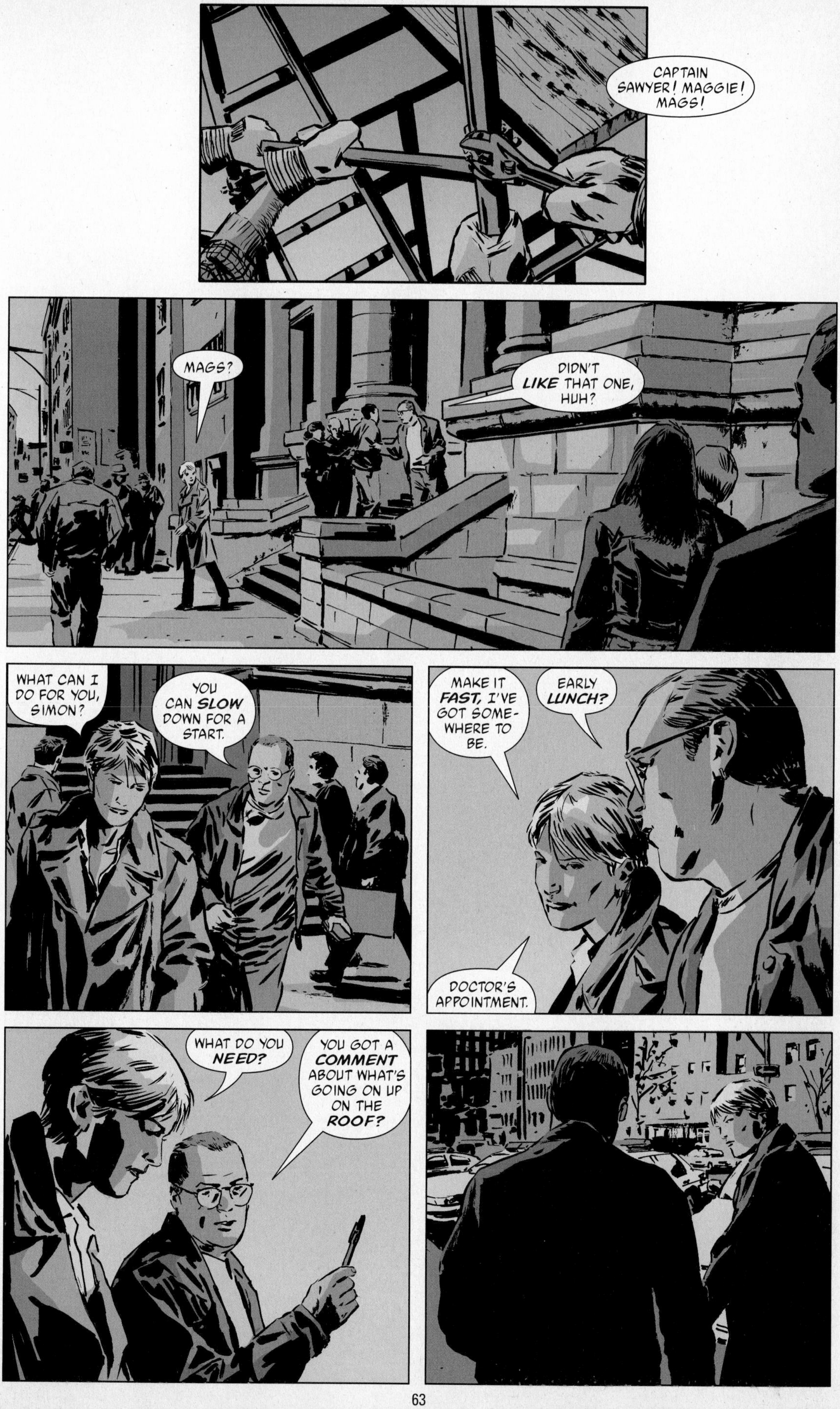
CAPTAIN SAWYER! MAGGIE! MAGS!
MAGS?
DIDN'T LIKE THAT ONE, HUH?
WHAT CAN I DO FOR YOU, SIMON?
YOU CAN SLOW DOWN FOR A START.
MAKE IT FAST, I'VE GOT SOME-WHERE TO BE.
EARLY LUNCH?
DOCTOR'S APPOINTMENT.
WHAT DO YOU NEED?
YOU GOT A COMMENT ABOUT WHAT'S GOING ON UP ON THE ROOF?

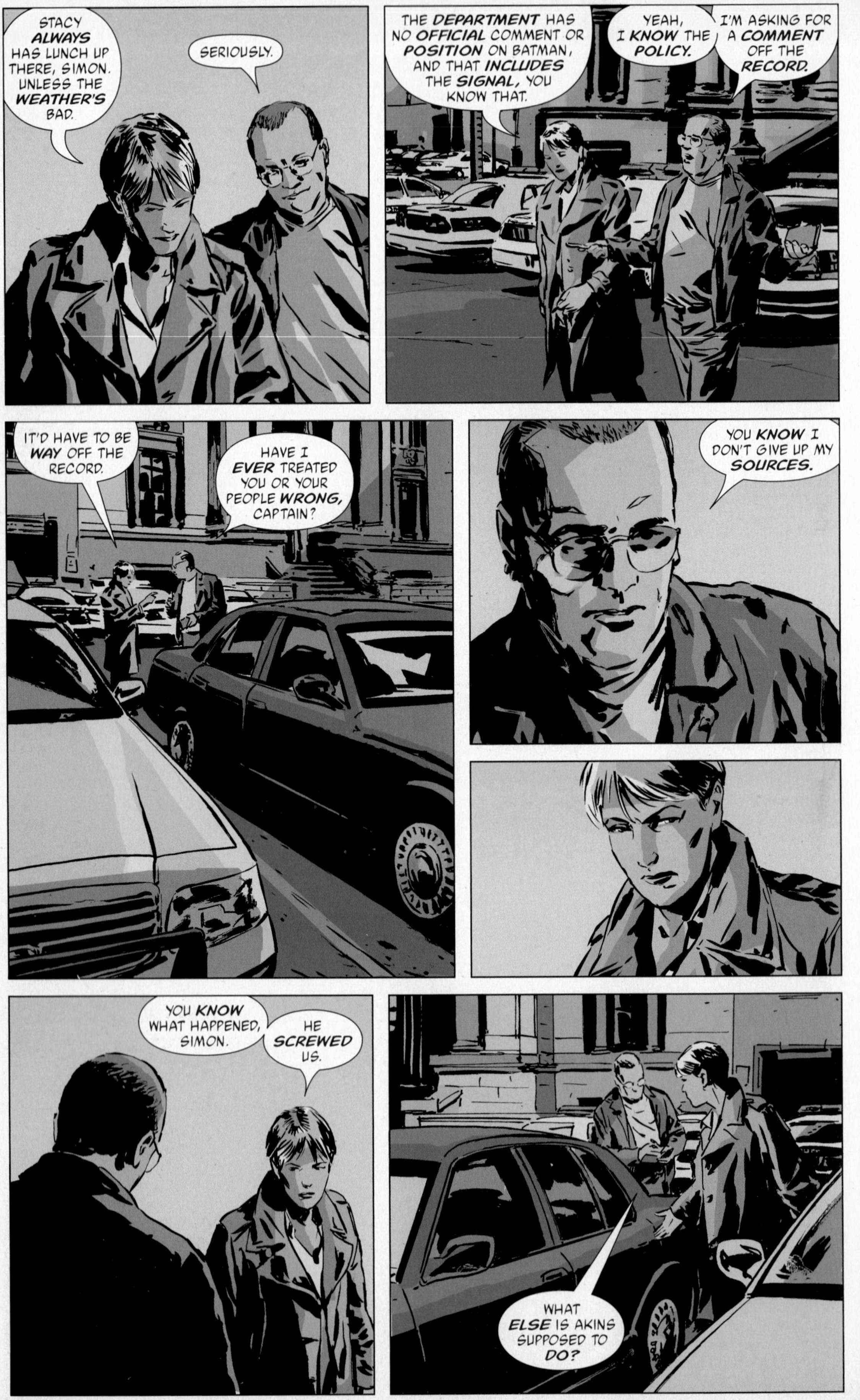
STACY ALWAYS HAS LUNCH UP THERE, SIMON. UNLESS THE WEATHER'S BAD.
SERIOUSLY.
THE DEPARTMENT HAS NO OFFICIAL COMMENT OR POSITION ON BATMAN, AND THAT INCLUDES THE SIGNAL, YOU KNOW THAT.
YEAH, I KNOW THE POLICY.
I'M ASKING FOR A COMMENT OFF THE RECORD.
IT'D HAVE TO BE WAY OFF THE RECORD.
HAVE I EVER TREATED YOU OR YOUR PEOPLE WRONG, CAPTAIN?
YOU KNOW I DON'T GIVE UP MY SOURCES.
YOU KNOW WHAT HAPPENED, SIMON.
HE SCREWED US.
WHAT ELSE IS AKINS SUPPOSED TO DO?

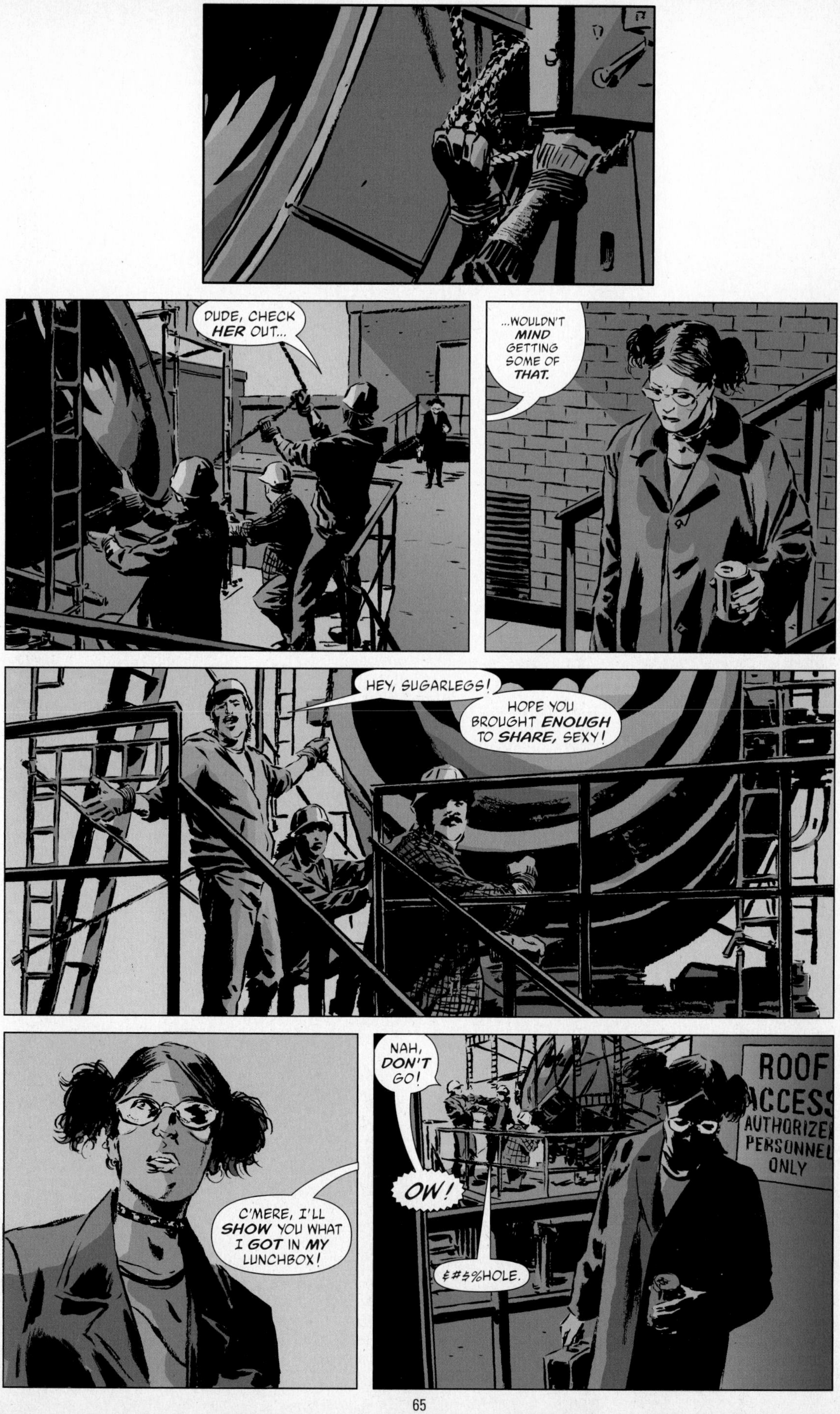
DUDE, CHECK HER OUT...
...WOULDN'T MIND GETTING SOME OF THAT.
HEY, SUGARLEGS!
HOPE YOU BROUGHT ENOUGH TO SHARE, SEXY!
C'MERE, I'LL SHOW YOU WHAT I GOT IN MY LUNCHBOX!
NAH, DON'T GO!
OW!
$#%%HOLE.
ROOF ACCESS AUTHORIZED PERSONNEL ONLY

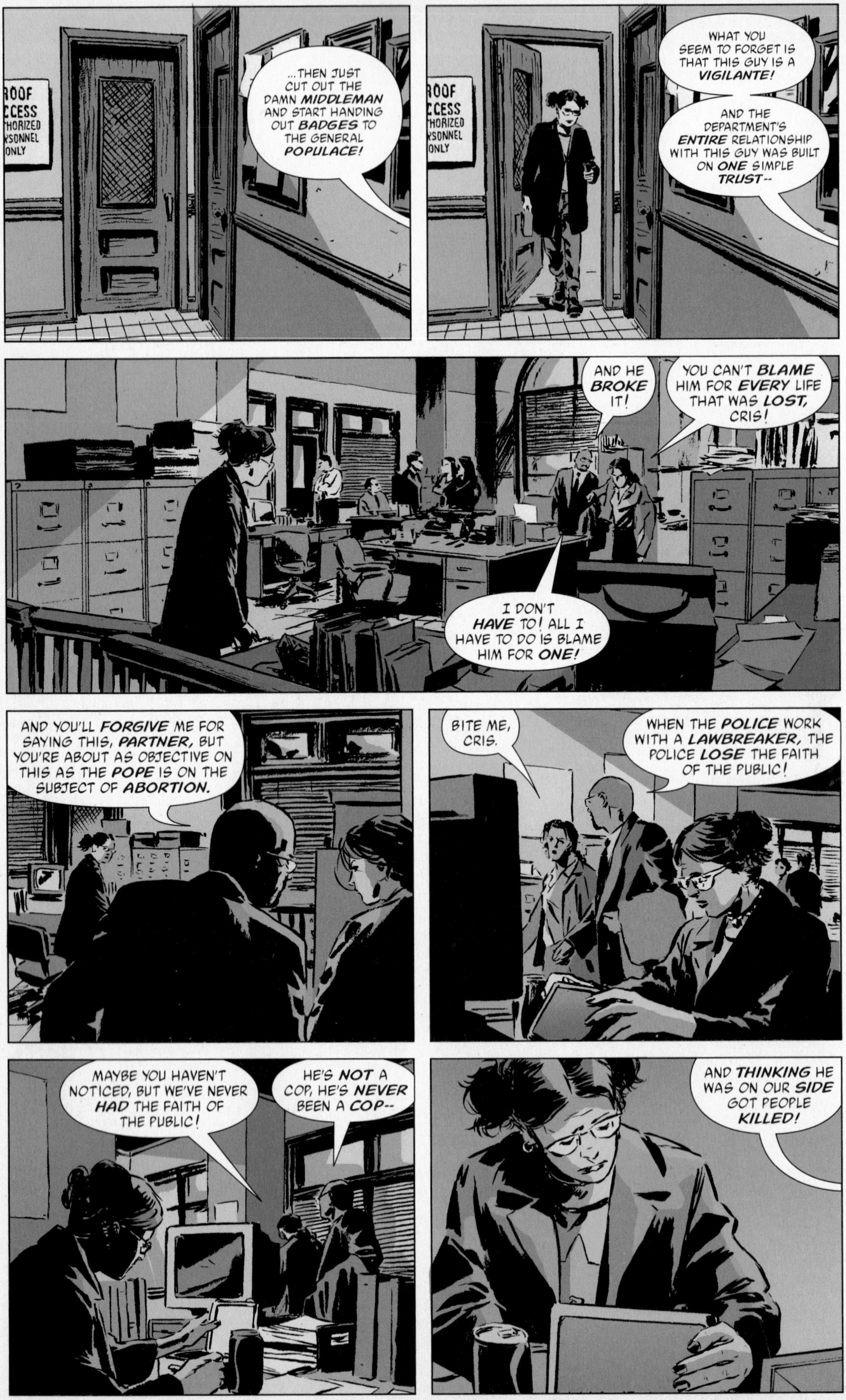
ROOF
CCESS
THORIZED
RSONNEL
ONLY
...THEN JUST CUT OUT THE DAMN MIDDLEMAN AND START HANDING OUT BADGES TO THE GENERAL POPULACE!
WHAT YOU SEEM TO FORGET IS THAT THIS GUY IS A VIGILANTE!
AND THE DEPARTMENT'S ENTIRE RELATIONSHIP WITH THIS GUY WAS BUILT ON ONE SIMPLE TRUST--
AND HE BROKE IT!
YOU CAN'T BLAME HIM FOR EVERY LIFE THAT WAS LOST, CRIS!
I DON'T HAVE TO! ALL I HAVE TO DO IS BLAME HIM FOR ONE!
AND YOU'LL FORGIVE ME FOR SAYING THIS, PARTNER, BUT YOU'RE ABOUT AS OBJECTIVE ON THIS AS THE POPE IS ON THE SUBJECT OF ABORTION.
BITE ME, CRIS.
WHEN THE POLICE WORK WITH A LAWBREAKER, THE POLICE LOSE THE FAITH OF THE PUBLIC!
MAYBE YOU HAVEN'T NOTICED, BUT WE'VE NEVER HAD THE FAITH OF THE PUBLIC!
HE'S NOT A COP, HE'S NEVER BEEN A COP--
AND THINKING HE WAS ON OUR SIDE GOT PEOPLE KILLED!

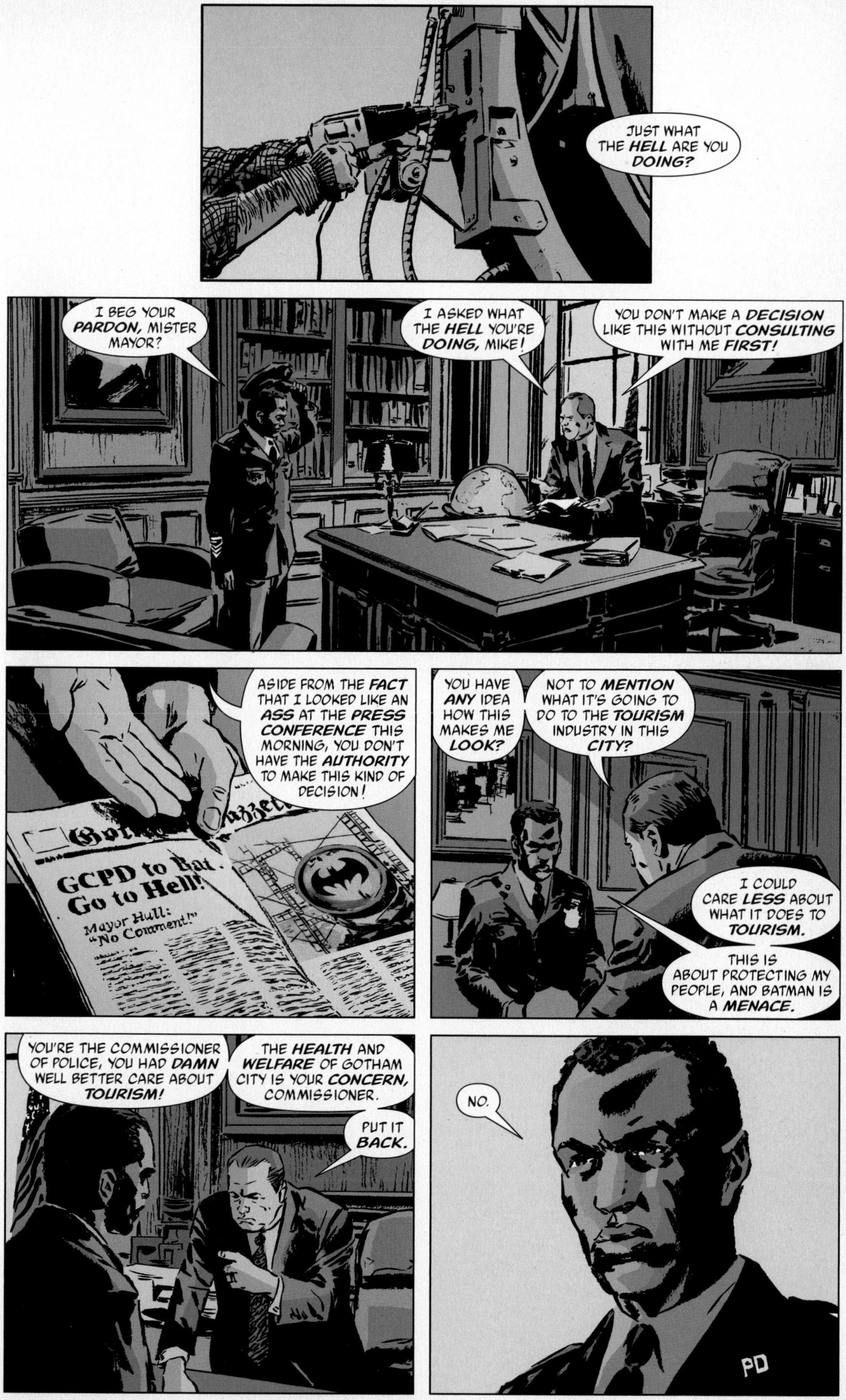
JUST WHAT THE HELL ARE YOU DOING?
I BEG YOUR PARDON, MISTER MAYOR?
I ASKED WHAT THE HELL YOU'RE DOING, MIKE!
YOU DON'T MAKE A DECISION LIKE THIS WITHOUT CONSULTING WITH ME FIRST!
GCPD to Bat Go to Hell!
Mayor Hull: "No Comment!"
ASIDE FROM THE FACT THAT I LOOKED LIKE AN ASS AT THE PRESS CONFERENCE THIS MORNING, YOU DON'T HAVE THE AUTHORITY TO MAKE THIS KIND OF DECISION!
YOU HAVE ANY IDEA HOW THIS MAKES ME LOOK?
NOT TO MENTION WHAT IT'S GOING TO DO TO THE TOURISM INDUSTRY IN THIS CITY?
I COULD CARE LESS ABOUT WHAT IT DOES TO TOURISM.
THIS IS ABOUT PROTECTING MY PEOPLE, AND BATMAN IS A MENACE.
YOU'RE THE COMMISSIONER OF POLICE, YOU HAD DAMN WELL BETTER CARE ABOUT TOURISM!
THE HEALTH AND WELFARE OF GOTHAM CITY IS YOUR CONCERN, COMMISSIONER.
PUT IT BACK.
NO.
PD

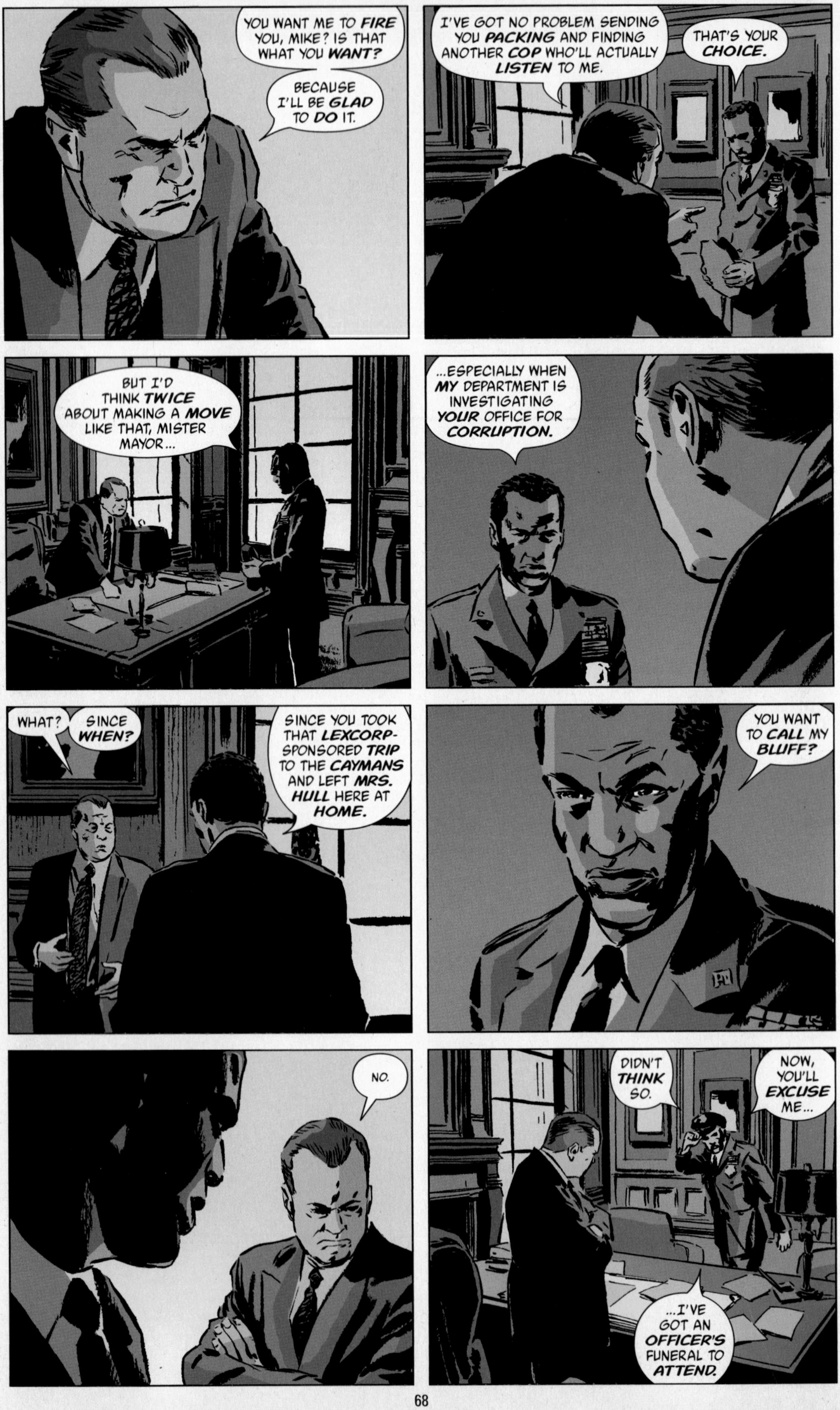
YOU WANT ME TO FIRE YOU, MIKE? IS THAT WHAT YOU WANT?
BECAUSE I'LL BE GLAD TO DO IT.
I'VE GOT NO PROBLEM SENDING YOU PACKING AND FINDING ANOTHER COP WHO'LL ACTUALLY LISTEN TO ME.
THAT'S YOUR CHOICE.
BUT I'D THINK TWICE ABOUT MAKING A MOVE LIKE THAT, MISTER MAYOR...
...ESPECIALLY WHEN MY DEPARTMENT IS INVESTIGATING YOUR OFFICE FOR CORRUPTION.
WHAT?
SINCE WHEN?
SINCE YOU TOOK THAT LEXCORP-SPONSORED TRIP TO THE CAYMANS AND LEFT MRS. HULL HERE AT HOME.
YOU WANT TO CALL MY BLUFF?
NO.
DIDN'T THINK SO.
NOW, YOU'LL EXCUSE ME...
...I'VE GOT AN OFFICER'S FUNERAL TO ATTEND.

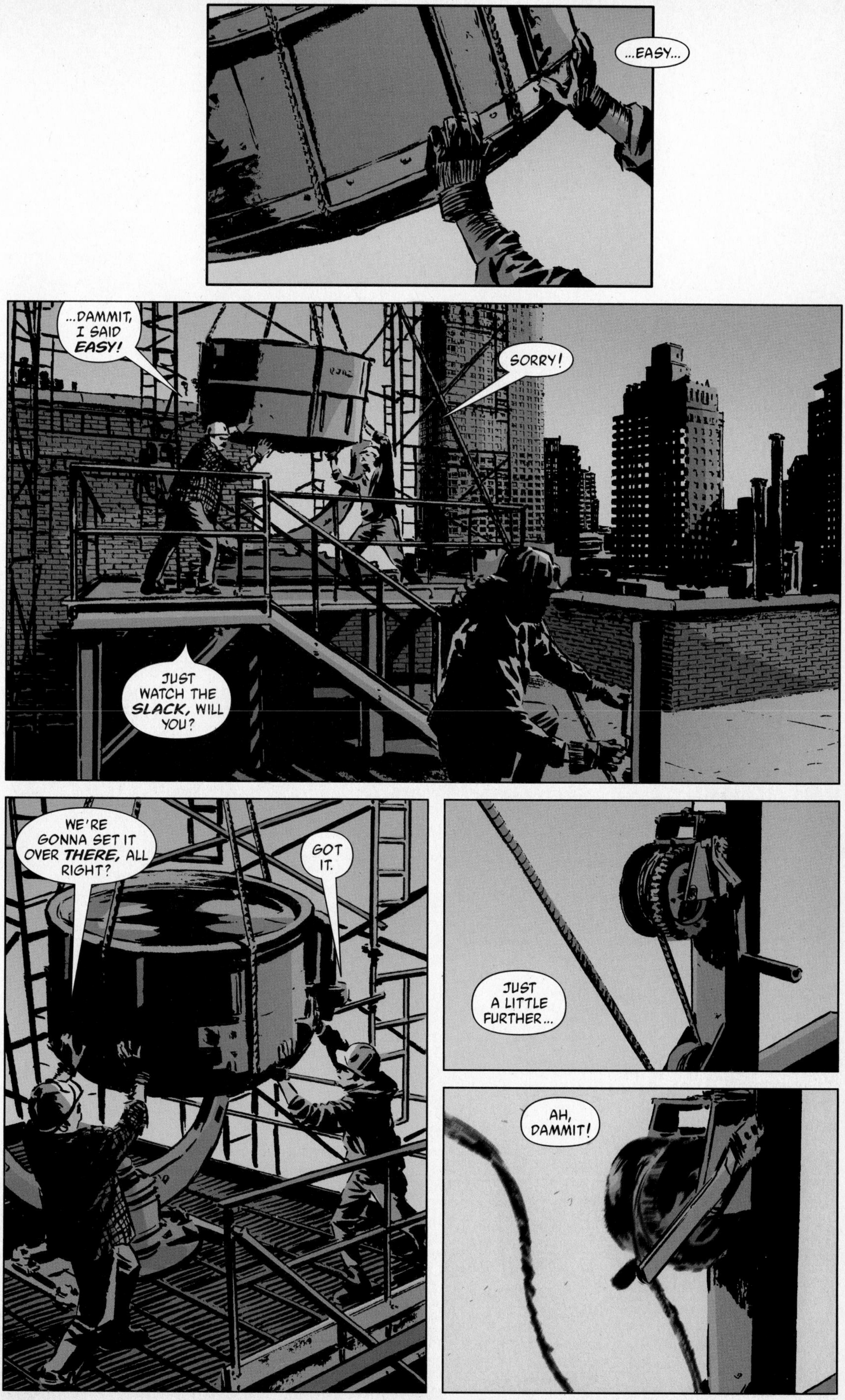
...EASY...
...DAMMIT, I SAID EASY!
SORRY!
JUST WATCH THE SLACK, WILL YOU?
WE'RE GONNA SET IT OVER THERE, ALL RIGHT?
GOT IT.
JUST A LITTLE FURTHER...
AH, DAMMIT!

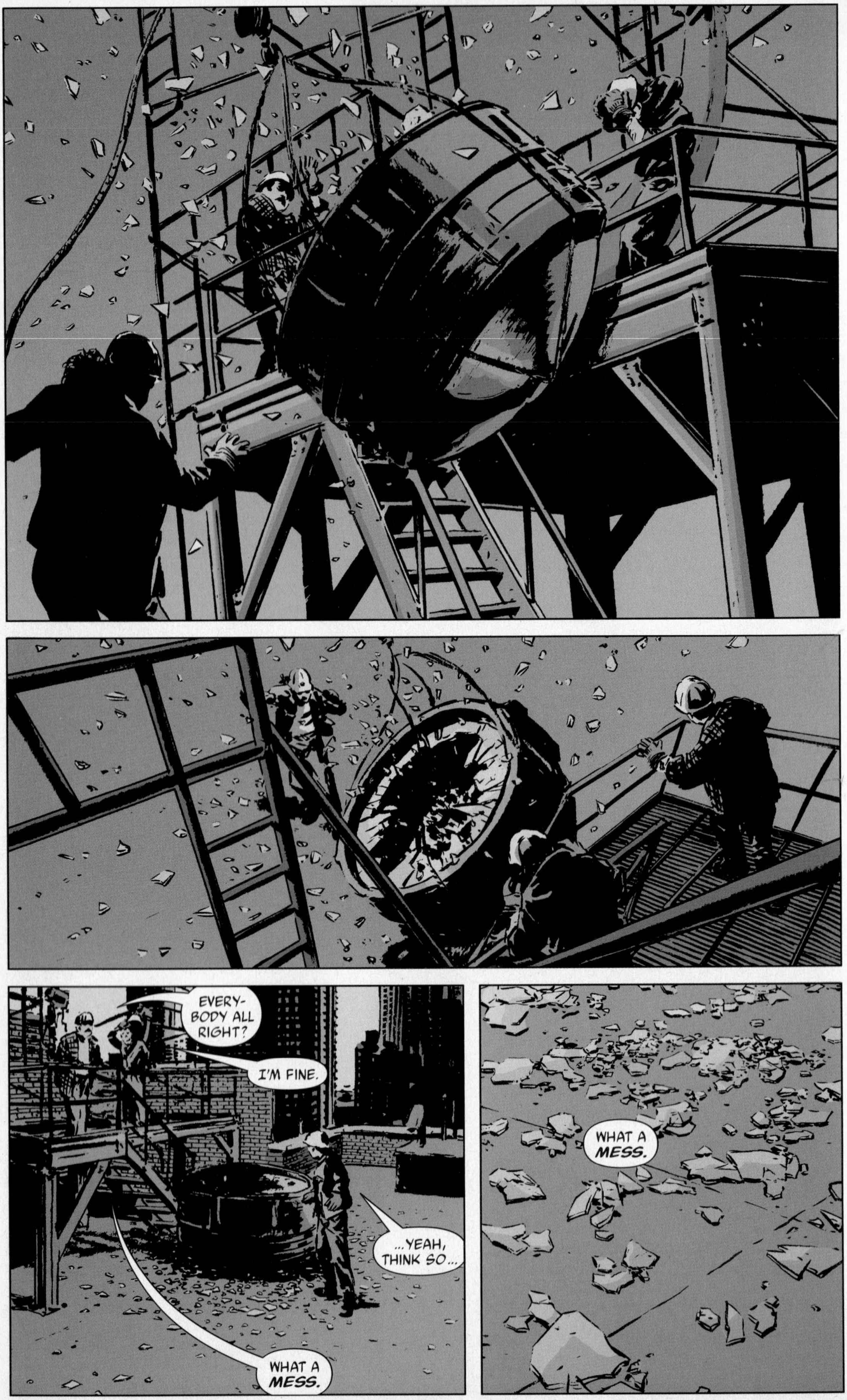
EVERY-
BODY ALL
RIGHT?
I'M FINE.
...YEAH,
THINK SO...
WHAT A
MESS.
WHAT A
MESS.

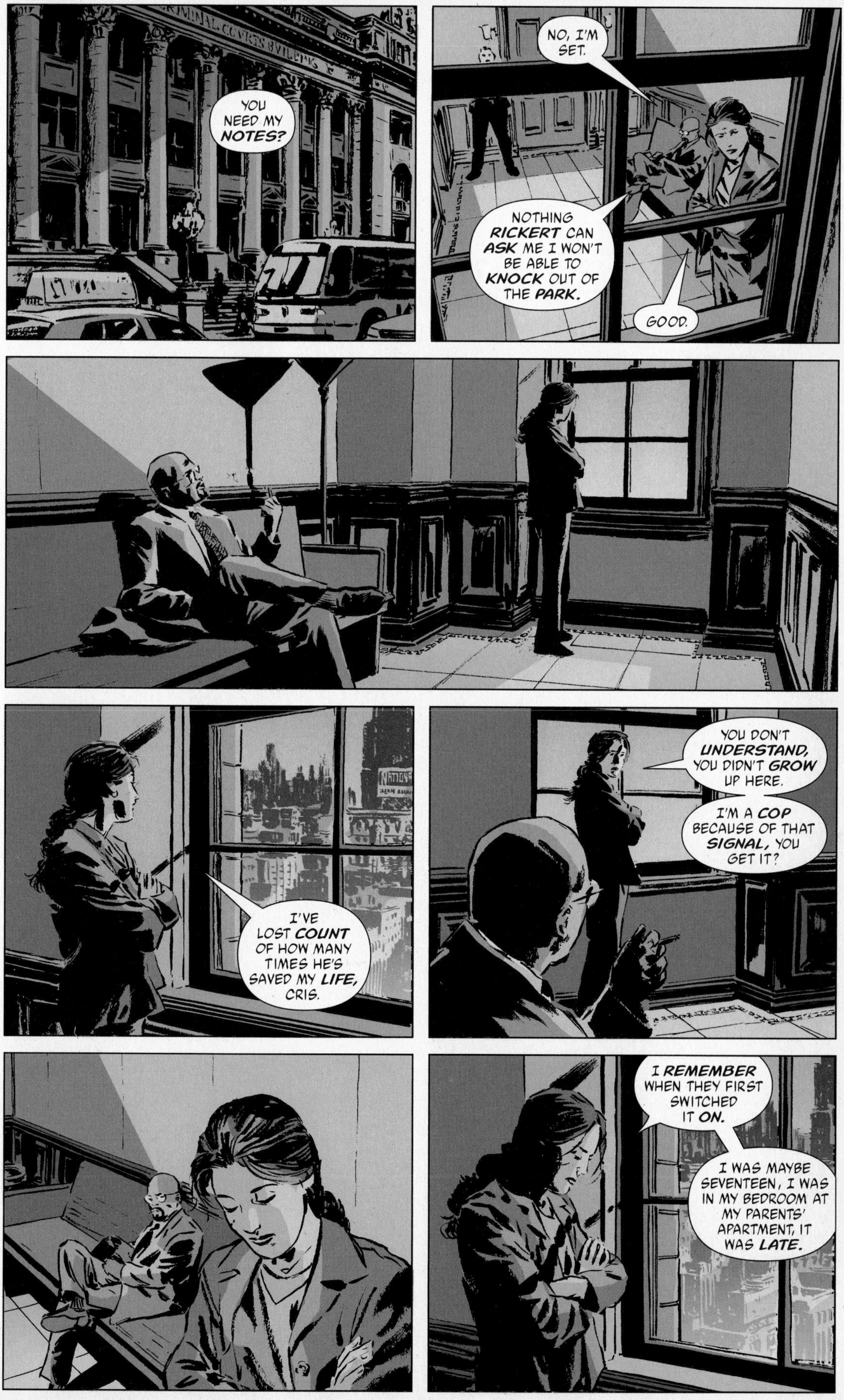
CRIMINAL COURTS BUILDING
YOU NEED MY NOTES?
NO, I'M SET.
NOTHING RICKERT CAN ASK ME I WON'T BE ABLE TO KNOCK OUT OF THE PARK.
GOOD.
I'VE LOST COUNT OF HOW MANY TIMES HE'S SAVED MY LIFE, CRIS.
YOU DON'T UNDERSTAND, YOU DIDN'T GROW UP HERE.
I'M A COP BECAUSE OF THAT SIGNAL, YOU GET IT?
I REMEMBER WHEN THEY FIRST SWITCHED IT ON.
I WAS MAYBE SEVENTEEN, I WAS IN MY BEDROOM AT MY PARENTS' APARTMENT, IT WAS LATE.

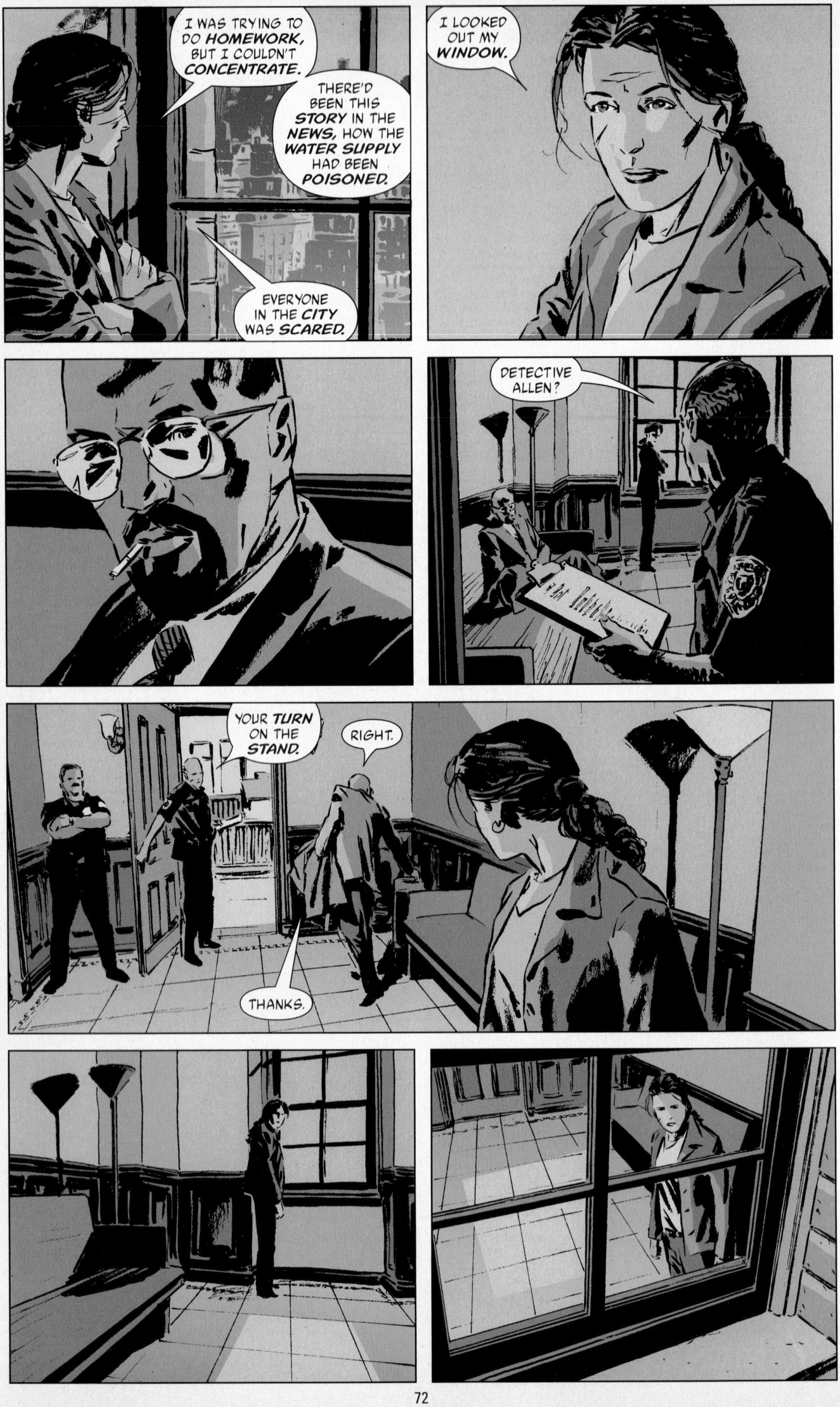
I WAS TRYING TO DO HOMEWORK, BUT I COULDN'T CONCENTRATE.
THERE'D BEEN THIS STORY IN THE NEWS, HOW THE WATER SUPPLY HAD BEEN POISONED.
EVERYONE IN THE CITY WAS SCARED.
I LOOKED OUT MY WINDOW.
DETECTIVE ALLEN?
YOUR TURN ON THE STAND.
RIGHT.
THANKS.

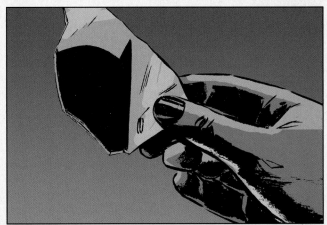

STACY?

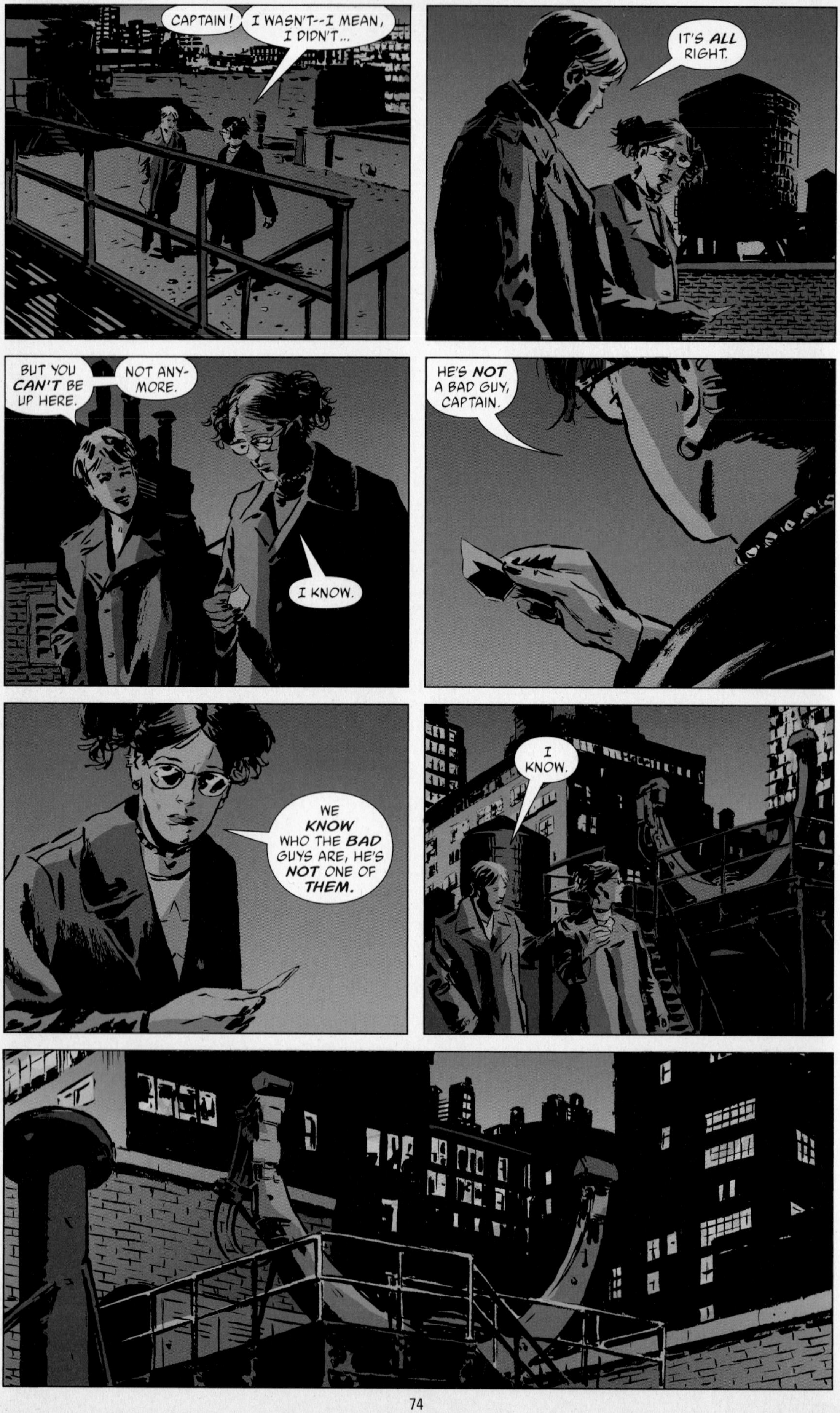
CAPTAIN!
I WASN'T--I MEAN, I DIDN'T...
IT'S ALL RIGHT.
BUT YOU CAN'T BE UP HERE.
NOT ANY-MORE.
I KNOW.
HE'S NOT A BAD GUY, CAPTAIN.
WE KNOW WHO THE BAD GUYS ARE, HE'S NOT ONE OF THEM.
I KNOW.

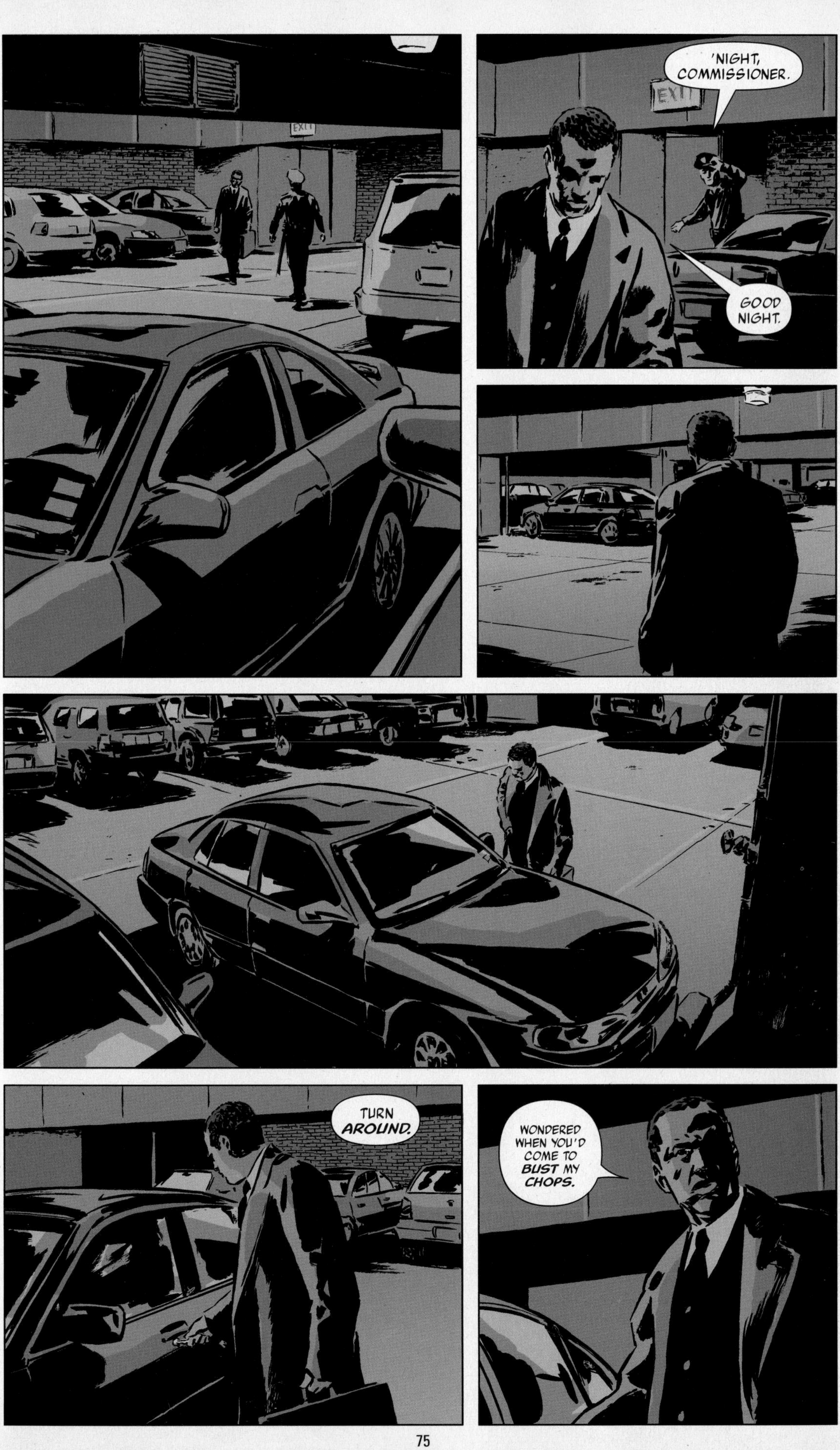
EXIT
'NIGHT, COMMISSIONER.
GOOD NIGHT.
TURN AROUND.
WONDERED WHEN YOU'D COME TO BUST MY CHOPS.

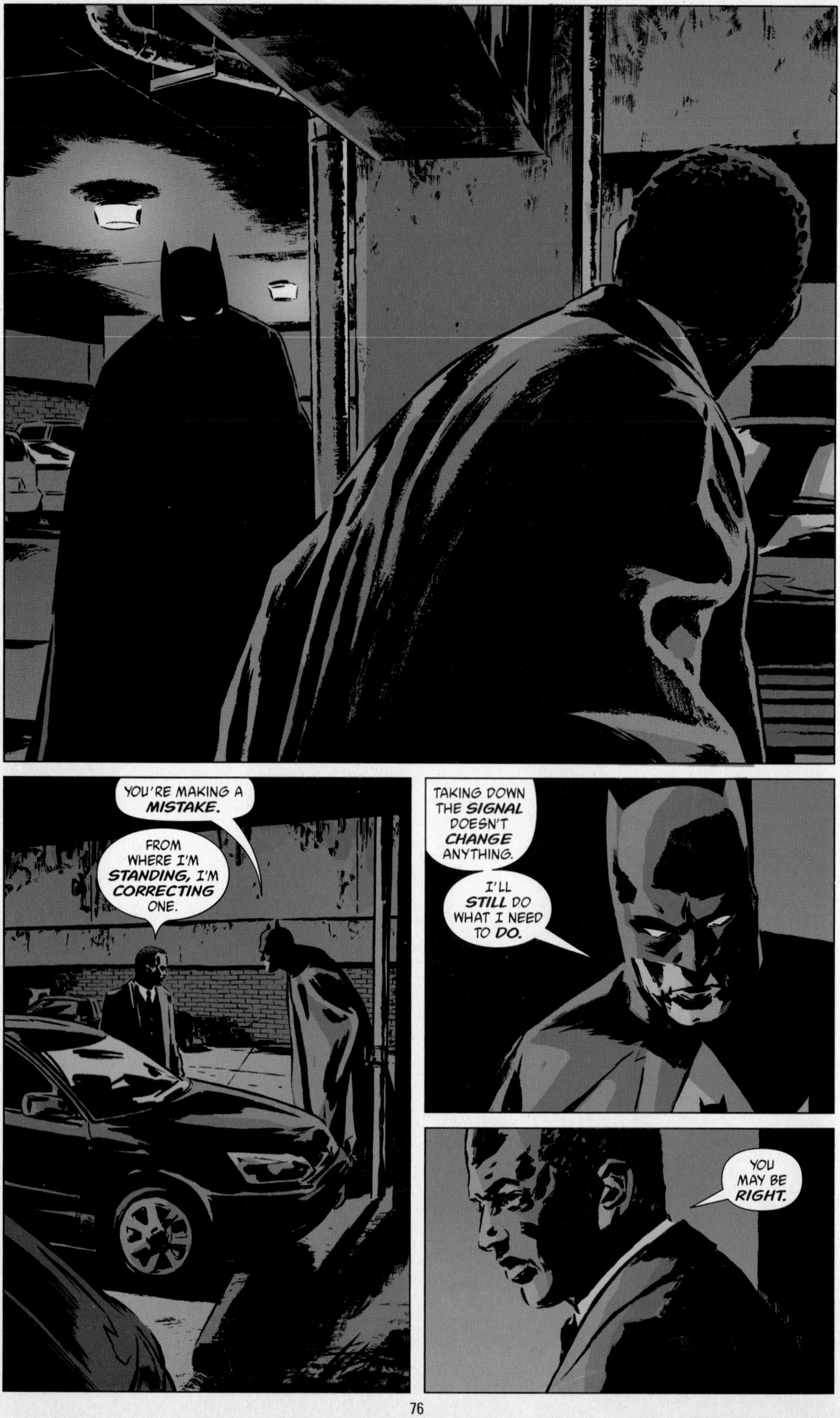
YOU'RE MAKING A MISTAKE.
FROM WHERE I'M STANDING, I'M CORRECTING ONE.
TAKING DOWN THE SIGNAL DOESN'T CHANGE ANYTHING.
I'LL STILL DO WHAT I NEED TO DO.
YOU MAY BE RIGHT.

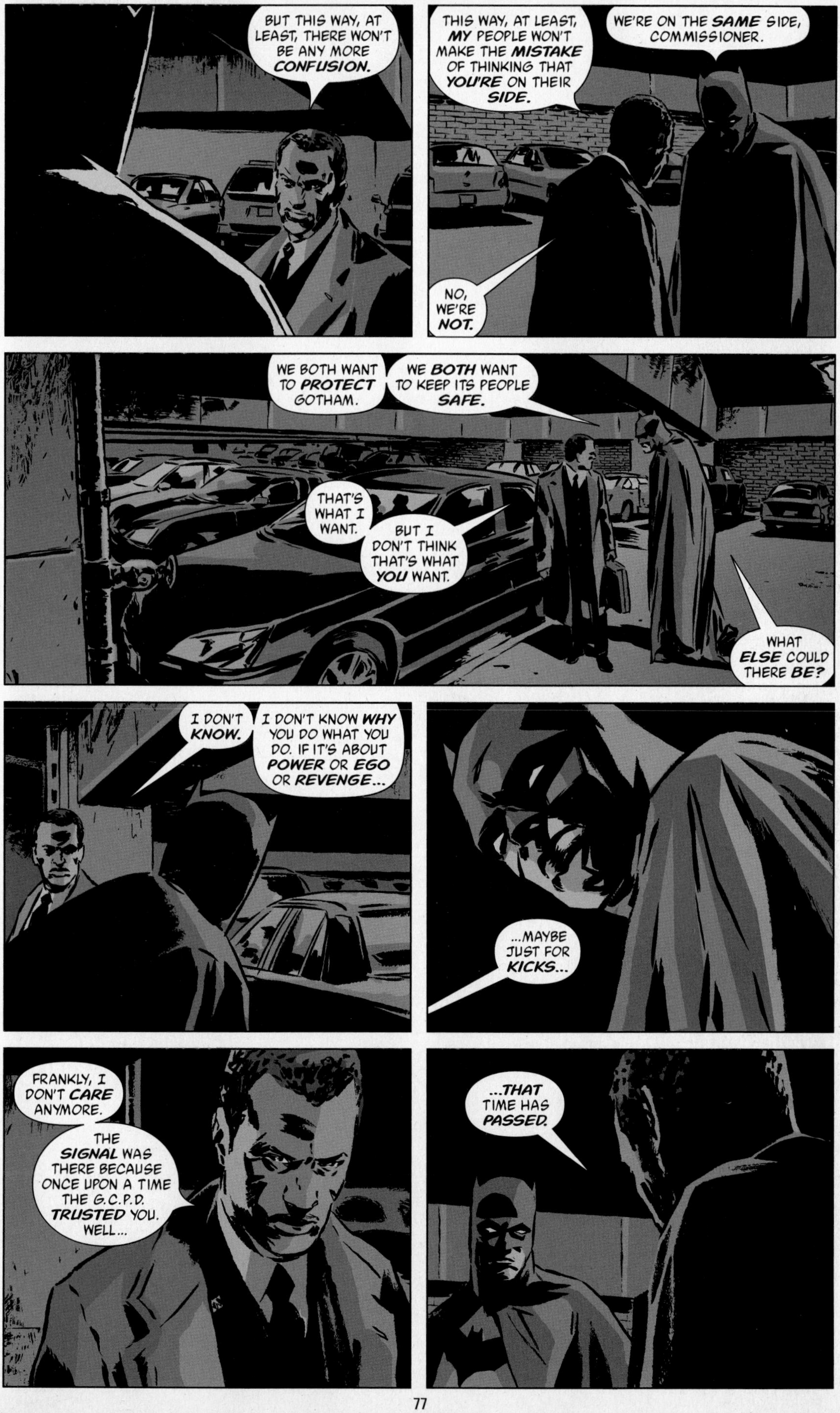
BUT THIS WAY, AT LEAST, THERE WON'T BE ANY MORE CONFUSION.
THIS WAY, AT LEAST, MY PEOPLE WON'T MAKE THE MISTAKE OF THINKING THAT YOU'RE ON THEIR SIDE.
WE'RE ON THE SAME SIDE, COMMISSIONER.
NO, WE'RE NOT.
WE BOTH WANT TO PROTECT GOTHAM.
WE BOTH WANT TO KEEP ITS PEOPLE SAFE.
THAT'S WHAT I WANT.
BUT I DON'T THINK THAT'S WHAT YOU WANT.
WHAT ELSE COULD THERE BE?
I DON'T KNOW.
I DON'T KNOW WHY YOU DO WHAT YOU DO. IF IT'S ABOUT POWER OR EGO OR REVENGE...
...MAYBE JUST FOR KICKS...
FRANKLY, I DON'T CARE ANYMORE.
THE SIGNAL WAS THERE BECAUSE ONCE UPON A TIME THE G.C.P.D. TRUSTED YOU. WELL...
...THAT TIME HAS PASSED.

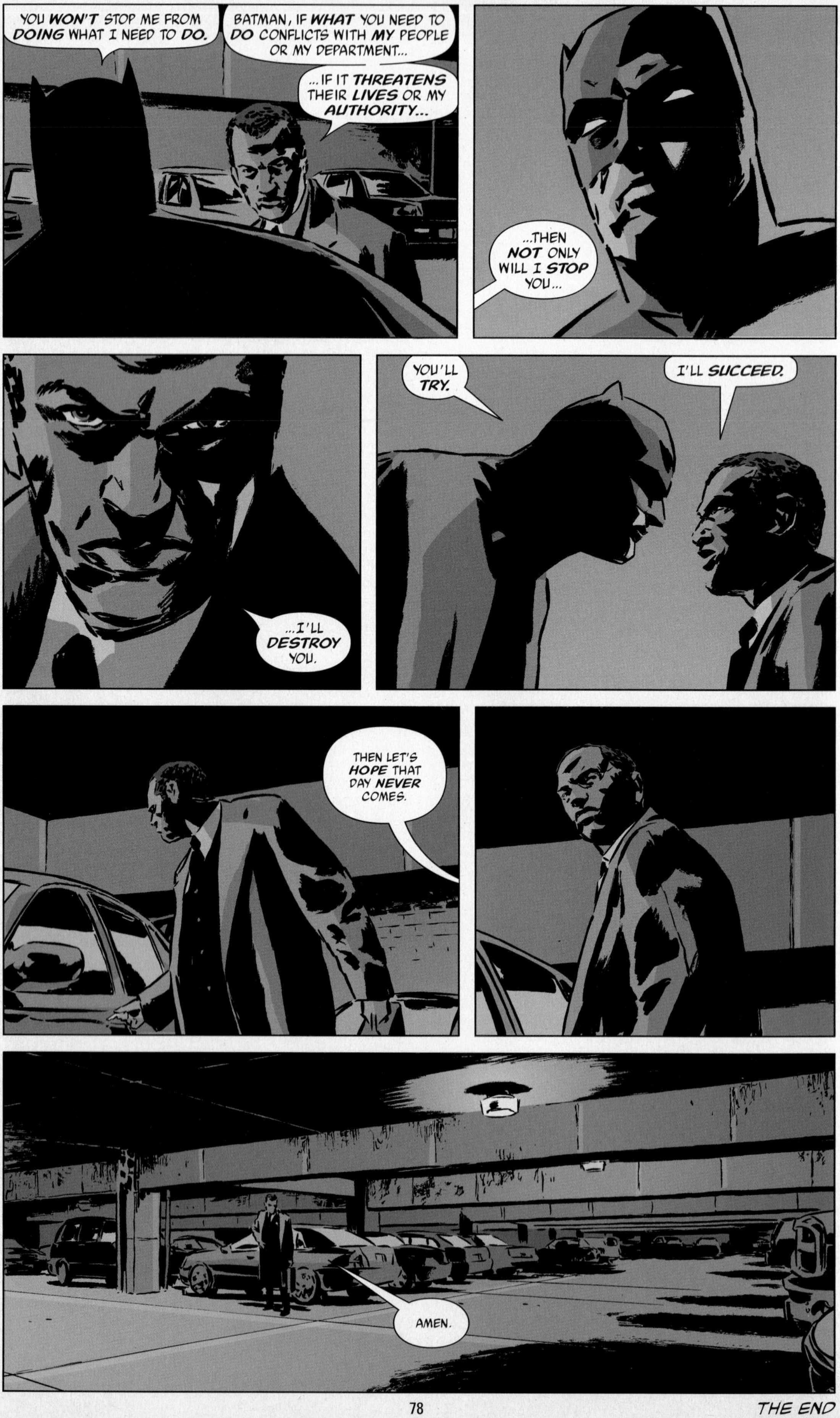
YOU WON'T STOP ME FROM DOING WHAT I NEED TO DO.
BATMAN, IF WHAT YOU NEED TO DO CONFLICTS WITH MY PEOPLE OR MY DEPARTMENT...
...IF IT THREATENS THEIR LIVES OR MY AUTHORITY...
...THEN NOT ONLY WILL I STOP YOU...
...I'LL DESTROY YOU.
YOU'LL TRY.
I'LL SUCCEED.
THEN LET'S HOPE THAT DAY NEVER COMES.
AMEN.

THE END

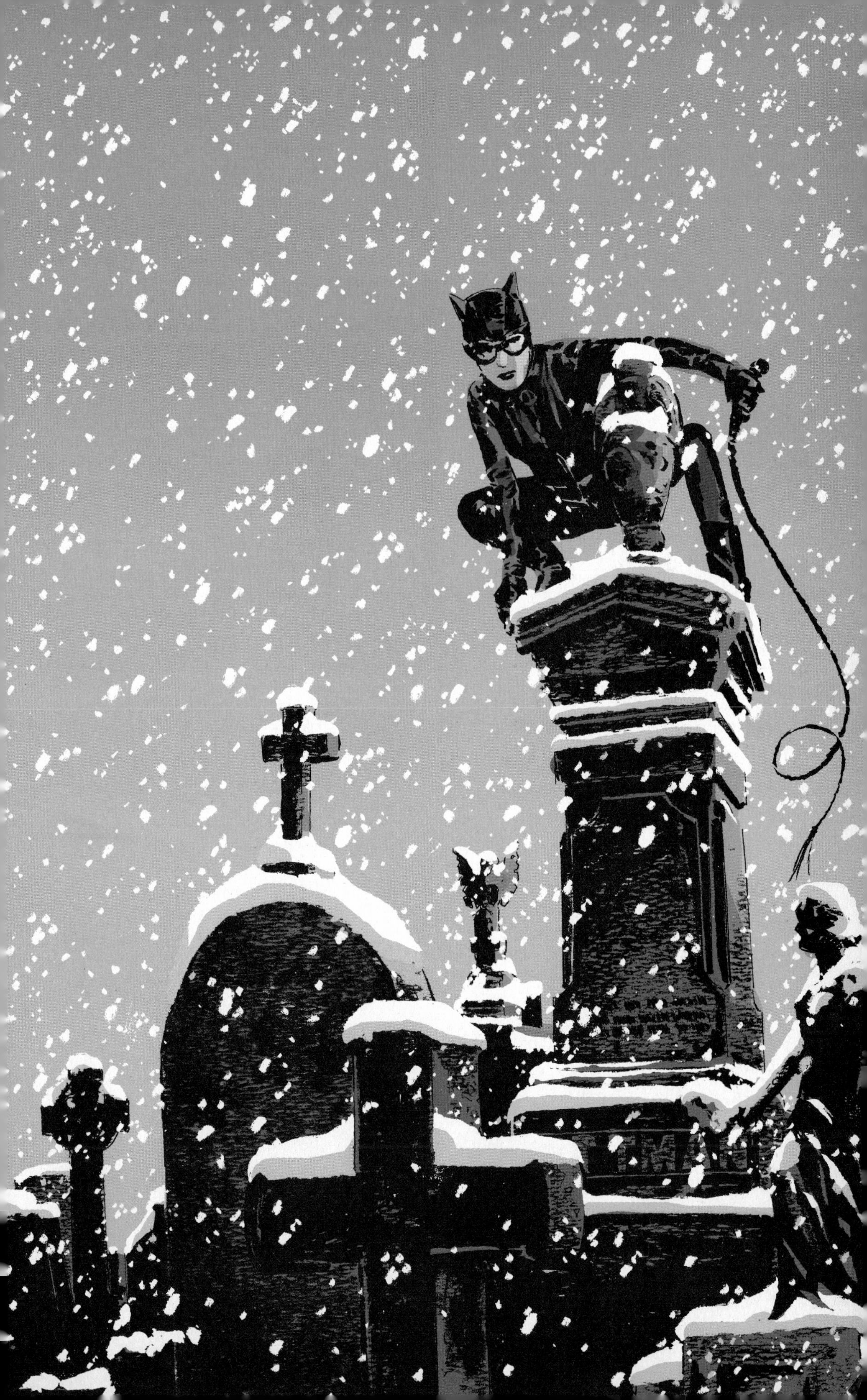

ON THE FREAK BEAT

Written by
ED BRUBAKER

Art by
JASON ALEXANDER

Colors by
LEE LOUGHRIDGE

Letters by
CLEM ROBINS

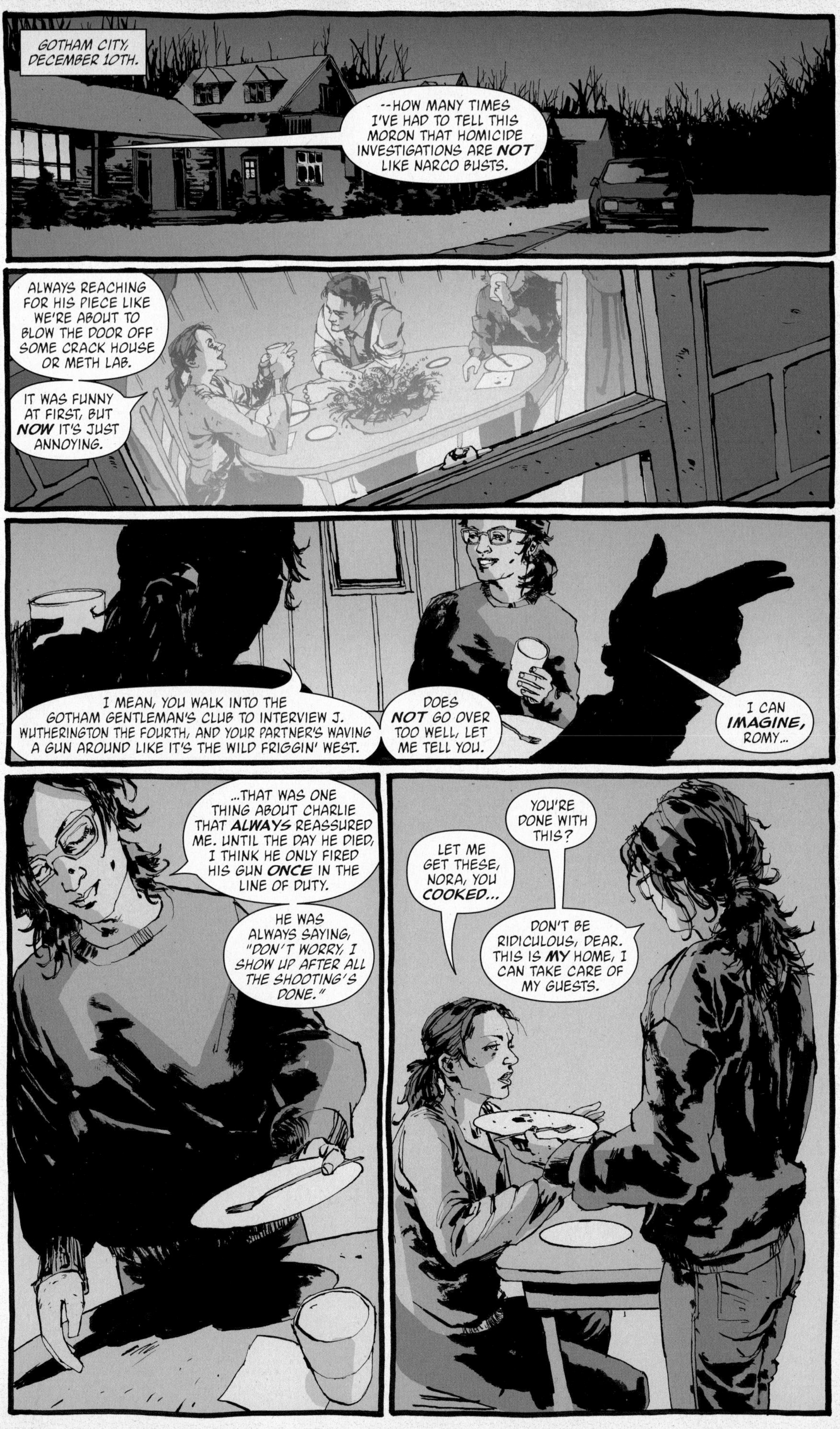
GOTHAM CITY, DECEMBER 10TH.
--HOW MANY TIMES I'VE HAD TO TELL THIS MORON THAT HOMICIDE INVESTIGATIONS ARE NOT LIKE NARCO BUSTS.
ALWAYS REACHING FOR HIS PIECE LIKE WE'RE ABOUT TO BLOW THE DOOR OFF SOME CRACK HOUSE OR METH LAB.
IT WAS FUNNY AT FIRST, BUT NOW IT'S JUST ANNOYING.
I MEAN, YOU WALK INTO THE GOTHAM GENTLEMAN'S CLUB TO INTERVIEW J. WUTHERINGTON THE FOURTH, AND YOUR PARTNER'S WAVING A GUN AROUND LIKE IT'S THE WILD FRIGGIN' WEST.
DOES NOT GO OVER TOO WELL, LET ME TELL YOU.
I CAN IMAGINE, ROMY...
...THAT WAS ONE THING ABOUT CHARLIE THAT ALWAYS REASSURED ME. UNTIL THE DAY HE DIED, I THINK HE ONLY FIRED HIS GUN ONCE IN THE LINE OF DUTY.
HE WAS ALWAYS SAYING, "DON'T WORRY, I SHOW UP AFTER ALL THE SHOOTING'S DONE."
LET ME GET THESE, NORA, YOU COOKED...
YOU'RE DONE WITH THIS?
DON'T BE RIDICULOUS, DEAR. THIS IS MY HOME, I CAN TAKE CARE OF MY GUESTS.

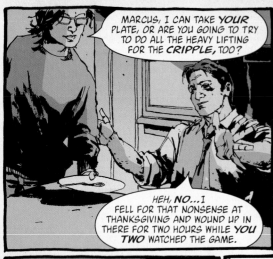

MARCUS, I CAN TAKE *YOUR* PLATE, OR ARE YOU GOING TO TRY TO DO ALL THE HEAVY LIFTING FOR THE *CRIPPLE,* TOO?

HEH, *NO...*I FELL FOR THAT NONSENSE AT THANKSGIVING AND WOUND UP IN THERE FOR TWO HOURS WHILE *YOU TWO* WATCHED THE GAME.

GAME?

YEAH, WE WATCHED THE *TWILIGHT ZONE* MARATHON. #€%$ THE *GAME.*

HEY, NOW I'M *REALLY* BURNED.

SO, NORA, I'VE REALLY BEEN MEANING TO ASK...SINCE YOU'RE ONLY CUTTING UP *DEAD PEOPLE,* CAN YOU STILL *WORK* WITH THE PROSTHETIC?

Y'KNOW, I NEVER THOUGHT TO TRY. I JUST TOOK THE PROMOTION TO SUPERVISOR AND FELT A WAVE OF RELIEF.

TEN YEARS IS ENOUGH TIME IN A MORGUE, DON'T YOU THINK?

BLEEDEL-DEET

OH, WHAT THE HELL? I'M ON IN AN HOUR ALREADY...

DRIVER HERE.

UH HUNH... YEAH...

DAMN IT, JOSIE...WHAT'VE I TOLD YOU ABOUT SHOWING UP FOR SHIFT EARLY?

PAPERWORK, RIGHT...BLAH BLAH BLAH...

YOU'RE SITTING AT A DESK, YOU'RE GONNA PICK UP A CASE.

WHAT IS IT?

BODY IN A PENTHOUSE, *UPTOWN...*

NO, NO... IT'S OKAY, JOSIE. I'LL MEET YOU THERE.

GET ROMY TO DROP ME.

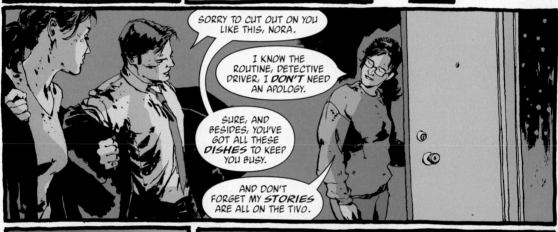

SORRY TO CUT OUT ON YOU LIKE THIS, NORA.

I KNOW THE ROUTINE, DETECTIVE DRIVER, I *DON'T* NEED AN APOLOGY.

SURE, AND BESIDES, YOU'VE GOT ALL THESE *DISHES* TO KEEP YOU BUSY.

AND DON'T FORGET MY *STORIES* ARE ALL ON THE TIVO.

BYE, NORA, SEE YOU NEXT WEEK.

OF COURSE, DEAR. TAKE CARE OF HIM.

I ALWAYS DO.

WHAT?

NOTHING. SHE'S JUST AMAZING.

YEAH, CHARLIE HAD GREAT TASTE.

SO, YOU GOT AN *ADDRESS* ON THIS BODY?

On The Freak Beat
Part One of Two

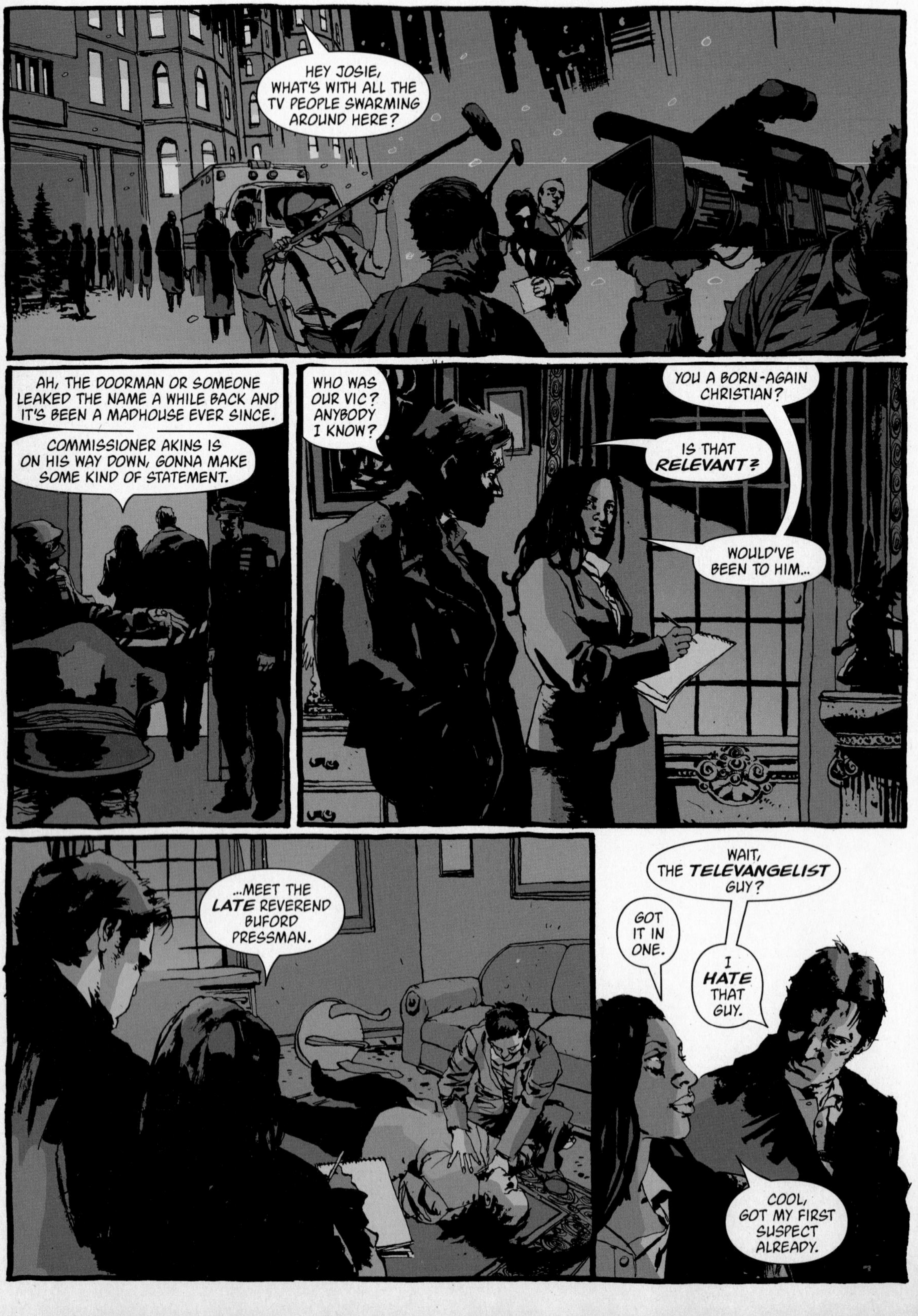

HEY JOSIE, WHAT'S WITH ALL THE TV PEOPLE SWARMING AROUND HERE?
AH, THE DOORMAN OR SOMEONE LEAKED THE NAME A WHILE BACK AND IT'S BEEN A MADHOUSE EVER SINCE.
COMMISSIONER AKINS IS ON HIS WAY DOWN, GONNA MAKE SOME KIND OF STATEMENT.
WHO WAS OUR VIC? ANYBODY I KNOW?
YOU A BORN-AGAIN CHRISTIAN?
IS THAT *RELEVANT?*
WOULD'VE BEEN TO HIM...
...MEET THE *LATE* REVEREND BUFORD PRESSMAN.
WAIT, THE *TELEVANGELIST* GUY?
GOT IT IN ONE.
I *HATE* THAT GUY.
COOL, GOT MY FIRST SUSPECT ALREADY.

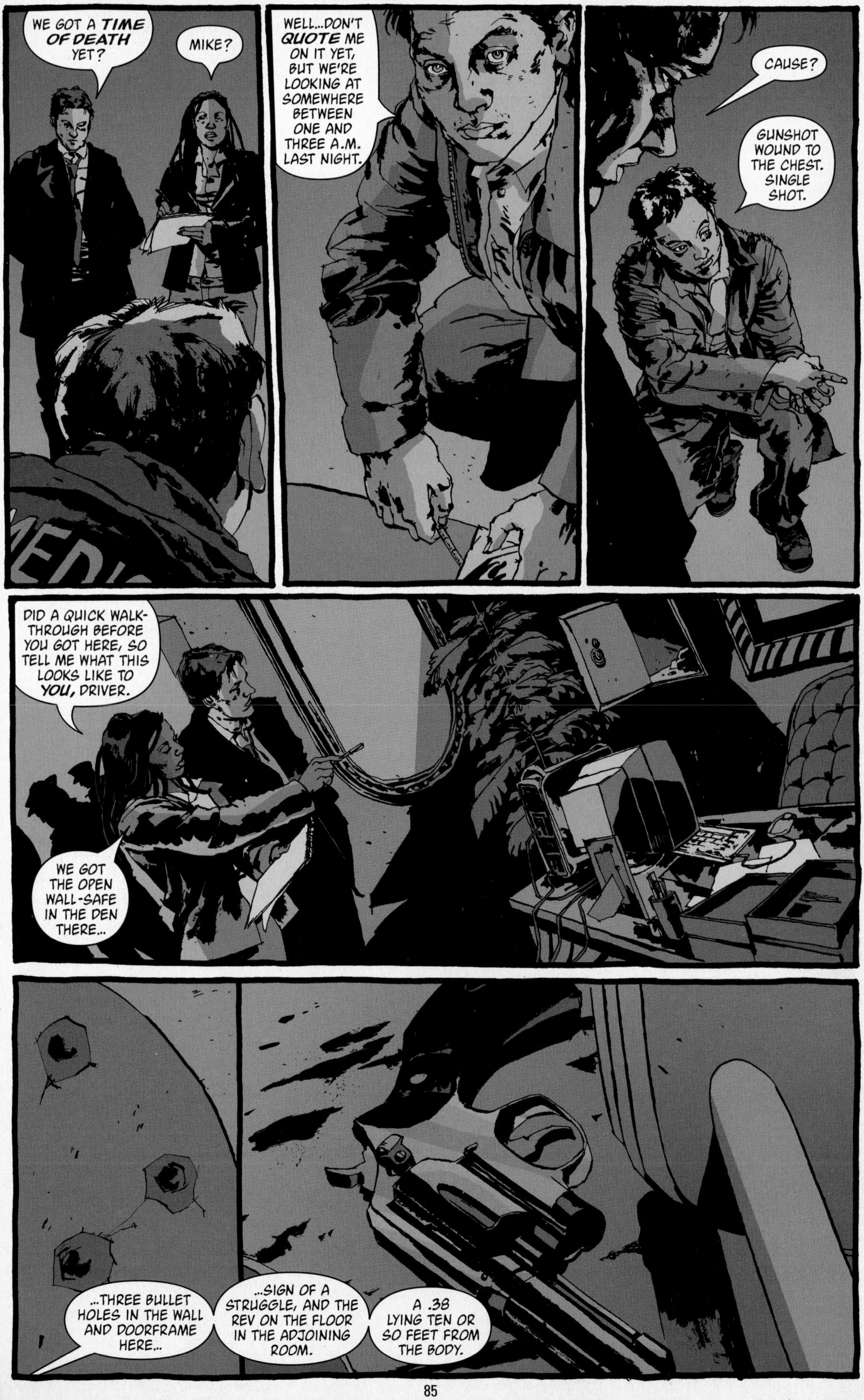

WE GOT A TIME OF DEATH YET?
MIKE?
WELL...DON'T QUOTE ME ON IT YET, BUT WE'RE LOOKING AT SOMEWHERE BETWEEN ONE AND THREE A.M. LAST NIGHT.
CAUSE?
GUNSHOT WOUND TO THE CHEST. SINGLE SHOT.
MEDIC
DID A QUICK WALK-THROUGH BEFORE YOU GOT HERE, SO TELL ME WHAT THIS LOOKS LIKE TO YOU, DRIVER.
WE GOT THE OPEN WALL-SAFE IN THE DEN THERE...
...THREE BULLET HOLES IN THE WALL AND DOORFRAME HERE...
...SIGN OF A STRUGGLE, AND THE REV ON THE FLOOR IN THE ADJOINING ROOM.
A .38 LYING TEN OR SO FEET FROM THE BODY.

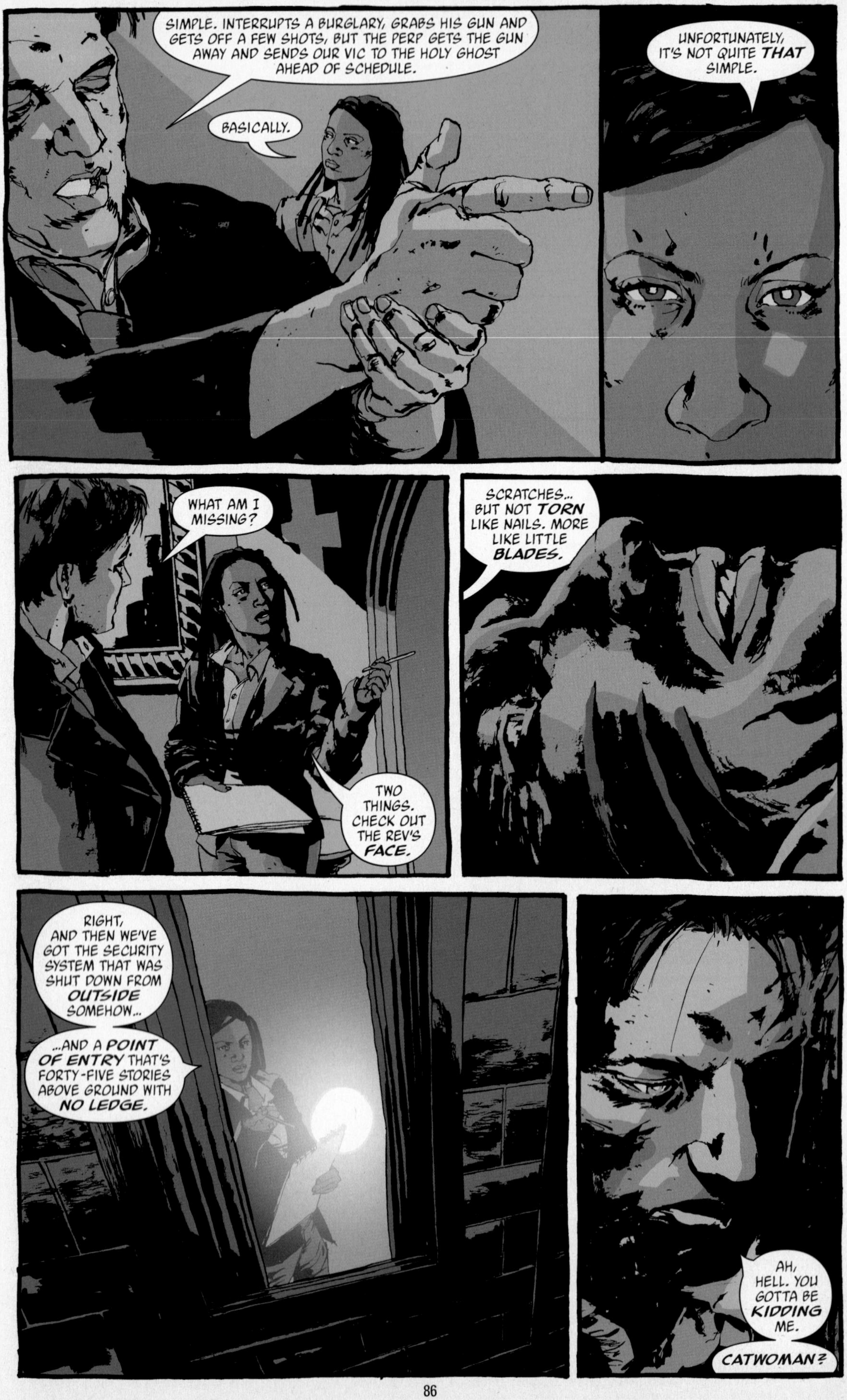
SIMPLE. INTERRUPTS A BURGLARY, GRABS HIS GUN AND GETS OFF A FEW SHOTS, BUT THE PERP GETS THE GUN AWAY AND SENDS OUR VIC TO THE HOLY GHOST AHEAD OF SCHEDULE.
BASICALLY.
UNFORTUNATELY, IT'S NOT QUITE THAT SIMPLE.
WHAT AM I MISSING?
TWO THINGS. CHECK OUT THE REV'S FACE.
SCRATCHES... BUT NOT TORN LIKE NAILS. MORE LIKE LITTLE BLADES.
RIGHT, AND THEN WE'VE GOT THE SECURITY SYSTEM THAT WAS SHUT DOWN FROM OUTSIDE SOMEHOW...
...AND A POINT OF ENTRY THAT'S FORTY-FIVE STORIES ABOVE GROUND WITH NO LEDGE.
AH, HELL. YOU GOTTA BE KIDDING ME.
CATWOMAN?

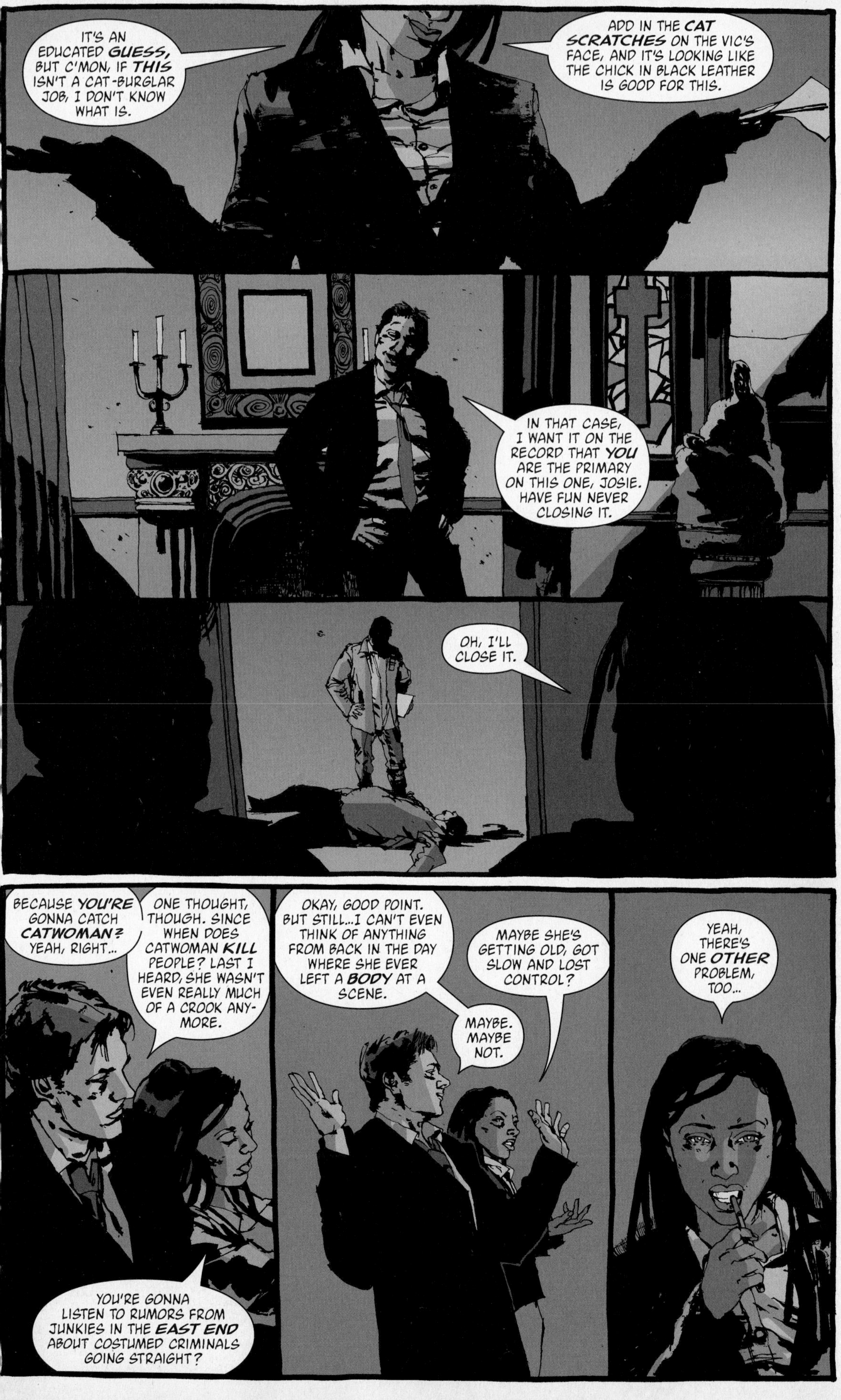
IT'S AN EDUCATED GUESS, BUT C'MON, IF THIS ISN'T A CAT-BURGLAR JOB, I DON'T KNOW WHAT IS.
ADD IN THE CAT SCRATCHES ON THE VIC'S FACE, AND IT'S LOOKING LIKE THE CHICK IN BLACK LEATHER IS GOOD FOR THIS.
IN THAT CASE, I WANT IT ON THE RECORD THAT YOU ARE THE PRIMARY ON THIS ONE, JOSIE. HAVE FUN NEVER CLOSING IT.
OH, I'LL CLOSE IT.
BECAUSE YOU'RE GONNA CATCH CATWOMAN? YEAH, RIGHT...
YOU'RE GONNA LISTEN TO RUMORS FROM JUNKIES IN THE EAST END ABOUT COSTUMED CRIMINALS GOING STRAIGHT?
ONE THOUGHT, THOUGH. SINCE WHEN DOES CATWOMAN KILL PEOPLE? LAST I HEARD, SHE WASN'T EVEN REALLY MUCH OF A CROOK ANYMORE.
OKAY, GOOD POINT. BUT STILL...I CAN'T EVEN THINK OF ANYTHING FROM BACK IN THE DAY WHERE SHE EVER LEFT A BODY AT A SCENE.
MAYBE SHE'S GETTING OLD, GOT SLOW AND LOST CONTROL?
MAYBE. MAYBE NOT.
YEAH, THERE'S ONE OTHER PROBLEM, TOO...

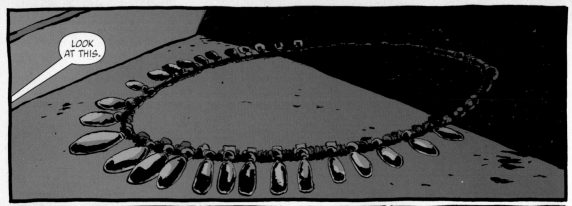

LOOK AT THIS.

THOSE *EMERALDS?*

I'M NOT AN EXPERT, BUT THAT'S WHAT *I'D* SAY, YEAH.

SO, SHE GETS *INTERRUPTED,* GETS IN A SCUFFLE, SHOOTS THE GUY AND ENDS UP LEAVING SOME JEWELS ON THE CARPET.

PROBABLY *DROPPED* THEM WHEN HE OPENED FIRE.

SHE'S GONNA LEAVE WITHOUT EVERYTHING SHE *CAME FOR?* THE REVEREND'S ALREADY DEAD, AND IF SHE CHECKED OUT THIS PLACE, SHE KNOWS IT'S SOUND-PROOF.

HELL, NO ONE EVEN FOUND THE *BODY* UNTIL TWO HOURS AGO, WHEN HIS SECRETARY CAME LOOKING FOR HIM.

CATWOMAN'S A PRO. I DON'T SEE HER LEAVING GEMS ON THE FLOOR AND RUNNING OFF SCATTER-BRAINED.

TALKING YOURSELF OUT OF YOUR *OWN* THEORY?

JUST A LITTLE. YOU'RE *RIGHT,* THOUGH, SHE NEVER *HAS* KILLED ANYONE, FAR AS I KNOW.

SO, MAYBE SHE FREAKED OUT AND RAN OFF, BUT STILL...

WHAT'S WRONG *NOW?*

I DON'T THINK THAT JEWELRY WAS ACTUALLY *IN* THAT SAFE. I THINK IT WAS *PLANTED.*

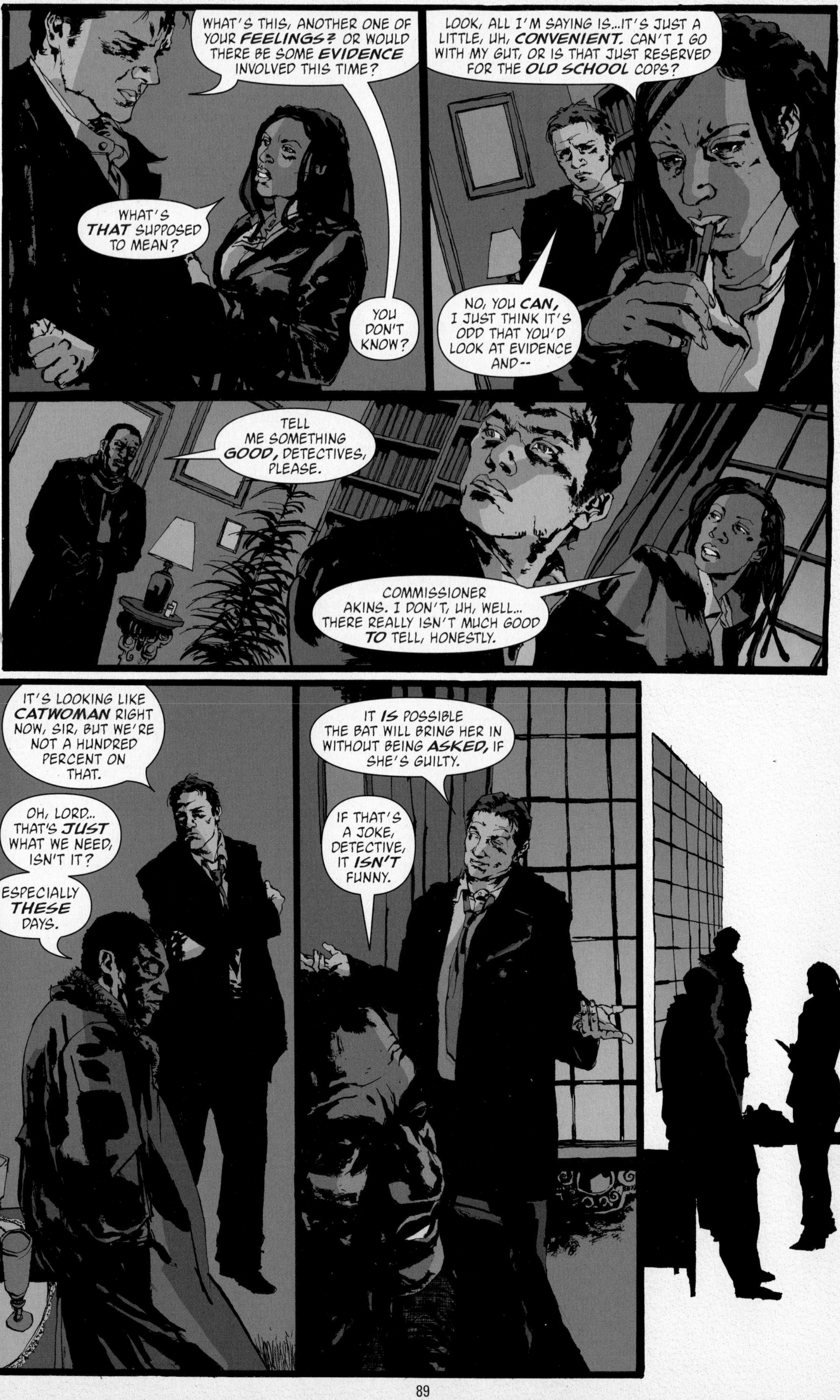
WHAT'S THIS, ANOTHER ONE OF YOUR FEELINGS? OR WOULD THERE BE SOME EVIDENCE INVOLVED THIS TIME?
WHAT'S THAT SUPPOSED TO MEAN?
YOU DON'T KNOW?
LOOK, ALL I'M SAYING IS...IT'S JUST A LITTLE, UH, CONVENIENT. CAN'T I GO WITH MY GUT, OR IS THAT JUST RESERVED FOR THE OLD SCHOOL COPS?
NO, YOU CAN, I JUST THINK IT'S ODD THAT YOU'D LOOK AT EVIDENCE AND--
TELL ME SOMETHING GOOD, DETECTIVES, PLEASE.
COMMISSIONER AKINS. I DON'T, UH, WELL... THERE REALLY ISN'T MUCH GOOD TO TELL, HONESTLY.
IT'S LOOKING LIKE CATWOMAN RIGHT NOW, SIR, BUT WE'RE NOT A HUNDRED PERCENT ON THAT.
OH, LORD... THAT'S JUST WHAT WE NEED, ISN'T IT?
ESPECIALLY THESE DAYS.
IT IS POSSIBLE THE BAT WILL BRING HER IN WITHOUT BEING ASKED, IF SHE'S GUILTY.
IF THAT'S A JOKE, DETECTIVE, IT ISN'T FUNNY.

EITHER OF YOU EVER **WATCH** THIS MAN ON TV?

NOT IF I CAN HELP IT.

I GET MY CHURCH IN CHURCH, SIR.

ARE THERE ANY **OTHER** POSSIBLES **BESIDES** CATWOMAN?

WE'RE BRINGING THE WIFE AND A FEW OF HIS ASSOCIATES DOWN TO CENTRAL TO HEAR WHAT THEY'VE GOT TO **SAY**, BUT AT THIS POINT IT'S WHAT YOU **SEE**, COMMISSIONER.

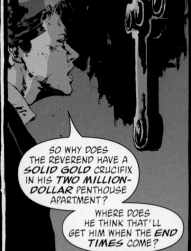

LET'S JUST KEEP A **LID** ON THIS WHOLE CATWOMAN ANGLE FOR THE **TIME BEING**, THEN.

AN IMPORTANT **COMMUNITY LEADER** GETS KILLED, LAST THING WE NEED IS TO SEE THE **FREAK ANGLE** PLAY OUT IN THE NEWS.

NOW I'VE GOT TO GO GIVE THESE VULTURES SOMETHING TO CHEW ON FOR THEIR NEXT NEWS-CYCLE. KEEP ME UPDATED ON YOUR PROGRESS...

OF COURSE, COMMISSIONER.

YOU KNOW WHAT'S **WEIRD**? DOESN'T IT SAY SOMEWHERE IN THE BIBLE ABOUT RICH MEN NOT BEING ABLE TO GET INTO HEAVEN?

SOME-THING LIKE THAT, YES.

SO WHY DOES THE REVEREND HAVE A **SOLID GOLD** CRUCIFIX IN HIS **TWO MILLION-DOLLAR** PENTHOUSE APARTMENT?

WHERE DOES HE THINK THAT'LL GET HIM WHEN THE **END TIMES** COME?

I DON'T KNOW. MAYBE THERE'S A **COVER CHARGE** FOR THE **WHITES-ONLY** SECTION OF HEAVEN.

SO YOU **HAVE** WATCHED THIS GUY'S SHOW.

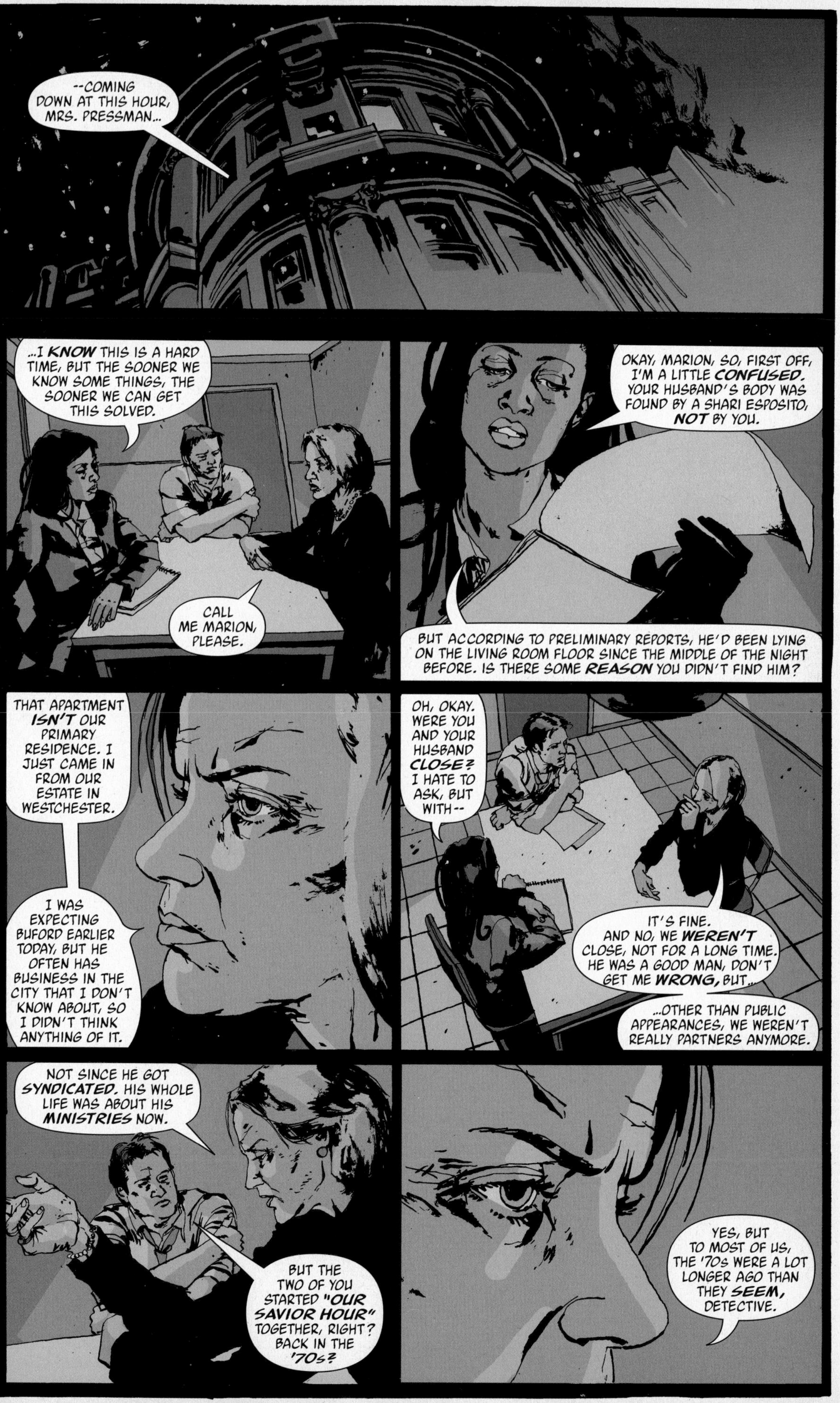
--COMING DOWN AT THIS HOUR, MRS. PRESSMAN...
...I KNOW THIS IS A HARD TIME, BUT THE SOONER WE KNOW SOME THINGS, THE SOONER WE CAN GET THIS SOLVED.
CALL ME MARION, PLEASE.
OKAY, MARION, SO, FIRST OFF, I'M A LITTLE CONFUSED. YOUR HUSBAND'S BODY WAS FOUND BY A SHARI ESPOSITO, NOT BY YOU.
BUT ACCORDING TO PRELIMINARY REPORTS, HE'D BEEN LYING ON THE LIVING ROOM FLOOR SINCE THE MIDDLE OF THE NIGHT BEFORE. IS THERE SOME REASON YOU DIDN'T FIND HIM?
THAT APARTMENT ISN'T OUR PRIMARY RESIDENCE. I JUST CAME IN FROM OUR ESTATE IN WESTCHESTER.
I WAS EXPECTING BUFORD EARLIER TODAY, BUT HE OFTEN HAS BUSINESS IN THE CITY THAT I DON'T KNOW ABOUT, SO I DIDN'T THINK ANYTHING OF IT.
OH, OKAY. WERE YOU AND YOUR HUSBAND CLOSE? I HATE TO ASK, BUT WITH--
IT'S FINE. AND NO, WE WEREN'T CLOSE, NOT FOR A LONG TIME. HE WAS A GOOD MAN, DON'T GET ME WRONG, BUT...
...OTHER THAN PUBLIC APPEARANCES, WE WEREN'T REALLY PARTNERS ANYMORE.
NOT SINCE HE GOT SYNDICATED. HIS WHOLE LIFE WAS ABOUT HIS MINISTRIES NOW.
BUT THE TWO OF YOU STARTED "OUR SAVIOR HOUR" TOGETHER, RIGHT? BACK IN THE '70s?
YES, BUT TO MOST OF US, THE '70s WERE A LOT LONGER AGO THAN THEY SEEM, DETECTIVE.

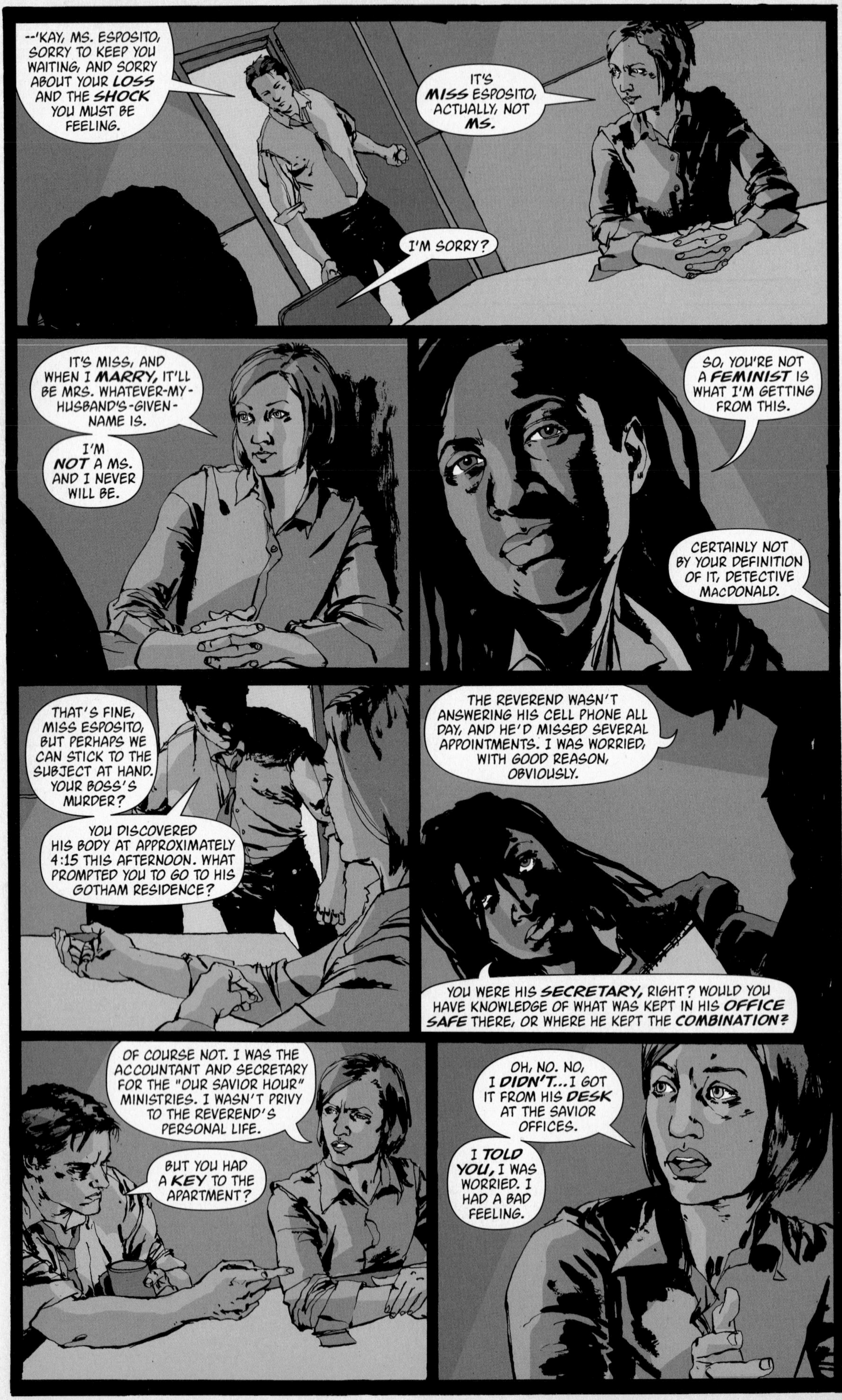
--'KAY, MS. ESPOSITO, SORRY TO KEEP YOU WAITING, AND SORRY ABOUT YOUR LOSS AND THE SHOCK YOU MUST BE FEELING.
IT'S MISS ESPOSITO, ACTUALLY, NOT MS.
I'M SORRY?
IT'S MISS, AND WHEN I MARRY, IT'LL BE MRS. WHATEVER-MY-HUSBAND'S-GIVEN-NAME IS.
I'M NOT A MS. AND I NEVER WILL BE.
SO, YOU'RE NOT A FEMINIST IS WHAT I'M GETTING FROM THIS.
CERTAINLY NOT BY YOUR DEFINITION OF IT, DETECTIVE MACDONALD.
THAT'S FINE, MISS ESPOSITO, BUT PERHAPS WE CAN STICK TO THE SUBJECT AT HAND. YOUR BOSS'S MURDER?
YOU DISCOVERED HIS BODY AT APPROXIMATELY 4:15 THIS AFTERNOON. WHAT PROMPTED YOU TO GO TO HIS GOTHAM RESIDENCE?
THE REVEREND WASN'T ANSWERING HIS CELL PHONE ALL DAY, AND HE'D MISSED SEVERAL APPOINTMENTS. I WAS WORRIED, WITH GOOD REASON, OBVIOUSLY.
YOU WERE HIS SECRETARY, RIGHT? WOULD YOU HAVE KNOWLEDGE OF WHAT WAS KEPT IN HIS OFFICE SAFE THERE, OR WHERE HE KEPT THE COMBINATION?
OF COURSE NOT. I WAS THE ACCOUNTANT AND SECRETARY FOR THE "OUR SAVIOR HOUR" MINISTRIES. I WASN'T PRIVY TO THE REVEREND'S PERSONAL LIFE.
BUT YOU HAD A KEY TO THE APARTMENT?
OH, NO. NO, I DIDN'T... I GOT IT FROM HIS DESK AT THE SAVIOR OFFICES.
I TOLD YOU, I WAS WORRIED. I HAD A BAD FEELING.

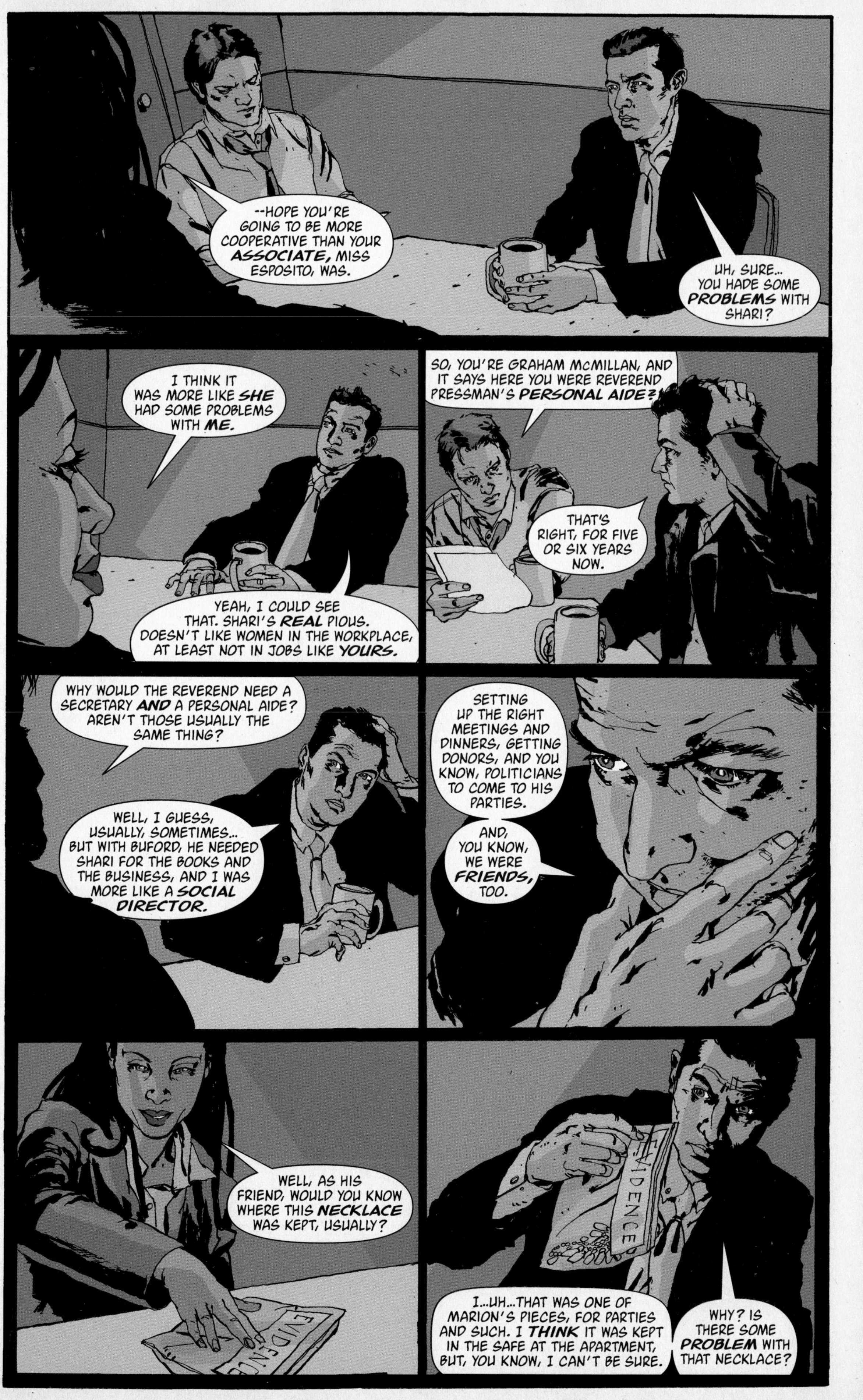
--HOPE YOU'RE GOING TO BE MORE COOPERATIVE THAN YOUR ASSOCIATE, MISS ESPOSITO, WAS.
UH, SURE... YOU HADE SOME PROBLEMS WITH SHARI?
I THINK IT WAS MORE LIKE SHE HAD SOME PROBLEMS WITH ME.
YEAH, I COULD SEE THAT. SHARI'S REAL PIOUS. DOESN'T LIKE WOMEN IN THE WORKPLACE, AT LEAST NOT IN JOBS LIKE YOURS.
SO, YOU'RE GRAHAM McMILLAN, AND IT SAYS HERE YOU WERE REVEREND PRESSMAN'S PERSONAL AIDE?
THAT'S RIGHT, FOR FIVE OR SIX YEARS NOW.
WHY WOULD THE REVEREND NEED A SECRETARY AND A PERSONAL AIDE? AREN'T THOSE USUALLY THE SAME THING?
WELL, I GUESS, USUALLY, SOMETIMES... BUT WITH BUFORD, HE NEEDED SHARI FOR THE BOOKS AND THE BUSINESS, AND I WAS MORE LIKE A SOCIAL DIRECTOR.
SETTING UP THE RIGHT MEETINGS AND DINNERS, GETTING DONORS, AND YOU KNOW, POLITICIANS TO COME TO HIS PARTIES.
AND, YOU KNOW, WE WERE FRIENDS, TOO.
WELL, AS HIS FRIEND, WOULD YOU KNOW WHERE THIS NECKLACE WAS KEPT, USUALLY?
EVIDENCE
EVIDENCE
I...UH...THAT WAS ONE OF MARION'S PIECES, FOR PARTIES AND SUCH. I THINK IT WAS KEPT IN THE SAFE AT THE APARTMENT, BUT, YOU KNOW, I CAN'T BE SURE.
WHY? IS THERE SOME PROBLEM WITH THAT NECKLACE?

WHAT, DRIVER? I SAID I WAS FOLLOWING MY *GUT* ON THIS THING.

I DIDN'T SAY A WORD.

LIKE YOU HAVE TO. I SAW THAT *LOOK* WHEN I PULLED OUT THE NECKLACE.

OKAY, FINE. I'D JUST LIKE TO KNOW WHERE THIS GUT FEELING *CAME FROM,* THAT'S ALL.

I SEE AN EXPENSIVE PIECE OF JEWELRY ON THE CARPET BY AN OPEN SAFE AT THE SCENE OF A ROBBERY/HOMICIDE, MY FIRST THOUGHT *ISN'T* THAT IT'S *PLANTED.*

MINE, EITHER. IT WAS MY *SECOND* THOUGHT.

BUT WHY?

I DON'T KNOW, I MEAN, LOOK AT THE GUY'S APARTMENT. IT'S LOADED WITH STUFF WORTH *JUST AS MUCH* AS THIS PIECE. SO WHY IS *THIS* IN A SAFE BUT THE REST IS ON DISPLAY?

MAYBE BECAUSE THAT NECKLACE IS SMALL ENOUGH TO *WALK AWAY* WITH?

HEY, GUYS, YOUR VIC WAS THAT TV *BORN-AGAIN* GUY, RIGHT?

HEY, ROMY...YEAH, WHY?

EARLY EDITION OF THE GAZETTE.

bings children

Grief: Iraqi man carries son killed in B

EVEREND PRESSMA MURDERED! CATWOMAN SUSPECTED

An Exclusive by SIMON LIPPM

The late Reverend Preston speaking at Cathedral Square last June

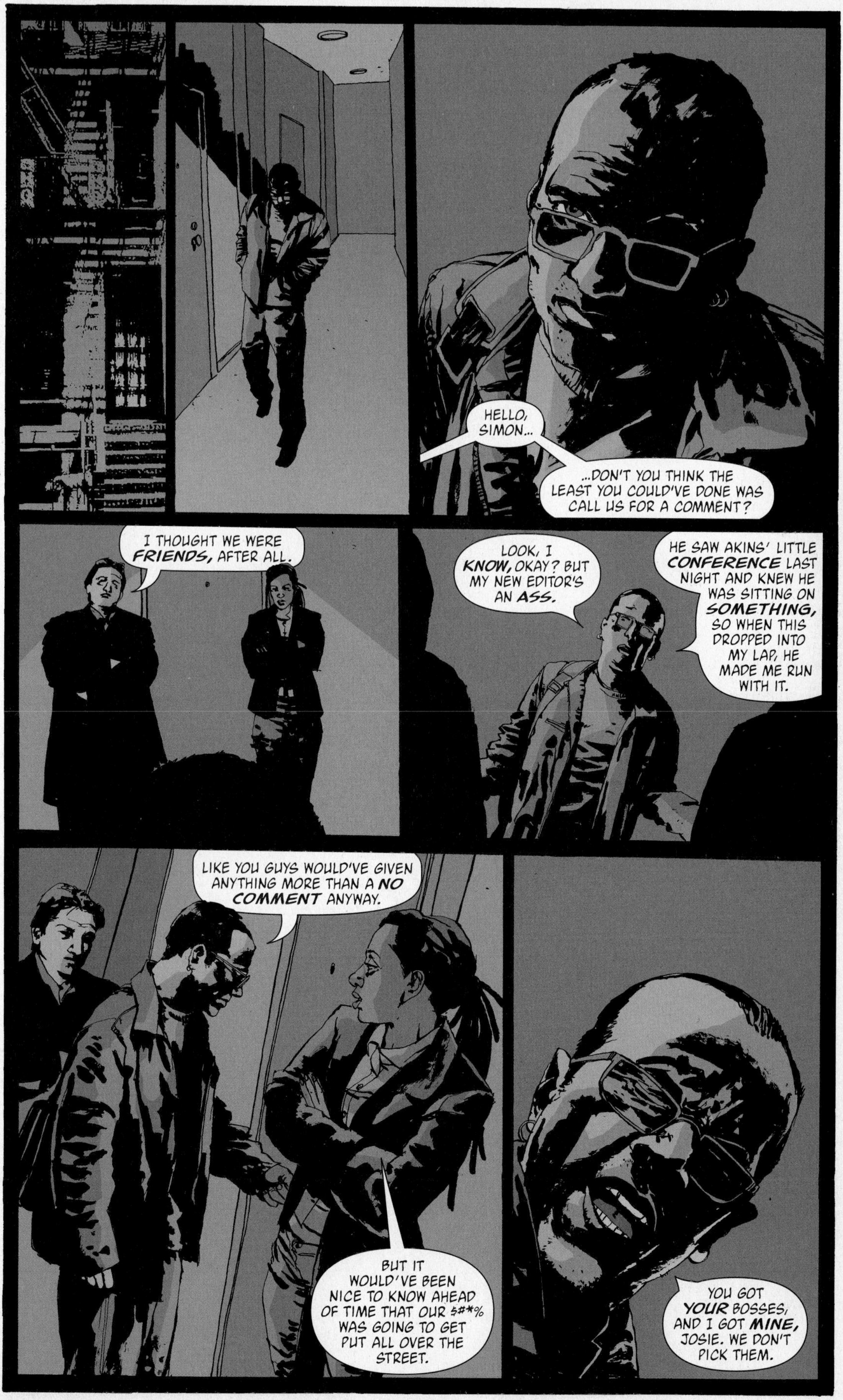
HELLO, SIMON...
...DON'T YOU THINK THE LEAST YOU COULD'VE DONE WAS CALL US FOR A COMMENT?
I THOUGHT WE WERE FRIENDS, AFTER ALL.
LOOK, I KNOW, OKAY? BUT MY NEW EDITOR'S AN ASS.
HE SAW AKINS' LITTLE CONFERENCE LAST NIGHT AND KNEW HE WAS SITTING ON SOMETHING, SO WHEN THIS DROPPED INTO MY LAP, HE MADE ME RUN WITH IT.
LIKE YOU GUYS WOULD'VE GIVEN ANYTHING MORE THAN A NO COMMENT ANYWAY.
BUT IT WOULD'VE BEEN NICE TO KNOW AHEAD OF TIME THAT OUR $#*% WAS GOING TO GET PUT ALL OVER THE STREET.
YOU GOT YOUR BOSSES, AND I GOT MINE, JOSIE. WE DON'T PICK THEM.

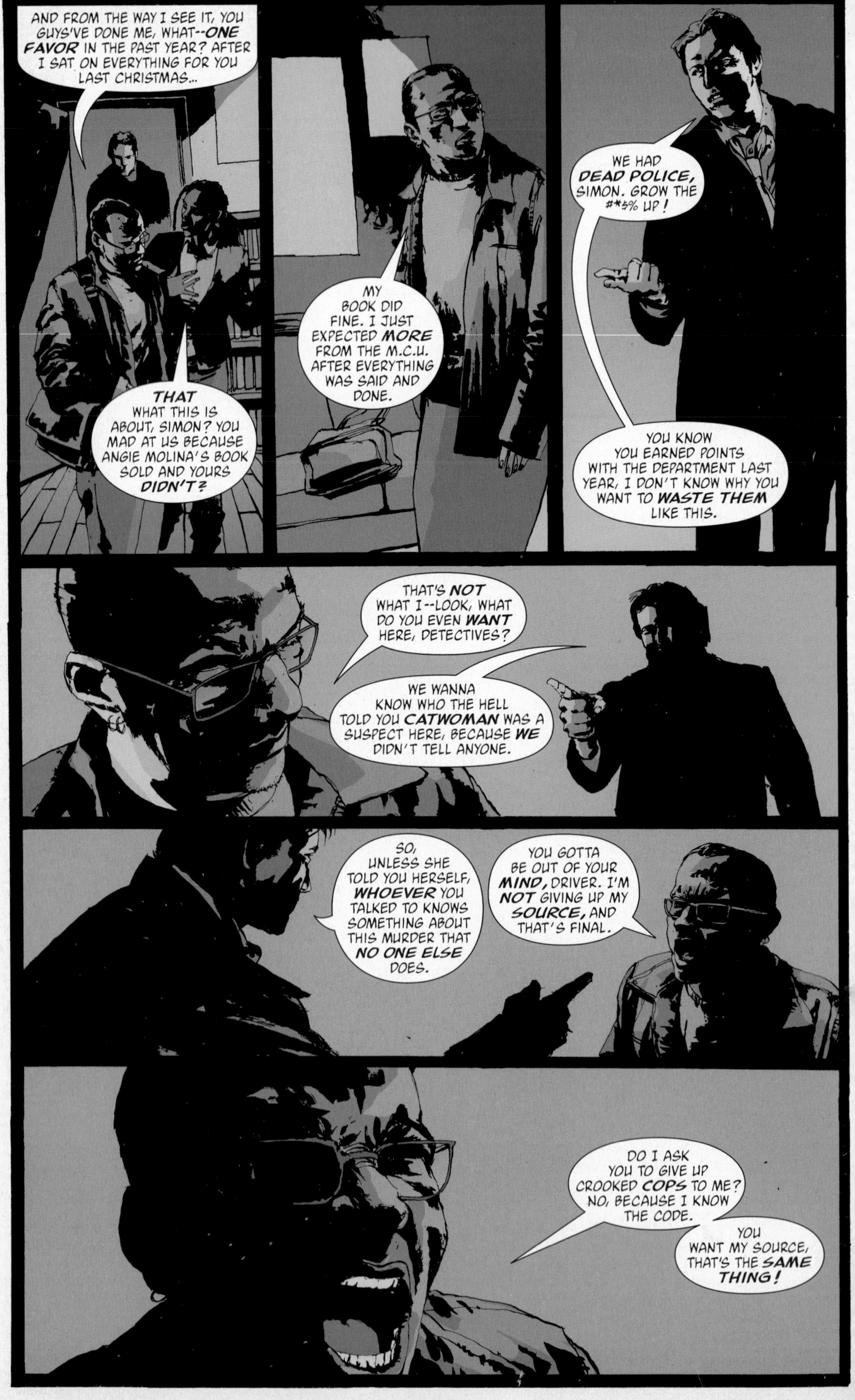
AND FROM THE WAY I SEE IT, YOU GUYS'VE DONE ME, WHAT--ONE FAVOR IN THE PAST YEAR? AFTER I SAT ON EVERYTHING FOR YOU LAST CHRISTMAS...
THAT WHAT THIS IS ABOUT, SIMON? YOU MAD AT US BECAUSE ANGIE MOLINA'S BOOK SOLD AND YOURS DIDN'T?
MY BOOK DID FINE. I JUST EXPECTED MORE FROM THE M.C.U. AFTER EVERYTHING WAS SAID AND DONE.
WE HAD DEAD POLICE, SIMON. GROW THE #*$% UP!
YOU KNOW YOU EARNED POINTS WITH THE DEPARTMENT LAST YEAR, I DON'T KNOW WHY YOU WANT TO WASTE THEM LIKE THIS.
THAT'S NOT WHAT I--LOOK, WHAT DO YOU EVEN WANT HERE, DETECTIVES?
WE WANNA KNOW WHO THE HELL TOLD YOU CATWOMAN WAS A SUSPECT HERE, BECAUSE WE DIDN'T TELL ANYONE.
SO, UNLESS SHE TOLD YOU HERSELF, WHOEVER YOU TALKED TO KNOWS SOMETHING ABOUT THIS MURDER THAT NO ONE ELSE DOES.
YOU GOTTA BE OUT OF YOUR MIND, DRIVER. I'M NOT GIVING UP MY SOURCE, AND THAT'S FINAL.
DO I ASK YOU TO GIVE UP CROOKED COPS TO ME? NO, BECAUSE I KNOW THE CODE.
YOU WANT MY SOURCE, THAT'S THE SAME THING!

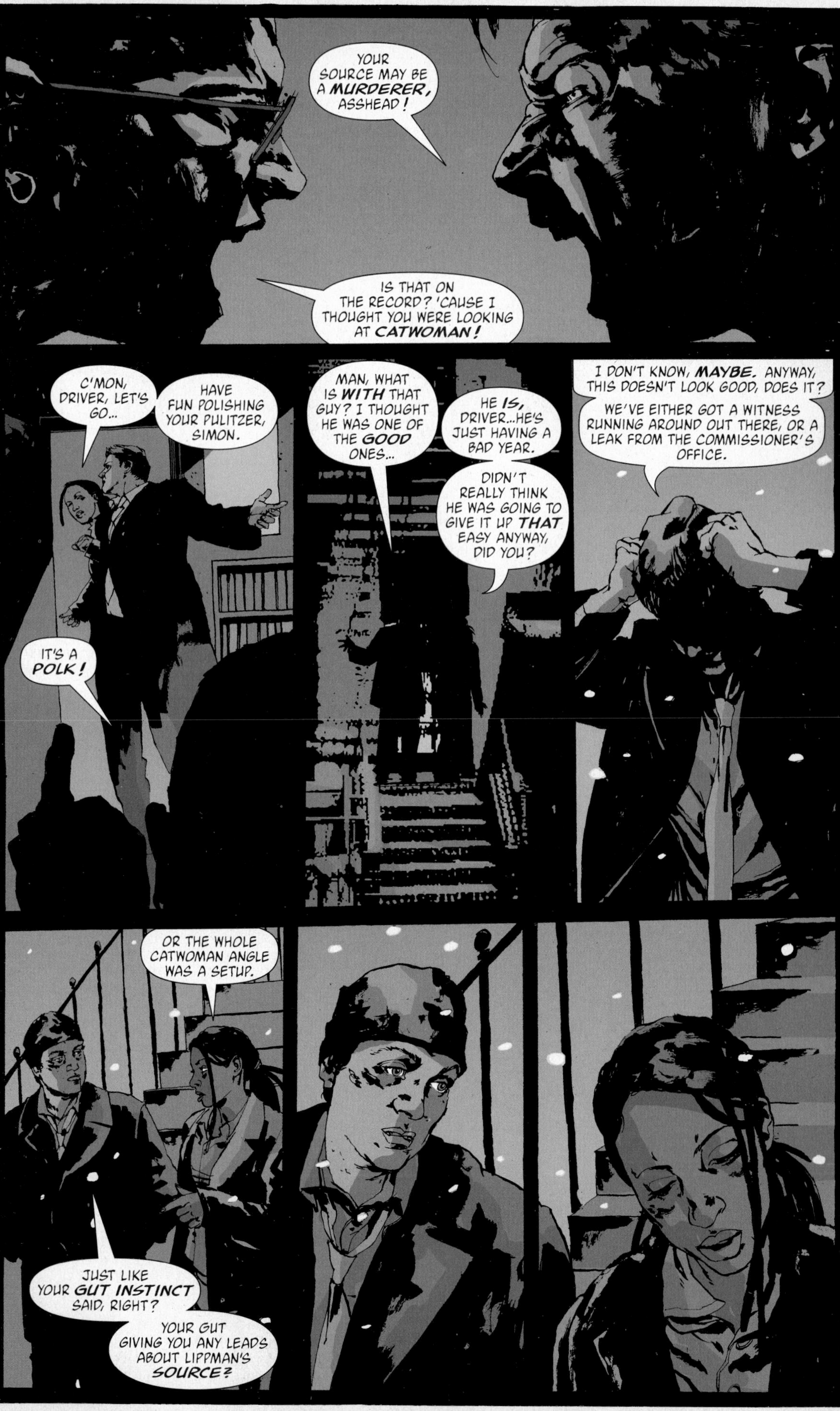
YOUR SOURCE MAY BE A MURDERER, ASSHEAD!
IS THAT ON THE RECORD? 'CAUSE I THOUGHT YOU WERE LOOKING AT CATWOMAN!
C'MON, DRIVER, LET'S GO...
HAVE FUN POLISHING YOUR PULITZER, SIMON.
IT'S A POLK!
MAN, WHAT IS WITH THAT GUY? I THOUGHT HE WAS ONE OF THE GOOD ONES...
HE IS, DRIVER...HE'S JUST HAVING A BAD YEAR.
DIDN'T REALLY THINK HE WAS GOING TO GIVE IT UP THAT EASY ANYWAY, DID YOU?
I DON'T KNOW, MAYBE. ANYWAY, THIS DOESN'T LOOK GOOD, DOES IT?
WE'VE EITHER GOT A WITNESS RUNNING AROUND OUT THERE, OR A LEAK FROM THE COMMISSIONER'S OFFICE.
OR THE WHOLE CATWOMAN ANGLE WAS A SETUP.
JUST LIKE YOUR GUT INSTINCT SAID, RIGHT?
YOUR GUT GIVING YOU ANY LEADS ABOUT LIPPMAN'S SOURCE?

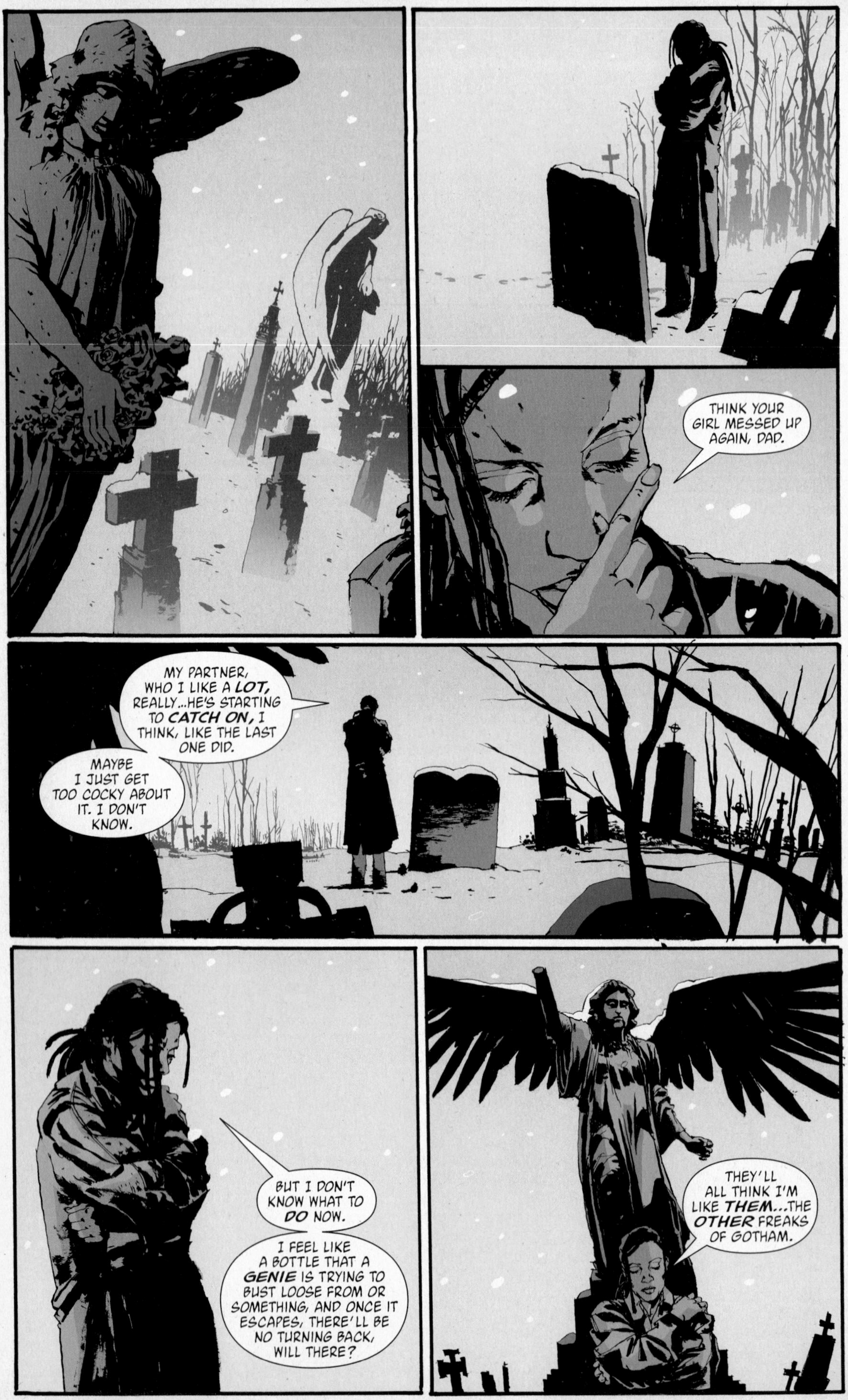
THINK YOUR GIRL MESSED UP AGAIN, DAD.
MY PARTNER, WHO I LIKE A LOT, REALLY...HE'S STARTING TO CATCH ON, I THINK, LIKE THE LAST ONE DID.
MAYBE I JUST GET TOO COCKY ABOUT IT. I DON'T KNOW.
BUT I DON'T KNOW WHAT TO DO NOW.
I FEEL LIKE A BOTTLE THAT A GENIE IS TRYING TO BUST LOOSE FROM OR SOMETHING, AND ONCE IT ESCAPES, THERE'LL BE NO TURNING BACK, WILL THERE?
THEY'LL ALL THINK I'M LIKE THEM...THE OTHER FREAKS OF GOTHAM.

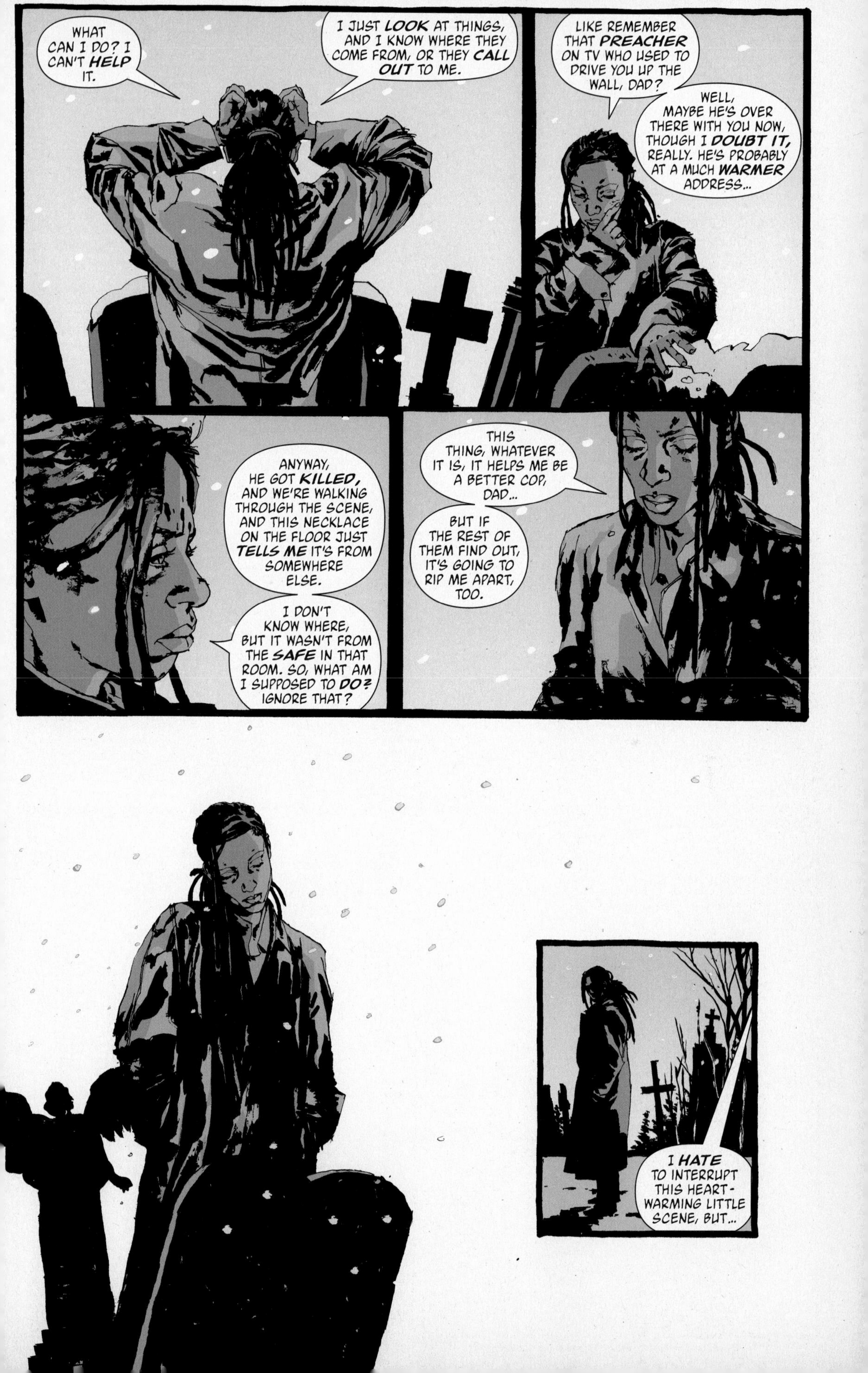
WHAT CAN I DO? I CAN'T HELP IT.
I JUST LOOK AT THINGS, AND I KNOW WHERE THEY COME FROM, OR THEY CALL OUT TO ME.
LIKE REMEMBER THAT PREACHER ON TV WHO USED TO DRIVE YOU UP THE WALL, DAD?
WELL, MAYBE HE'S OVER THERE WITH YOU NOW, THOUGH I DOUBT IT, REALLY. HE'S PROBABLY AT A MUCH WARMER ADDRESS...
ANYWAY, HE GOT KILLED, AND WE'RE WALKING THROUGH THE SCENE, AND THIS NECKLACE ON THE FLOOR JUST TELLS ME IT'S FROM SOMEWHERE ELSE.
I DON'T KNOW WHERE, BUT IT WASN'T FROM THE SAFE IN THAT ROOM. SO, WHAT AM I SUPPOSED TO DO? IGNORE THAT?
THIS THING, WHATEVER IT IS, IT HELPS ME BE A BETTER COP, DAD...
BUT IF THE REST OF THEM FIND OUT, IT'S GOING TO RIP ME APART, TOO.
I HATE TO INTERRUPT THIS HEART-WARMING LITTLE SCENE, BUT...

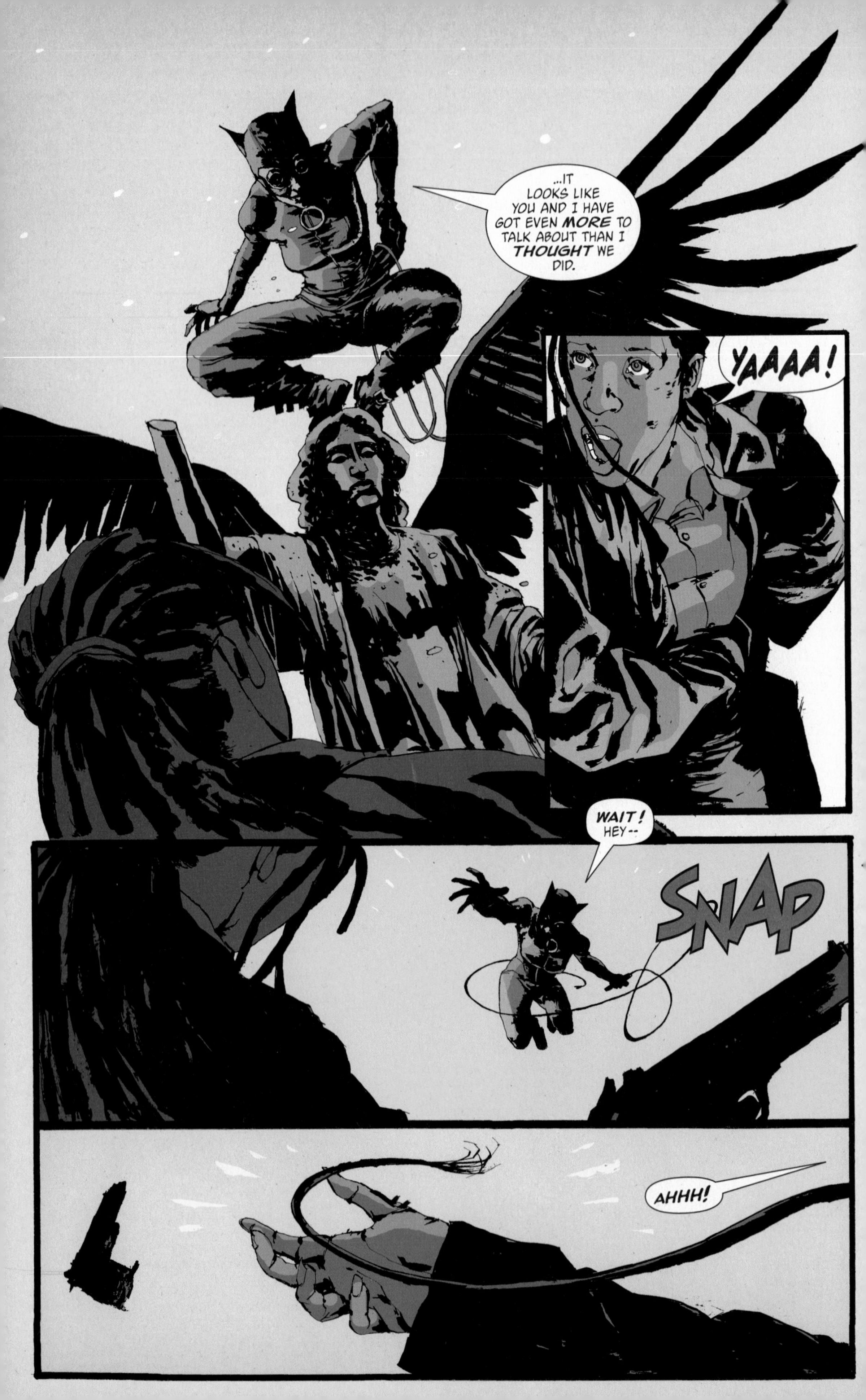

...IT LOOKS LIKE YOU AND I HAVE GOT EVEN MORE TO TALK ABOUT THAN I THOUGHT WE DID.
YAAAA!
WAIT! HEY--
SNAP
AHHH!

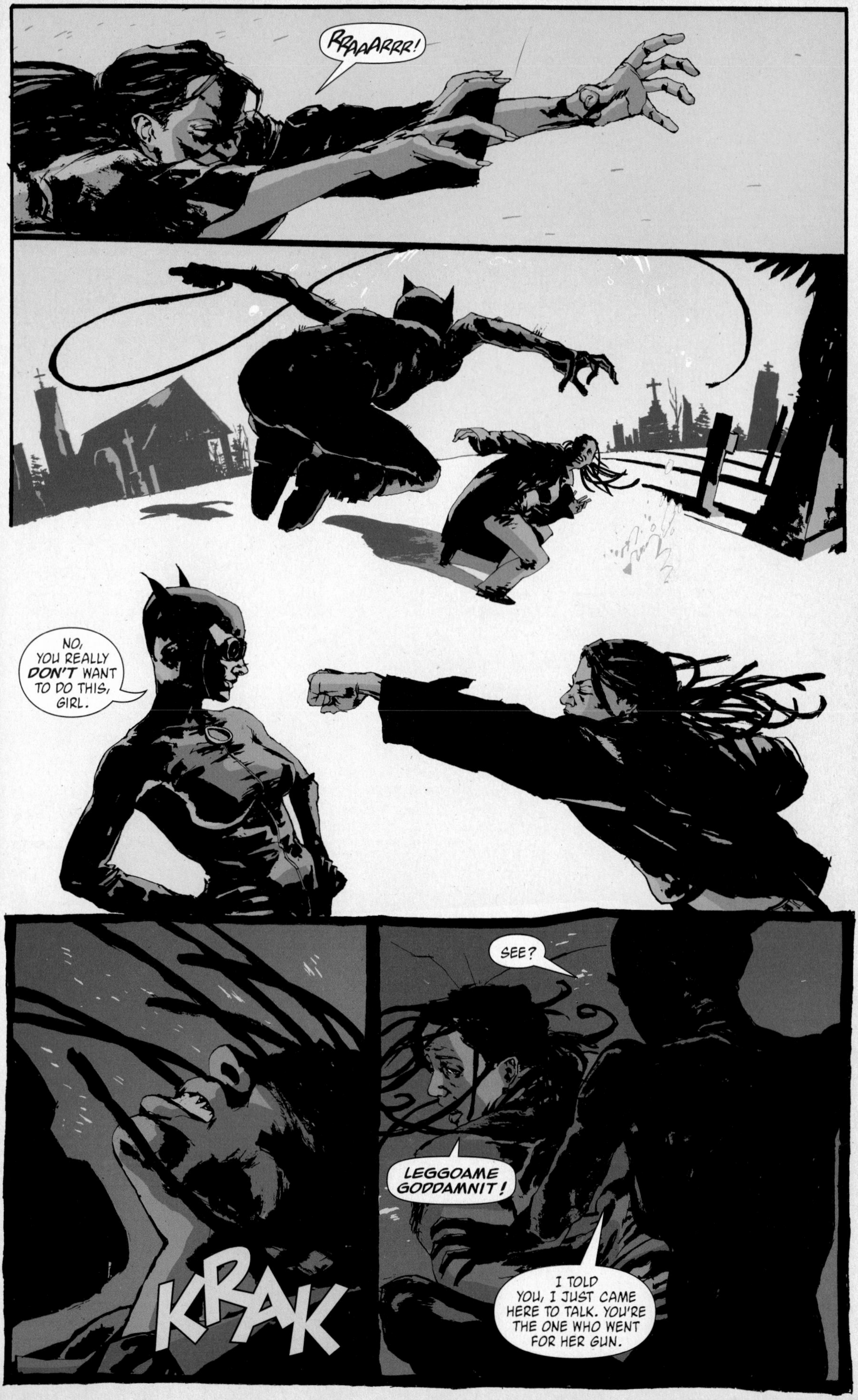
RRAAARRR!
NO, YOU REALLY DON'T WANT TO DO THIS, GIRL.
KRAK
SEE?
LEGGOAME GODDAMNIT!
I TOLD YOU, I JUST CAME HERE TO TALK. YOU'RE THE ONE WHO WENT FOR HER GUN.

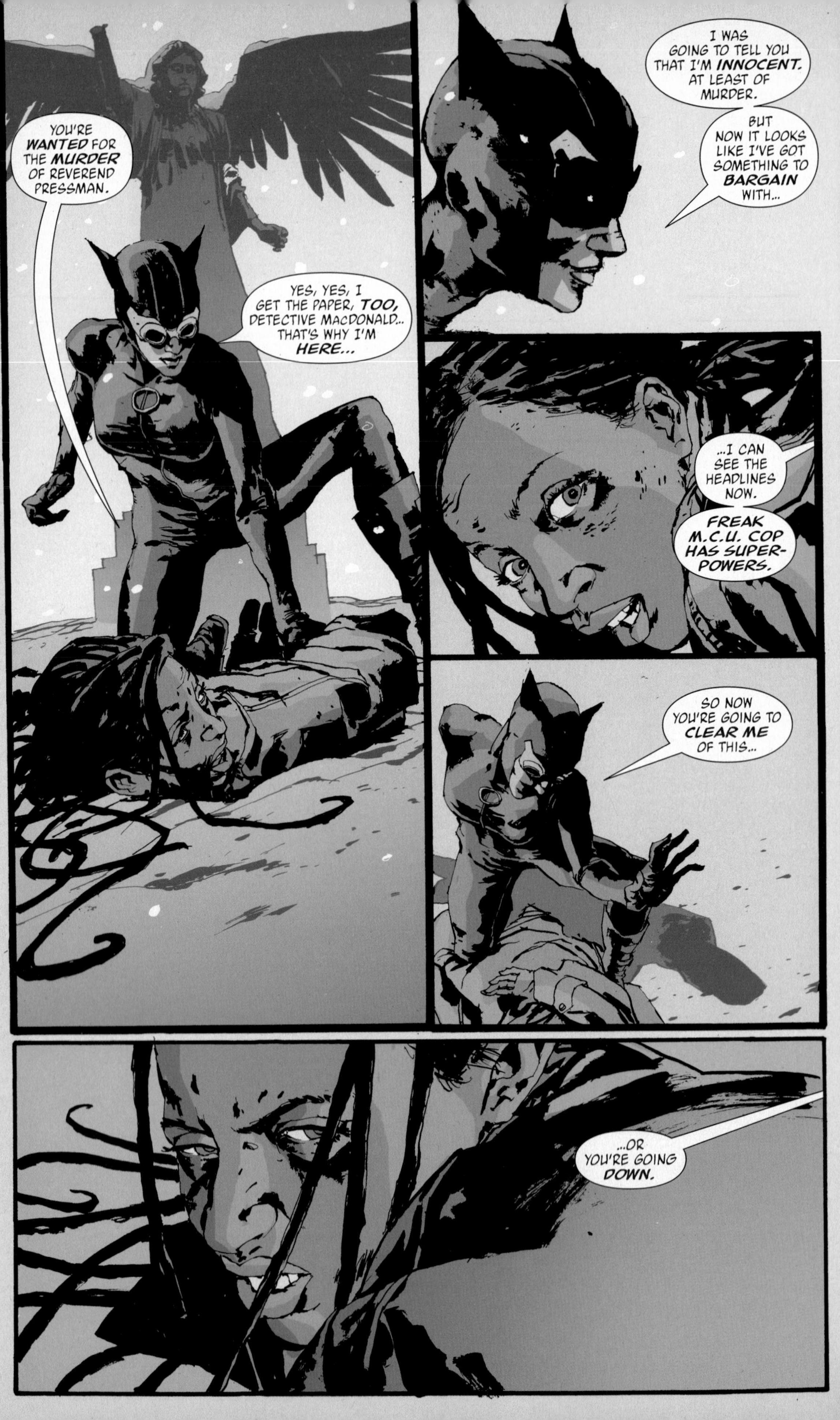
YOU'RE WANTED FOR THE MURDER OF REVEREND PRESSMAN.
YES, YES, I GET THE PAPER, TOO, DETECTIVE MACDONALD... THAT'S WHY I'M HERE...
I WAS GOING TO TELL YOU THAT I'M INNOCENT. AT LEAST OF MURDER.
BUT NOW IT LOOKS LIKE I'VE GOT SOMETHING TO BARGAIN WITH...
...I CAN SEE THE HEADLINES NOW.
FREAK M.C.U. COP HAS SUPER-POWERS.
SO NOW YOU'RE GOING TO CLEAR ME OF THIS...
...OR YOU'RE GOING DOWN.

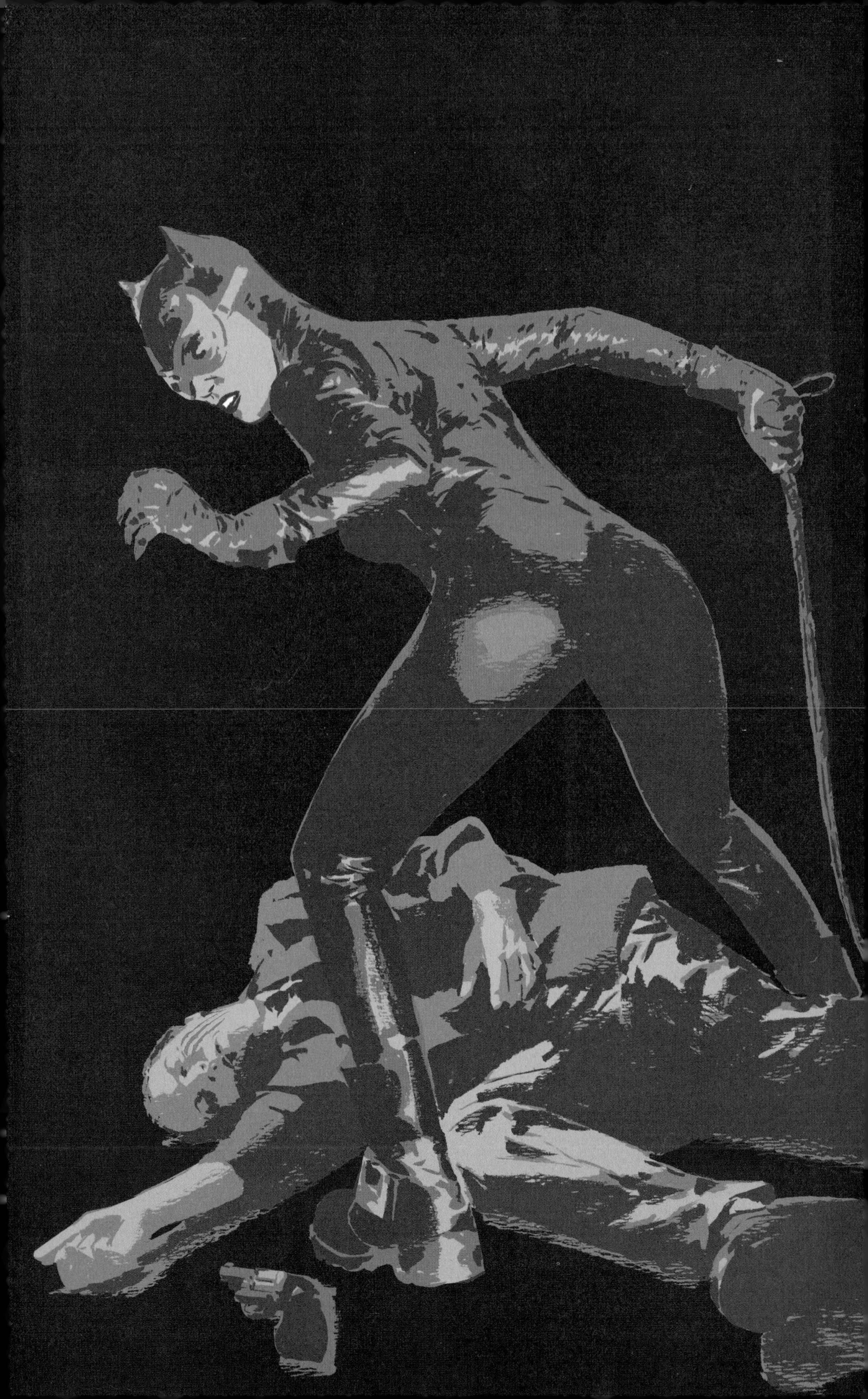

GTHAM CITY
LICE DEPARTMENT   INITIAL REPORT   XXX FOLLOW

/14/05

E NAME LAST, FIRST, M.I.

STRUCTION OF OCCURRENCE - SUSPECT NAME/NICKNAME/ALIAS - INCLUDE METHOD OF ENTRY AND ESCAPE - INCLUDE UNIQUE AND UN

PREVIOUSLY IN GOTHAM CENTRAL...

A little over a year ago Detective Josephine MacDonald (usually just Josie Mac, to her friends), transferred to the Major Crimes Unit, and has spent most of that year partnered with Marcus Driver. But Josie is keeping a secret from him and everyone else on the force, that she has a strange psychic ability. Josie can tell when things are out of place, and objects often tell her where they are supposed to be. This ability has helped make her one of the best cops on the squad, but her fear of being found out by her fellow Detectives has been eating her up inside, and a new case has brought it all to the surface.

The Reverend Buford Pressman was murdered in his penthouse apartment, and all signs point to Catwoman as the perp. Despite attempts by the police to keep this from the public, it leaks, and now the whole city knows Catwoman is suspect number one. That would be bad enough, but Catwoman has also discovered Josie's secret and is threatening to out her...Unless Josie can clear her of these murder charges.

On The Freak Beat Part Two of Two

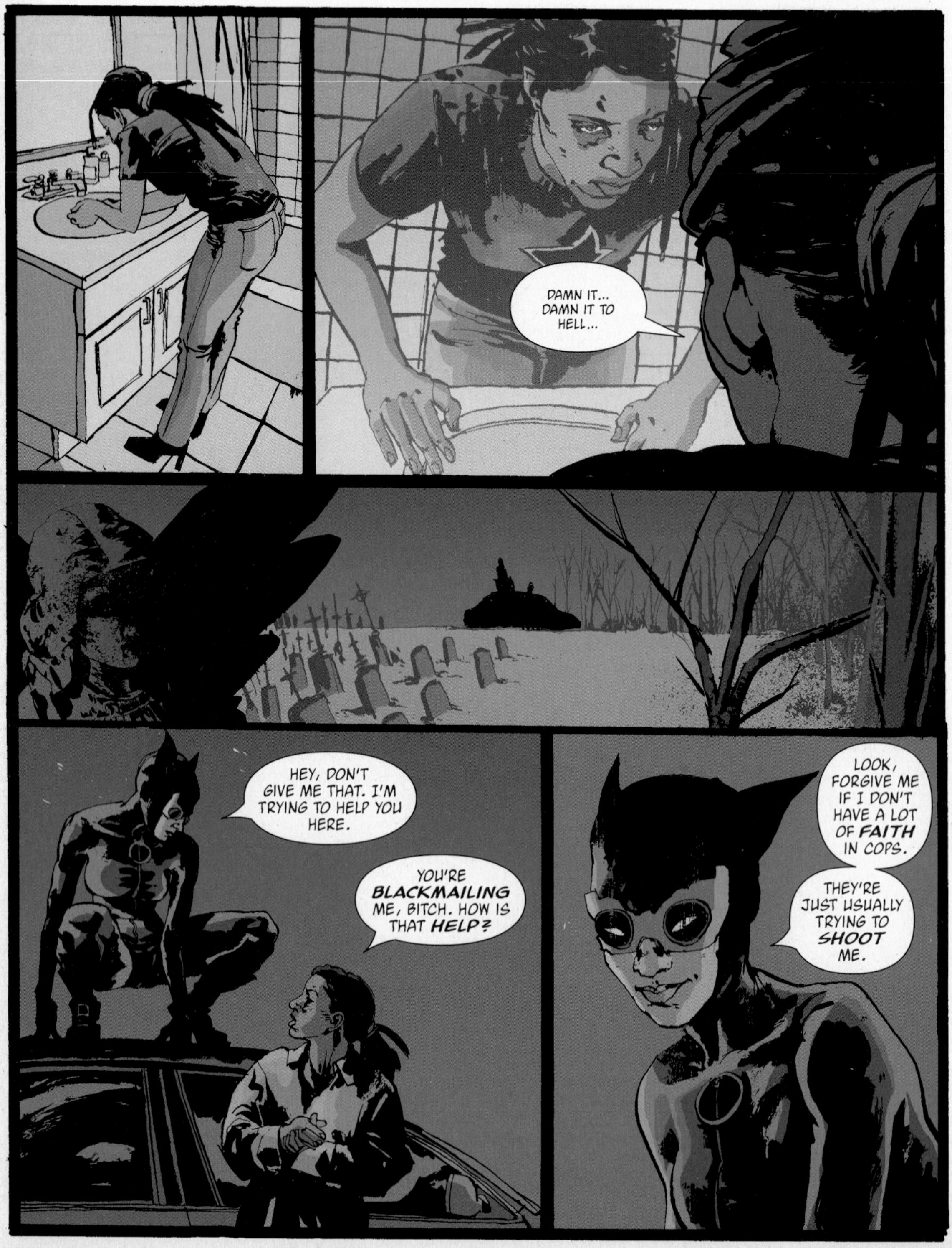
DAMN IT... DAMN IT TO HELL...
HEY, DON'T GIVE ME THAT. I'M TRYING TO HELP YOU HERE.
YOU'RE BLACKMAILING ME, BITCH. HOW IS THAT HELP?
LOOK, FORGIVE ME IF I DON'T HAVE A LOT OF FAITH IN COPS.
THEY'RE JUST USUALLY TRYING TO SHOOT ME.

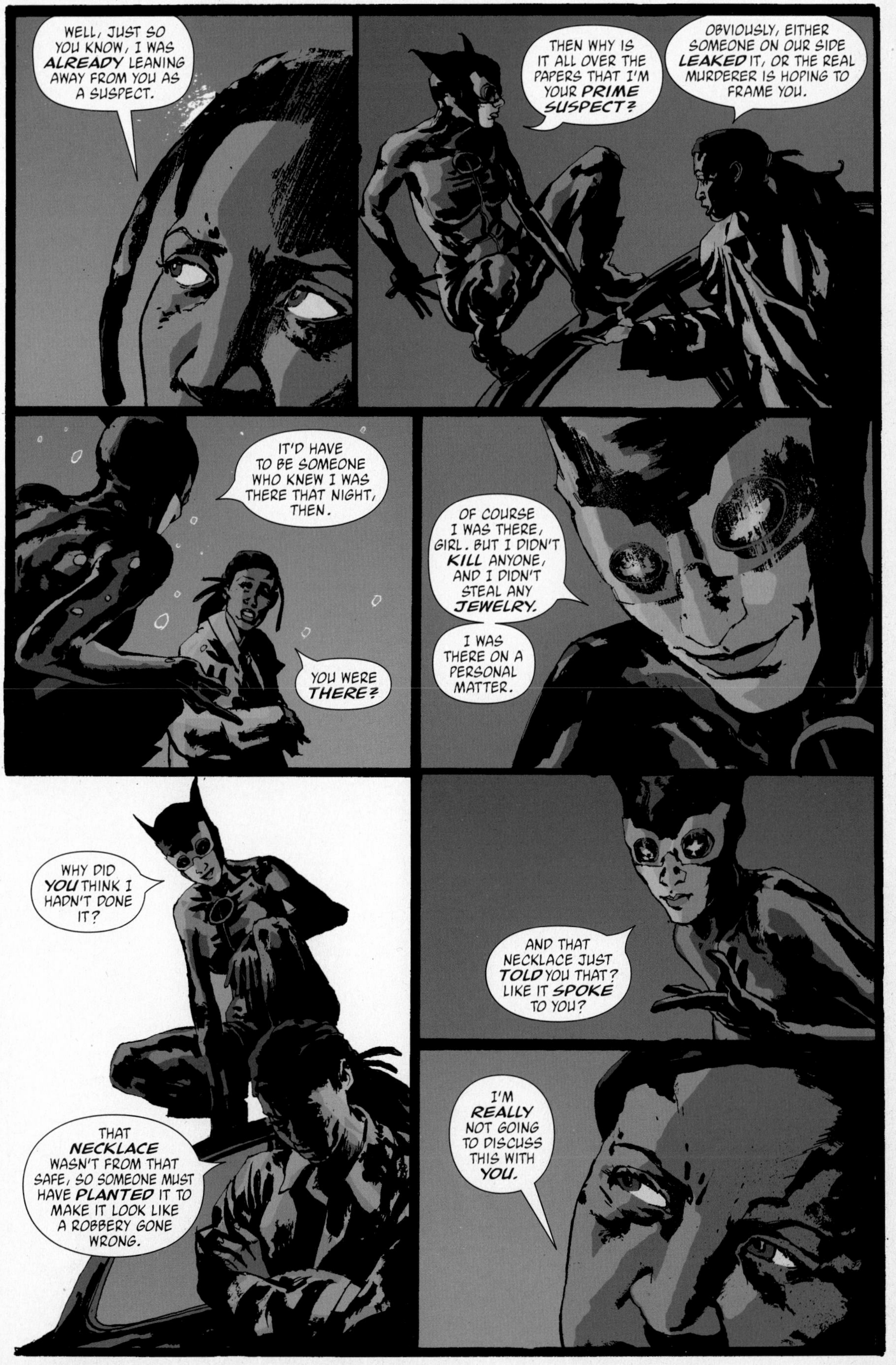
WELL, JUST SO YOU KNOW, I WAS ALREADY LEANING AWAY FROM YOU AS A SUSPECT.
THEN WHY IS IT ALL OVER THE PAPERS THAT I'M YOUR PRIME SUSPECT?
OBVIOUSLY, EITHER SOMEONE ON OUR SIDE LEAKED IT, OR THE REAL MURDERER IS HOPING TO FRAME YOU.
IT'D HAVE TO BE SOMEONE WHO KNEW I WAS THERE THAT NIGHT, THEN.
YOU WERE THERE?
OF COURSE I WAS THERE, GIRL. BUT I DIDN'T KILL ANYONE, AND I DIDN'T STEAL ANY JEWELRY.
I WAS THERE ON A PERSONAL MATTER.
WHY DID YOU THINK I HADN'T DONE IT?
THAT NECKLACE WASN'T FROM THAT SAFE, SO SOMEONE MUST HAVE PLANTED IT TO MAKE IT LOOK LIKE A ROBBERY GONE WRONG.
AND THAT NECKLACE JUST TOLD YOU THAT? LIKE IT SPOKE TO YOU?
I'M REALLY NOT GOING TO DISCUSS THIS WITH YOU.

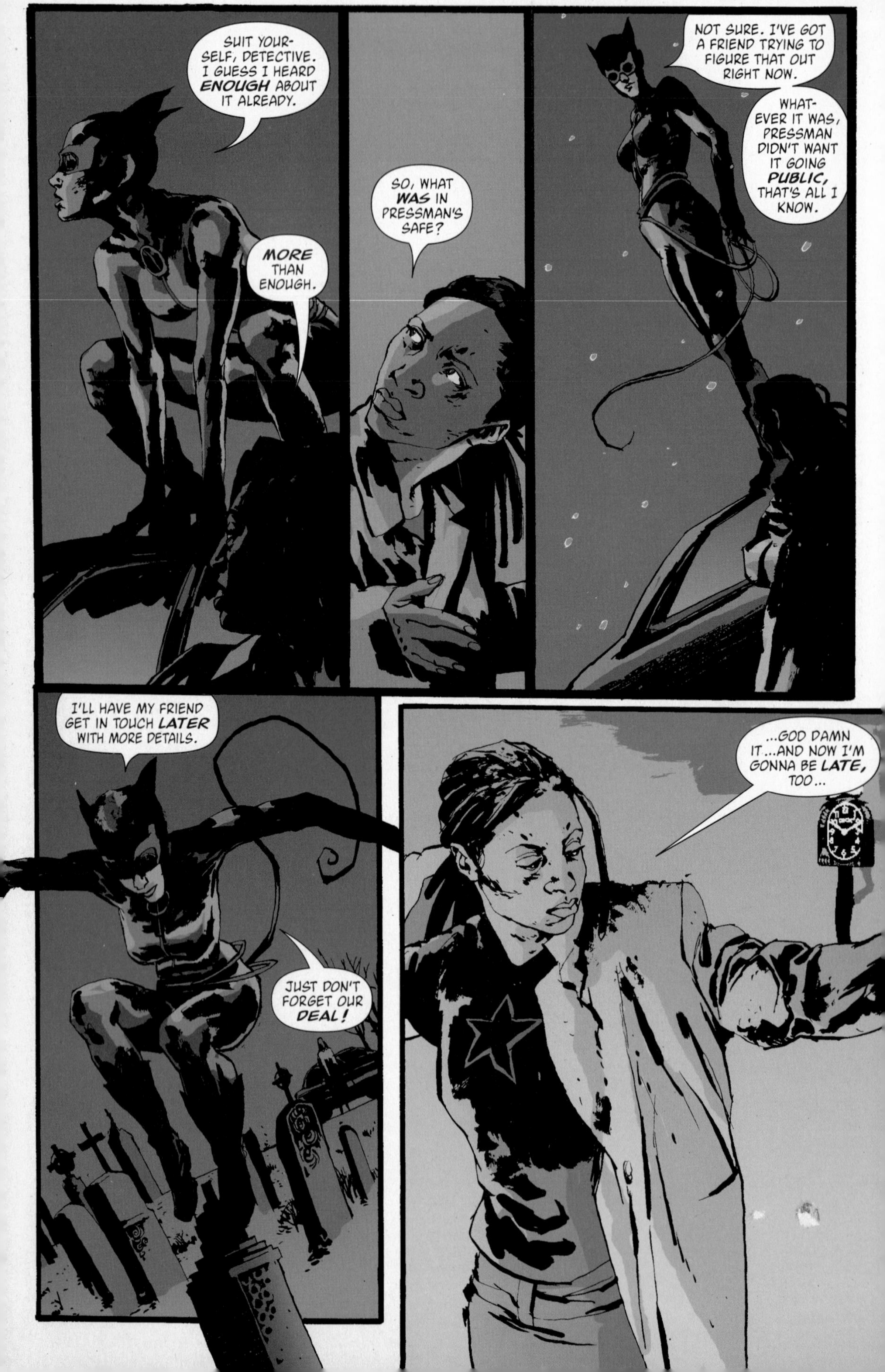
SUIT YOUR-SELF, DETECTIVE. I GUESS I HEARD ENOUGH ABOUT IT ALREADY.
MORE THAN ENOUGH.
SO, WHAT WAS IN PRESSMAN'S SAFE?
NOT SURE. I'VE GOT A FRIEND TRYING TO FIGURE THAT OUT RIGHT NOW.
WHAT-EVER IT WAS, PRESSMAN DIDN'T WANT IT GOING PUBLIC, THAT'S ALL I KNOW.
I'LL HAVE MY FRIEND GET IN TOUCH LATER WITH MORE DETAILS.
JUST DON'T FORGET OUR DEAL!
...GOD DAMN IT...AND NOW I'M GONNA BE LATE, TOO...

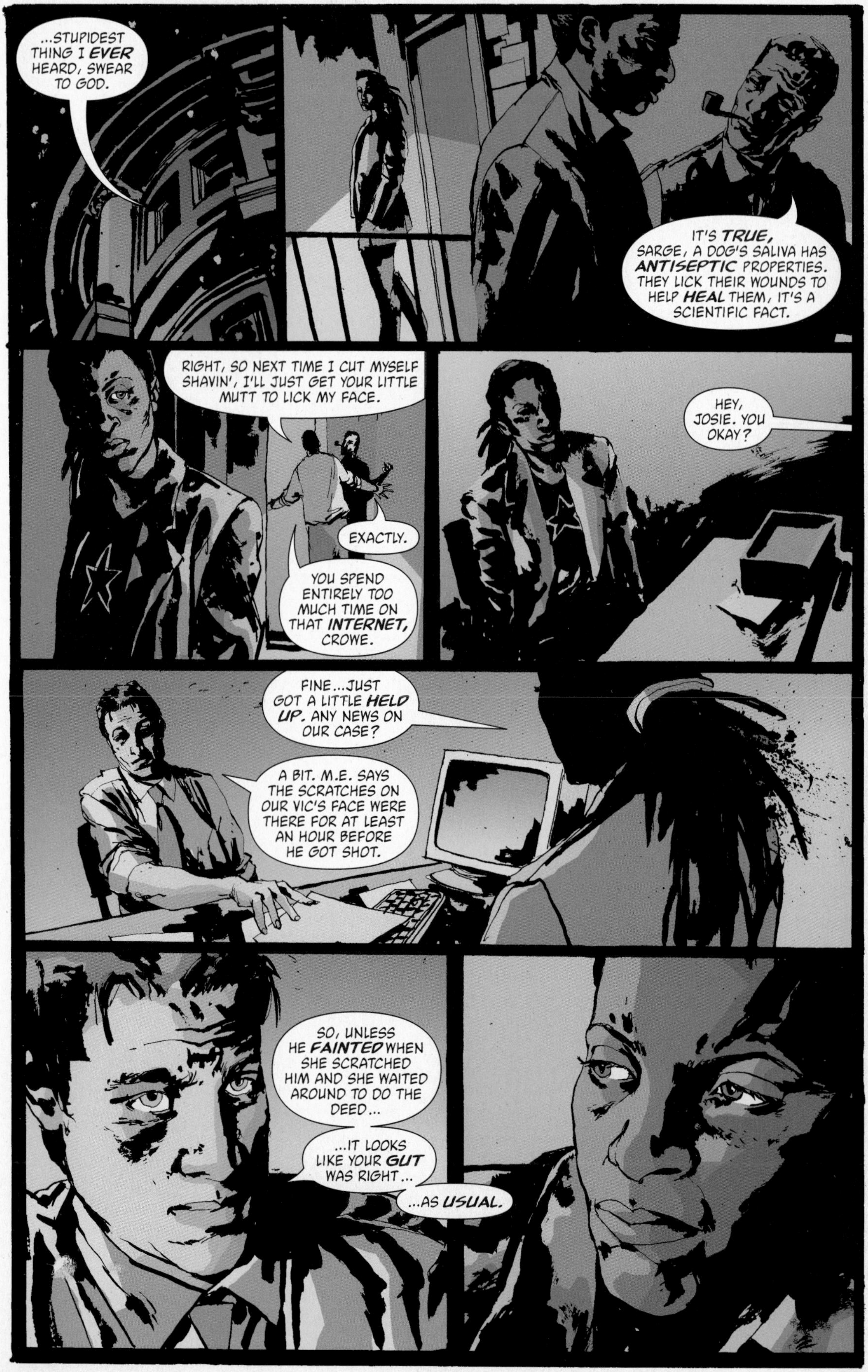
...STUPIDEST THING I EVER HEARD, SWEAR TO GOD.
IT'S TRUE, SARGE, A DOG'S SALIVA HAS ANTISEPTIC PROPERTIES. THEY LICK THEIR WOUNDS TO HELP HEAL THEM, IT'S A SCIENTIFIC FACT.
RIGHT, SO NEXT TIME I CUT MYSELF SHAVIN', I'LL JUST GET YOUR LITTLE MUTT TO LICK MY FACE.
EXACTLY.
YOU SPEND ENTIRELY TOO MUCH TIME ON THAT INTERNET, CROWE.
HEY, JOSIE. YOU OKAY?
FINE...JUST GOT A LITTLE HELD UP. ANY NEWS ON OUR CASE?
A BIT. M.E. SAYS THE SCRATCHES ON OUR VIC'S FACE WERE THERE FOR AT LEAST AN HOUR BEFORE HE GOT SHOT.
SO, UNLESS HE FAINTED WHEN SHE SCRATCHED HIM AND SHE WAITED AROUND TO DO THE DEED...
...IT LOOKS LIKE YOUR GUT WAS RIGHT...
...AS USUAL.

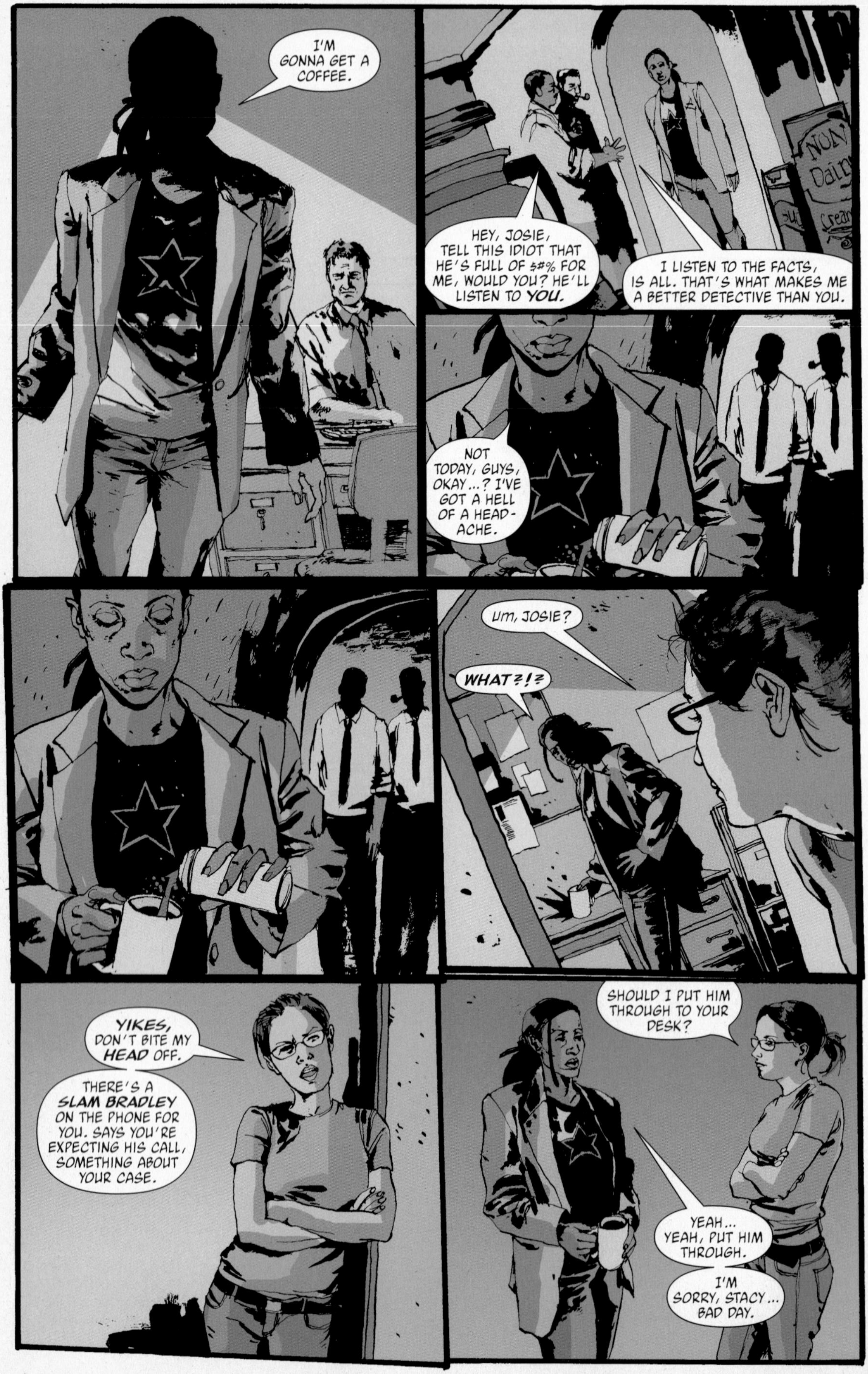
I'M GONNA GET A COFFEE.
HEY, JOSIE, TELL THIS IDIOT THAT HE'S FULL OF $#% FOR ME, WOULD YOU? HE'LL LISTEN TO YOU.
I LISTEN TO THE FACTS, IS ALL. THAT'S WHAT MAKES ME A BETTER DETECTIVE THAN YOU.
NOT TODAY, GUYS, OKAY...? I'VE GOT A HELL OF A HEAD-ACHE.
UM, JOSIE?
WHAT?!?
YIKES, DON'T BITE MY HEAD OFF.
THERE'S A SLAM BRADLEY ON THE PHONE FOR YOU. SAYS YOU'RE EXPECTING HIS CALL, SOMETHING ABOUT YOUR CASE.
SHOULD I PUT HIM THROUGH TO YOUR DESK?
YEAH... YEAH, PUT HIM THROUGH.
I'M SORRY, STACY... BAD DAY.

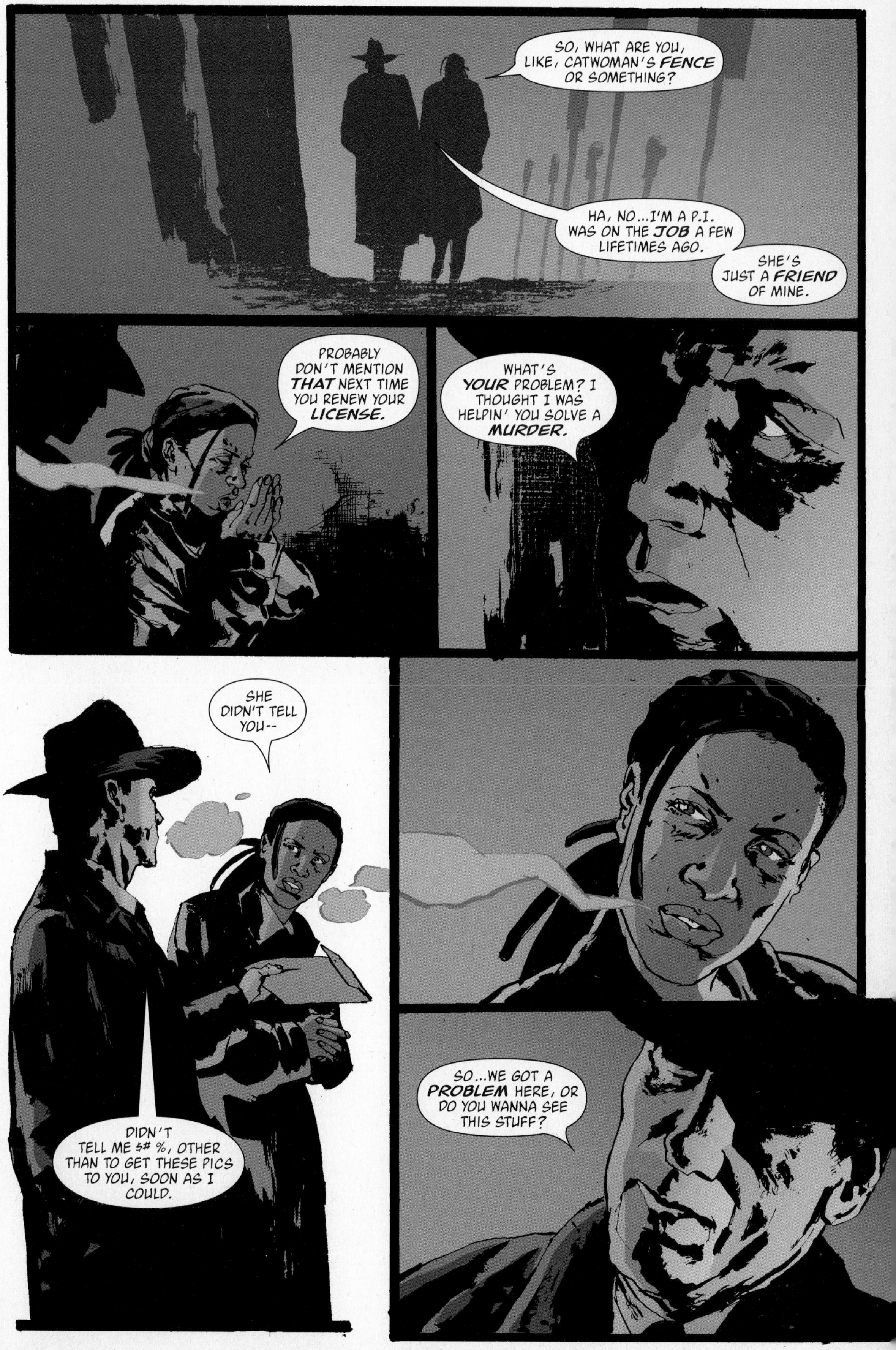

SO, WHAT ARE YOU, LIKE, CATWOMAN'S FENCE OR SOMETHING?
HA, NO...I'M A P.I. WAS ON THE JOB A FEW LIFETIMES AGO.
SHE'S JUST A FRIEND OF MINE.
PROBABLY DON'T MENTION THAT NEXT TIME YOU RENEW YOUR LICENSE.
WHAT'S YOUR PROBLEM? I THOUGHT I WAS HELPIN' YOU SOLVE A MURDER.
SHE DIDN'T TELL YOU--
DIDN'T TELL ME $# %, OTHER THAN TO GET THESE PICS TO YOU, SOON AS I COULD.
SO...WE GOT A PROBLEM HERE, OR DO YOU WANNA SEE THIS STUFF?

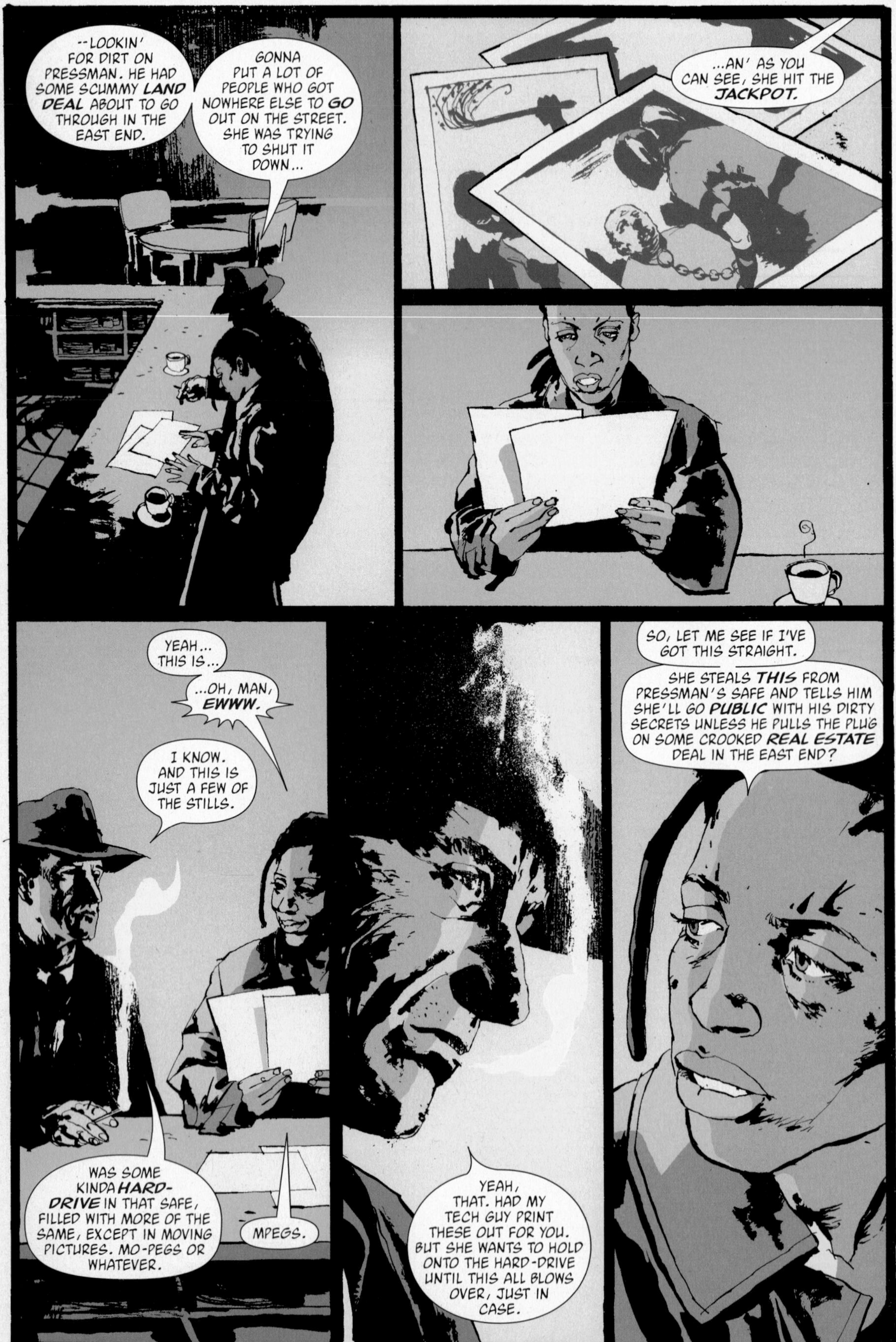
--LOOKIN' FOR DIRT ON PRESSMAN. HE HAD SOME SCUMMY LAND DEAL ABOUT TO GO THROUGH IN THE EAST END.
GONNA PUT A LOT OF PEOPLE WHO GOT NOWHERE ELSE TO GO OUT ON THE STREET. SHE WAS TRYING TO SHUT IT DOWN...
...AN' AS YOU CAN SEE, SHE HIT THE JACKPOT.
YEAH... THIS IS...
...OH, MAN, EWWW.
I KNOW. AND THIS IS JUST A FEW OF THE STILLS.
WAS SOME KINDA HARD-DRIVE IN THAT SAFE, FILLED WITH MORE OF THE SAME, EXCEPT IN MOVING PICTURES. MO-PEGS OR WHATEVER.
MPEGS.
YEAH, THAT. HAD MY TECH GUY PRINT THESE OUT FOR YOU. BUT SHE WANTS TO HOLD ONTO THE HARD-DRIVE UNTIL THIS ALL BLOWS OVER, JUST IN CASE.
SO, LET ME SEE IF I'VE GOT THIS STRAIGHT.
SHE STEALS THIS FROM PRESSMAN'S SAFE AND TELLS HIM SHE'LL GO PUBLIC WITH HIS DIRTY SECRETS UNLESS HE PULLS THE PLUG ON SOME CROOKED REAL ESTATE DEAL IN THE EAST END?

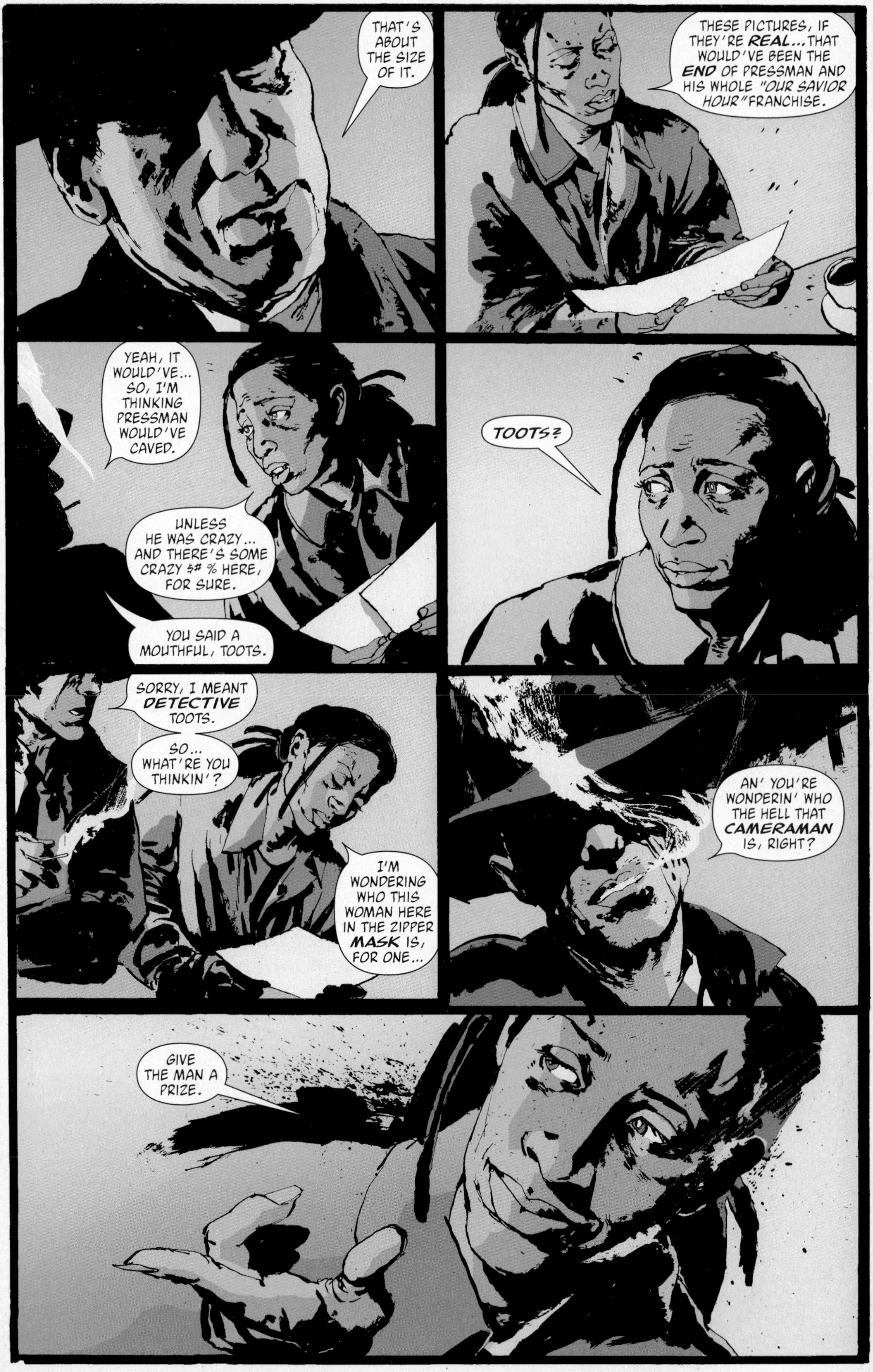
THAT'S ABOUT THE SIZE OF IT.
THESE PICTURES, IF THEY'RE REAL... THAT WOULD'VE BEEN THE END OF PRESSMAN AND HIS WHOLE "OUR SAVIOR HOUR" FRANCHISE.
YEAH, IT WOULD'VE... SO, I'M THINKING PRESSMAN WOULD'VE CAVED.
UNLESS HE WAS CRAZY... AND THERE'S SOME CRAZY $# % HERE, FOR SURE.
YOU SAID A MOUTHFUL, TOOTS.
TOOTS?
SORRY, I MEANT DETECTIVE TOOTS.
SO... WHAT'RE YOU THINKIN'?
I'M WONDERING WHO THIS WOMAN HERE IN THE ZIPPER MASK IS, FOR ONE...
AN' YOU'RE WONDERIN' WHO THE HELL THAT CAMERAMAN IS, RIGHT?
GIVE THE MAN A PRIZE.

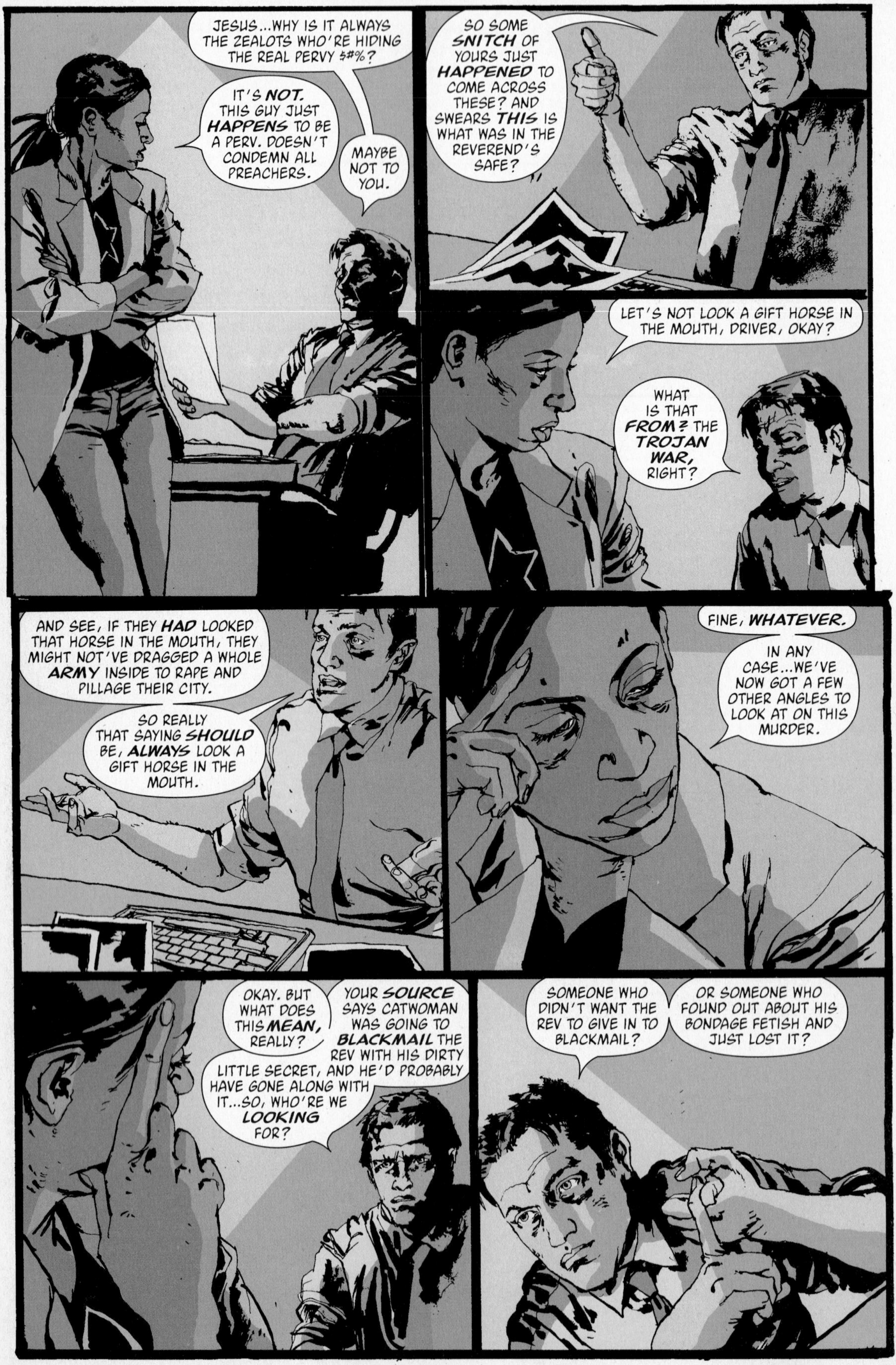
JESUS...WHY IS IT ALWAYS THE ZEALOTS WHO'RE HIDING THE REAL PERVY $#%?
IT'S NOT. THIS GUY JUST HAPPENS TO BE A PERV. DOESN'T CONDEMN ALL PREACHERS.
MAYBE NOT TO YOU.
SO SOME SNITCH OF YOURS JUST HAPPENED TO COME ACROSS THESE? AND SWEARS THIS IS WHAT WAS IN THE REVEREND'S SAFE?
LET'S NOT LOOK A GIFT HORSE IN THE MOUTH, DRIVER, OKAY?
WHAT IS THAT FROM? THE TROJAN WAR, RIGHT?
AND SEE, IF THEY HAD LOOKED THAT HORSE IN THE MOUTH, THEY MIGHT NOT'VE DRAGGED A WHOLE ARMY INSIDE TO RAPE AND PILLAGE THEIR CITY.
SO REALLY THAT SAYING SHOULD BE, ALWAYS LOOK A GIFT HORSE IN THE MOUTH.
FINE, WHATEVER.
IN ANY CASE...WE'VE NOW GOT A FEW OTHER ANGLES TO LOOK AT ON THIS MURDER.
OKAY. BUT WHAT DOES THIS MEAN, REALLY?
YOUR SOURCE SAYS CATWOMAN WAS GOING TO BLACKMAIL THE REV WITH HIS DIRTY LITTLE SECRET, AND HE'D PROBABLY HAVE GONE ALONG WITH IT...SO, WHO'RE WE LOOKING FOR?
SOMEONE WHO DIDN'T WANT THE REV TO GIVE IN TO BLACKMAIL?
OR SOMEONE WHO FOUND OUT ABOUT HIS BONDAGE FETISH AND JUST LOST IT?

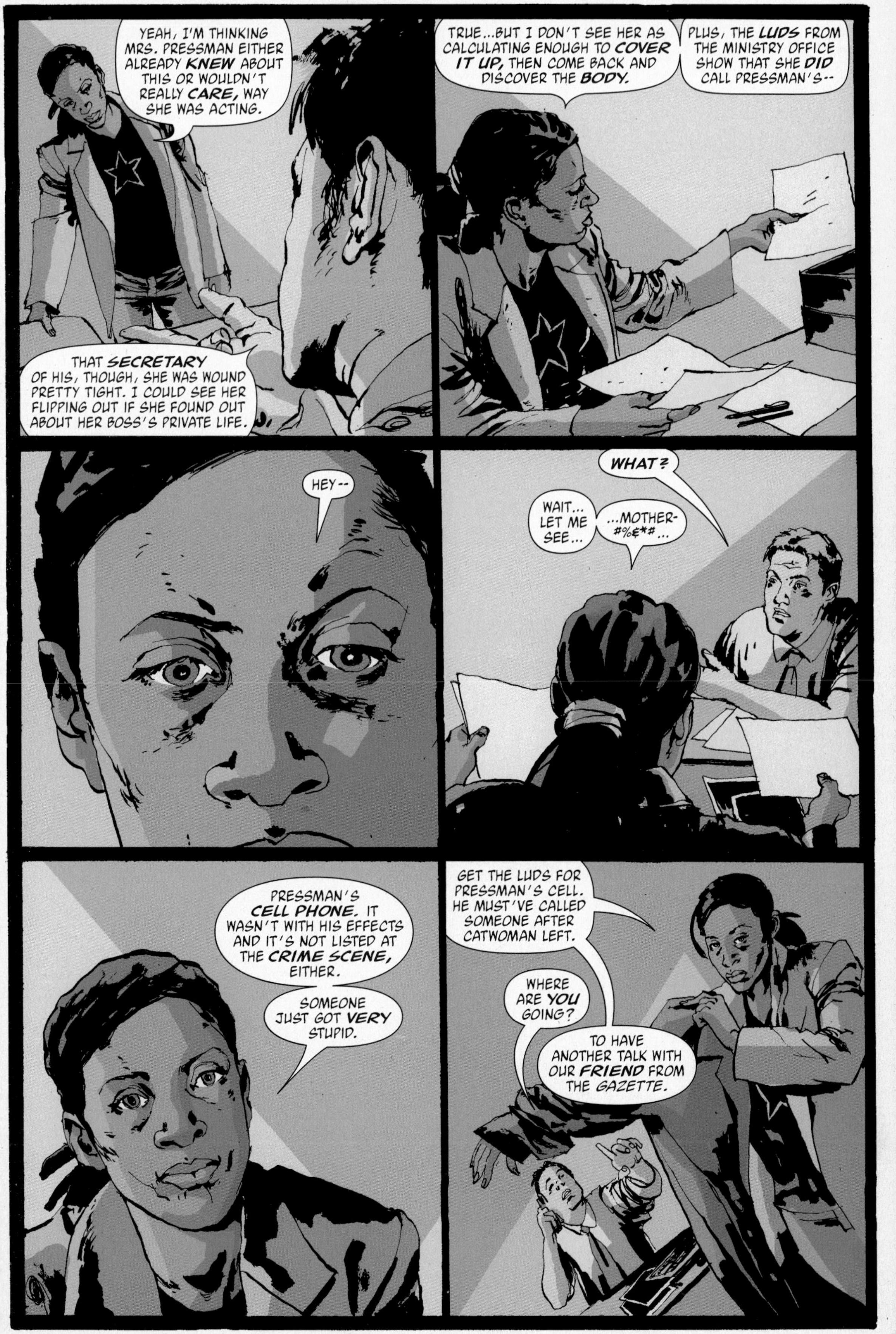

YEAH, I'M THINKING MRS. PRESSMAN EITHER ALREADY **KNEW** ABOUT THIS OR WOULDN'T REALLY **CARE,** WAY SHE WAS ACTING.
THAT **SECRETARY** OF HIS, THOUGH, SHE WAS WOUND PRETTY TIGHT. I COULD SEE HER FLIPPING OUT IF SHE FOUND OUT ABOUT HER BOSS'S PRIVATE LIFE.
TRUE...BUT I DON'T SEE HER AS CALCULATING ENOUGH TO **COVER IT UP,** THEN COME BACK AND DISCOVER THE **BODY.**
PLUS, THE **LUDS** FROM THE MINISTRY OFFICE SHOW THAT SHE **DID** CALL PRESSMAN'S--
HEY--
WHAT?
WAIT... LET ME SEE...
...MOTHER-#%€*#...
PRESSMAN'S **CELL PHONE.** IT WASN'T WITH HIS EFFECTS AND IT'S NOT LISTED AT THE **CRIME SCENE,** EITHER.
SOMEONE JUST GOT **VERY** STUPID.
GET THE LUDS FOR PRESSMAN'S CELL. HE MUST'VE CALLED SOMEONE AFTER CATWOMAN LEFT.
WHERE ARE **YOU** GOING?
TO HAVE ANOTHER TALK WITH OUR **FRIEND** FROM THE *GAZETTE.*

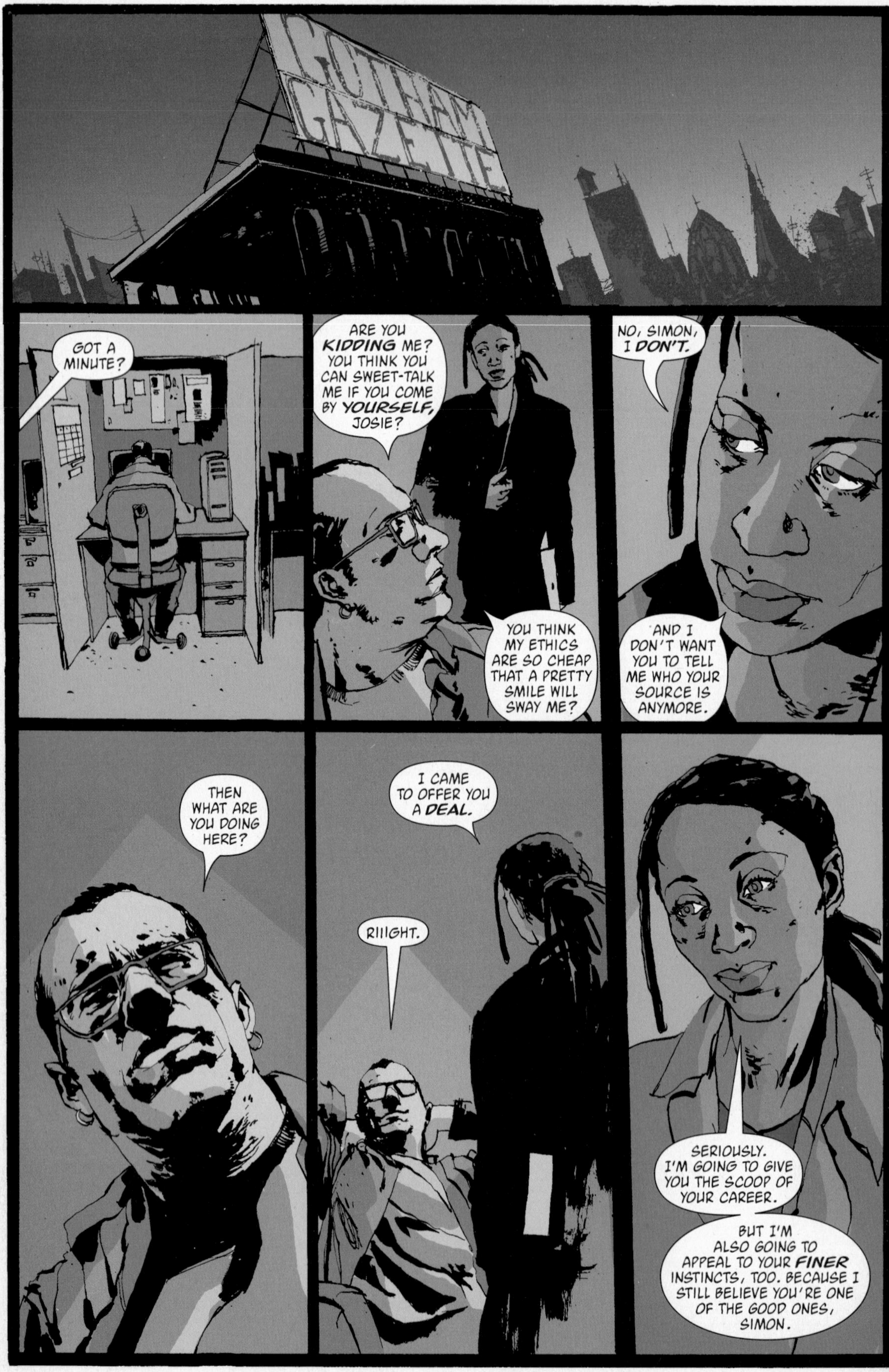
GOTHAM GAZETTE
GOT A MINUTE?
ARE YOU KIDDING ME? YOU THINK YOU CAN SWEET-TALK ME IF YOU COME BY YOURSELF, JOSIE?
YOU THINK MY ETHICS ARE SO CHEAP THAT A PRETTY SMILE WILL SWAY ME?
NO, SIMON, I DON'T.
AND I DON'T WANT YOU TO TELL ME WHO YOUR SOURCE IS ANYMORE.
THEN WHAT ARE YOU DOING HERE?
I CAME TO OFFER YOU A DEAL.
RIIIGHT.
SERIOUSLY. I'M GOING TO GIVE YOU THE SCOOP OF YOUR CAREER.
BUT I'M ALSO GOING TO APPEAL TO YOUR FINER INSTINCTS, TOO. BECAUSE I STILL BELIEVE YOU'RE ONE OF THE GOOD ONES, SIMON.

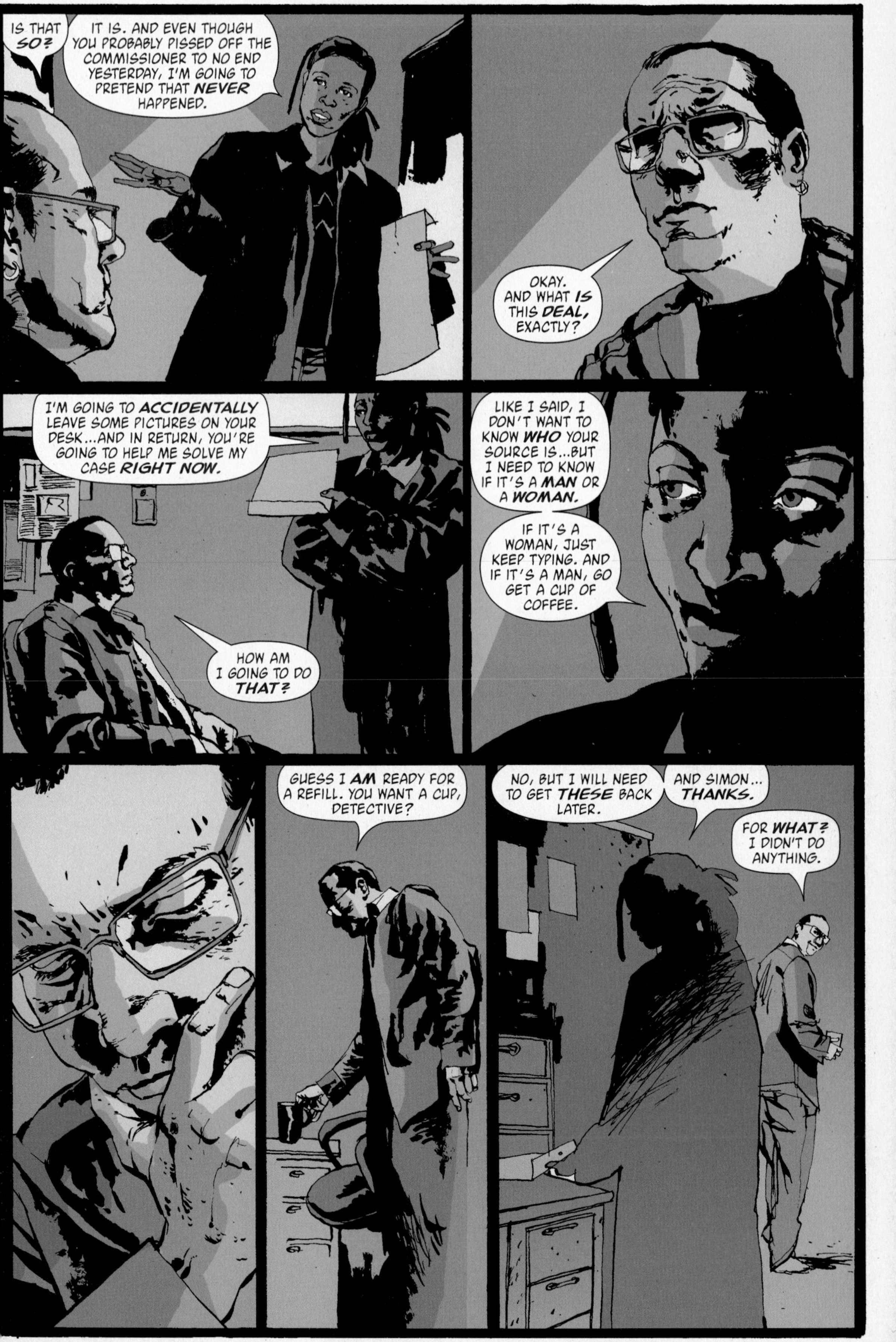
IS THAT SO?
IT IS. AND EVEN THOUGH YOU PROBABLY PISSED OFF THE COMMISSIONER TO NO END YESTERDAY, I'M GOING TO PRETEND THAT NEVER HAPPENED.
OKAY. AND WHAT IS THIS DEAL, EXACTLY?
I'M GOING TO ACCIDENTALLY LEAVE SOME PICTURES ON YOUR DESK...AND IN RETURN, YOU'RE GOING TO HELP ME SOLVE MY CASE RIGHT NOW.
HOW AM I GOING TO DO THAT?
LIKE I SAID, I DON'T WANT TO KNOW WHO YOUR SOURCE IS...BUT I NEED TO KNOW IF IT'S A MAN OR A WOMAN.
IF IT'S A WOMAN, JUST KEEP TYPING. AND IF IT'S A MAN, GO GET A CUP OF COFFEE.
GUESS I AM READY FOR A REFILL. YOU WANT A CUP, DETECTIVE?
NO, BUT I WILL NEED TO GET THESE BACK LATER.
AND SIMON... THANKS.
FOR WHAT? I DIDN'T DO ANYTHING.

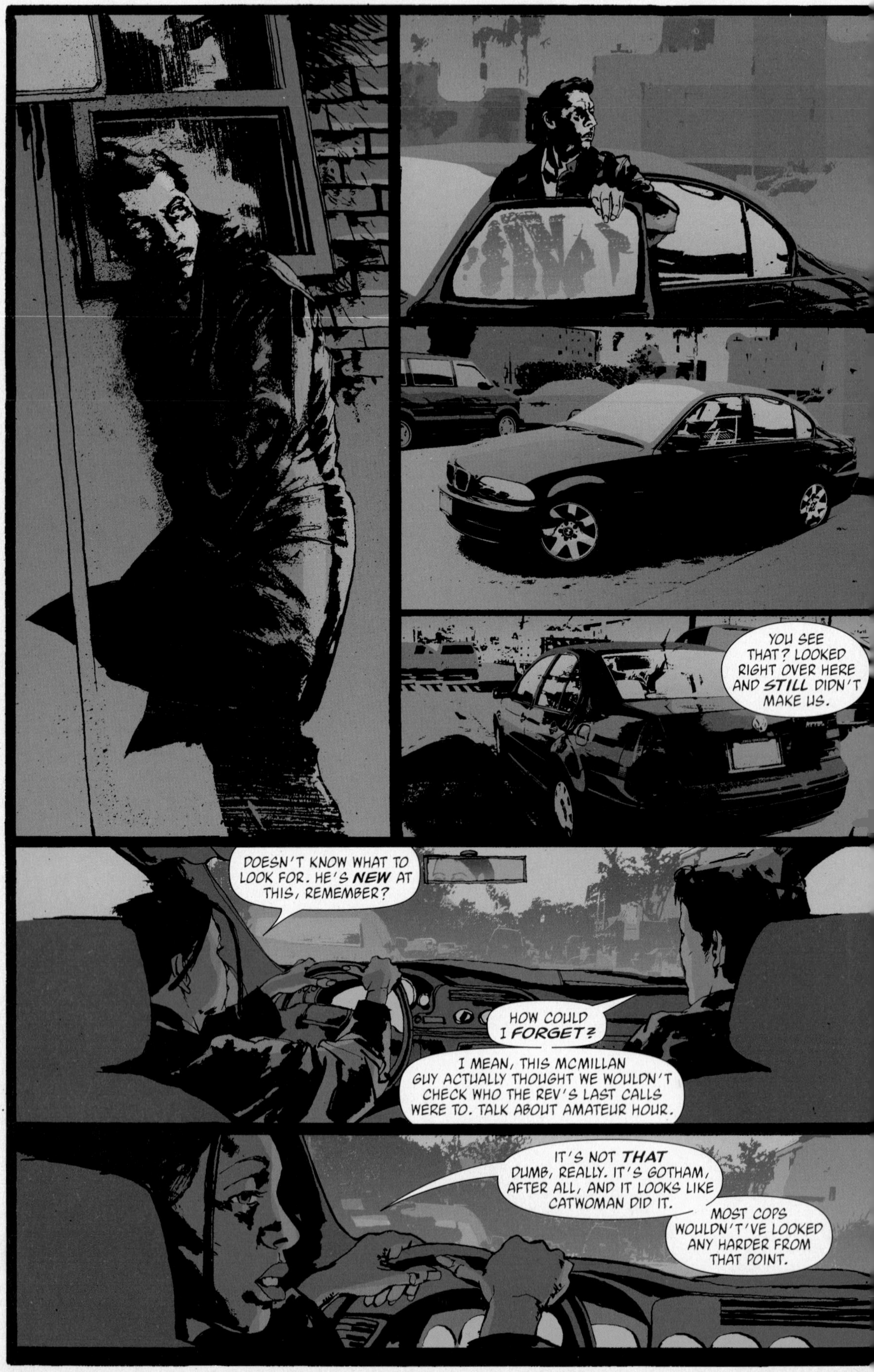
YOU SEE THAT? LOOKED RIGHT OVER HERE AND **STILL** DIDN'T MAKE US.
DOESN'T KNOW WHAT TO LOOK FOR. HE'S **NEW** AT THIS, REMEMBER?
HOW COULD I **FORGET**?
I MEAN, THIS MCMILLAN GUY ACTUALLY THOUGHT WE WOULDN'T CHECK WHO THE REV'S LAST CALLS WERE TO. TALK ABOUT AMATEUR HOUR.
IT'S NOT **THAT** DUMB, REALLY. IT'S GOTHAM, AFTER ALL, AND IT LOOKS LIKE CATWOMAN DID IT.
MOST COPS WOULDN'T'VE LOOKED ANY HARDER FROM THAT POINT.

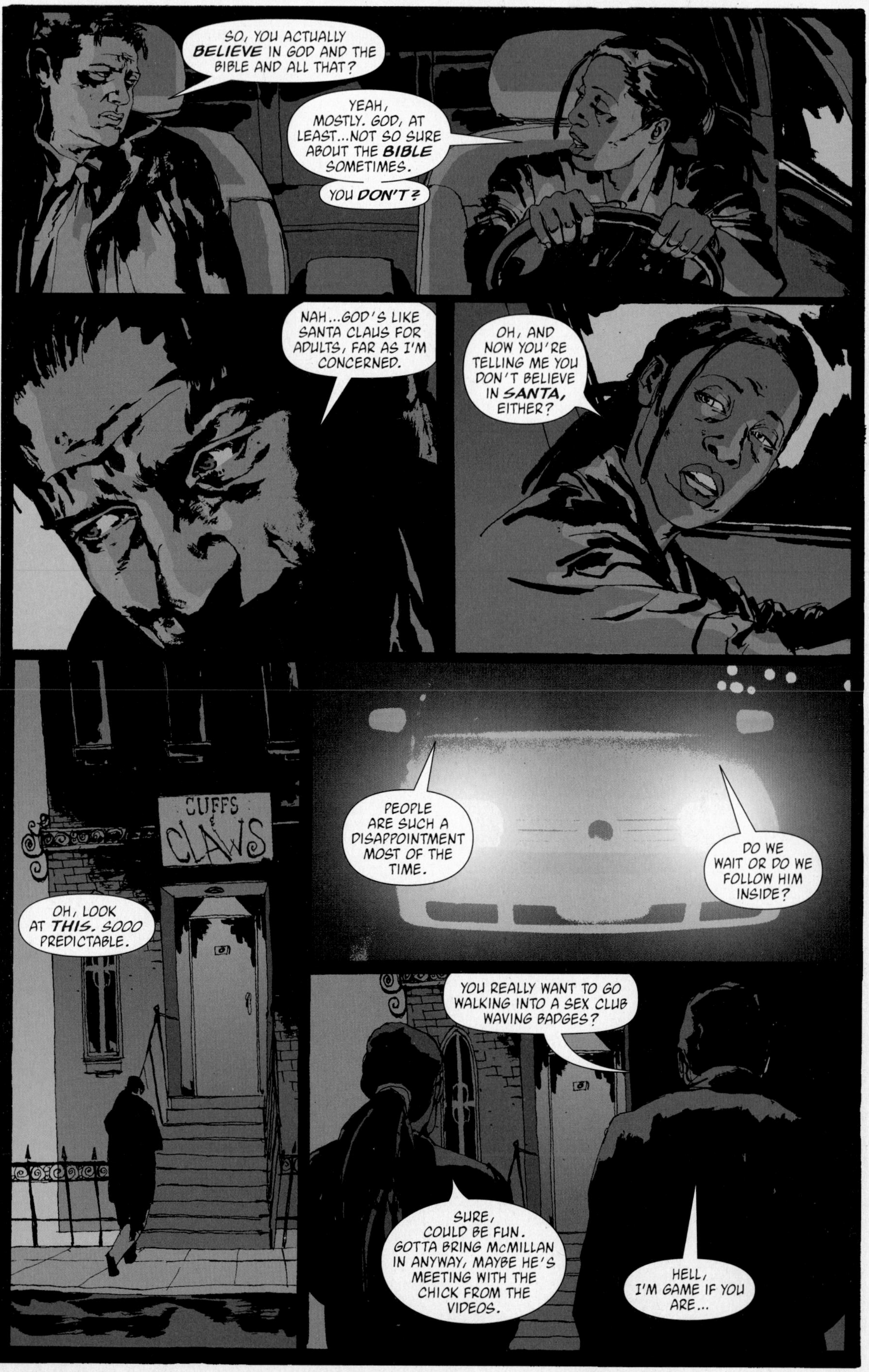
SO, YOU ACTUALLY BELIEVE IN GOD AND THE BIBLE AND ALL THAT?
YEAH, MOSTLY. GOD, AT LEAST...NOT SO SURE ABOUT THE BIBLE SOMETIMES.
YOU DON'T?
NAH...GOD'S LIKE SANTA CLAUS FOR ADULTS, FAR AS I'M CONCERNED.
OH, AND NOW YOU'RE TELLING ME YOU DON'T BELIEVE IN SANTA, EITHER?
CUFFS CLAWS
OH, LOOK AT THIS. SOOO PREDICTABLE.
PEOPLE ARE SUCH A DISAPPOINTMENT MOST OF THE TIME.
DO WE WAIT OR DO WE FOLLOW HIM INSIDE?
YOU REALLY WANT TO GO WALKING INTO A SEX CLUB WAVING BADGES?
SURE, COULD BE FUN. GOTTA BRING McMILLAN IN ANYWAY, MAYBE HE'S MEETING WITH THE CHICK FROM THE VIDEOS.
HELL, I'M GAME IF YOU ARE...

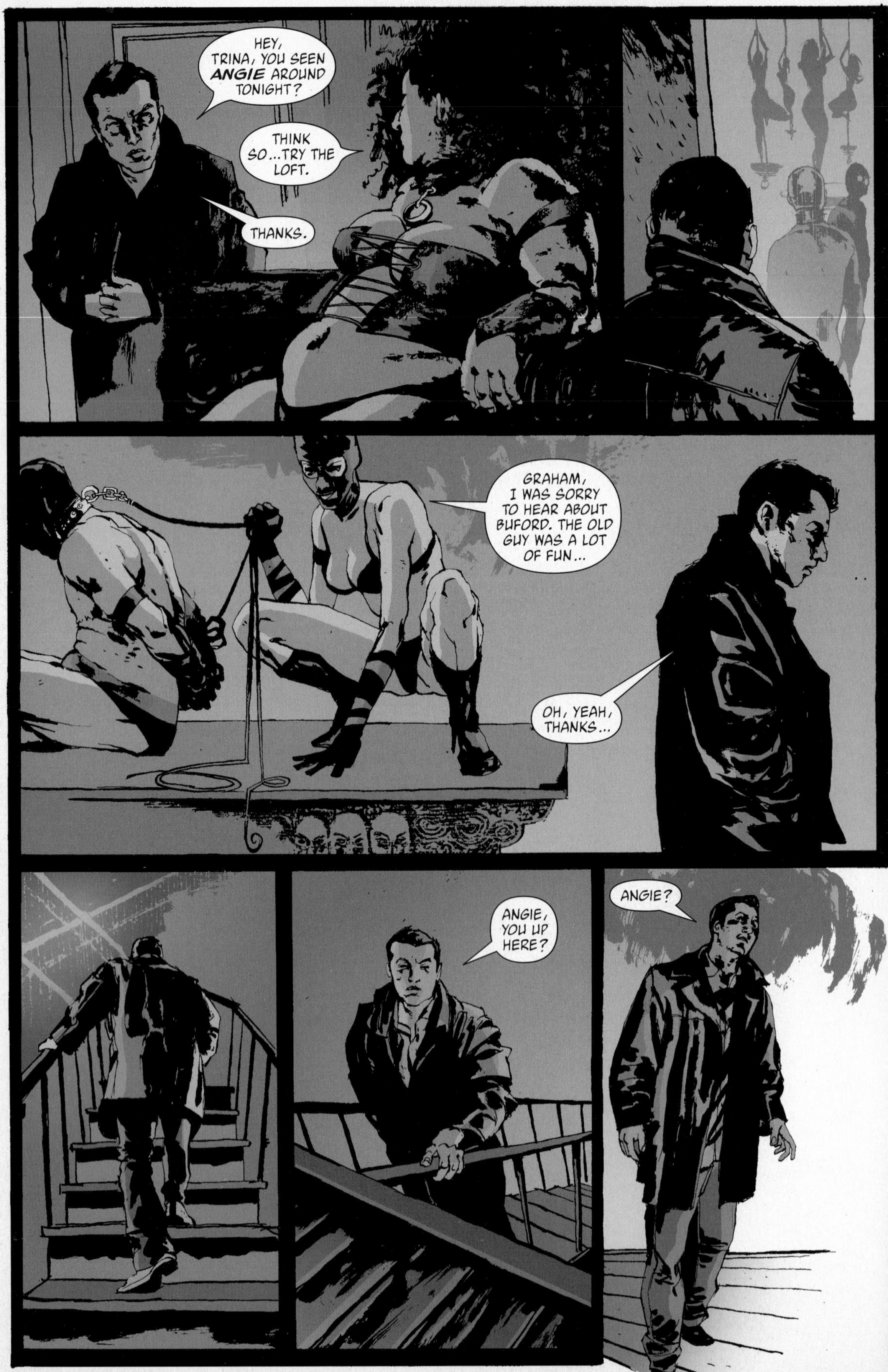
HEY, TRINA, YOU SEEN ANGIE AROUND TONIGHT?
THINK SO...TRY THE LOFT.
THANKS.
GRAHAM, I WAS SORRY TO HEAR ABOUT BUFORD. THE OLD GUY WAS A LOT OF FUN...
OH, YEAH, THANKS...
ANGIE, YOU UP HERE?
ANGIE?

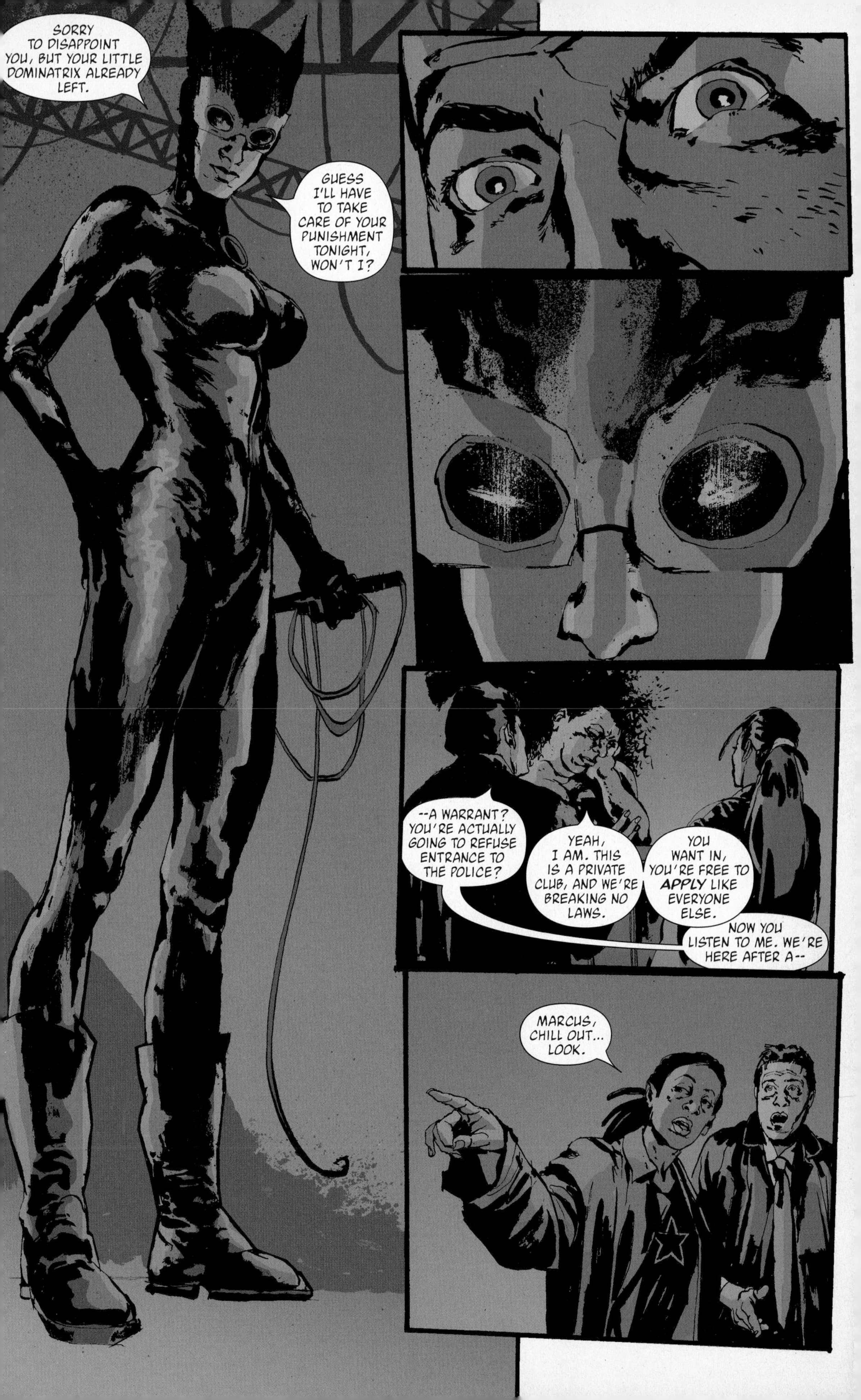
SORRY TO DISAPPOINT YOU, BUT YOUR LITTLE DOMINATRIX ALREADY LEFT.
GUESS I'LL HAVE TO TAKE CARE OF YOUR PUNISHMENT TONIGHT, WON'T I?
--A WARRANT? YOU'RE ACTUALLY GOING TO REFUSE ENTRANCE TO THE POLICE?
YEAH, I AM. THIS IS A PRIVATE CLUB, AND WE'RE BREAKING NO LAWS.
YOU WANT IN, YOU'RE FREE TO APPLY LIKE EVERYONE ELSE.
NOW YOU LISTEN TO ME. WE'RE HERE AFTER A--
MARCUS, CHILL OUT... LOOK.

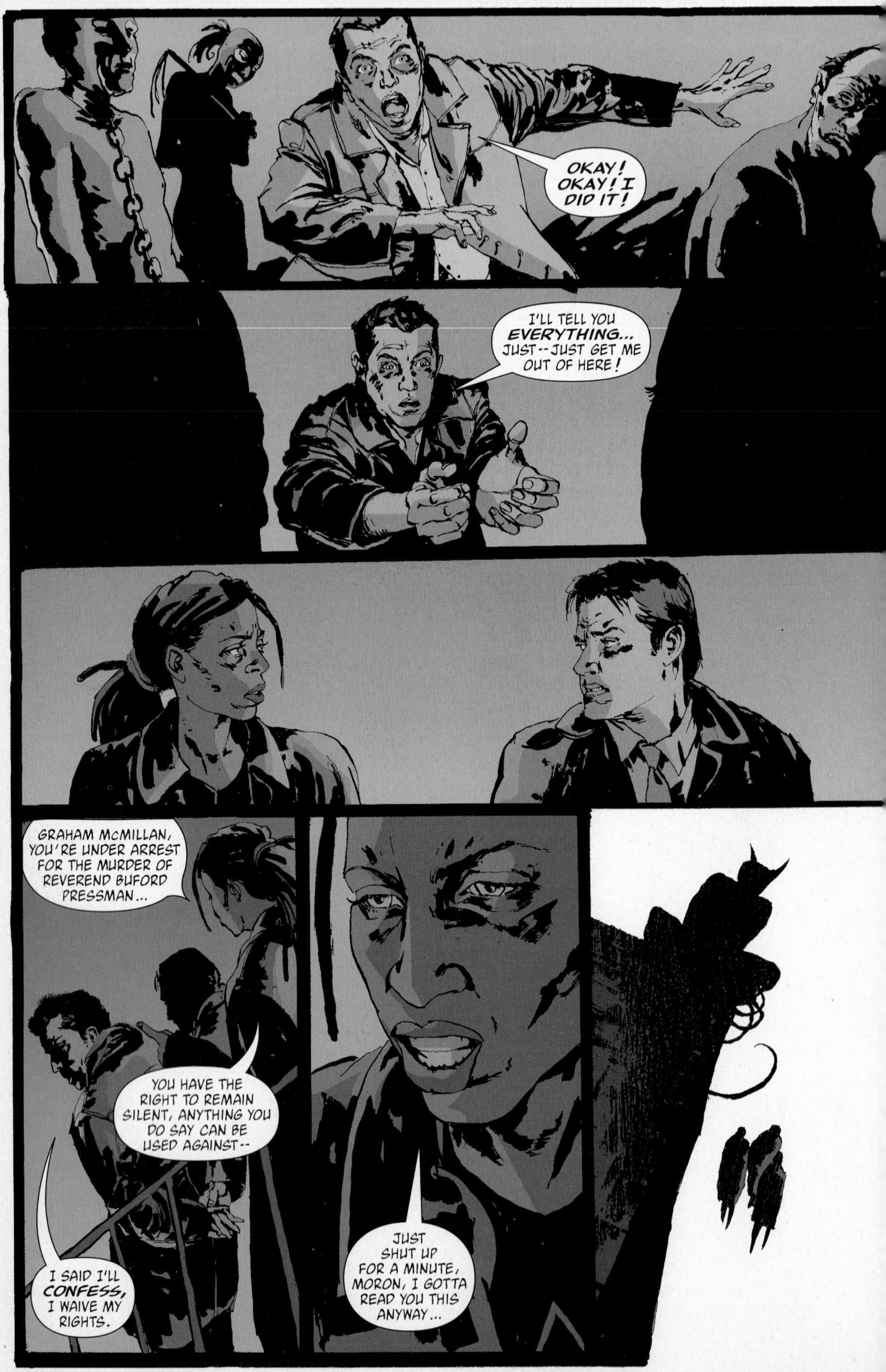
OKAY! OKAY! I DID IT!
I'LL TELL YOU EVERYTHING... JUST-- JUST GET ME OUT OF HERE!
GRAHAM McMILLAN, YOU'RE UNDER ARREST FOR THE MURDER OF REVEREND BUFORD PRESSMAN...
YOU HAVE THE RIGHT TO REMAIN SILENT, ANYTHING YOU DO SAY CAN BE USED AGAINST--
I SAID I'LL CONFESS, I WAIVE MY RIGHTS.
JUST SHUT UP FOR A MINUTE, MORON, I GOTTA READ YOU THIS ANYWAY...

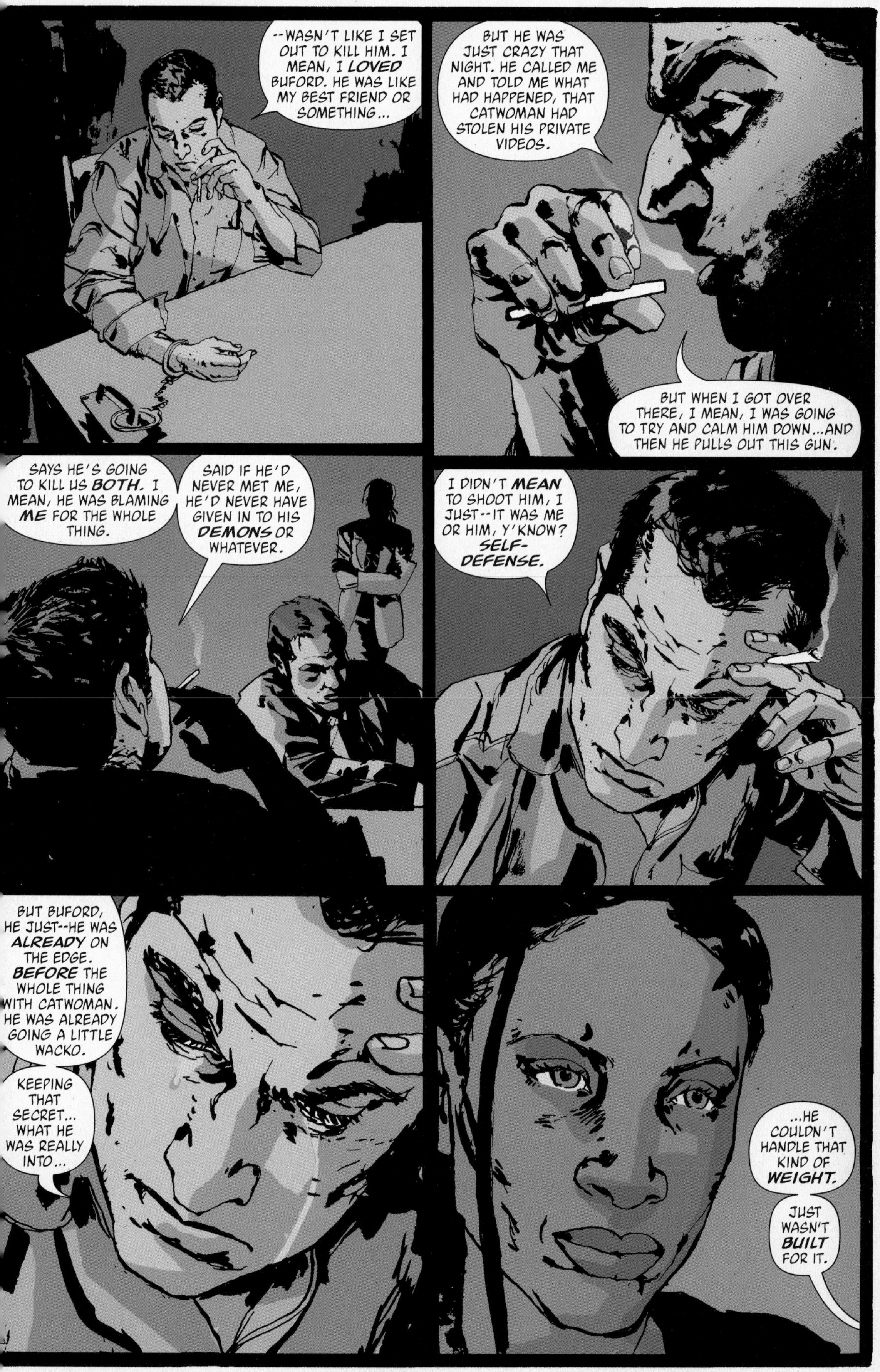
--WASN'T LIKE I SET OUT TO KILL HIM. I MEAN, I LOVED BUFORD. HE WAS LIKE MY BEST FRIEND OR SOMETHING...
BUT HE WAS JUST CRAZY THAT NIGHT. HE CALLED ME AND TOLD ME WHAT HAD HAPPENED, THAT CATWOMAN HAD STOLEN HIS PRIVATE VIDEOS.
BUT WHEN I GOT OVER THERE, I MEAN, I WAS GOING TO TRY AND CALM HIM DOWN...AND THEN HE PULLS OUT THIS GUN.
SAYS HE'S GOING TO KILL US BOTH. I MEAN, HE WAS BLAMING ME FOR THE WHOLE THING.
SAID IF HE'D NEVER MET ME, HE'D NEVER HAVE GIVEN IN TO HIS DEMONS OR WHATEVER.
I DIDN'T MEAN TO SHOOT HIM, I JUST--IT WAS ME OR HIM, Y'KNOW? SELF-DEFENSE.
BUT BUFORD, HE JUST--HE WAS ALREADY ON THE EDGE. BEFORE THE WHOLE THING WITH CATWOMAN. HE WAS ALREADY GOING A LITTLE WACKO.
KEEPING THAT SECRET... WHAT HE WAS REALLY INTO...
...HE COULDN'T HANDLE THAT KIND OF WEIGHT.
JUST WASN'T BUILT FOR IT.

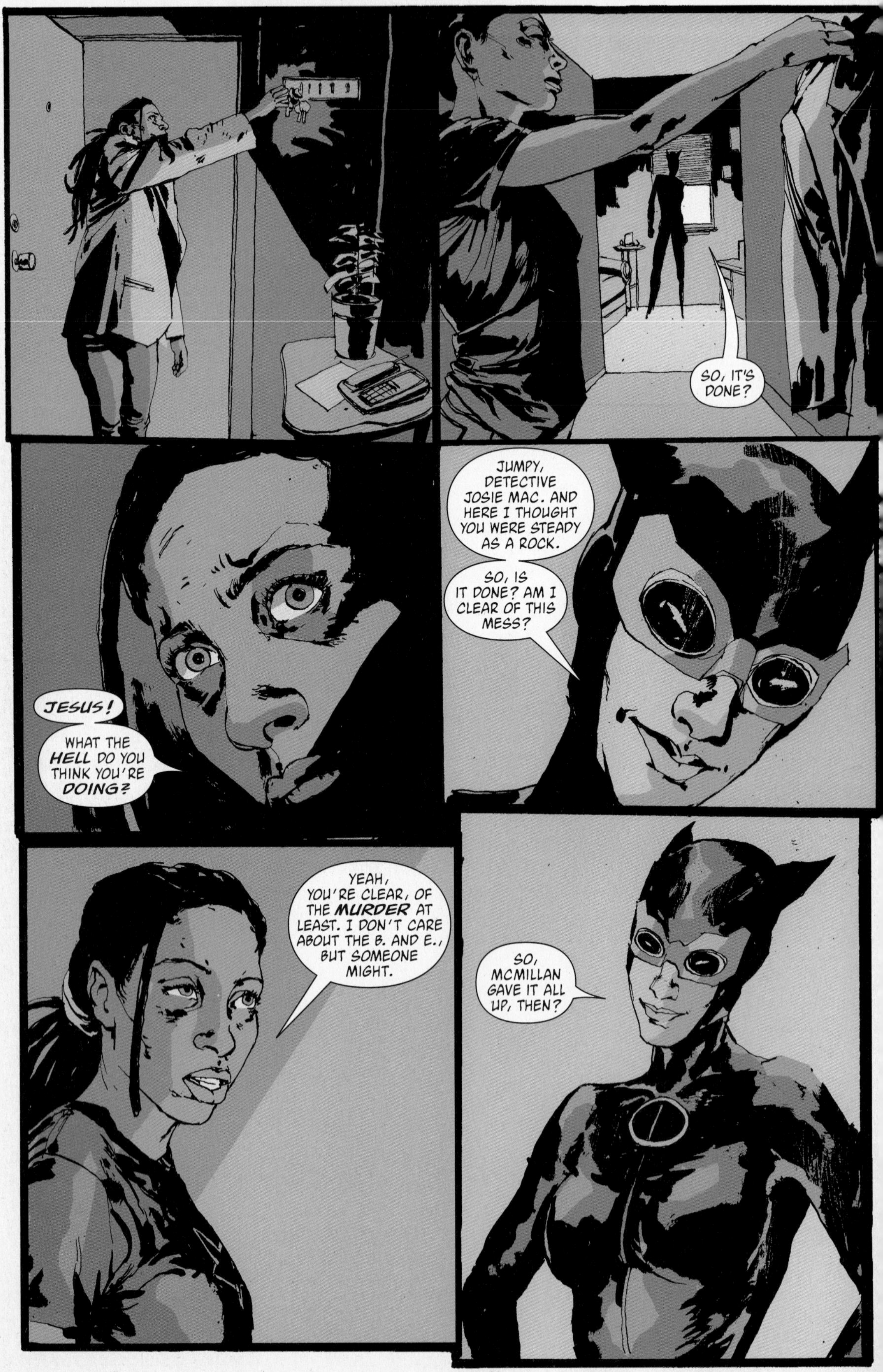
SO, IT'S DONE?
JESUS!
WHAT THE HELL DO YOU THINK YOU'RE DOING?
JUMPY, DETECTIVE JOSIE MAC. AND HERE I THOUGHT YOU WERE STEADY AS A ROCK.
SO, IS IT DONE? AM I CLEAR OF THIS MESS?
YEAH, YOU'RE CLEAR, OF THE MURDER AT LEAST. I DON'T CARE ABOUT THE B. AND E., BUT SOMEONE MIGHT.
SO, MCMILLAN GAVE IT ALL UP, THEN?

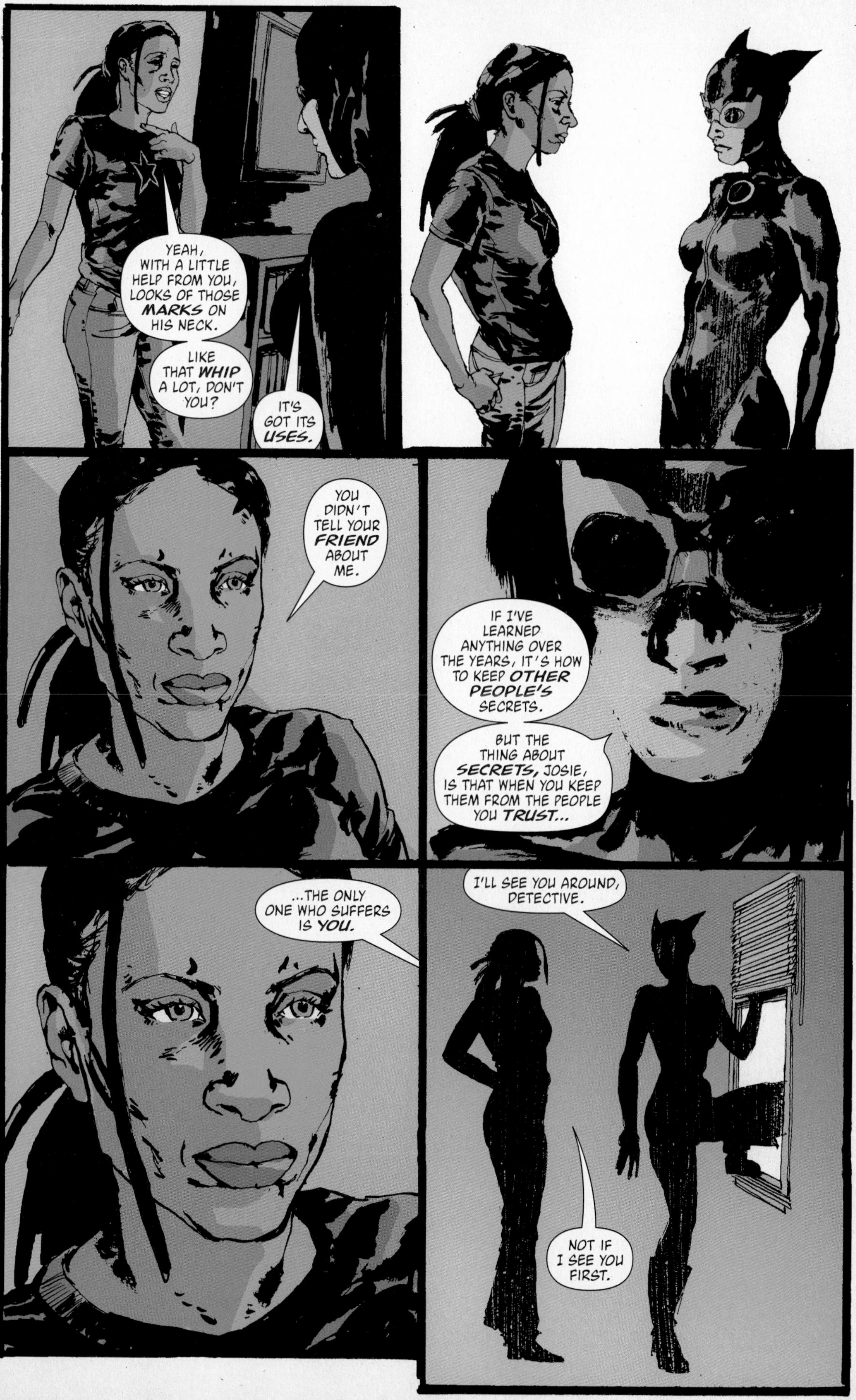
YEAH, WITH A LITTLE HELP FROM YOU, LOOKS OF THOSE MARKS ON HIS NECK.
LIKE THAT WHIP A LOT, DON'T YOU?
IT'S GOT ITS USES.
YOU DIDN'T TELL YOUR FRIEND ABOUT ME.
IF I'VE LEARNED ANYTHING OVER THE YEARS, IT'S HOW TO KEEP OTHER PEOPLE'S SECRETS.
BUT THE THING ABOUT SECRETS, JOSIE, IS THAT WHEN YOU KEEP THEM FROM THE PEOPLE YOU TRUST...
...THE ONLY ONE WHO SUFFERS IS YOU.
I'LL SEE YOU AROUND, DETECTIVE.
NOT IF I SEE YOU FIRST.

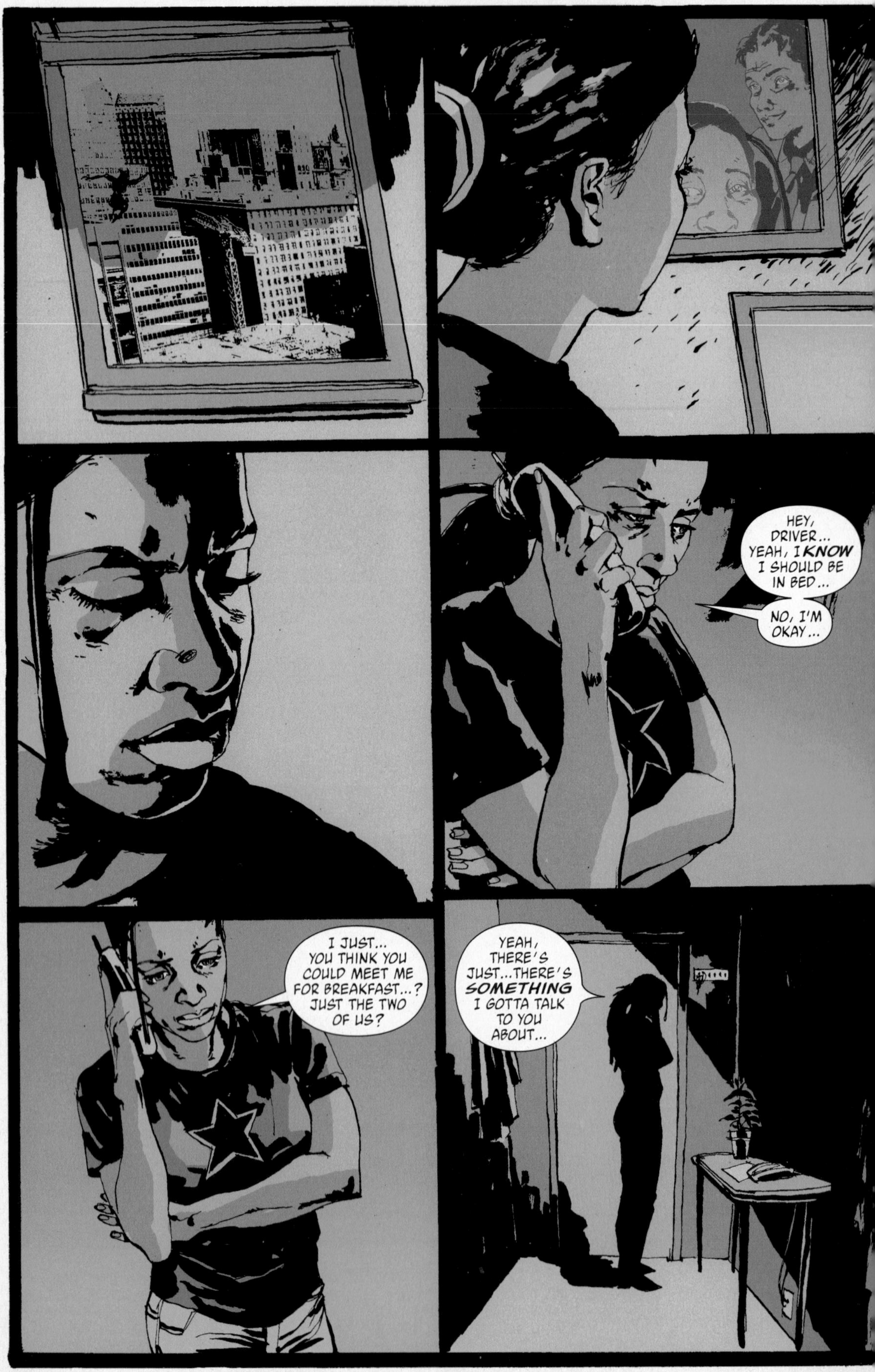
HEY, DRIVER... YEAH, I KNOW I SHOULD BE IN BED...
NO, I'M OKAY...
I JUST... YOU THINK YOU COULD MEET ME FOR BREAKFAST...? JUST THE TWO OF US?
YEAH, THERE'S JUST...THERE'S SOMETHING I GOTTA TALK TO YOU ABOUT...

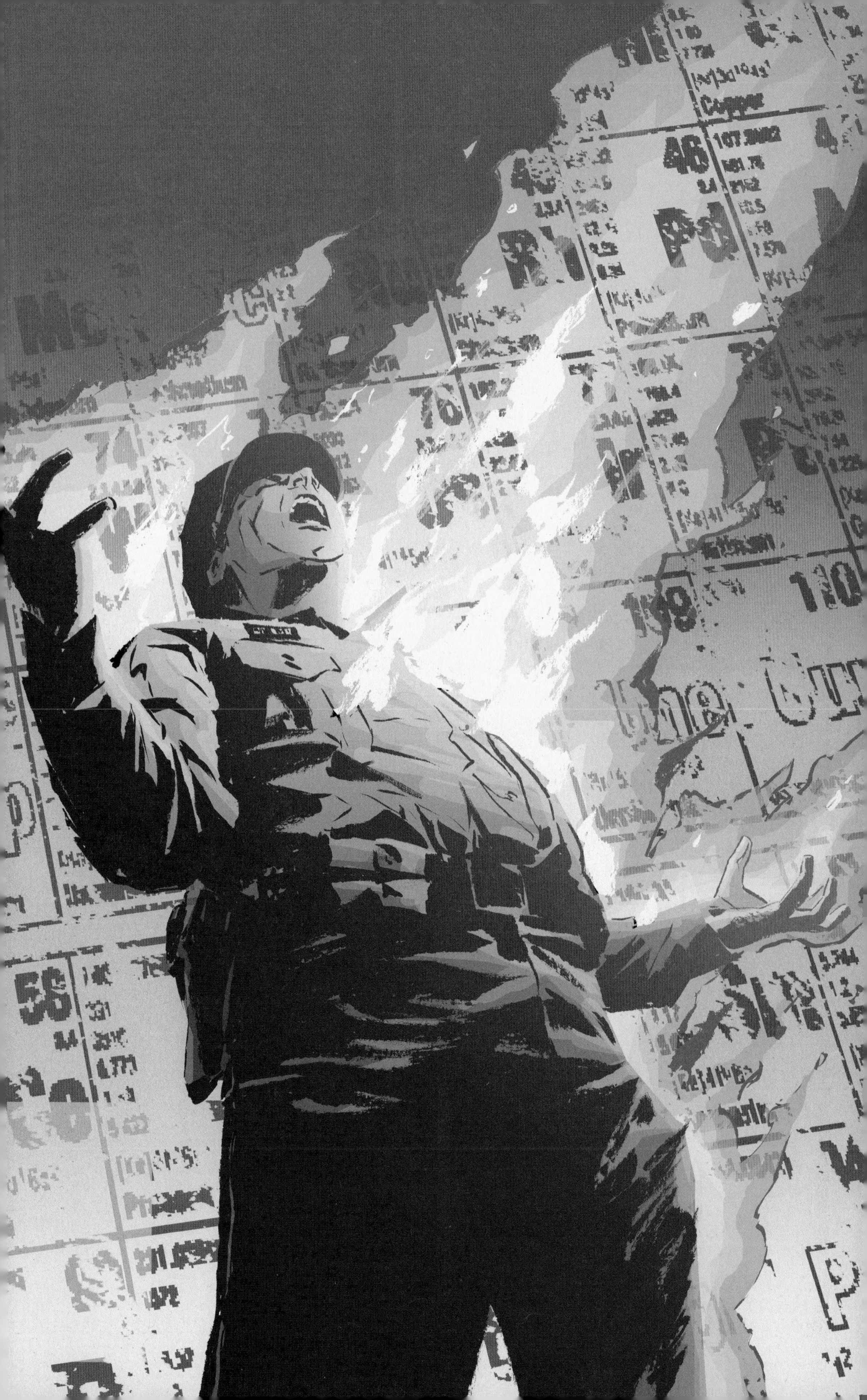

Copper
46
Pd
76
74
110
56

KEYSTONE KOPS

Written by
GREG RUCKA

Pencils by
STEFANO GAUDIANO

Inks by
GAUDIANO *(Part One & Two)*, **KANO** *(Part Three)*, **AND GARY AMARO** *(Part Four)*

Colors by
LEE LOUGHRIDGE

Letters by
CLEM ROBINS

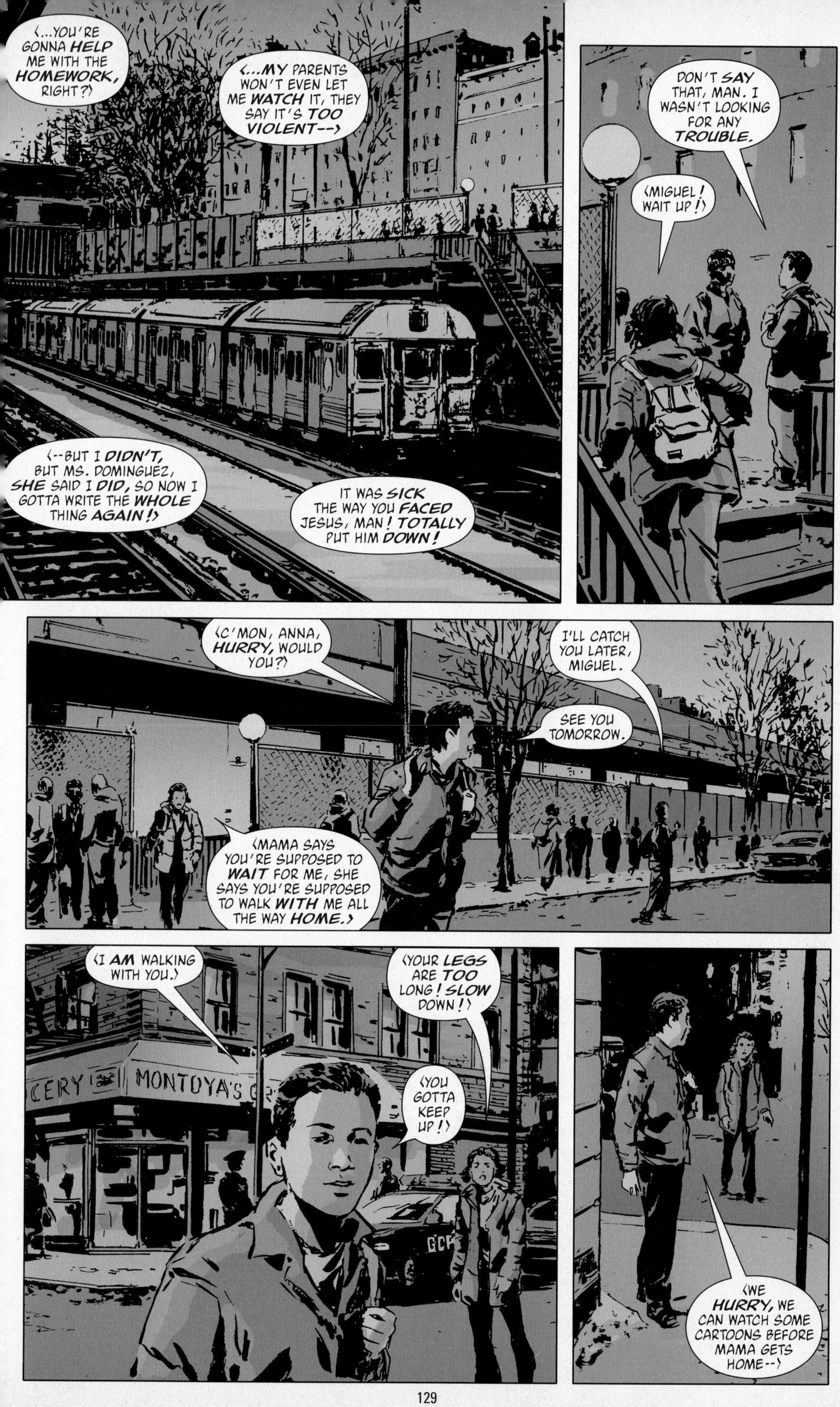
‹...YOU'RE GONNA HELP ME WITH THE HOMEWORK, RIGHT?›
‹...MY PARENTS WON'T EVEN LET ME WATCH IT, THEY SAY IT'S TOO VIOLENT--›
‹--BUT I DIDN'T, BUT MS. DOMINGUEZ, SHE SAID I DID, SO NOW I GOTTA WRITE THE WHOLE THING AGAIN!›
IT WAS SICK THE WAY YOU FACED JESUS, MAN! TOTALLY PUT HIM DOWN!
DON'T SAY THAT, MAN. I WASN'T LOOKING FOR ANY TROUBLE.
‹MIGUEL! WAIT UP!›
‹C'MON, ANNA, HURRY, WOULD YOU?›
I'LL CATCH YOU LATER, MIGUEL.
SEE YOU TOMORROW.
‹MAMA SAYS YOU'RE SUPPOSED TO WAIT FOR ME, SHE SAYS YOU'RE SUPPOSED TO WALK WITH ME ALL THE WAY HOME.›
‹I AM WALKING WITH YOU.›
‹YOUR LEGS ARE TOO LONG! SLOW DOWN!›
‹YOU GOTTA KEEP UP!›
CERY
MONTOYA'S G
GCP
‹WE HURRY, WE CAN WATCH SOME CARTOONS BEFORE MAMA GETS HOME--›

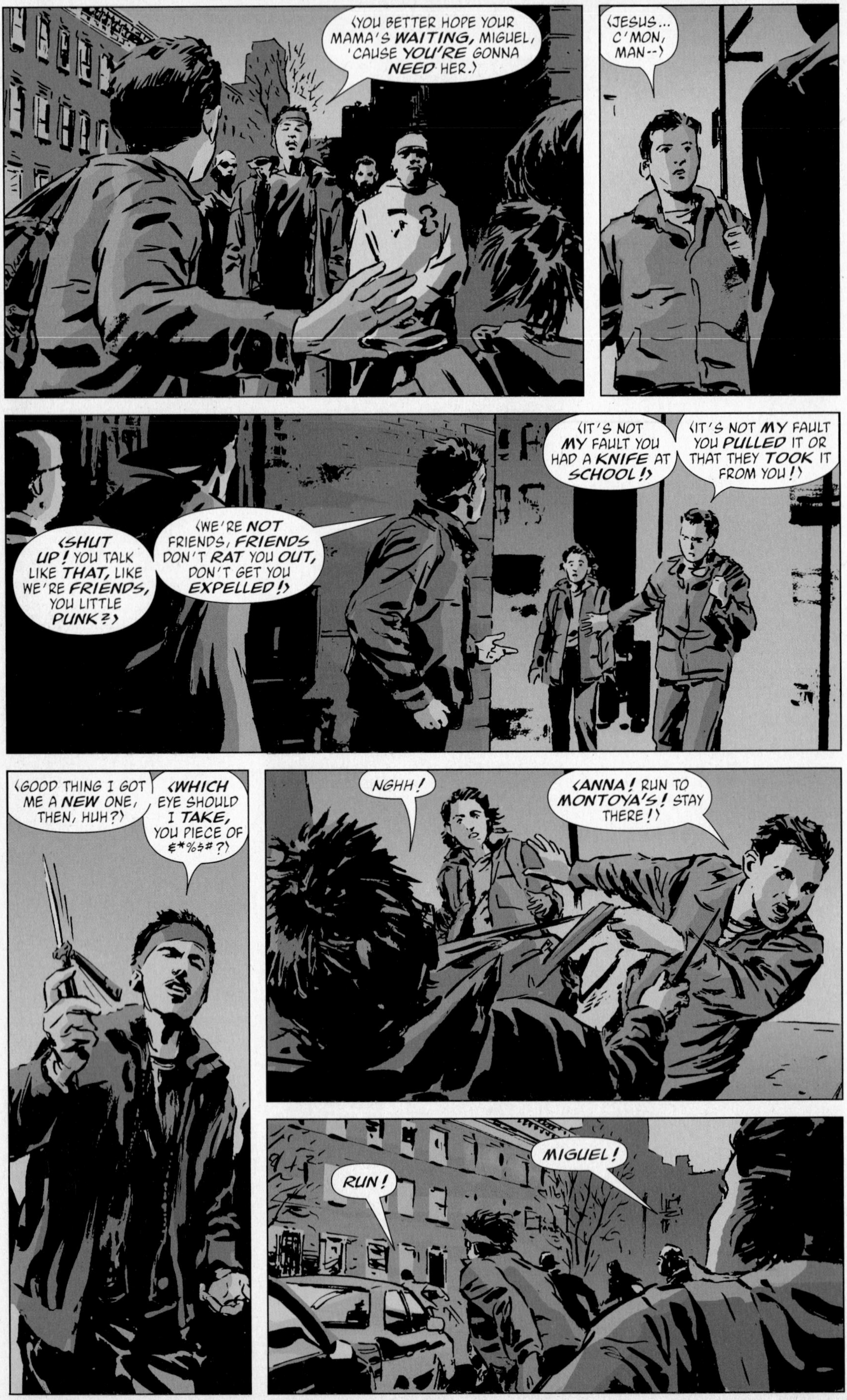

<YOU BETTER HOPE YOUR MAMA'S WAITING, MIGUEL, 'CAUSE YOU'RE GONNA NEED HER.>
<JESUS... C'MON, MAN-->
<SHUT UP! YOU TALK LIKE THAT, LIKE WE'RE FRIENDS, YOU LITTLE PUNK?>
<WE'RE NOT FRIENDS, FRIENDS DON'T RAT YOU OUT, DON'T GET YOU EXPELLED!>
<IT'S NOT MY FAULT YOU HAD A KNIFE AT SCHOOL!>
<IT'S NOT MY FAULT YOU PULLED IT OR THAT THEY TOOK IT FROM YOU!>
<GOOD THING I GOT ME A NEW ONE, THEN, HUH?>
<WHICH EYE SHOULD I TAKE, YOU PIECE OF &*%$#?>
NGHH!
<ANNA! RUN TO MONTOYA'S! STAY THERE!>
MIGUEL!
RUN!

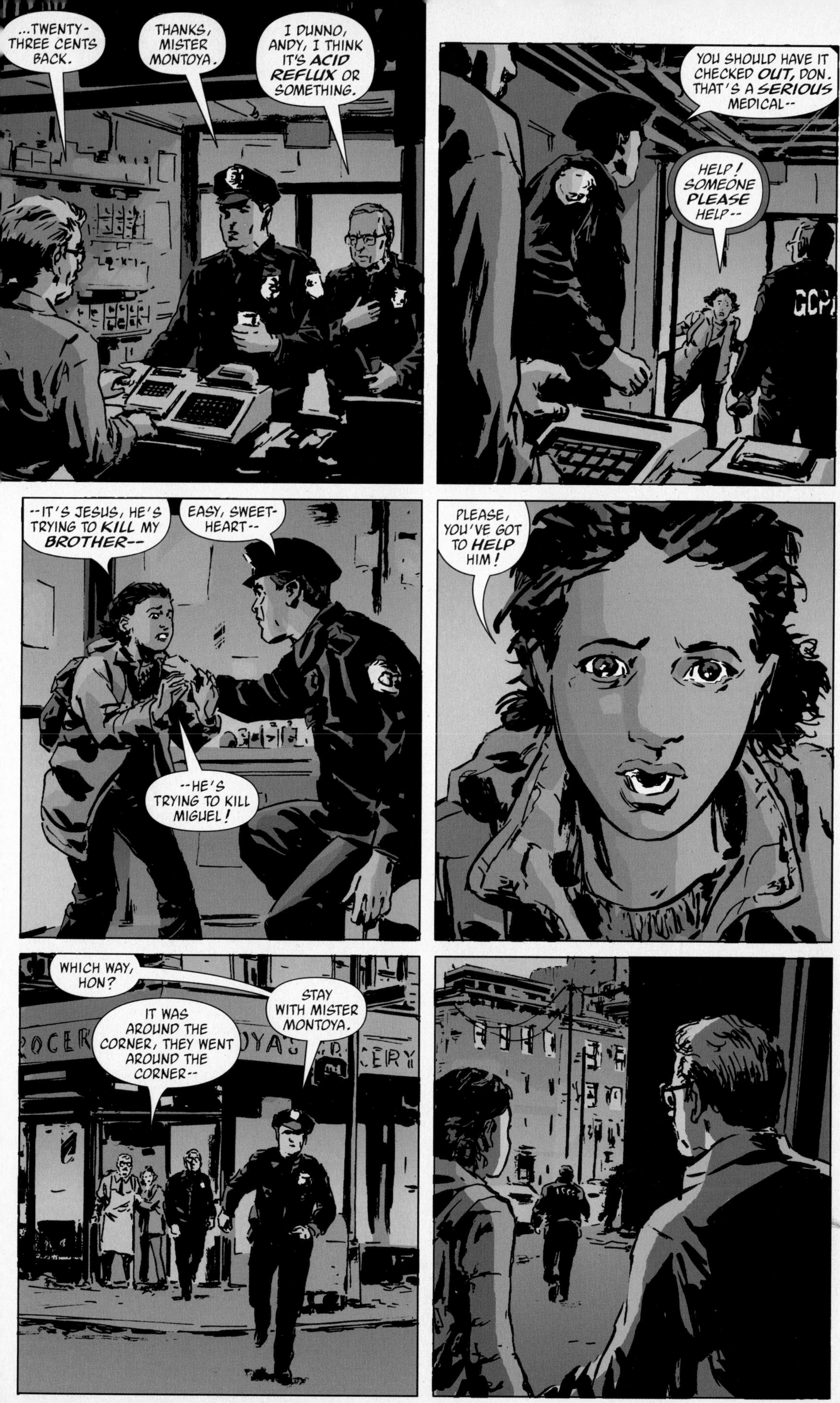

...TWENTY-THREE CENTS BACK.
THANKS, MISTER MONTOYA.
I DUNNO, ANDY, I THINK IT'S ACID REFLUX OR SOMETHING.
YOU SHOULD HAVE IT CHECKED OUT, DON. THAT'S A SERIOUS MEDICAL--
HELP! SOMEONE PLEASE HELP--
--IT'S JESUS, HE'S TRYING TO KILL MY BROTHER--
EASY, SWEET-HEART--
--HE'S TRYING TO KILL MIGUEL!
PLEASE, YOU'VE GOT TO HELP HIM!
WHICH WAY, HON?
IT WAS AROUND THE CORNER, THEY WENT AROUND THE CORNER--
STAY WITH MISTER MONTOYA.

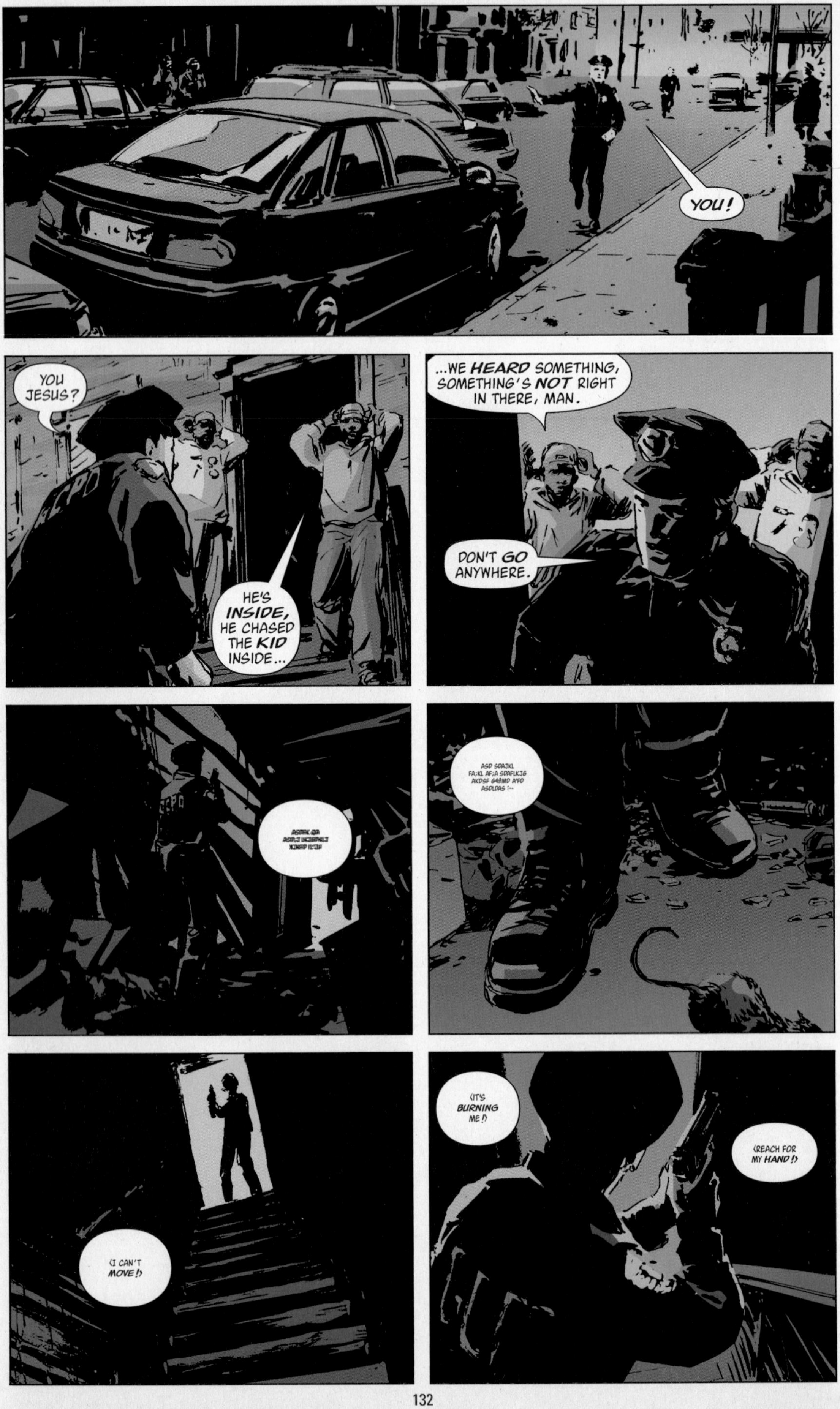
YOU!
YOU JESUS?
HE'S INSIDE, HE CHASED THE KID INSIDE...
...WE HEARD SOMETHING, SOMETHING'S NOT RIGHT IN THERE, MAN.
DON'T GO ANYWHERE.
<I CAN'T MOVE!>
<IT'S BURNING ME!>
<REACH FOR MY HAND!>

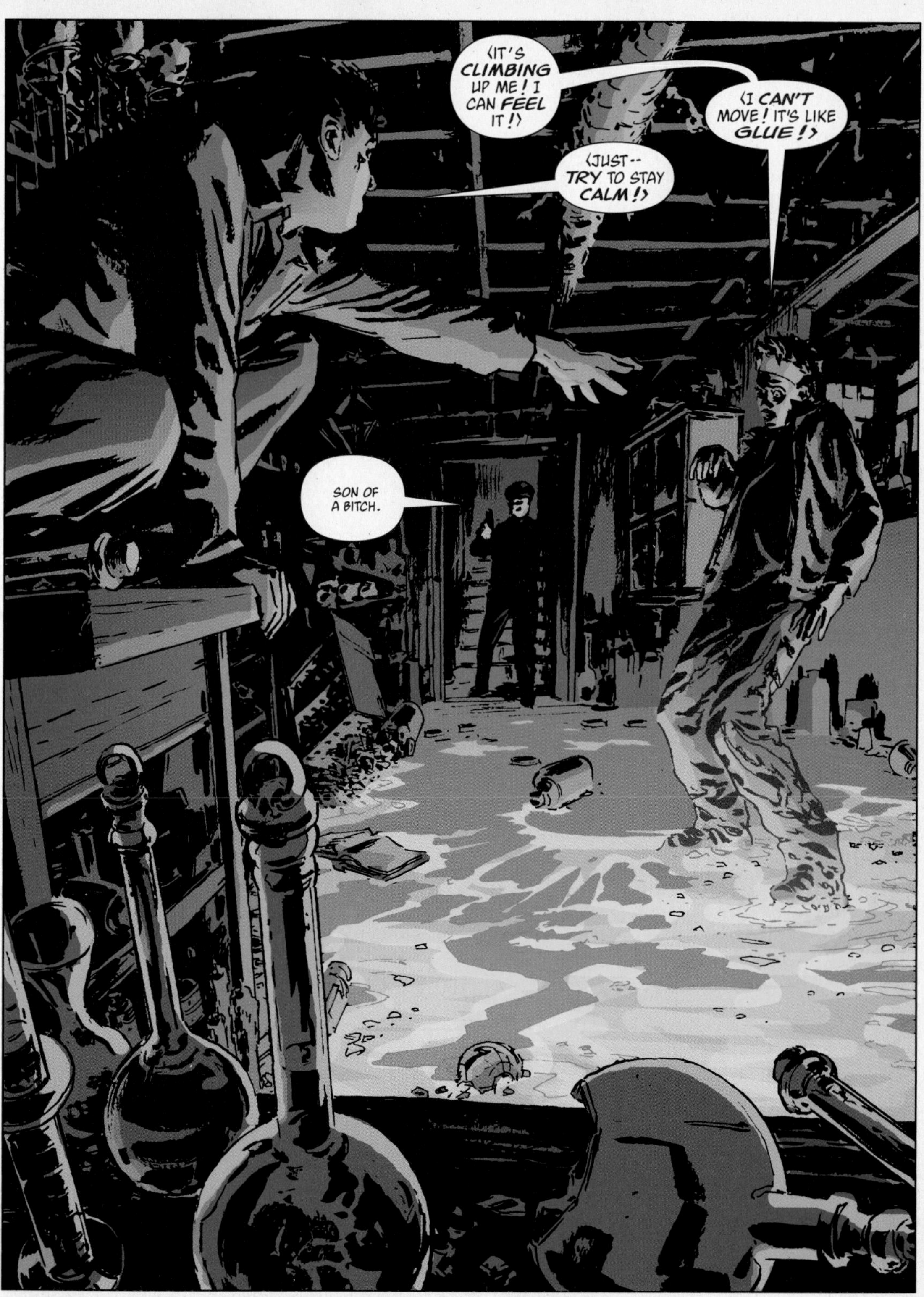
⟨IT'S CLIMBING UP ME! I CAN FEEL IT!⟩
⟨I CAN'T MOVE! IT'S LIKE GLUE!⟩
⟨JUST-- TRY TO STAY CALM!⟩
SON OF A BITCH.

Keystone Kops Part One

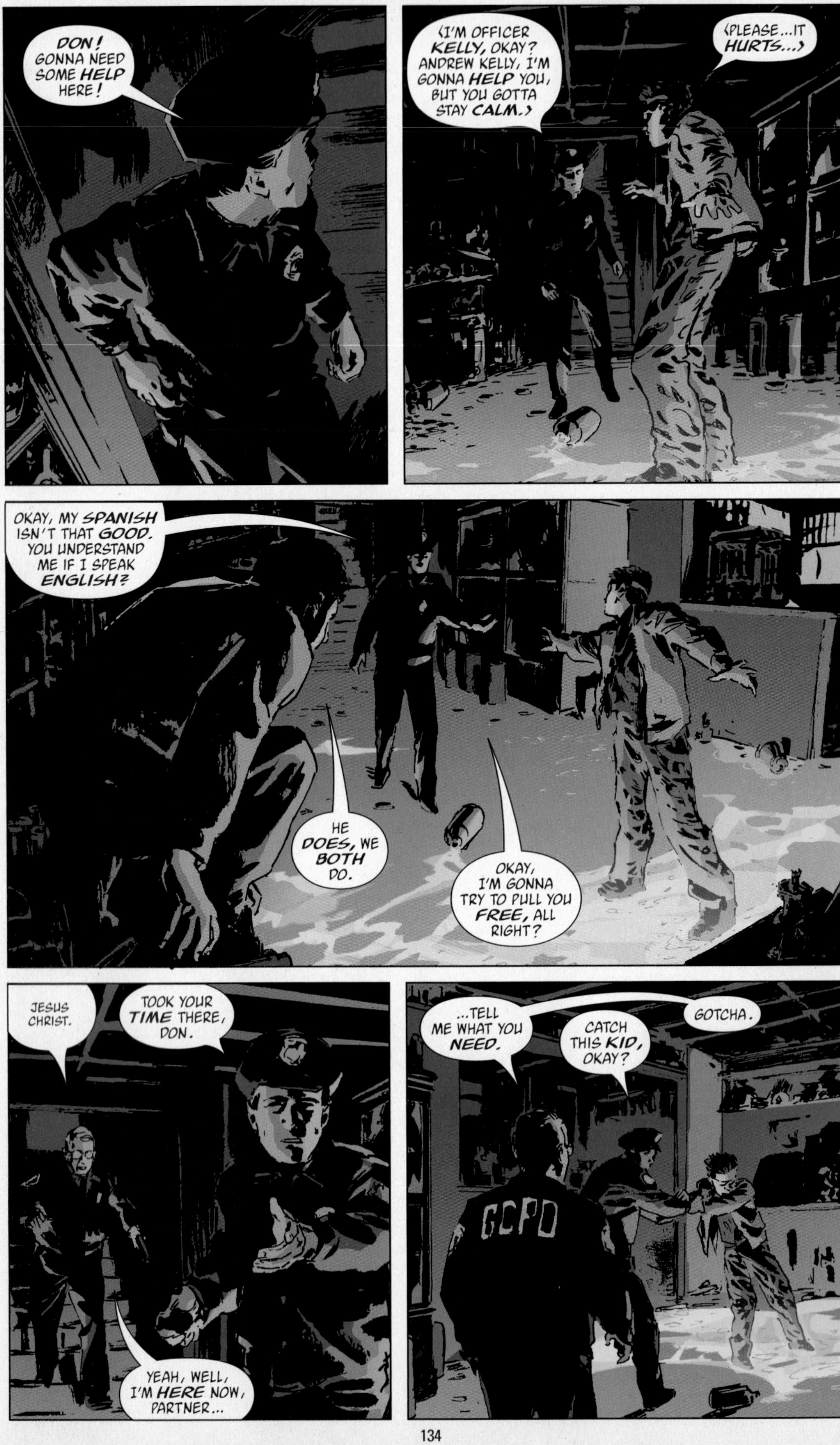
DON! GONNA NEED SOME HELP HERE!
‹I'M OFFICER KELLY, OKAY? ANDREW KELLY, I'M GONNA HELP YOU, BUT YOU GOTTA STAY CALM.›
‹PLEASE...IT HURTS...›
OKAY, MY SPANISH ISN'T THAT GOOD. YOU UNDERSTAND ME IF I SPEAK ENGLISH?
HE DOES, WE BOTH DO.
OKAY, I'M GONNA TRY TO PULL YOU FREE, ALL RIGHT?
JESUS CHRIST.
TOOK YOUR TIME THERE, DON.
YEAH, WELL, I'M HERE NOW, PARTNER...
...TELL ME WHAT YOU NEED.
CATCH THIS KID, OKAY?
GOTCHA.
GCPD

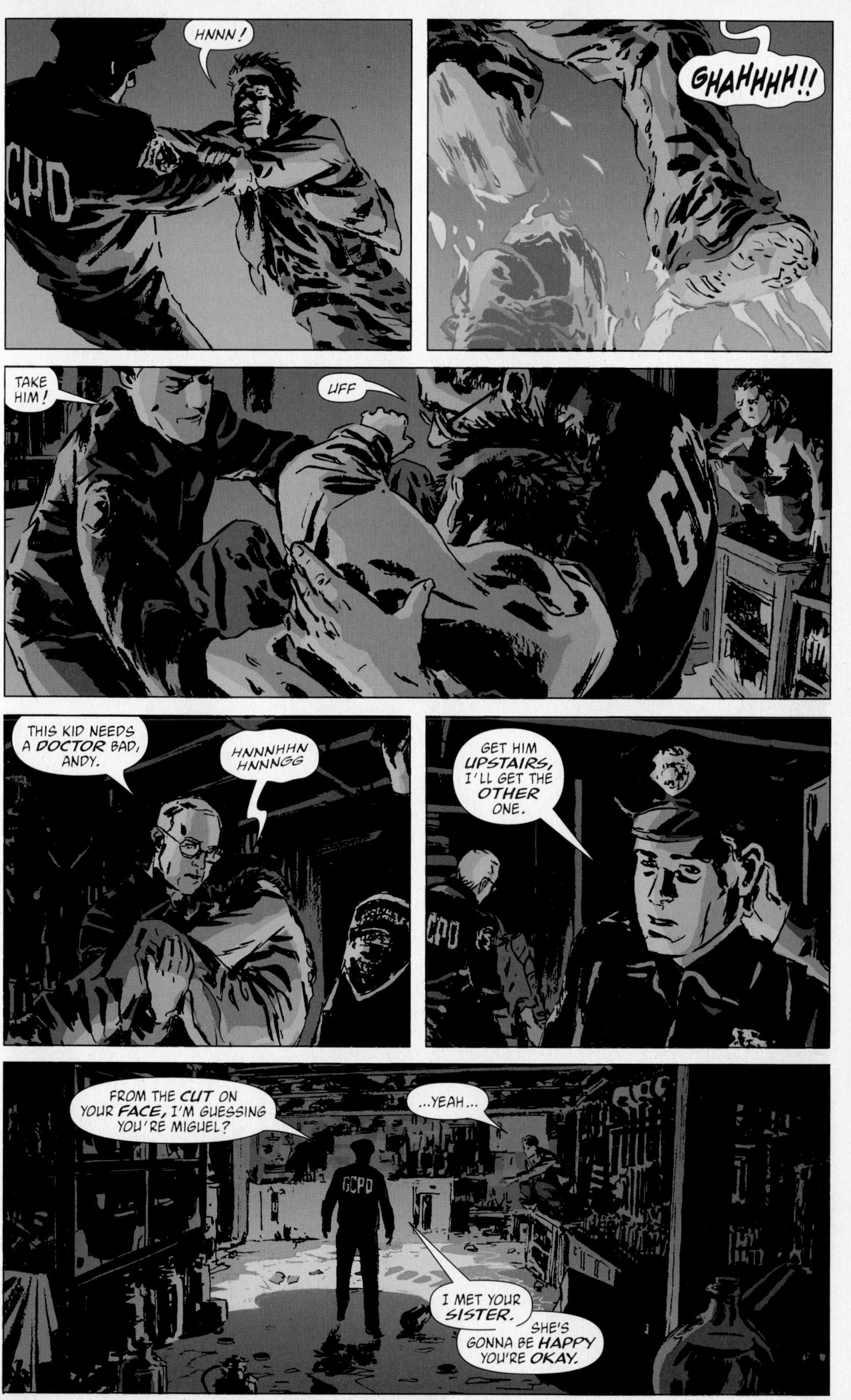

HNNN!
GHAHHHH!!
TAKE HIM!
UFF
THIS KID NEEDS A DOCTOR BAD, ANDY.
HNNNHHN HNNNGG
GET HIM UPSTAIRS, I'LL GET THE OTHER ONE.
FROM THE CUT ON YOUR FACE, I'M GUESSING YOU'RE MIGUEL?
...YEAH...
I MET YOUR SISTER.
SHE'S GONNA BE HAPPY YOU'RE OKAY.

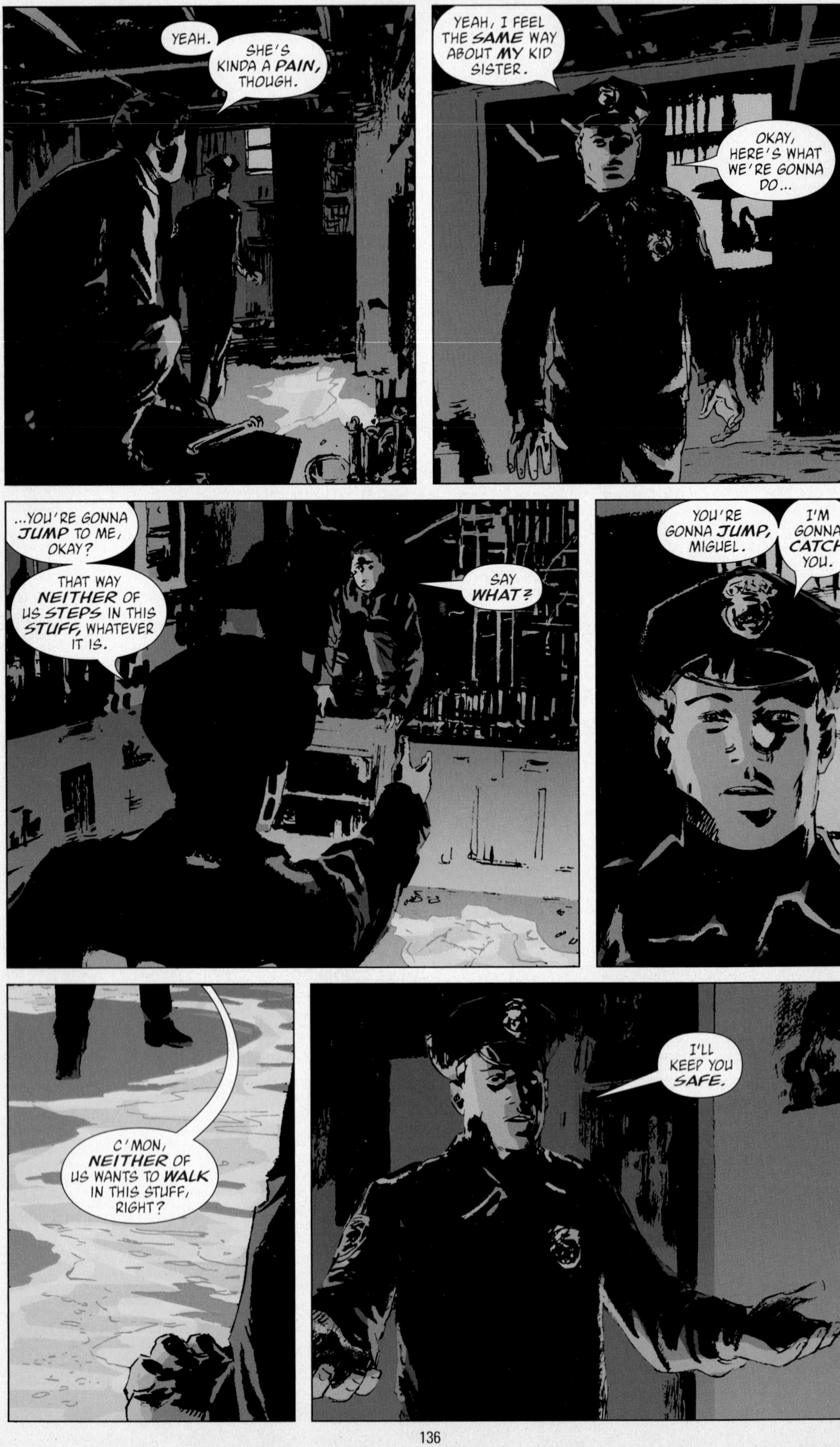
YEAH.
SHE'S KINDA A PAIN, THOUGH.
YEAH, I FEEL THE SAME WAY ABOUT MY KID SISTER.
OKAY, HERE'S WHAT WE'RE GONNA DO...
...YOU'RE GONNA JUMP TO ME, OKAY?
THAT WAY NEITHER OF US STEPS IN THIS STUFF, WHATEVER IT IS.
SAY WHAT?
YOU'RE GONNA JUMP, MIGUEL.
I'M GONNA CATCH YOU.
C'MON, NEITHER OF US WANTS TO WALK IN THIS STUFF, RIGHT?
I'LL KEEP YOU SAFE.

MY MAMA, SHE SAYS *COPS*, THEY JUST WANT *MONEY*.

YEAH. I'M *NOT* ONE OF *THOSE*.

YOU CAN *TRUST* ME. COME ON...

...YOU CAN *DO* IT...

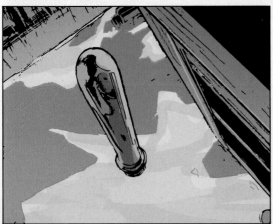

KSSSH

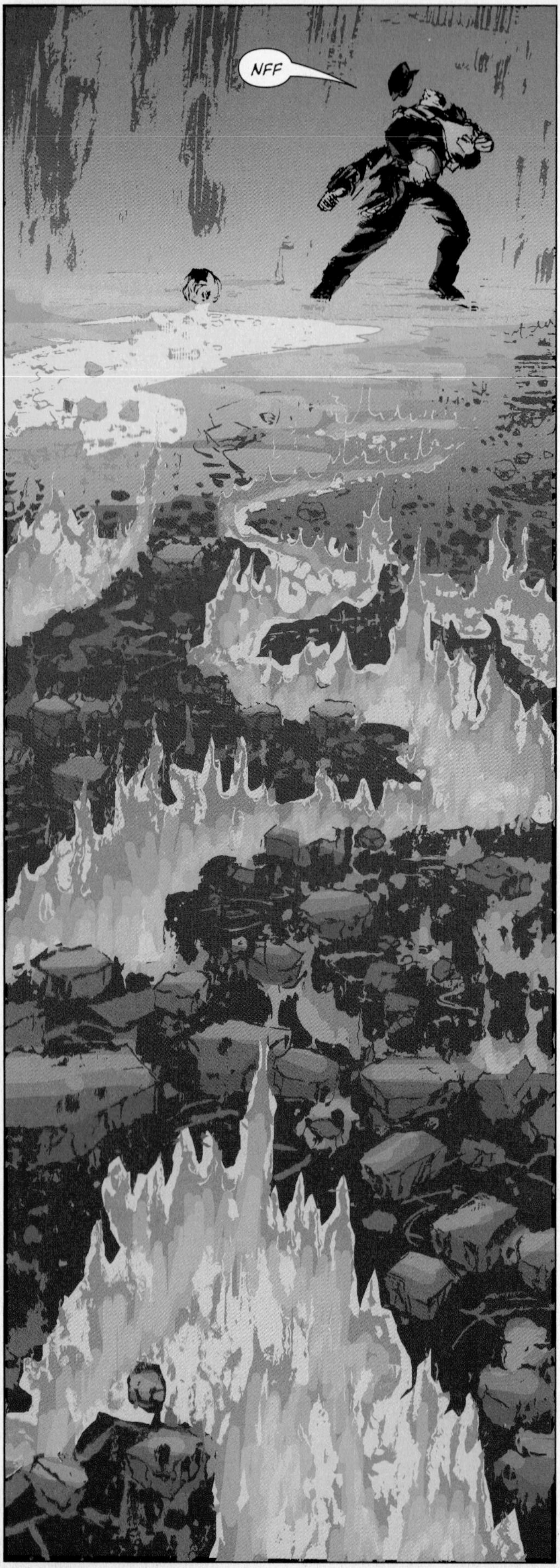
NFF

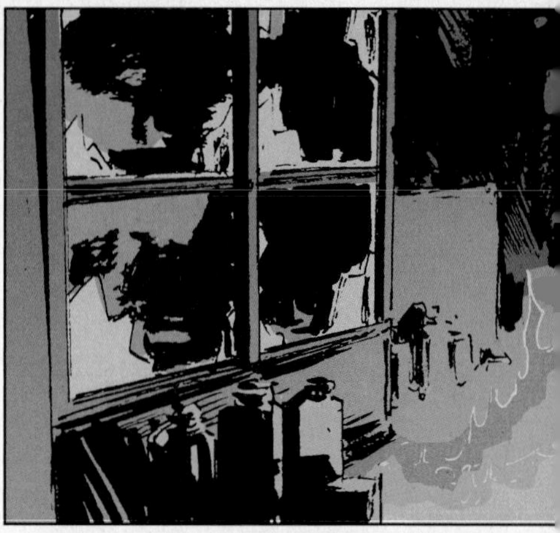

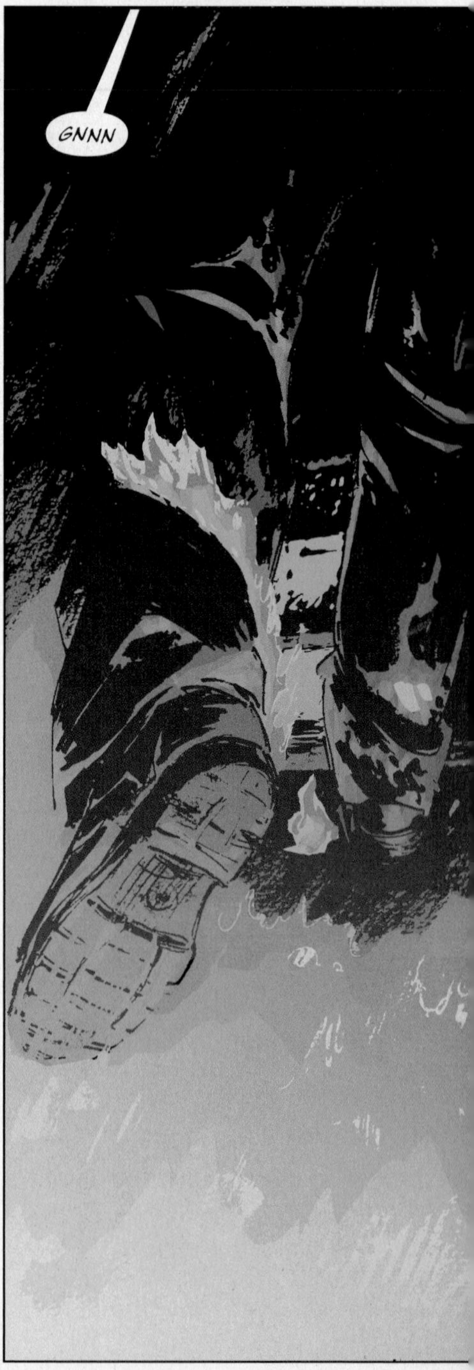
GNNN

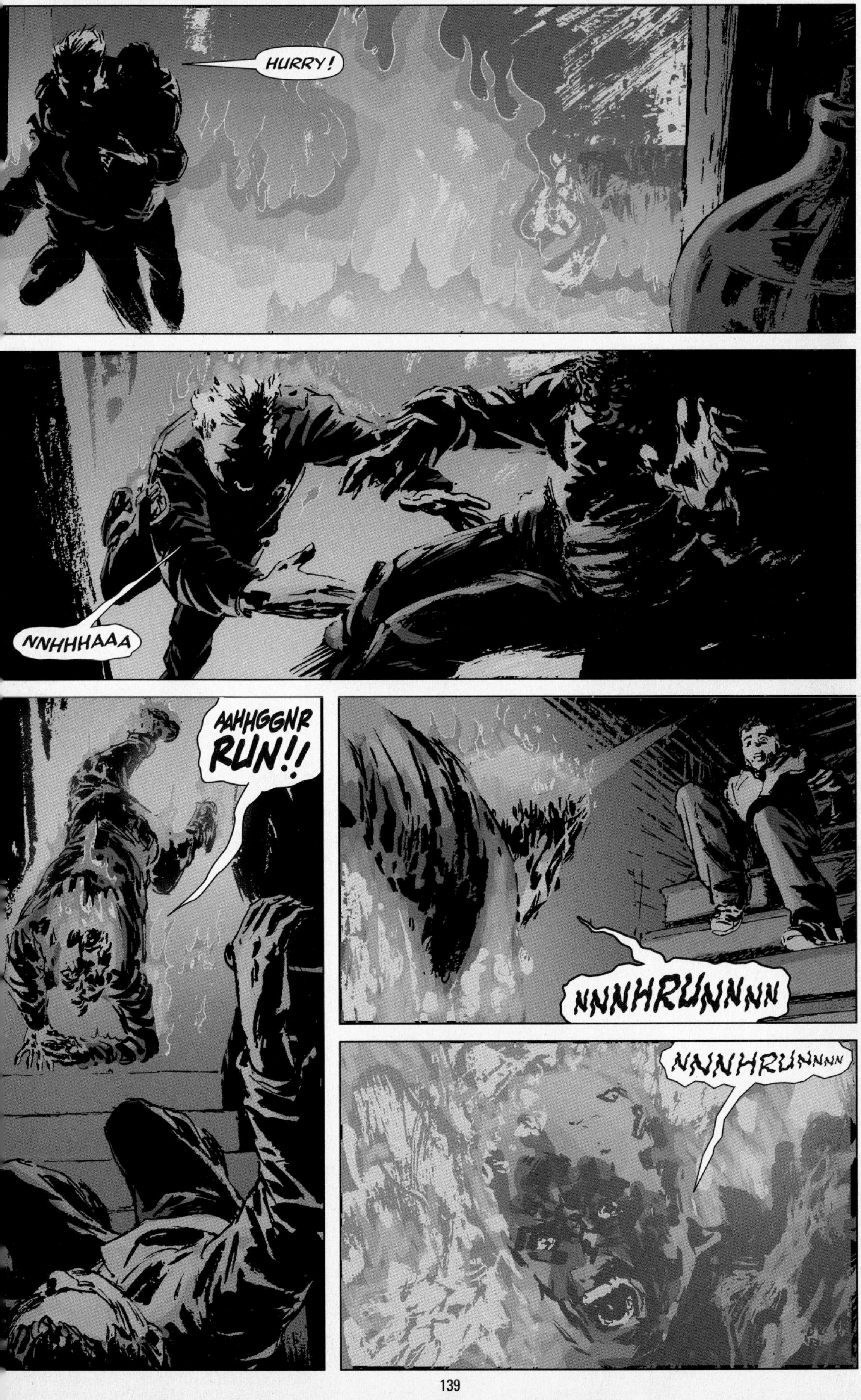
HURRY!
NNHHHAAA
AAHHGGNR RUN!!
NNNHRUNNNN
NNNHRUNnnn

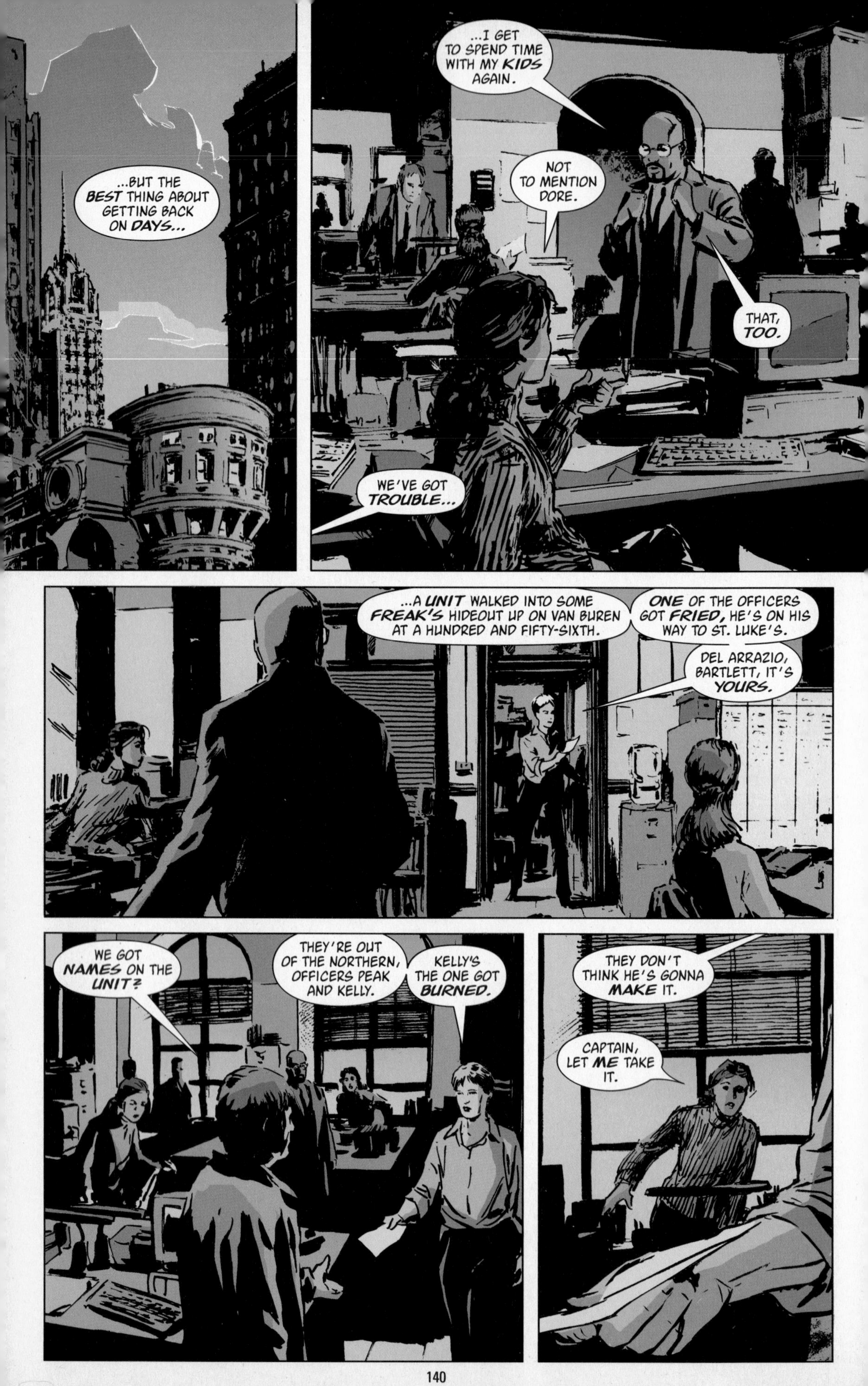
...BUT THE BEST THING ABOUT GETTING BACK ON DAYS...
...I GET TO SPEND TIME WITH MY KIDS AGAIN.
NOT TO MENTION DORE.
THAT, TOO.
WE'VE GOT TROUBLE...
...A UNIT WALKED INTO SOME FREAK'S HIDEOUT UP ON VAN BUREN AT A HUNDRED AND FIFTY-SIXTH.
ONE OF THE OFFICERS GOT FRIED, HE'S ON HIS WAY TO ST. LUKE'S.
DEL ARRAZIO, BARTLETT, IT'S YOURS.
WE GOT NAMES ON THE UNIT?
THEY'RE OUT OF THE NORTHERN, OFFICERS PEAK AND KELLY.
KELLY'S THE ONE GOT BURNED.
THEY DON'T THINK HE'S GONNA MAKE IT.
CAPTAIN, LET ME TAKE IT.

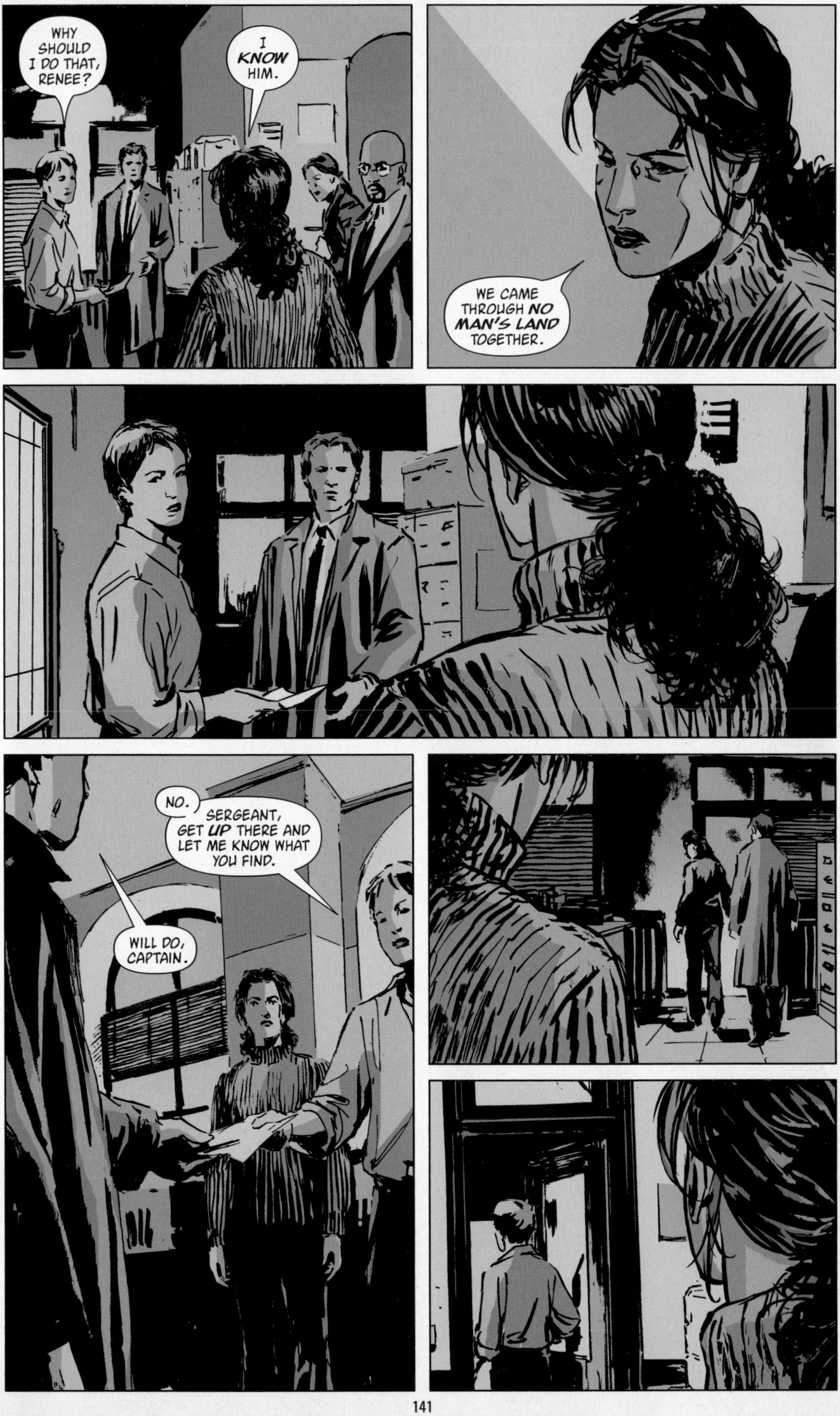
WHY SHOULD I DO THAT, RENEE?
I KNOW HIM.
WE CAME THROUGH NO MAN'S LAND TOGETHER.
NO.
SERGEANT, GET UP THERE AND LET ME KNOW WHAT YOU FIND.
WILL DO, CAPTAIN.

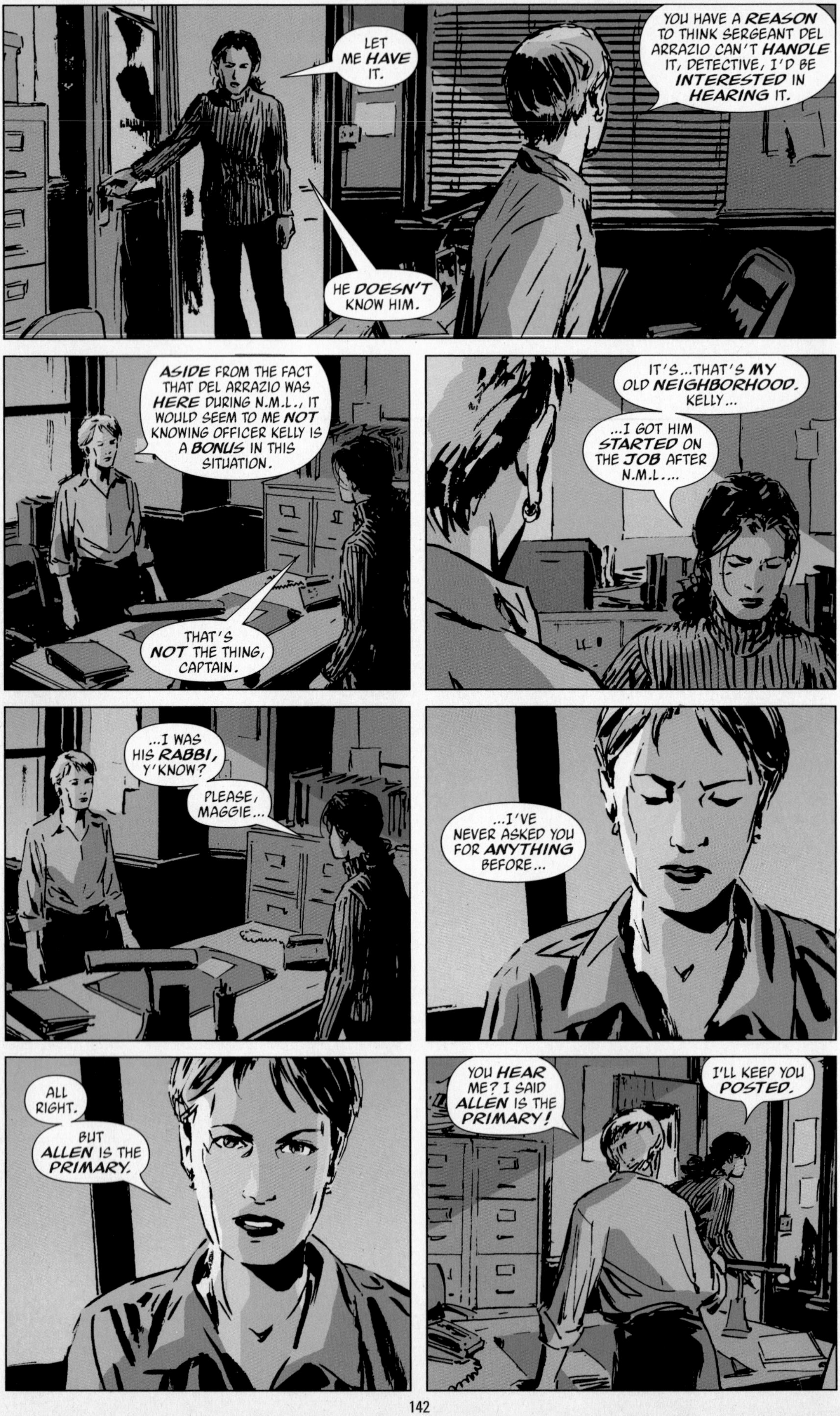
LET ME HAVE IT.
YOU HAVE A REASON TO THINK SERGEANT DEL ARRAZIO CAN'T HANDLE IT, DETECTIVE, I'D BE INTERESTED IN HEARING IT.
HE DOESN'T KNOW HIM.
ASIDE FROM THE FACT THAT DEL ARRAZIO WAS HERE DURING N.M.L., IT WOULD SEEM TO ME NOT KNOWING OFFICER KELLY IS A BONUS IN THIS SITUATION.
THAT'S NOT THE THING, CAPTAIN.
IT'S...THAT'S MY OLD NEIGHBORHOOD. KELLY...
...I GOT HIM STARTED ON THE JOB AFTER N.M.L....
...I WAS HIS RABBI, Y'KNOW?
PLEASE, MAGGIE...
...I'VE NEVER ASKED YOU FOR ANYTHING BEFORE...
ALL RIGHT.
BUT ALLEN IS THE PRIMARY.
YOU HEAR ME? I SAID ALLEN IS THE PRIMARY!
I'LL KEEP YOU POSTED.

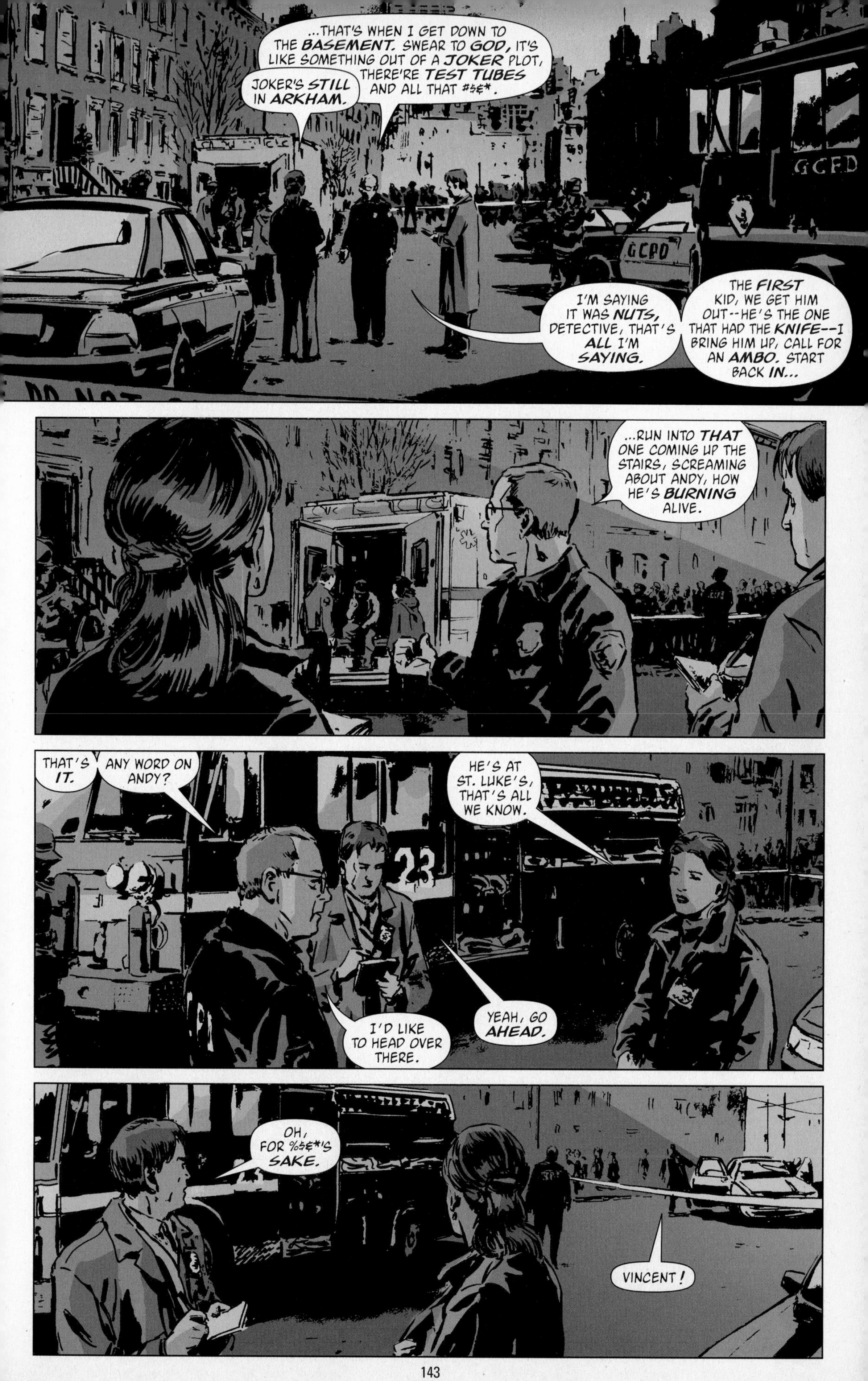
...THAT'S WHEN I GET DOWN TO THE BASEMENT. SWEAR TO GOD, IT'S LIKE SOMETHING OUT OF A JOKER PLOT, THERE'RE TEST TUBES AND ALL THAT #$&*.
JOKER'S STILL IN ARKHAM.
GCFD
GCPD
I'M SAYING IT WAS NUTS, DETECTIVE, THAT'S ALL I'M SAYING.
THE FIRST KID, WE GET HIM OUT--HE'S THE ONE THAT HAD THE KNIFE--I BRING HIM UP, CALL FOR AN AMBO. START BACK IN...
...RUN INTO THAT ONE COMING UP THE STAIRS, SCREAMING ABOUT ANDY, HOW HE'S BURNING ALIVE.
THAT'S IT.
ANY WORD ON ANDY?
HE'S AT ST. LUKE'S, THAT'S ALL WE KNOW.
23
I'D LIKE TO HEAD OVER THERE.
YEAH, GO AHEAD.
OH, FOR %$&*'S SAKE.
VINCENT!

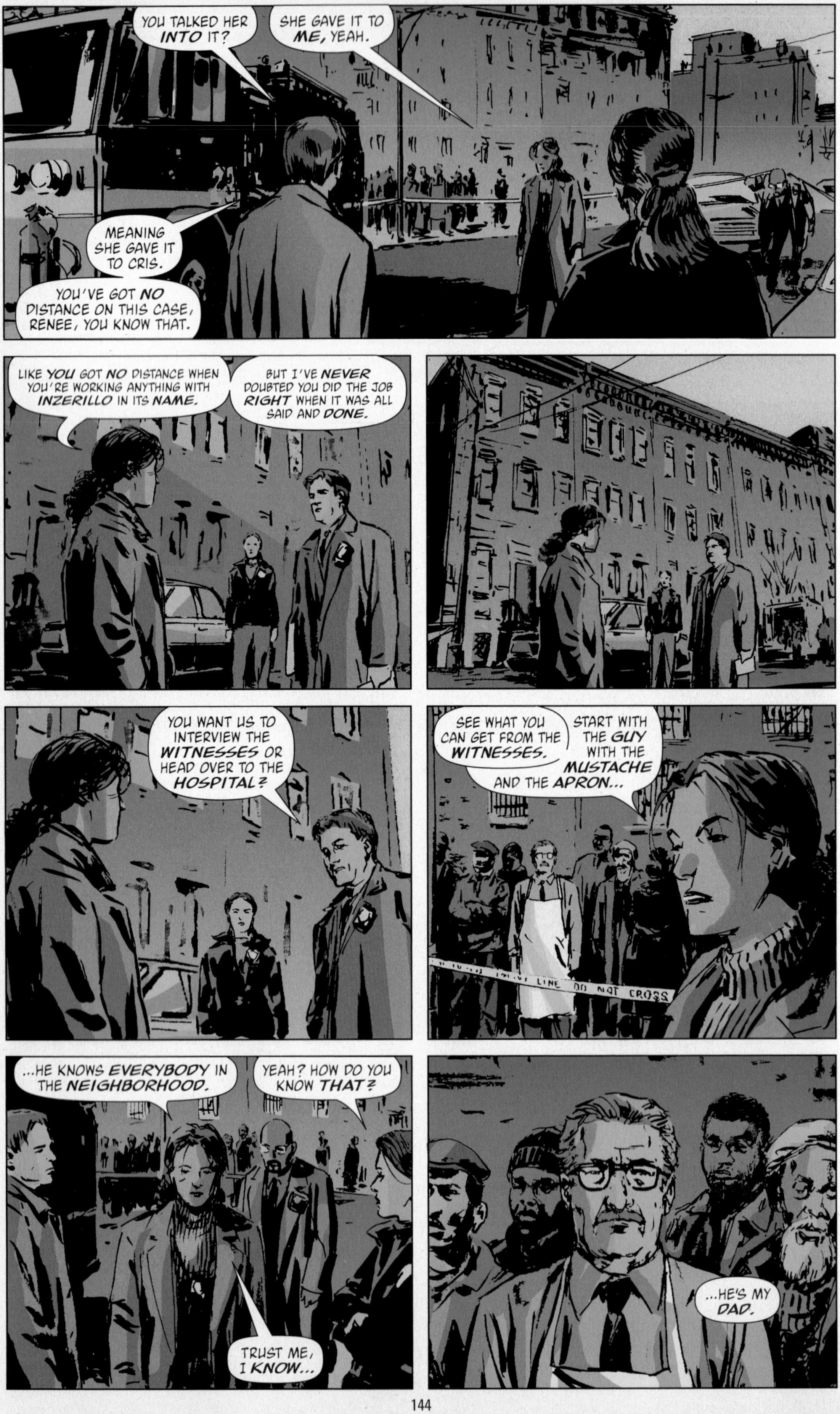
YOU TALKED HER INTO IT?
SHE GAVE IT TO ME, YEAH.
MEANING SHE GAVE IT TO CRIS.
YOU'VE GOT NO DISTANCE ON THIS CASE, RENEE, YOU KNOW THAT.
LIKE YOU GOT NO DISTANCE WHEN YOU'RE WORKING ANYTHING WITH INZERILLO IN ITS NAME.
BUT I'VE NEVER DOUBTED YOU DID THE JOB RIGHT WHEN IT WAS ALL SAID AND DONE.
YOU WANT US TO INTERVIEW THE WITNESSES OR HEAD OVER TO THE HOSPITAL?
SEE WHAT YOU CAN GET FROM THE WITNESSES.
START WITH THE GUY WITH THE MUSTACHE AND THE APRON...
LINE DO NOT CROSS
...HE KNOWS EVERYBODY IN THE NEIGHBORHOOD.
YEAH? HOW DO YOU KNOW THAT?
TRUST ME, I KNOW...
...HE'S MY DAD.

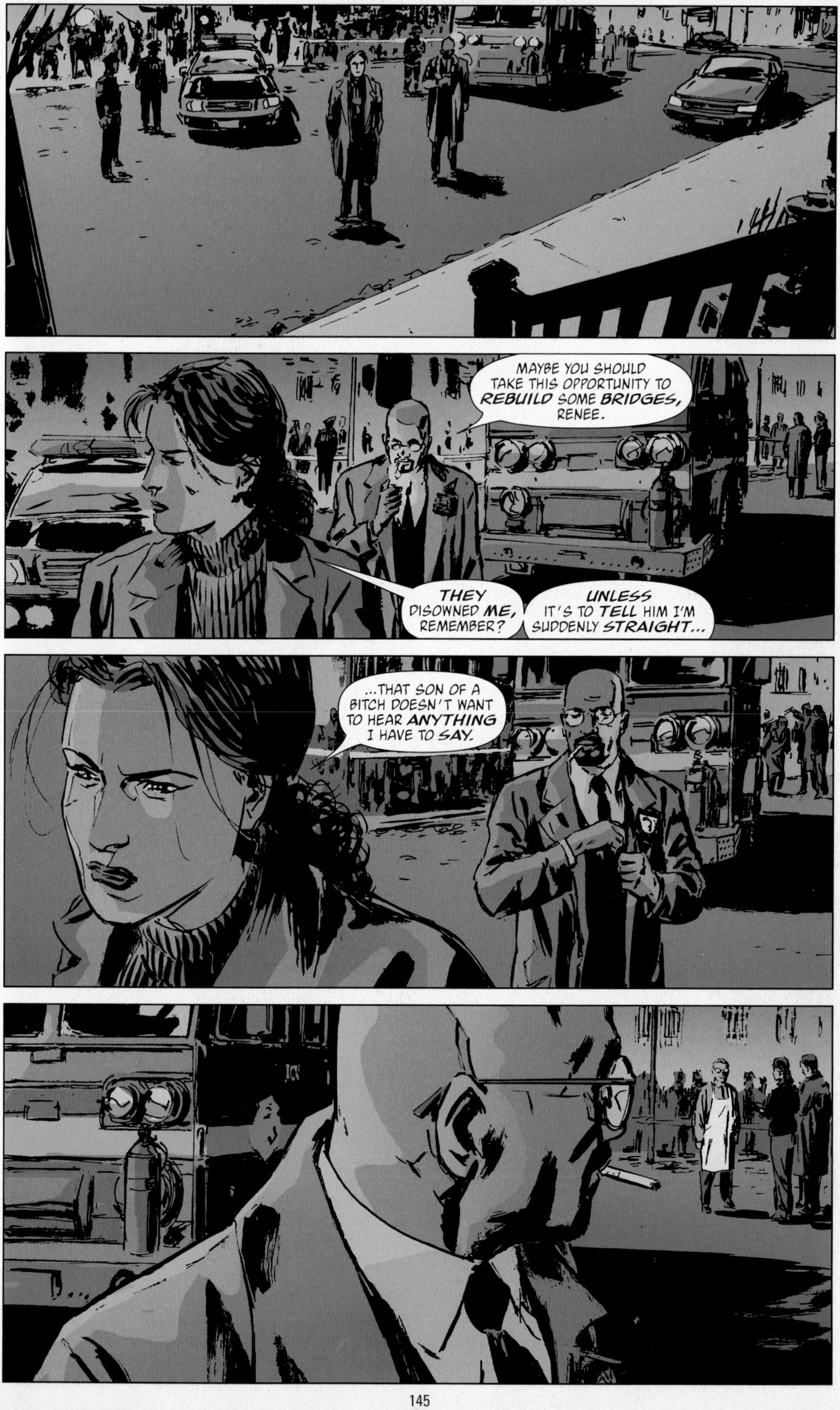
MAYBE YOU SHOULD TAKE THIS OPPORTUNITY TO REBUILD SOME BRIDGES, RENEE.
THEY DISOWNED ME, REMEMBER?
UNLESS IT'S TO TELL HIM I'M SUDDENLY STRAIGHT...
...THAT SON OF A BITCH DOESN'T WANT TO HEAR ANYTHING I HAVE TO SAY.

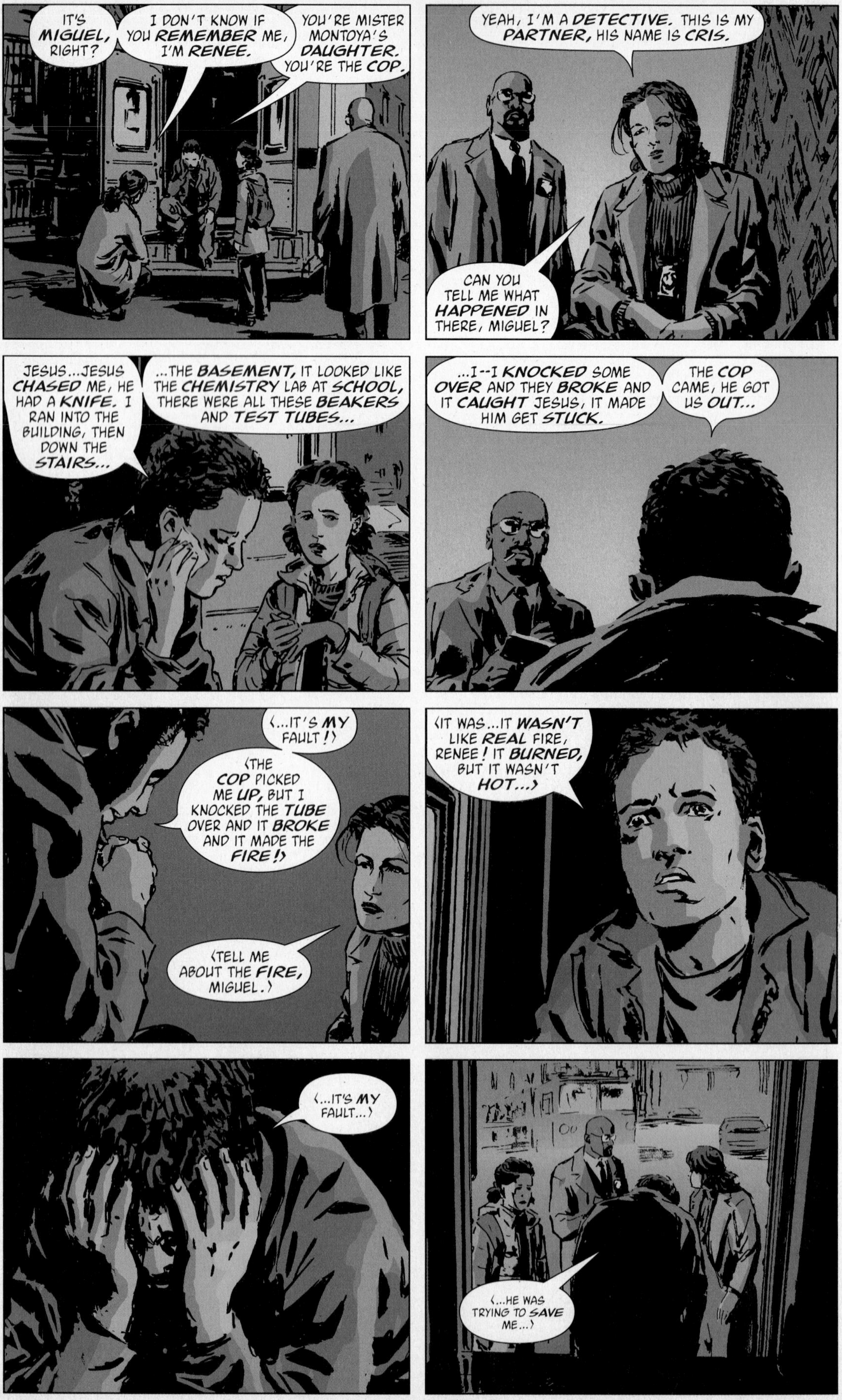
IT'S MIGUEL, RIGHT?
I DON'T KNOW IF YOU REMEMBER ME, I'M RENEE.
YOU'RE MISTER MONTOYA'S DAUGHTER. YOU'RE THE COP.
YEAH, I'M A DETECTIVE. THIS IS MY PARTNER, HIS NAME IS CRIS.
CAN YOU TELL ME WHAT HAPPENED IN THERE, MIGUEL?
JESUS...JESUS CHASED ME, HE HAD A KNIFE. I RAN INTO THE BUILDING, THEN DOWN THE STAIRS...
...THE BASEMENT, IT LOOKED LIKE THE CHEMISTRY LAB AT SCHOOL, THERE WERE ALL THESE BEAKERS AND TEST TUBES...
...I--I KNOCKED SOME OVER AND THEY BROKE AND IT CAUGHT JESUS, IT MADE HIM GET STUCK.
THE COP CAME, HE GOT US OUT...
‹...IT'S MY FAULT!›
‹THE COP PICKED ME UP, BUT I KNOCKED THE TUBE OVER AND IT BROKE AND IT MADE THE FIRE!›
‹TELL ME ABOUT THE FIRE, MIGUEL.›
‹IT WAS...IT WASN'T LIKE REAL FIRE, RENEE! IT BURNED, BUT IT WASN'T HOT...›
‹...IT'S MY FAULT...›
‹...HE WAS TRYING TO SAVE ME...›

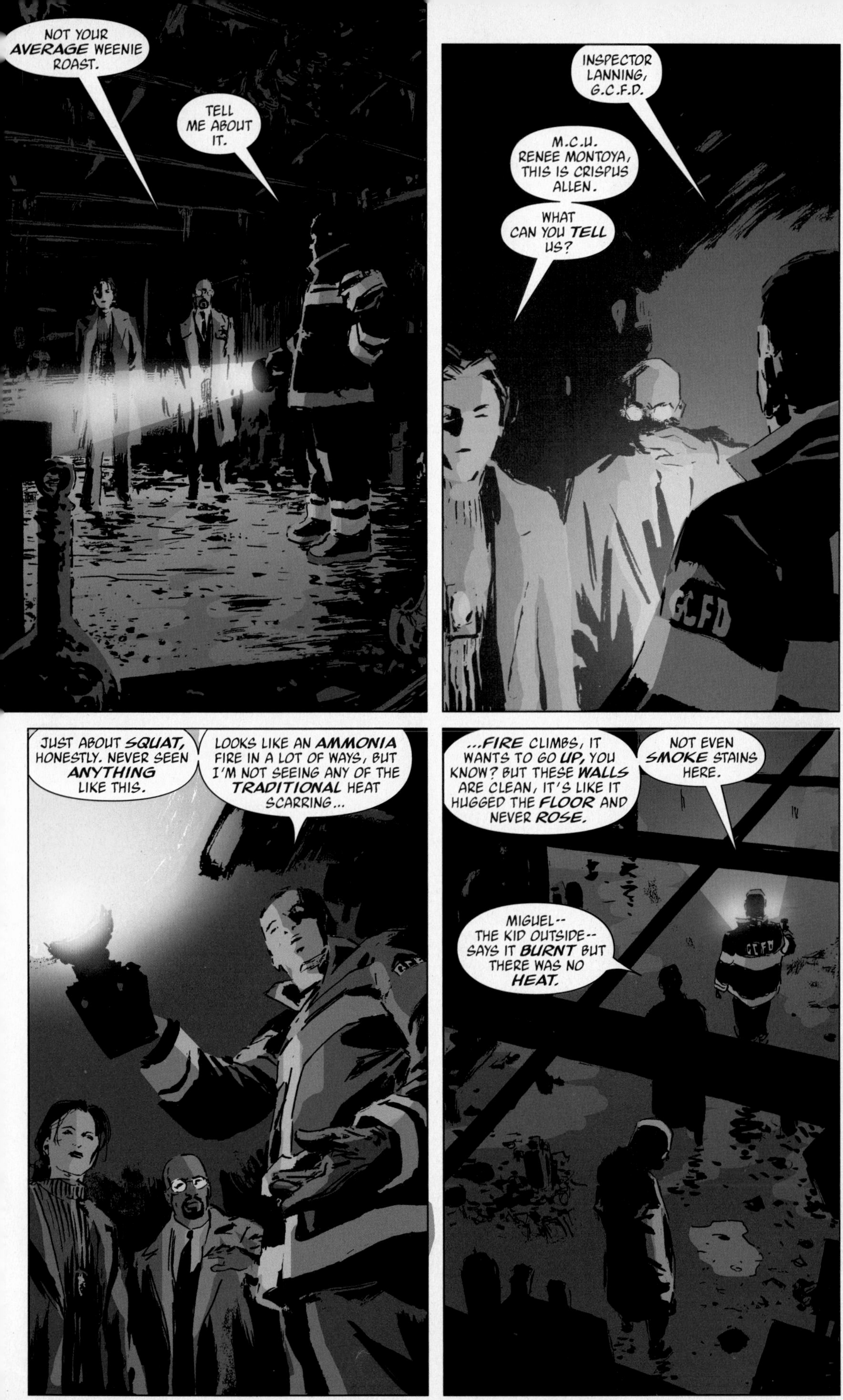
NOT YOUR AVERAGE WEENIE ROAST.
TELL ME ABOUT IT.
INSPECTOR LANNING, G.C.F.D.
M.C.U. RENEE MONTOYA, THIS IS CRISPUS ALLEN.
WHAT CAN YOU TELL US?
GCFD
JUST ABOUT SQUAT, HONESTLY. NEVER SEEN ANYTHING LIKE THIS.
LOOKS LIKE AN AMMONIA FIRE IN A LOT OF WAYS, BUT I'M NOT SEEING ANY OF THE TRADITIONAL HEAT SCARRING...
...FIRE CLIMBS, IT WANTS TO GO UP, YOU KNOW? BUT THESE WALLS ARE CLEAN, IT'S LIKE IT HUGGED THE FLOOR AND NEVER ROSE.
NOT EVEN SMOKE STAINS HERE.
MIGUEL-- THE KID OUTSIDE-- SAYS IT BURNT BUT THERE WAS NO HEAT.

KID'S A *MORON*, IT'S *NOT* POSSIBLE.

HE'S A *GOOD* KID, I KNOW HIS *MOTHER*.

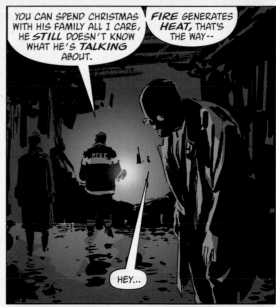

YOU CAN SPEND CHRISTMAS WITH HIS FAMILY ALL I CARE, HE *STILL* DOESN'T KNOW WHAT HE'S *TALKING* ABOUT.

FIRE GENERATES *HEAT*, THAT'S THE WAY--

HEY...

COULD YOU MAYBE *SHINE* THAT *LIGHT* AT MY FEET INSTEAD OF AT MY *FACE*, LANNING?

YOU GOT SOME-THING?

YEAH, MAYBE...

...LOOKS LIKE THE *PERIODIC TABLE*...

THE WHAT?

THE *ELEMENTS*, YOU KNOW, IT WAS ON THE WALL OF YOUR CHEMISTRY CLASS IN HIGH SCHOOL?

I *CUT* CHEM.

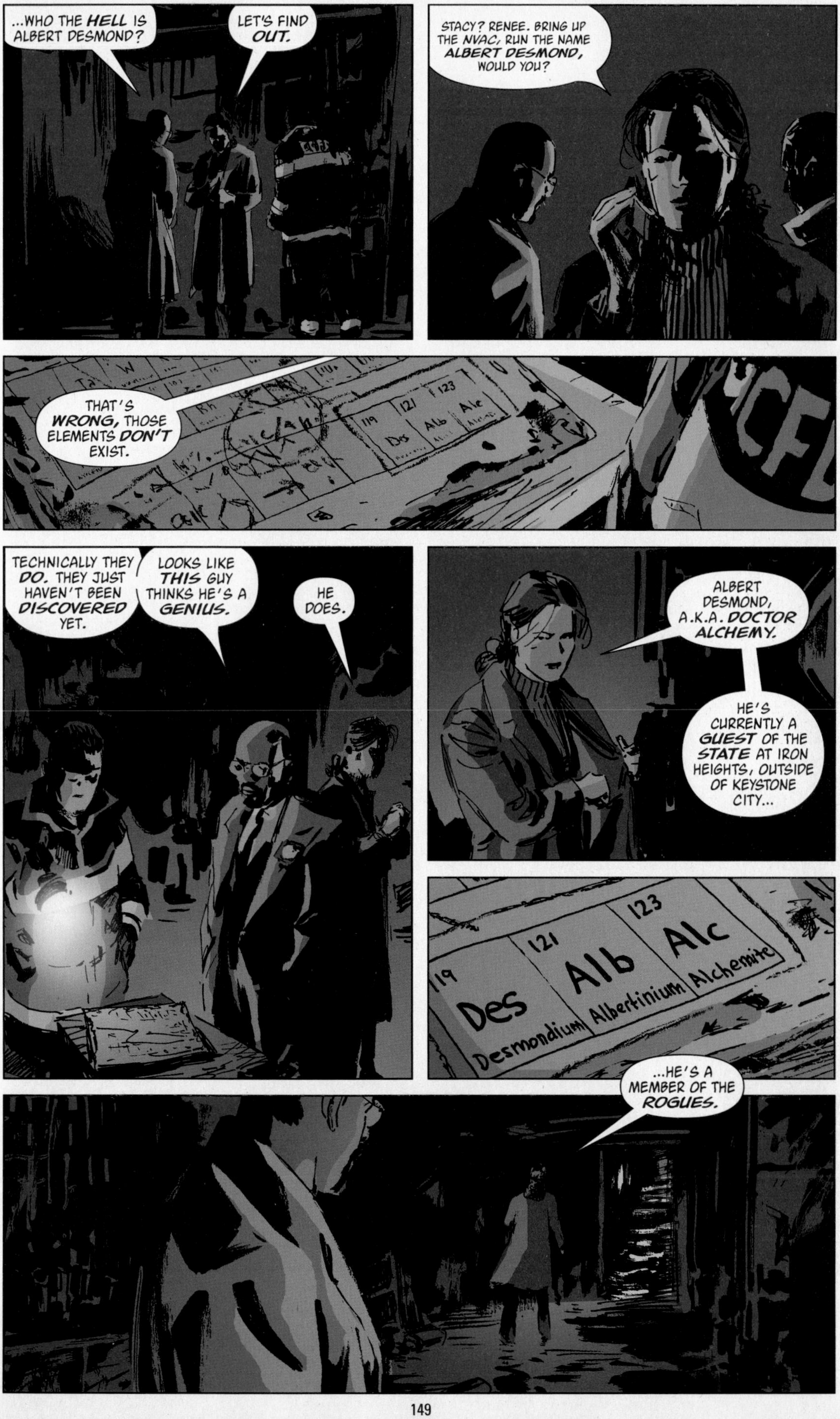
...WHO THE HELL IS ALBERT DESMOND?
LET'S FIND OUT.
STACY? RENEE. BRING UP THE NVAC, RUN THE NAME ALBERT DESMOND, WOULD YOU?
THAT'S WRONG, THOSE ELEMENTS DON'T EXIST.
CFD
TECHNICALLY THEY DO. THEY JUST HAVEN'T BEEN DISCOVERED YET.
LOOKS LIKE THIS GUY THINKS HE'S A GENIUS.
HE DOES.
ALBERT DESMOND, A.K.A. DOCTOR ALCHEMY.
HE'S CURRENTLY A GUEST OF THE STATE AT IRON HEIGHTS, OUTSIDE OF KEYSTONE CITY...
119 121 123
Des Alb Alc
Desmondium Albertinium Alchemite
...HE'S A MEMBER OF THE ROGUES.

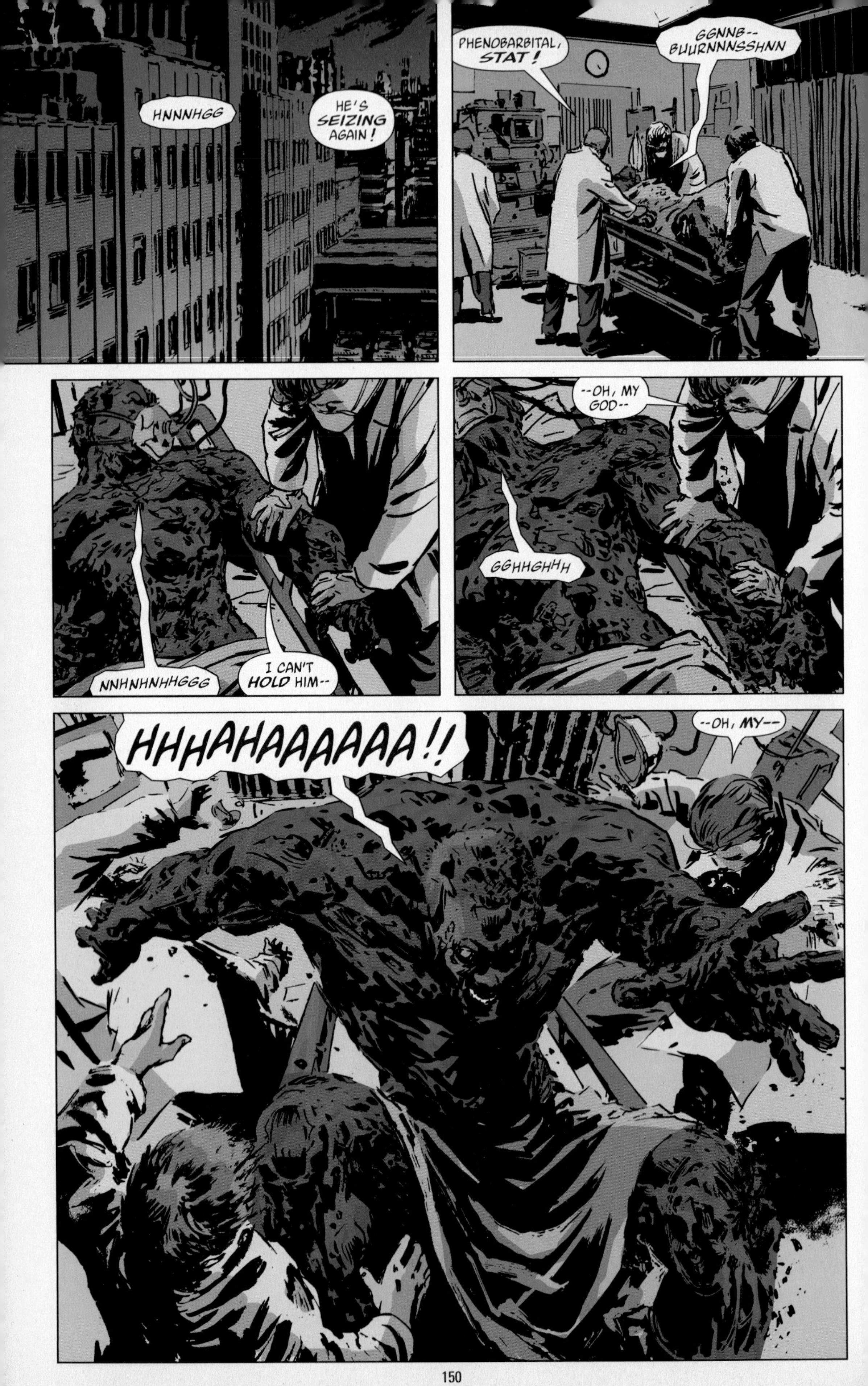
HNNNHGG
HE'S SEIZING AGAIN!
PHENOBARBITAL, STAT!
GGNNB-- BUURNNNSSHNN
NNHNHNHHGGG
I CAN'T HOLD HIM--
--OH, MY GOD--
GGHHGHHH
HHHAHAAAAAAA!!
--OH, MY--

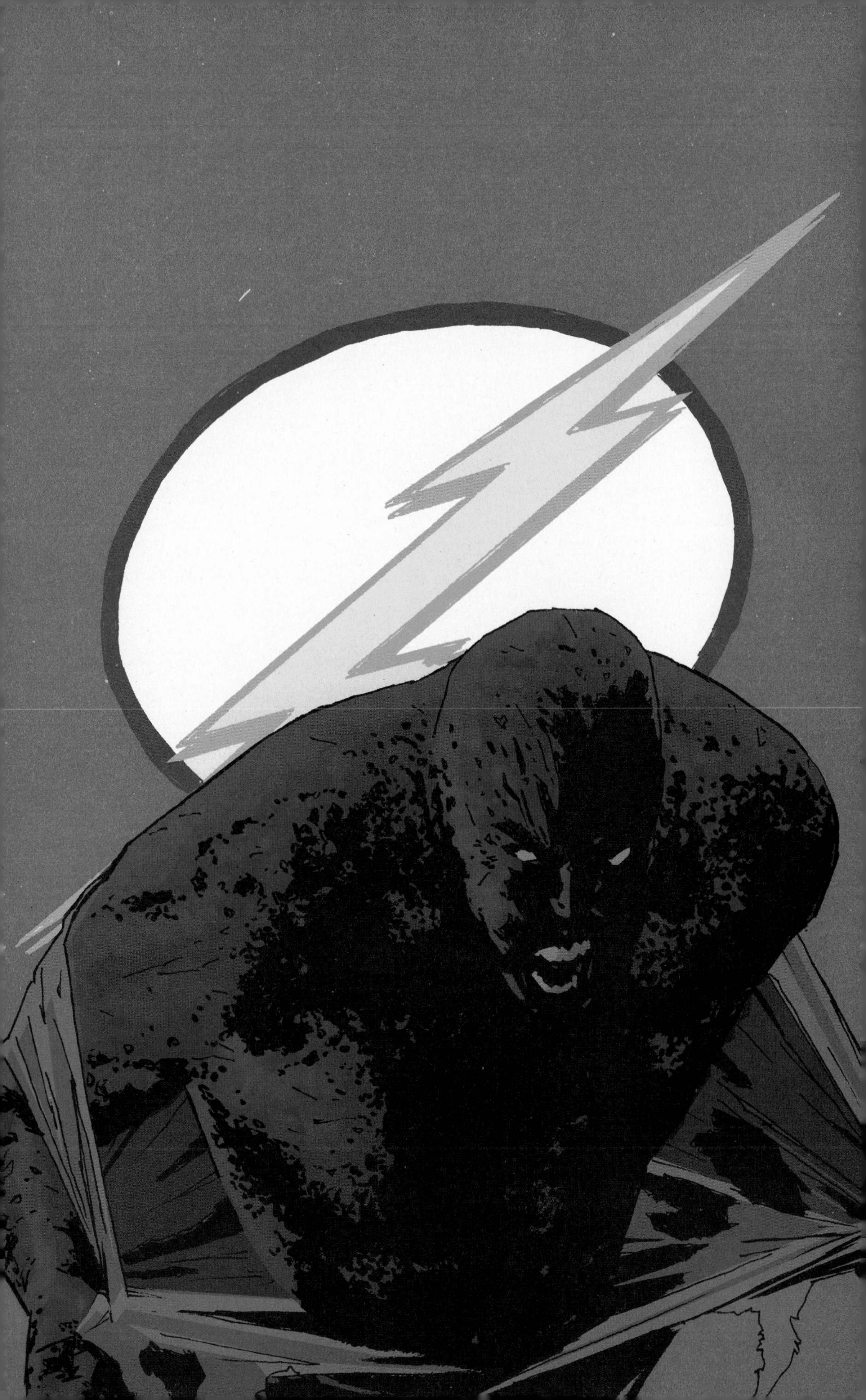

Keystone Kops Part Two

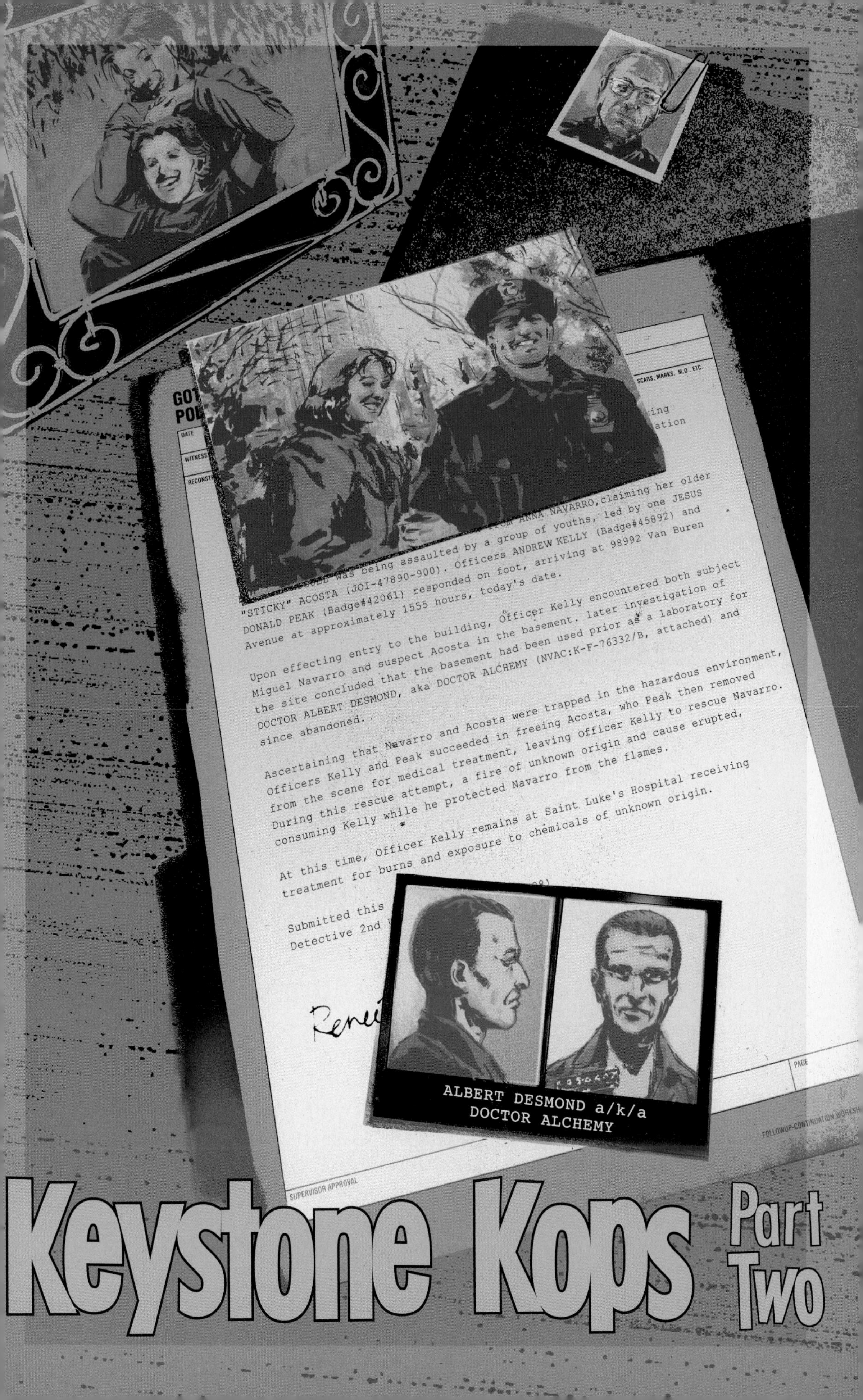
SCARS, MARKS, M.O., ETC.
DATE
WITNESS
ANNA NAVARRO,claiming her older
was being assaulted by a group of youths, led by one JESUS
"STICKY" ACOSTA (JOI-47890-900). Officers ANDREW KELLY (Badge#45892) and
DONALD PEAK (Badge#42061) responded on foot, arriving at 98992 Van Buren
Avenue at approximately 1555 hours, today's date.
Upon effecting entry to the building, Officer Kelly encountered both subject
Miguel Navarro and suspect Acosta in the basement. later investigation of
the site concluded that the basement had been used prior as a laboratory for
DOCTOR ALBERT DESMOND, aka DOCTOR ALCHEMY (NVAC:K-F-76332/B, attached) and
since abandoned.
Ascertaining that Navarro and Acosta were trapped in the hazardous environment,
Officers Kelly and Peak succeeded in freeing Acosta, who Peak then removed
from the scene for medical treatment, leaving Officer Kelly to rescue Navarro.
During this rescue attempt, a fire of unknown origin and cause erupted,
consuming Kelly while he protected Navarro from the flames.
At this time, Officer Kelly remains at Saint Luke's Hospital receiving
treatment for burns and exposure to chemicals of unknown origin.
Submitted this
Detective 2nd
Renee
PAGE
ALBERT DESMOND a/k/a
DOCTOR ALCHEMY
SUPERVISOR APPROVAL

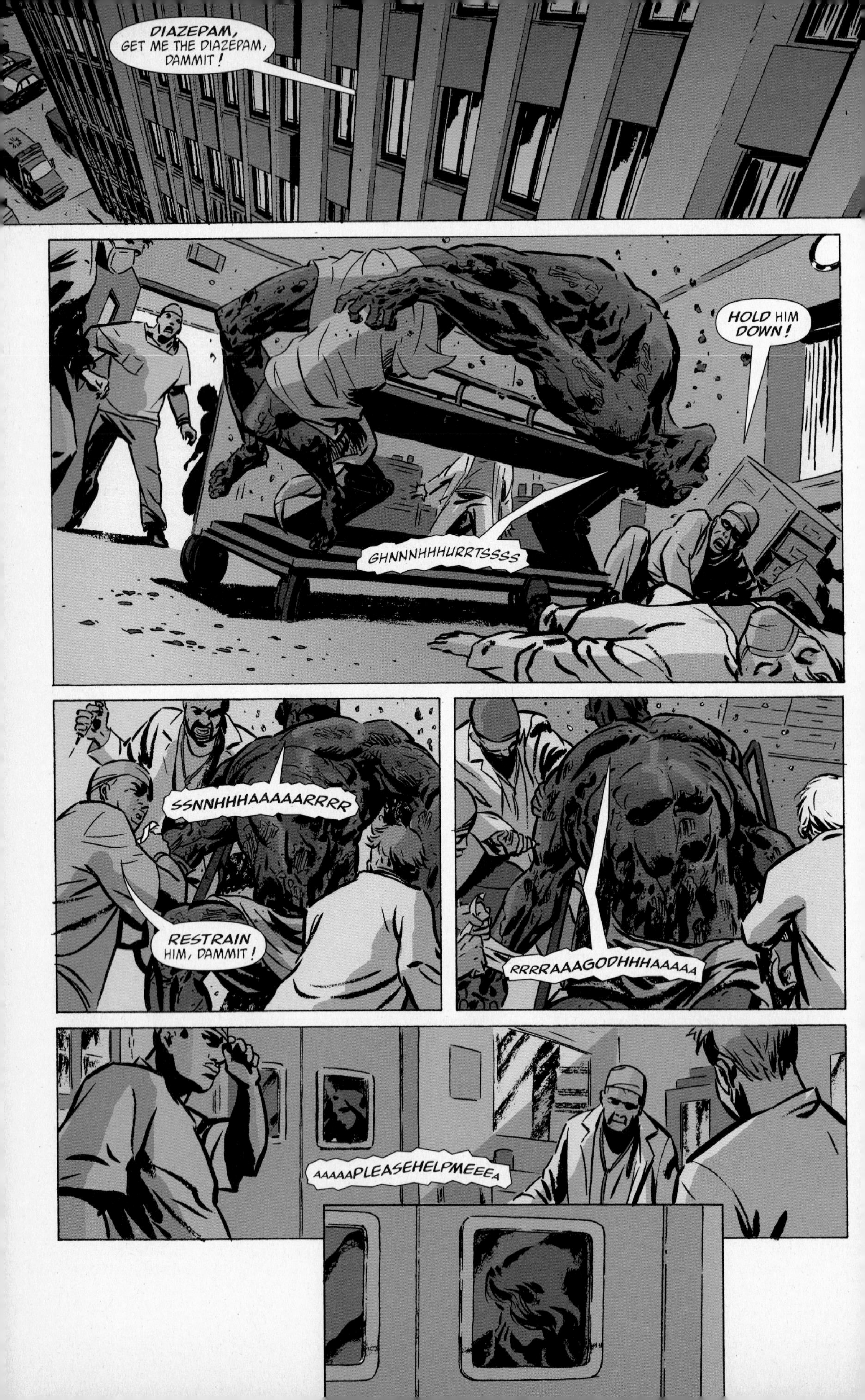
DIAZEPAM, GET ME THE DIAZEPAM, DAMMIT!
HOLD HIM DOWN!
GHNNNHHHURRTSSSS
SSNNHHHAAAAARRRR
RESTRAIN HIM, DAMMIT!
RRRRAAAGODHHHAAAAA
AAAAAPLEASEHELPMEEEA

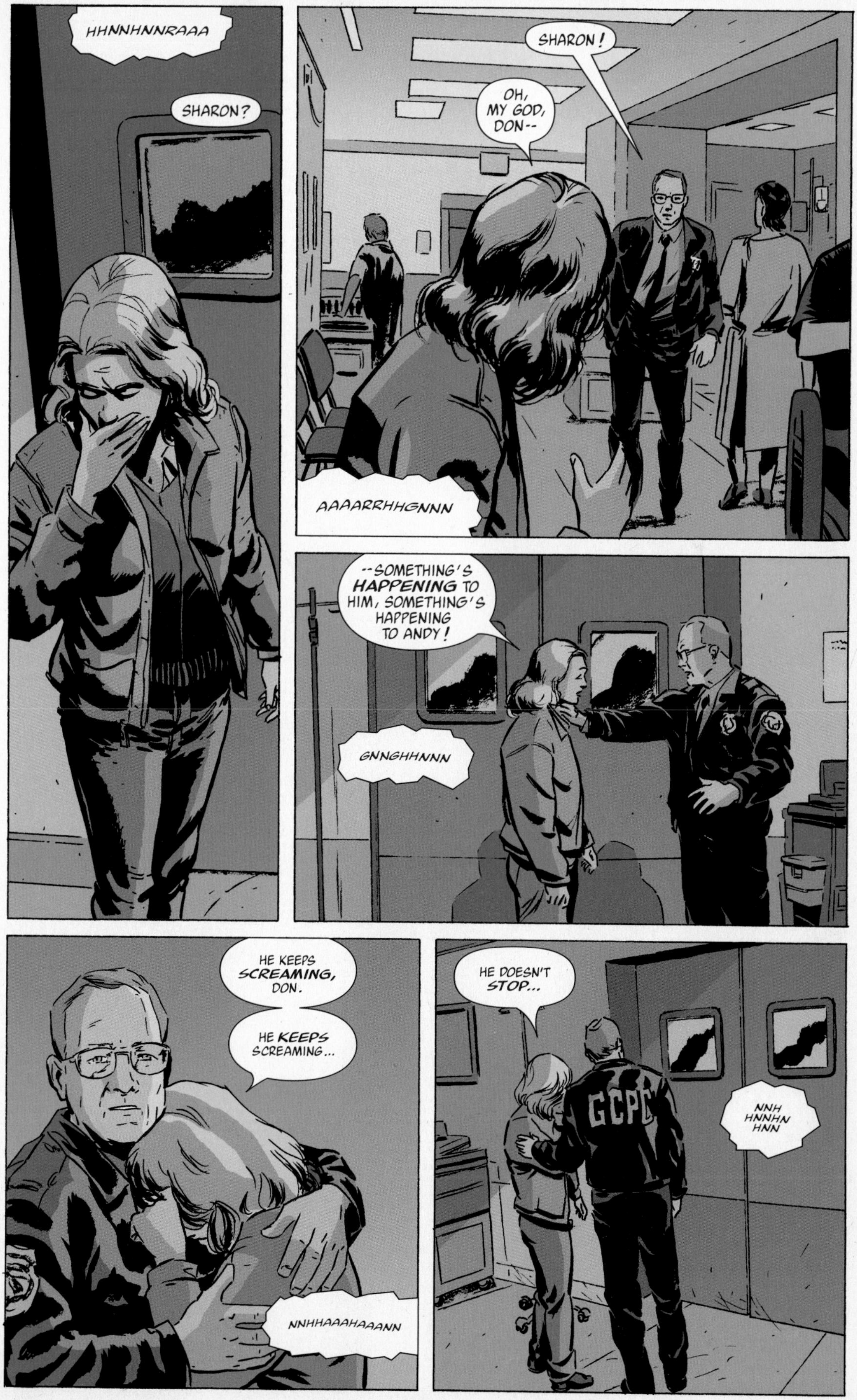
HHNNHNNRAAA
SHARON?
SHARON!
OH, MY GOD, DON--
AAAARRHHGNNN
--SOMETHING'S HAPPENING TO HIM, SOMETHING'S HAPPENING TO ANDY!
GNNGHHNNN
HE KEEPS SCREAMING, DON.
HE KEEPS SCREAMING...
NNHHAAAHAAANN
HE DOESN'T STOP...
GCPD
NNH HNNHN HNN

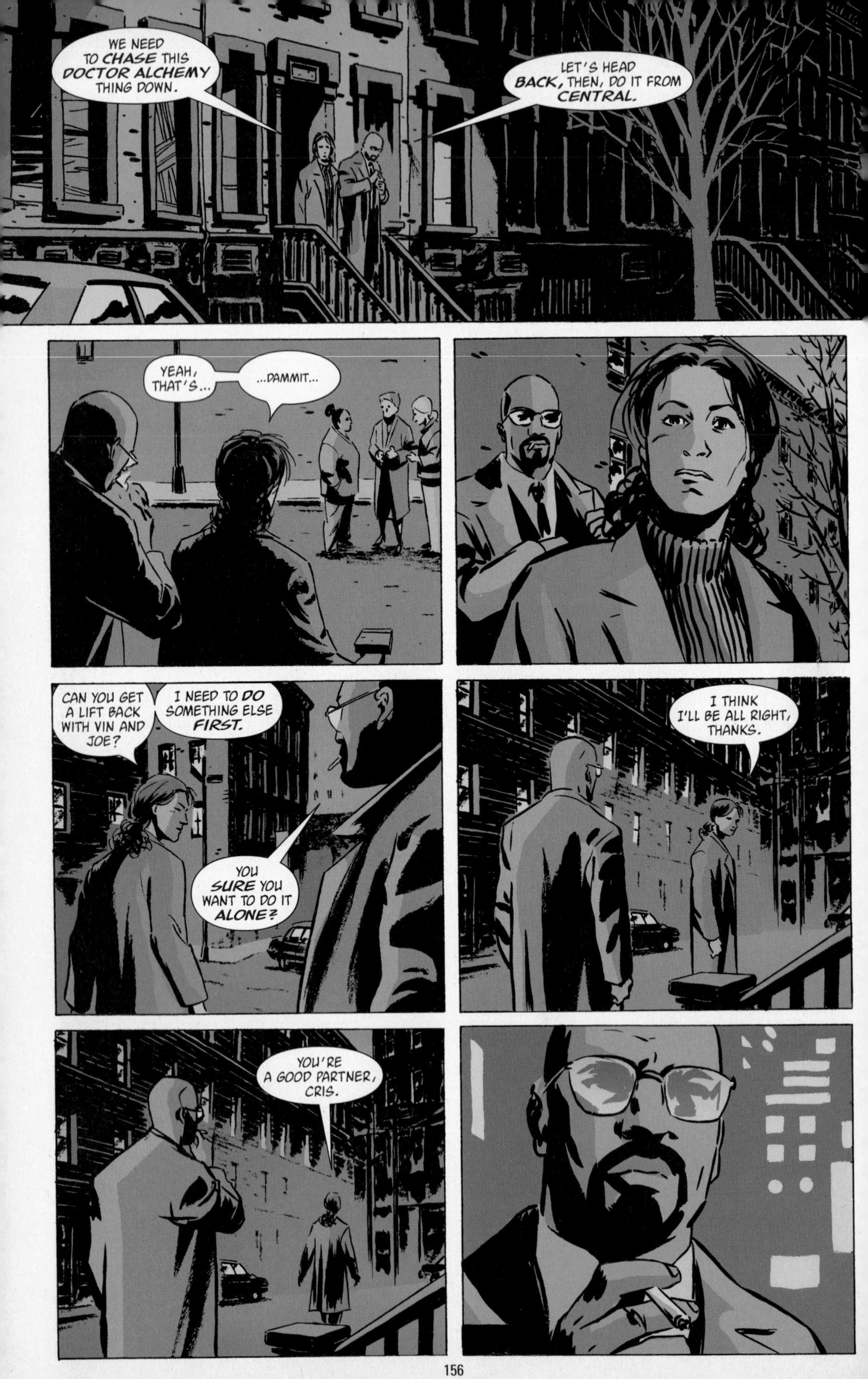
WE NEED TO CHASE THIS DOCTOR ALCHEMY THING DOWN.
LET'S HEAD BACK, THEN, DO IT FROM CENTRAL.
YEAH, THAT'S...
...DAMMIT...
CAN YOU GET A LIFT BACK WITH VIN AND JOE?
I NEED TO DO SOMETHING ELSE FIRST.
YOU SURE YOU WANT TO DO IT ALONE?
I THINK I'LL BE ALL RIGHT, THANKS.
YOU'RE A GOOD PARTNER, CRIS.

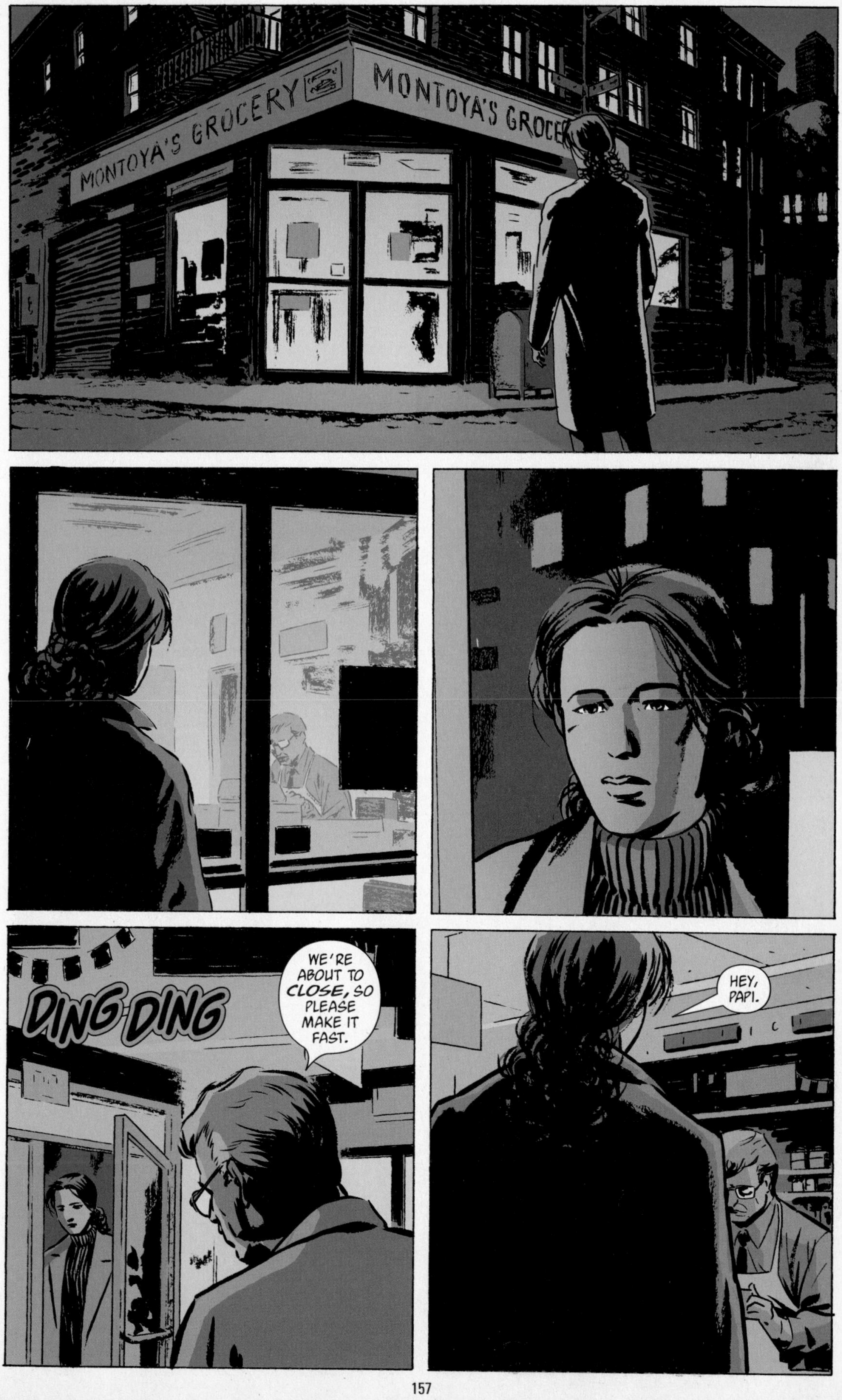
MONTOYA'S GROCERY
MONTOYA'S GROCERY
MONTOYA'S GROCE
DING DING
WE'RE ABOUT TO CLOSE, SO PLEASE MAKE IT FAST.
HEY, PAPI.

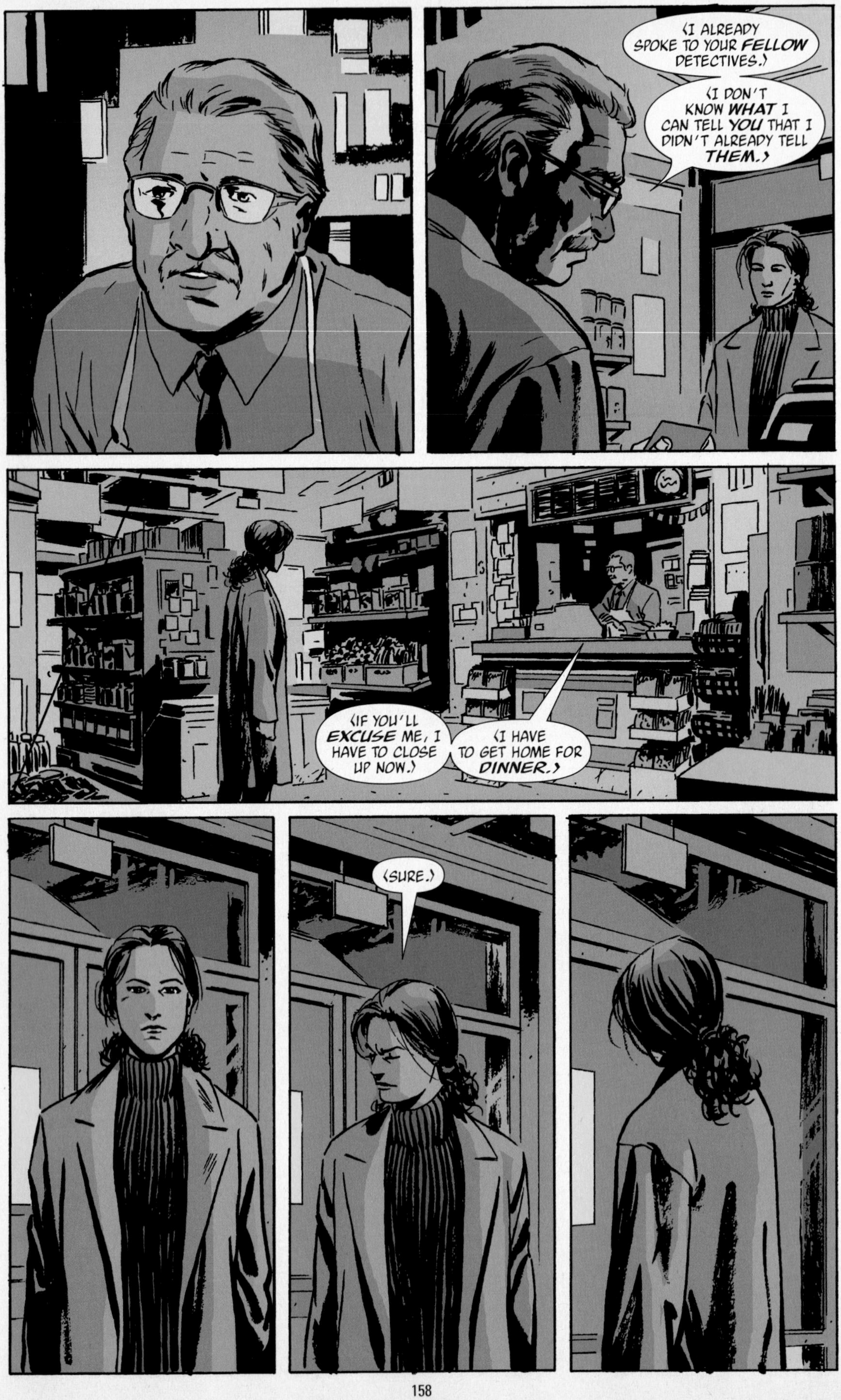
‹I ALREADY SPOKE TO YOUR FELLOW DETECTIVES.›
‹I DON'T KNOW WHAT I CAN TELL YOU THAT I DIDN'T ALREADY TELL THEM.›
‹IF YOU'LL EXCUSE ME, I HAVE TO CLOSE UP NOW.›
‹I HAVE TO GET HOME FOR DINNER.›
‹SURE.›

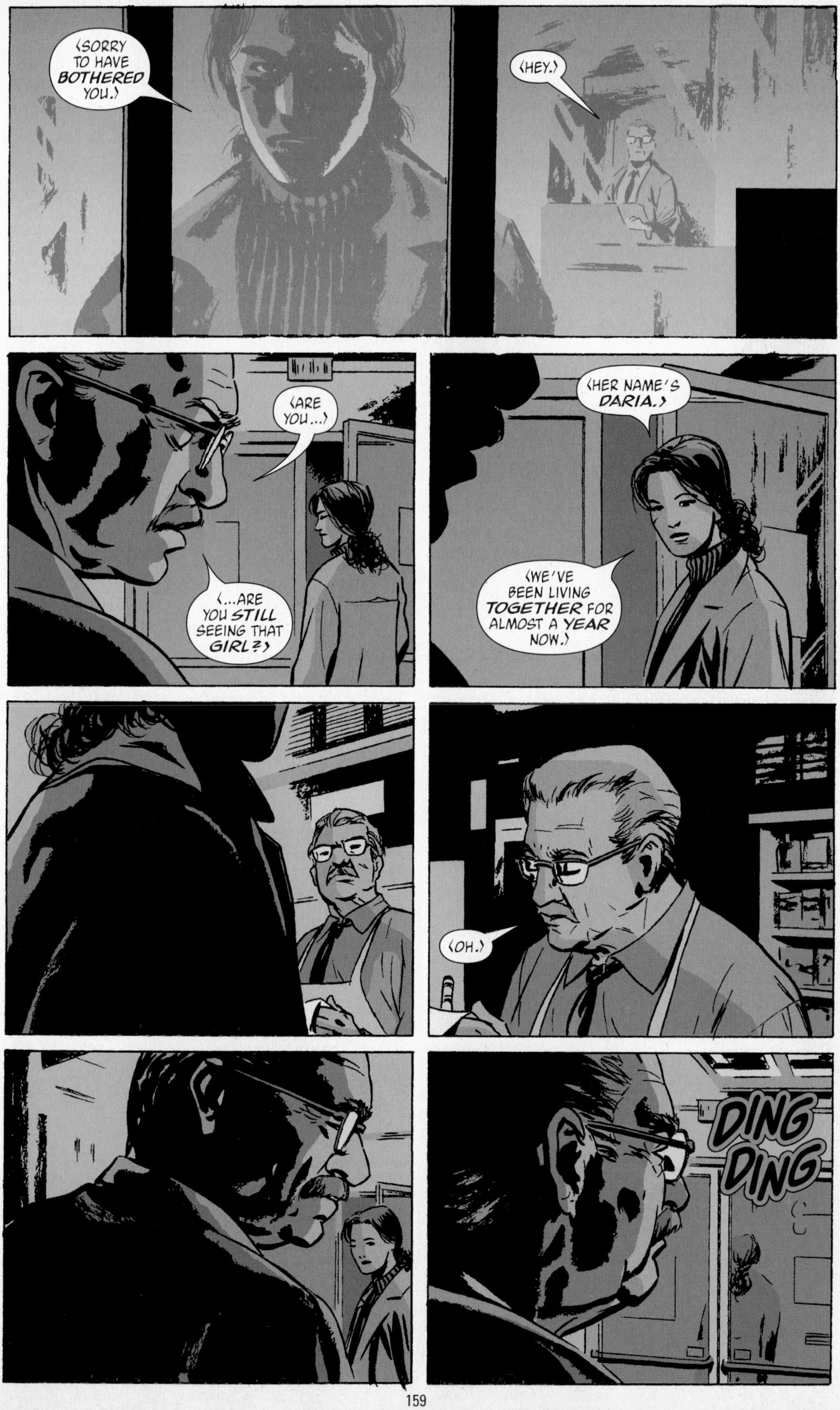
‹SORRY TO HAVE BOTHERED YOU.›
‹HEY.›
‹ARE YOU...›
‹...ARE YOU STILL SEEING THAT GIRL?›
‹HER NAME'S DARIA.›
‹WE'VE BEEN LIVING TOGETHER FOR ALMOST A YEAR NOW.›
‹OH.›
DING DING

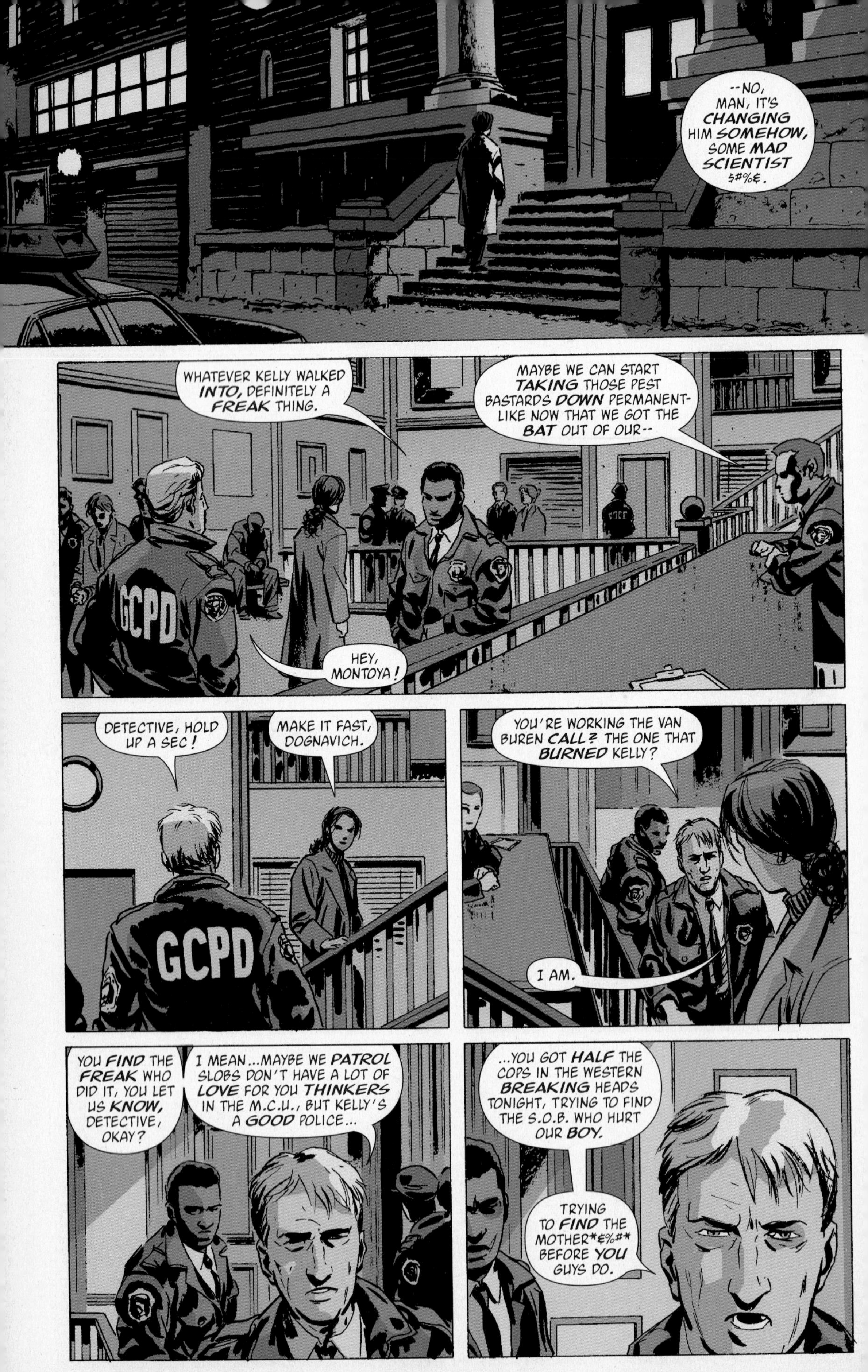
--NO, MAN, IT'S CHANGING HIM SOMEHOW, SOME MAD SCIENTIST $#%&.
WHATEVER KELLY WALKED INTO, DEFINITELY A FREAK THING.
MAYBE WE CAN START TAKING THOSE PEST BASTARDS DOWN PERMANENT-LIKE NOW THAT WE GOT THE BAT OUT OF OUR--
HEY, MONTOYA!
GCPD
DETECTIVE, HOLD UP A SEC!
MAKE IT FAST, DOGNAVICH.
GCPD
YOU'RE WORKING THE VAN BUREN CALL? THE ONE THAT BURNED KELLY?
I AM.
YOU FIND THE FREAK WHO DID IT, YOU LET US KNOW, DETECTIVE, OKAY?
I MEAN...MAYBE WE PATROL SLOBS DON'T HAVE A LOT OF LOVE FOR YOU THINKERS IN THE M.C.U., BUT KELLY'S A GOOD POLICE...
...YOU GOT HALF THE COPS IN THE WESTERN BREAKING HEADS TONIGHT, TRYING TO FIND THE S.O.B. WHO HURT OUR BOY.
TRYING TO FIND THE MOTHER*&%#* BEFORE YOU GUYS DO.

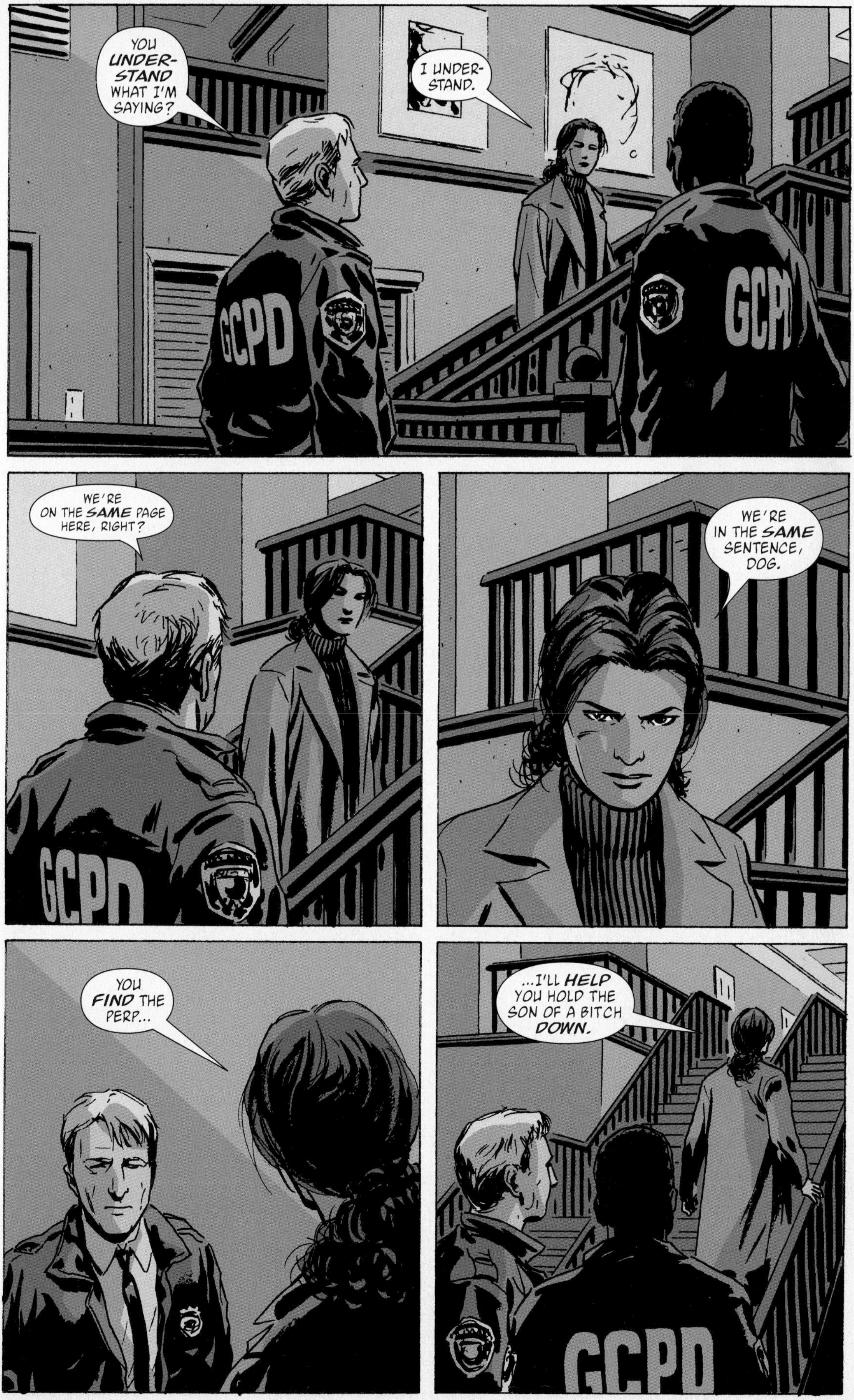

YOU UNDERSTAND WHAT I'M SAYING?
I UNDERSTAND.
WE'RE ON THE SAME PAGE HERE, RIGHT?
WE'RE IN THE SAME SENTENCE, DOG.
YOU FIND THE PERP...
...I'LL HELP YOU HOLD THE SON OF A BITCH DOWN.
GCPD
GCPD
GCPD
GCPD

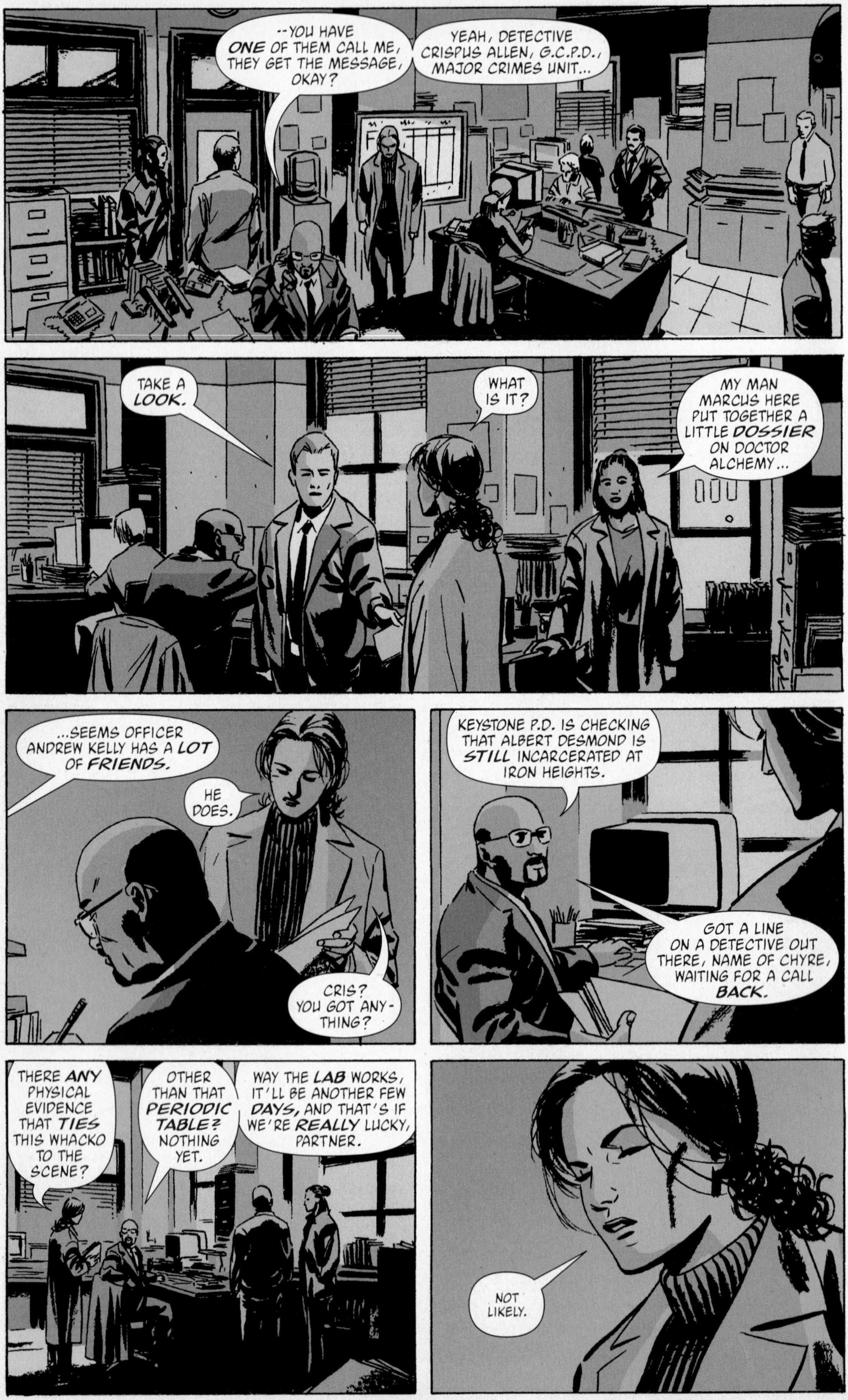
--YOU HAVE ONE OF THEM CALL ME, THEY GET THE MESSAGE, OKAY?
YEAH, DETECTIVE CRISPUS ALLEN, G.C.P.D., MAJOR CRIMES UNIT...
TAKE A LOOK.
WHAT IS IT?
MY MAN MARCUS HERE PUT TOGETHER A LITTLE DOSSIER ON DOCTOR ALCHEMY...
...SEEMS OFFICER ANDREW KELLY HAS A LOT OF FRIENDS.
HE DOES.
CRIS? YOU GOT ANY-THING?
KEYSTONE P.D. IS CHECKING THAT ALBERT DESMOND IS STILL INCARCERATED AT IRON HEIGHTS.
GOT A LINE ON A DETECTIVE OUT THERE, NAME OF CHYRE, WAITING FOR A CALL BACK.
THERE ANY PHYSICAL EVIDENCE THAT TIES THIS WHACKO TO THE SCENE?
OTHER THAN THAT PERIODIC TABLE? NOTHING YET.
WAY THE LAB WORKS, IT'LL BE ANOTHER FEW DAYS, AND THAT'S IF WE'RE REALLY LUCKY, PARTNER.
NOT LIKELY.

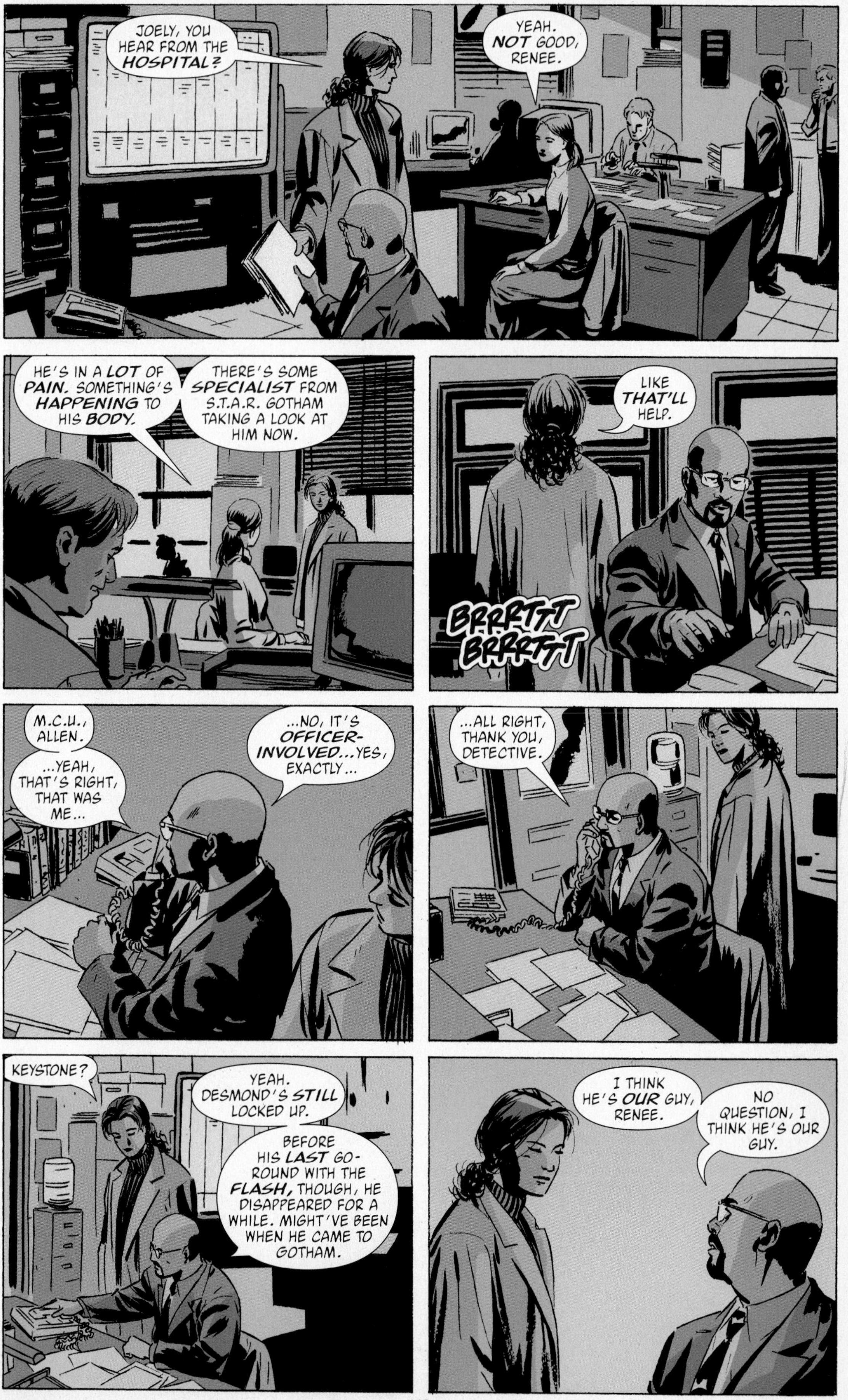
JOELY, YOU HEAR FROM THE HOSPITAL?
YEAH. NOT GOOD, RENEE.
HE'S IN A LOT OF PAIN. SOMETHING'S HAPPENING TO HIS BODY.
THERE'S SOME SPECIALIST FROM S.T.A.R. GOTHAM TAKING A LOOK AT HIM NOW.
LIKE THAT'LL HELP.
BRRRTTT BRRRTTT
M.C.U., ALLEN.
...NO, IT'S OFFICER-INVOLVED...YES, EXACTLY...
...YEAH, THAT'S RIGHT, THAT WAS ME...
...ALL RIGHT, THANK YOU, DETECTIVE.
KEYSTONE?
YEAH. DESMOND'S STILL LOCKED UP.
BEFORE HIS LAST GO-ROUND WITH THE FLASH, THOUGH, HE DISAPPEARED FOR A WHILE. MIGHT'VE BEEN WHEN HE CAME TO GOTHAM.
I THINK HE'S OUR GUY, RENEE.
NO QUESTION, I THINK HE'S OUR GUY.

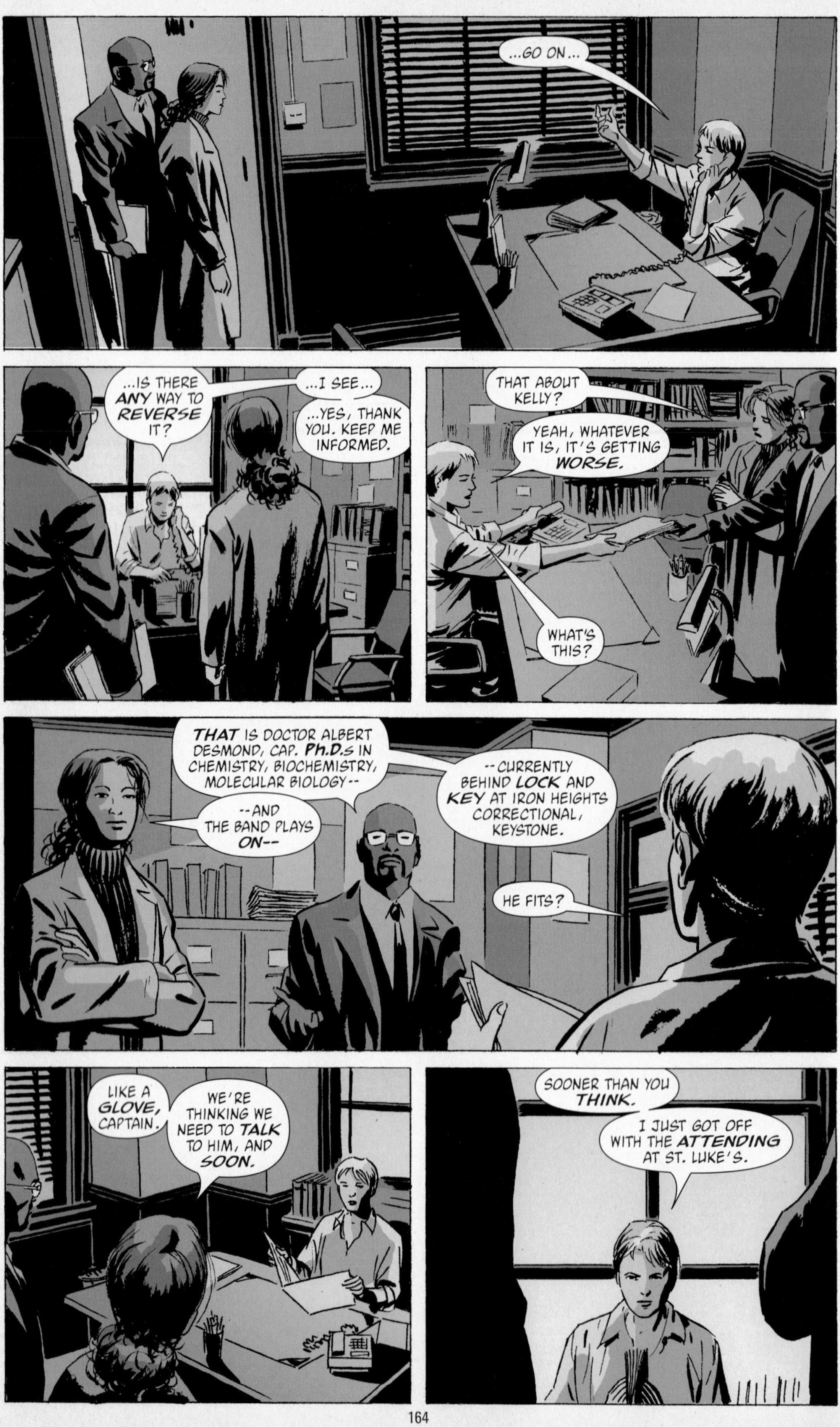
...GO ON...
...I SEE...
...YES, THANK YOU. KEEP ME INFORMED.
...IS THERE ANY WAY TO REVERSE IT?
THAT ABOUT KELLY?
YEAH, WHATEVER IT IS, IT'S GETTING WORSE.
WHAT'S THIS?
THAT IS DOCTOR ALBERT DESMOND, CAP. Ph.D.s IN CHEMISTRY, BIOCHEMISTRY, MOLECULAR BIOLOGY--
--AND THE BAND PLAYS ON--
--CURRENTLY BEHIND LOCK AND KEY AT IRON HEIGHTS CORRECTIONAL, KEYSTONE.
HE FITS?
LIKE A GLOVE, CAPTAIN.
WE'RE THINKING WE NEED TO TALK TO HIM, AND SOON.
SOONER THAN YOU THINK.
I JUST GOT OFF WITH THE ATTENDING AT ST. LUKE'S.

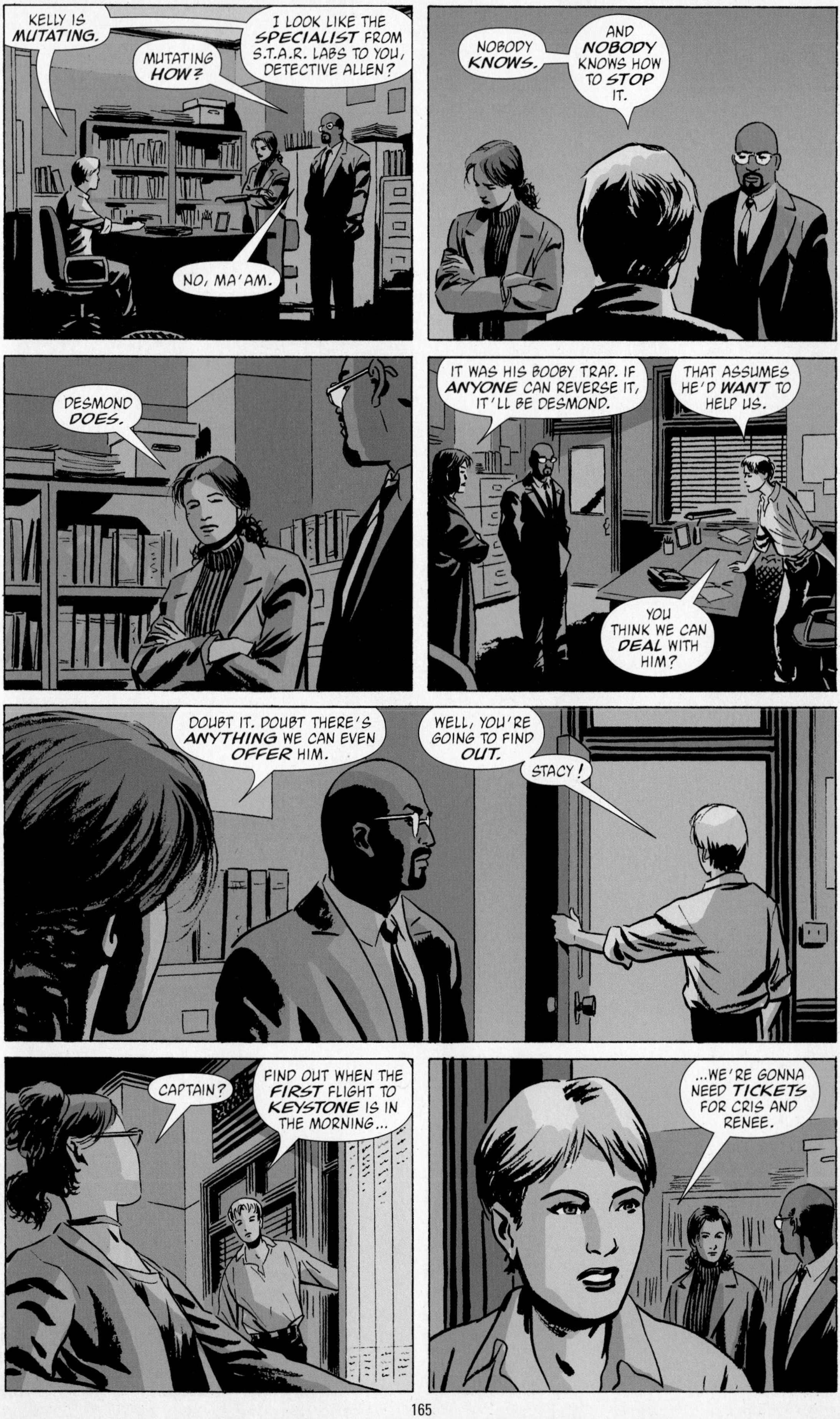
KELLY IS MUTATING.
MUTATING HOW?
I LOOK LIKE THE SPECIALIST FROM S.T.A.R. LABS TO YOU, DETECTIVE ALLEN?
NO, MA'AM.
NOBODY KNOWS.
AND NOBODY KNOWS HOW TO STOP IT.
DESMOND DOES.
IT WAS HIS BOOBY TRAP. IF ANYONE CAN REVERSE IT, IT'LL BE DESMOND.
THAT ASSUMES HE'D WANT TO HELP US.
YOU THINK WE CAN DEAL WITH HIM?
DOUBT IT. DOUBT THERE'S ANYTHING WE CAN EVEN OFFER HIM.
WELL, YOU'RE GOING TO FIND OUT.
STACY!
CAPTAIN?
FIND OUT WHEN THE FIRST FLIGHT TO KEYSTONE IS IN THE MORNING...
...WE'RE GONNA NEED TICKETS FOR CRIS AND RENEE.

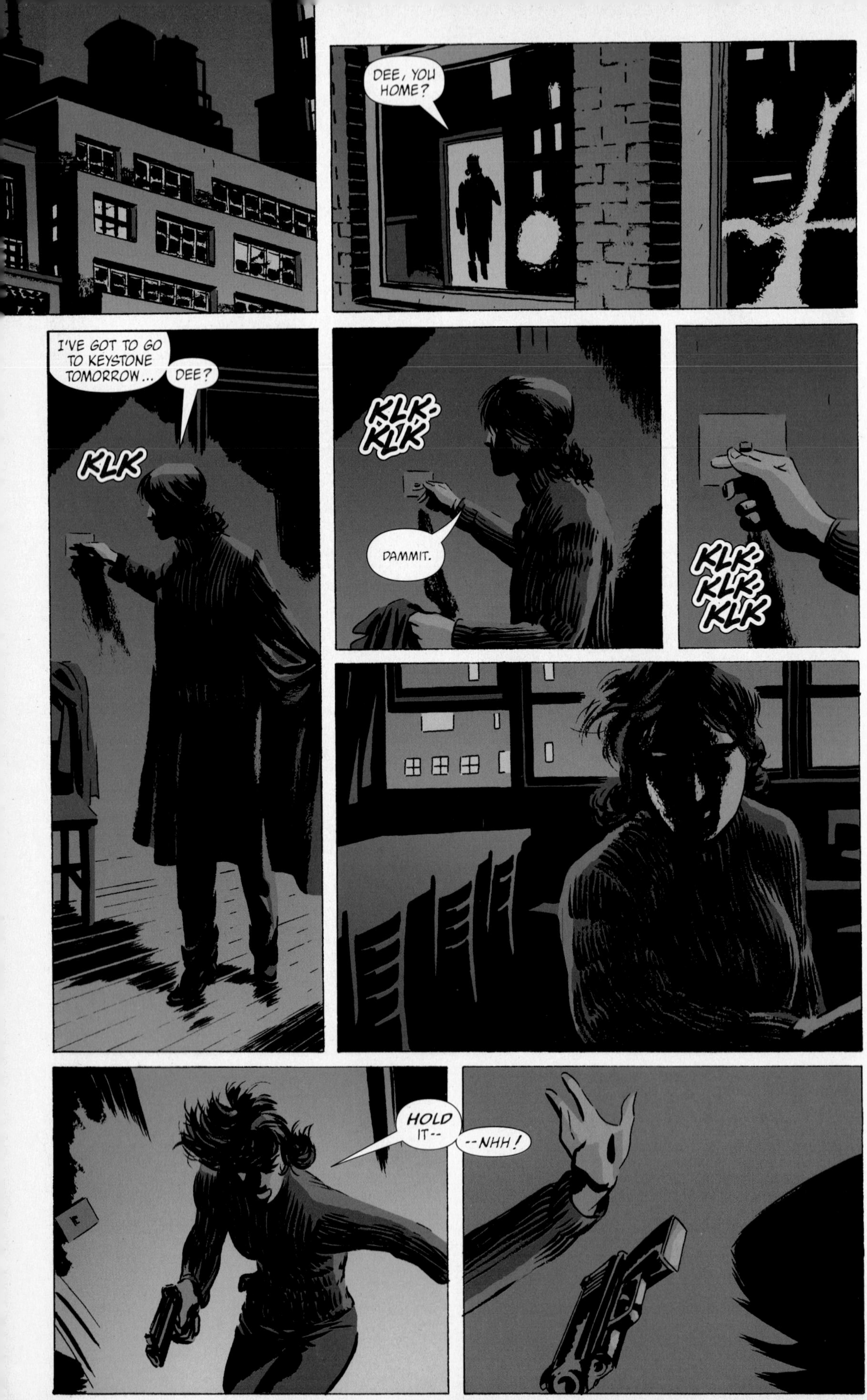

DEE, YOU HOME?
I'VE GOT TO GO TO KEYSTONE TOMORROW...
DEE?
KLK
KLK-KLK
DAMMIT.
KLK-KLK-KLK
HOLD IT--
--NHH!

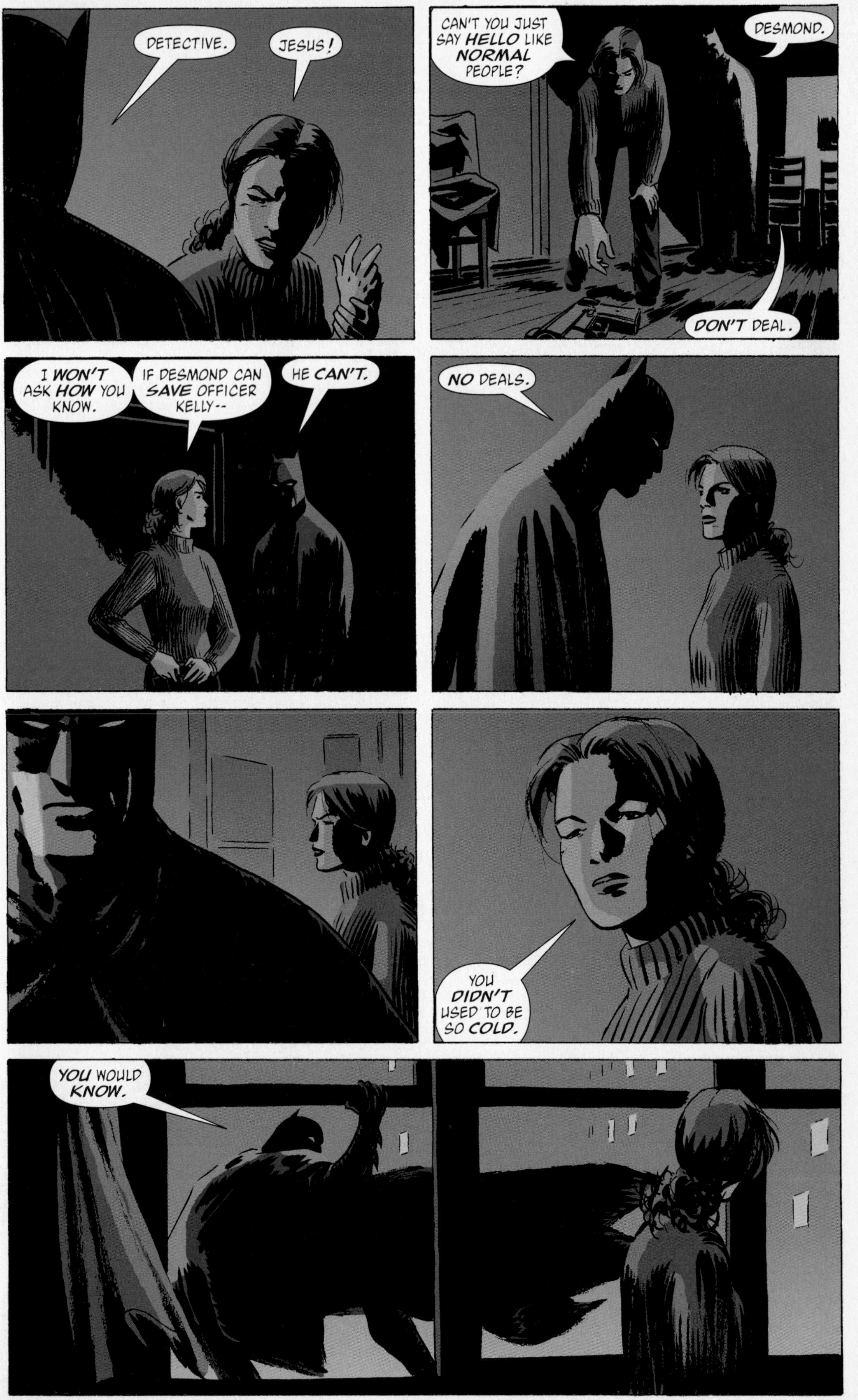

DETECTIVE.
JESUS!
CAN'T YOU JUST SAY HELLO LIKE NORMAL PEOPLE?
DESMOND.
DON'T DEAL.
I WON'T ASK HOW YOU KNOW.
IF DESMOND CAN SAVE OFFICER KELLY--
HE CAN'T.
NO DEALS.
YOU DIDN'T USED TO BE SO COLD.
YOU WOULD KNOW.

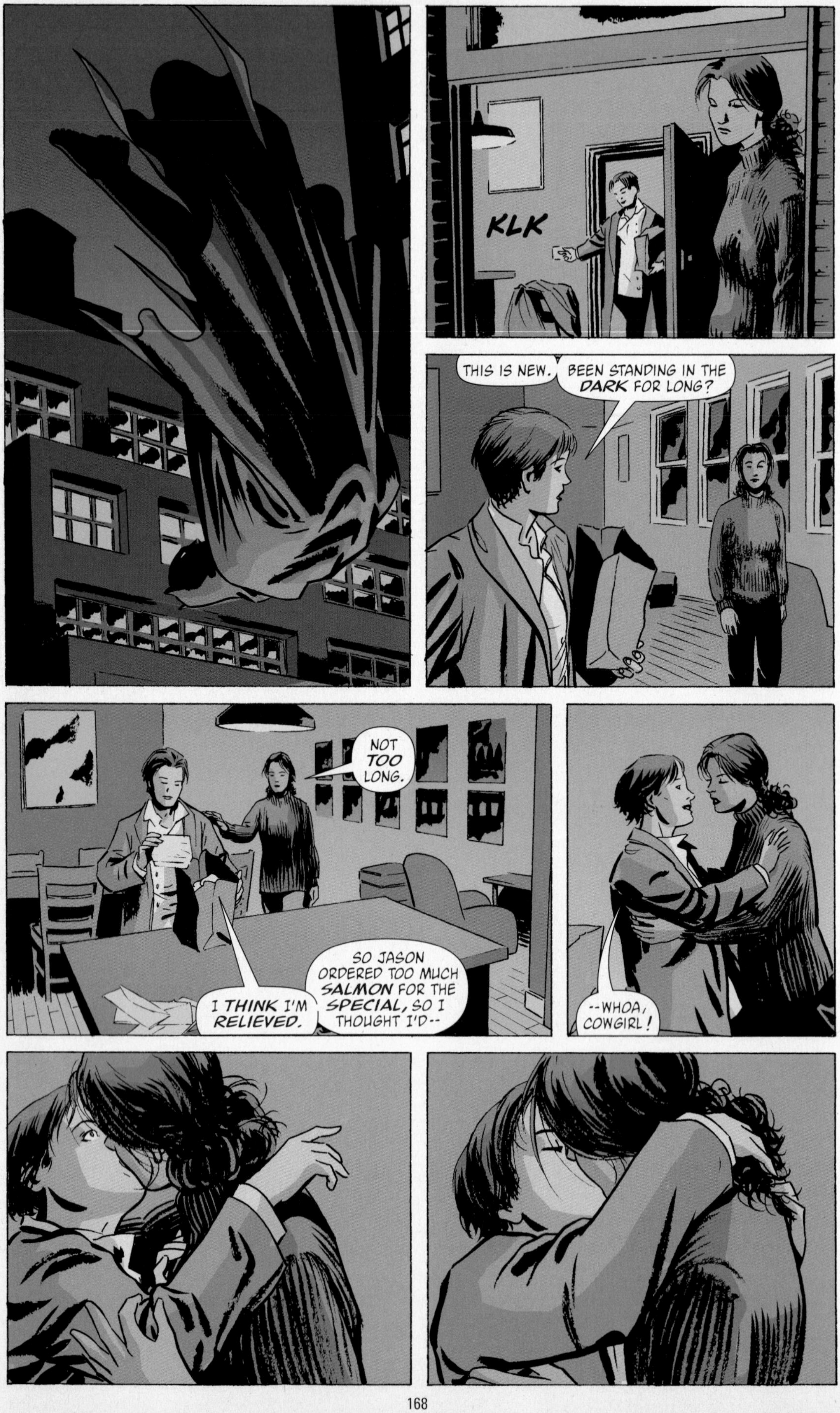
KLK
THIS IS NEW.
BEEN STANDING IN THE DARK FOR LONG?
NOT TOO LONG.
I THINK I'M RELIEVED.
SO JASON ORDERED TOO MUCH SALMON FOR THE SPECIAL, SO I THOUGHT I'D--
--WHOA, COWGIRL!

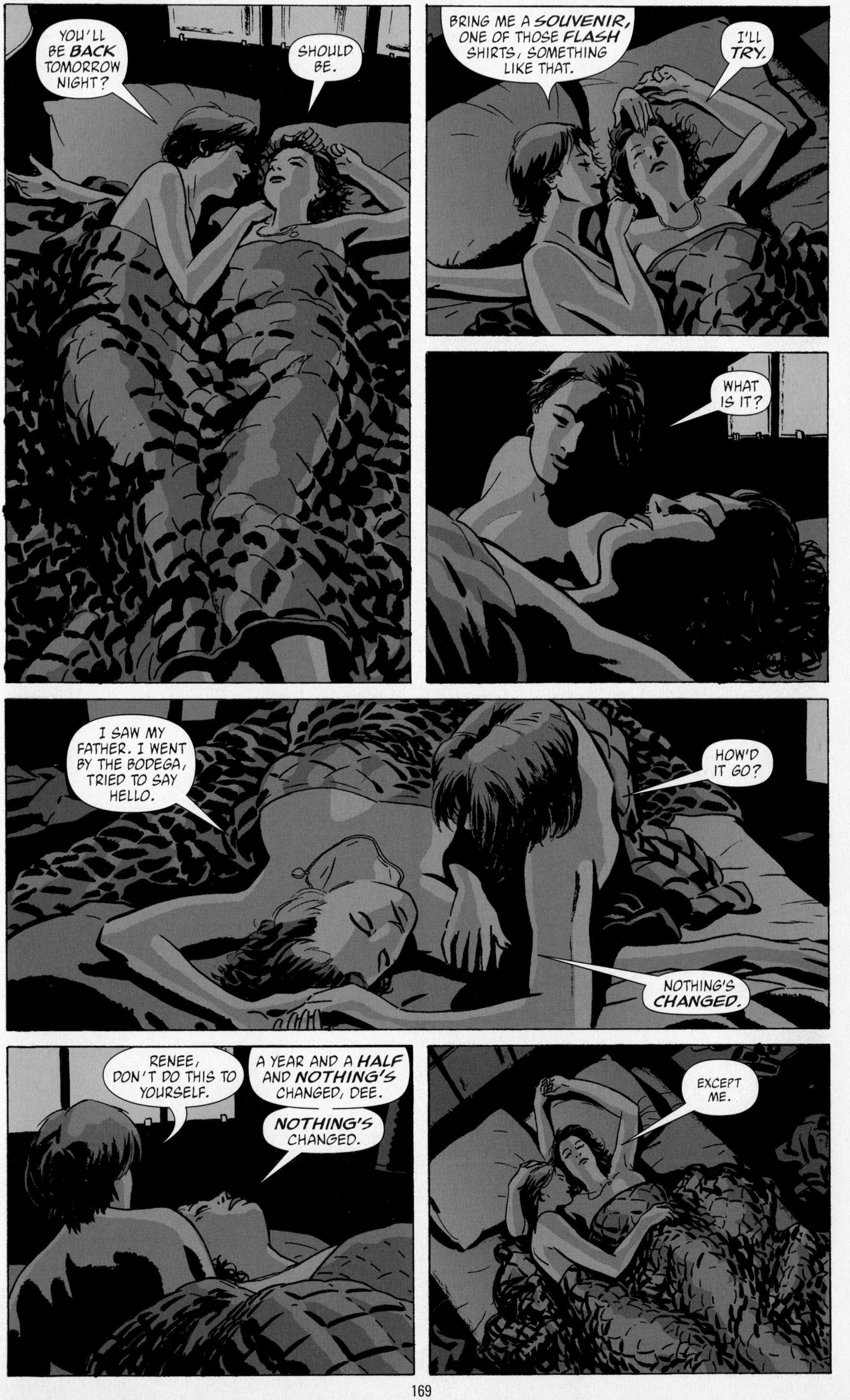
YOU'LL BE BACK TOMORROW NIGHT?
SHOULD BE.
BRING ME A SOUVENIR, ONE OF THOSE FLASH SHIRTS, SOMETHING LIKE THAT.
I'LL TRY.
WHAT IS IT?
I SAW MY FATHER. I WENT BY THE BODEGA, TRIED TO SAY HELLO.
HOW'D IT GO?
NOTHING'S CHANGED.
RENEE, DON'T DO THIS TO YOURSELF.
A YEAR AND A HALF AND NOTHING'S CHANGED, DEE.
NOTHING'S CHANGED.
EXCEPT ME.

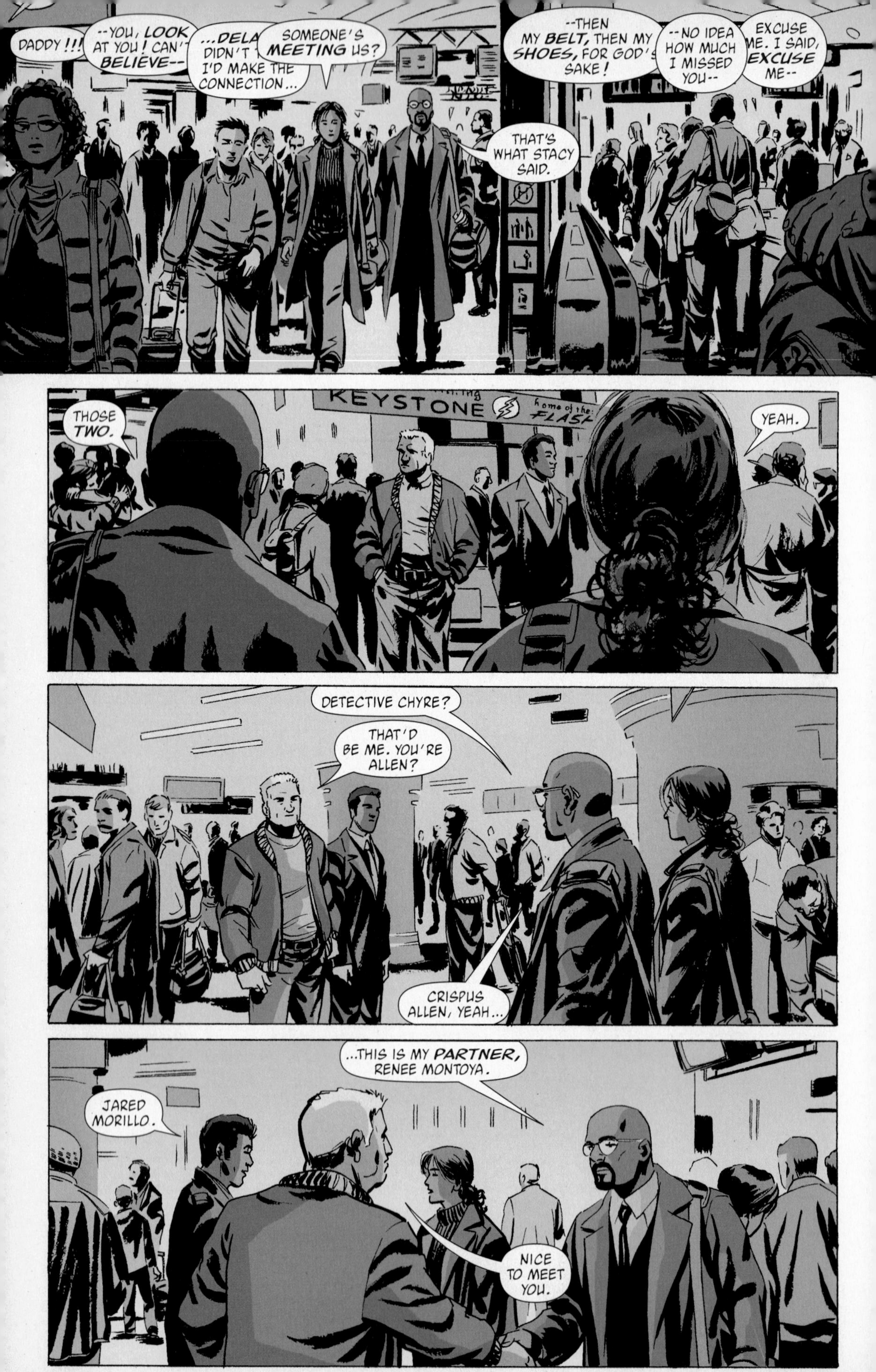
DADDY!!!
--YOU, LOOK AT YOU! CAN'T BELIEVE--
...DELA DIDN'T I'D MAKE THE CONNECTION...
SOMEONE'S MEETING US?
THAT'S WHAT STACY SAID.
--THEN MY BELT, THEN MY SHOES, FOR GOD'S SAKE!
--NO IDEA HOW MUCH I MISSED YOU--
EXCUSE ME. I SAID, EXCUSE ME--
KEYSTONE
home of the FLASH
THOSE TWO.
YEAH.
DETECTIVE CHYRE?
THAT'D BE ME. YOU'RE ALLEN?
CRISPUS ALLEN, YEAH...
...THIS IS MY PARTNER, RENEE MONTOYA.
JARED MORILLO.
NICE TO MEET YOU.

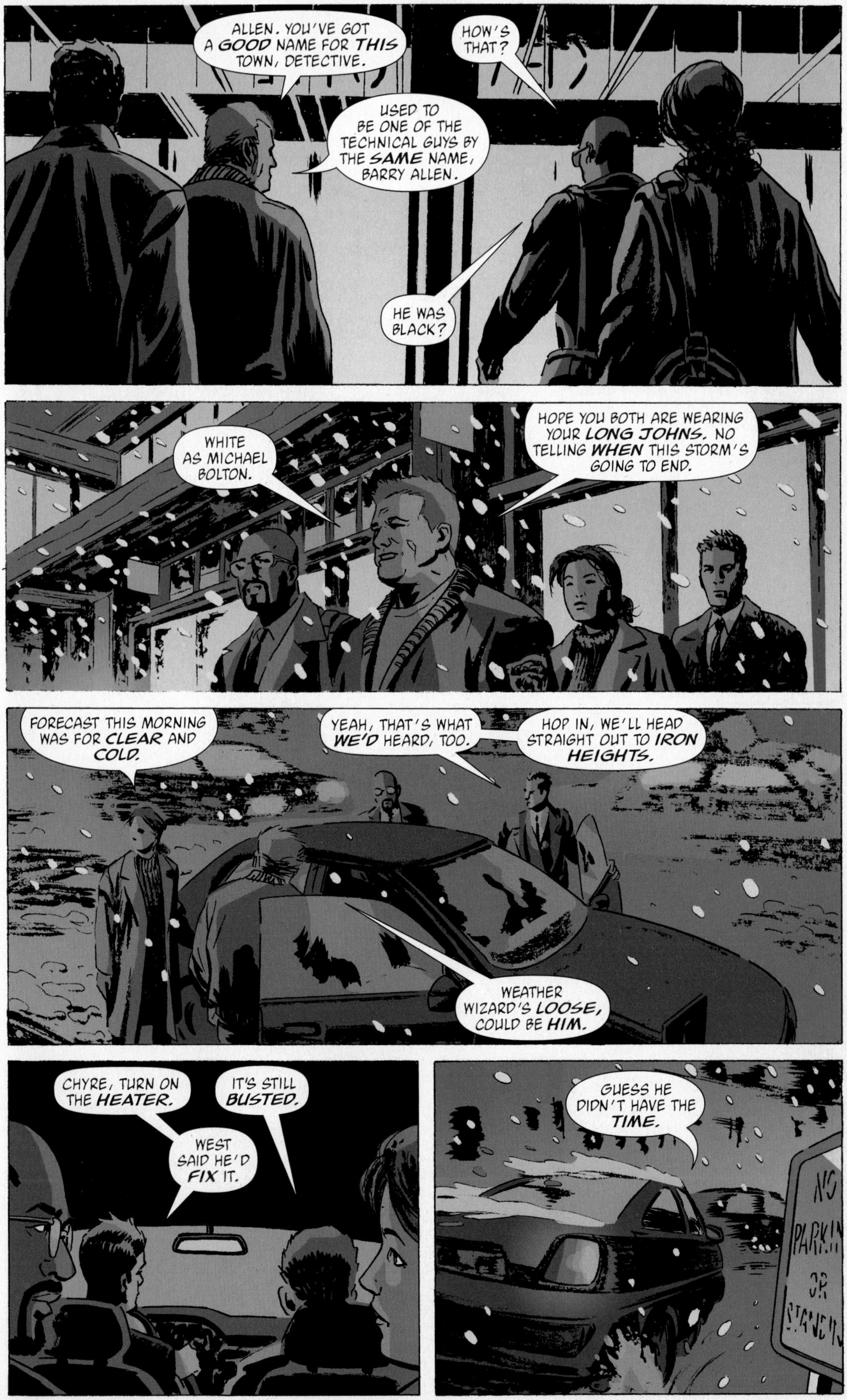
ALLEN. YOU'VE GOT A GOOD NAME FOR THIS TOWN, DETECTIVE.
HOW'S THAT?
USED TO BE ONE OF THE TECHNICAL GUYS BY THE SAME NAME, BARRY ALLEN.
HE WAS BLACK?
WHITE AS MICHAEL BOLTON.
HOPE YOU BOTH ARE WEARING YOUR LONG JOHNS. NO TELLING WHEN THIS STORM'S GOING TO END.
FORECAST THIS MORNING WAS FOR CLEAR AND COLD.
YEAH, THAT'S WHAT WE'D HEARD, TOO.
HOP IN, WE'LL HEAD STRAIGHT OUT TO IRON HEIGHTS.
WEATHER WIZARD'S LOOSE, COULD BE HIM.
CHYRE, TURN ON THE HEATER.
IT'S STILL BUSTED.
WEST SAID HE'D FIX IT.
GUESS HE DIDN'T HAVE THE TIME.

YOU HEARD FROM OUR **CAPTAIN?**

THE D.A.s ARE **TALKING.** I THINK IT'S A **BAD** IDEA, THOUGH, CUTTING A **DEAL** WITH HIM.

DESMOND'S ONE OF THE **SMARTEST** OF THE ROGUES. NUTS, BUT **BRILLIANT.**

"ROGUES"?

YEAH, THEY'RE A GROUP OF **METAS,** WORK TOGETHER TO MAKE **OUR** LIVES **MISERABLE.**

CHRIST, THEY'VE **UNIONIZED?**

YOUR GUYS DON'T DO THAT?

GUNS AND SHIELDS, KIDS.

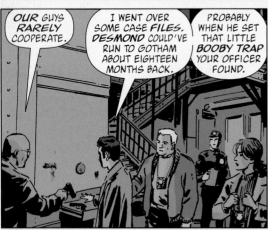

OUR GUYS **RARELY** COOPERATE.

I WENT OVER SOME CASE **FILES. DESMOND** COULD'VE RUN TO GOTHAM ABOUT EIGHTEEN MONTHS BACK.

PROBABLY WHEN HE SET THAT LITTLE **BOOBY TRAP** YOUR OFFICER FOUND.

DOCTOR ZOLOMON IS WAITING FOR YOU INSIDE.

THANKS, GEOFF.

ALL RIGHT, WE'RE GOOD. IT'S **THIS** WAY--

GIMME A SECOND.

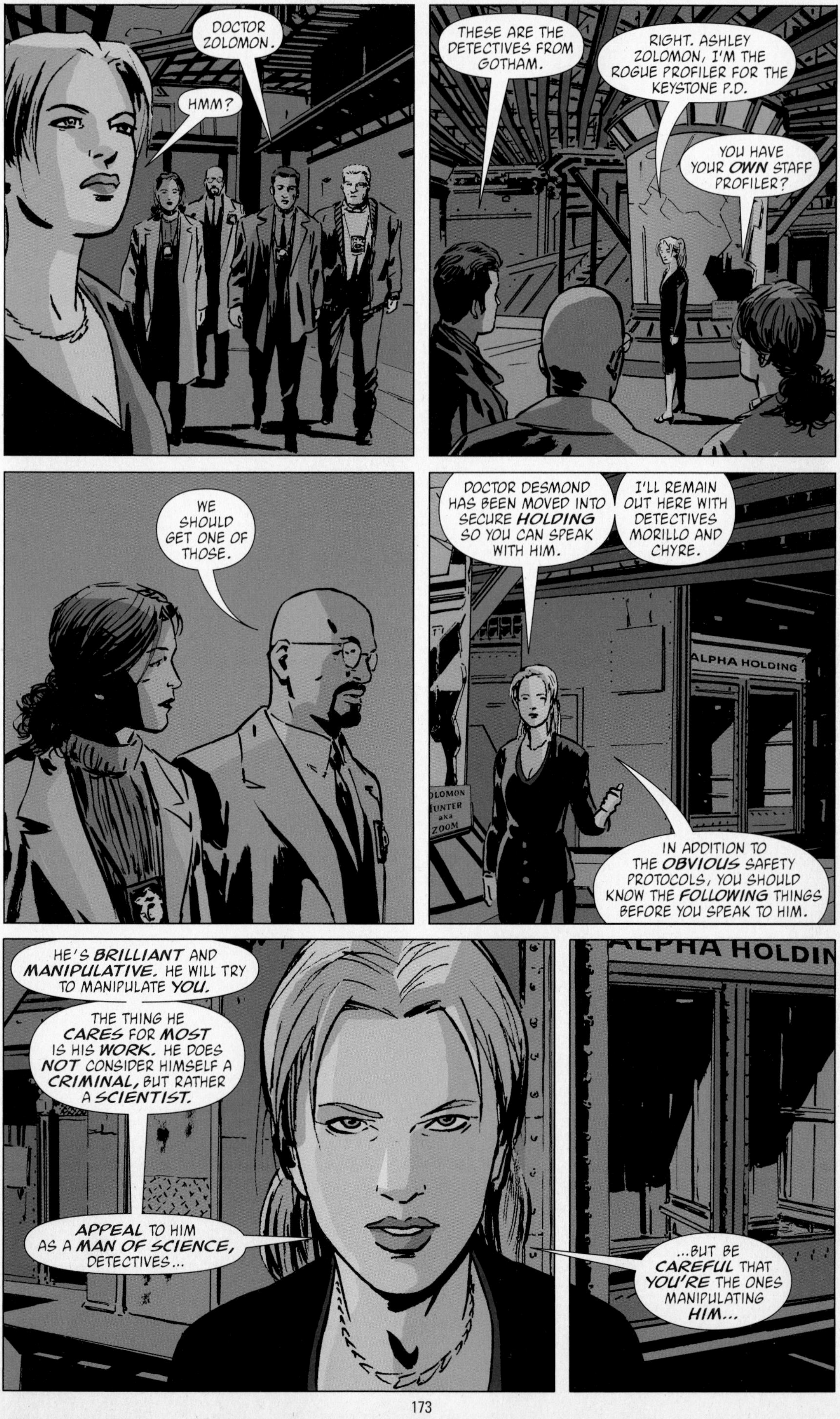
DOCTOR ZOLOMON.
HMM?
THESE ARE THE DETECTIVES FROM GOTHAM.
RIGHT. ASHLEY ZOLOMON, I'M THE ROGUE PROFILER FOR THE KEYSTONE P.D.
YOU HAVE YOUR OWN STAFF PROFILER?
WE SHOULD GET ONE OF THOSE.
DOCTOR DESMOND HAS BEEN MOVED INTO SECURE HOLDING SO YOU CAN SPEAK WITH HIM.
I'LL REMAIN OUT HERE WITH DETECTIVES MORILLO AND CHYRE.
ALPHA HOLDING
IN ADDITION TO THE OBVIOUS SAFETY PROTOCOLS, YOU SHOULD KNOW THE FOLLOWING THINGS BEFORE YOU SPEAK TO HIM.
HE'S BRILLIANT AND MANIPULATIVE. HE WILL TRY TO MANIPULATE YOU.
THE THING HE CARES FOR MOST IS HIS WORK. HE DOES NOT CONSIDER HIMSELF A CRIMINAL, BUT RATHER A SCIENTIST.
APPEAL TO HIM AS A MAN OF SCIENCE, DETECTIVES...
...BUT BE CAREFUL THAT YOU'RE THE ONES MANIPULATING HIM...

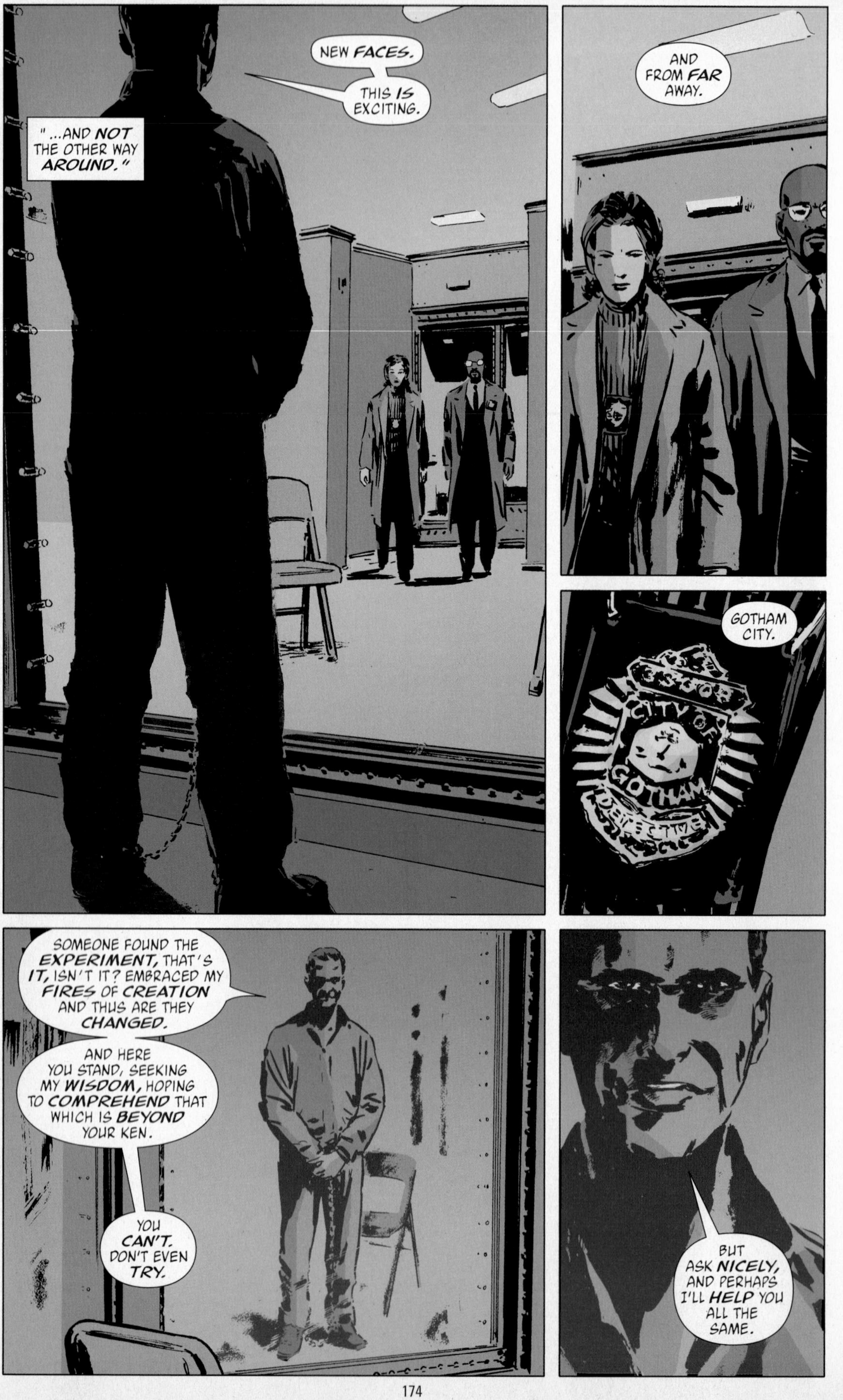
"...AND NOT THE OTHER WAY AROUND."
NEW FACES.
THIS IS EXCITING.
AND FROM FAR AWAY.
GOTHAM CITY.
SOMEONE FOUND THE EXPERIMENT, THAT'S IT, ISN'T IT? EMBRACED MY FIRES OF CREATION AND THUS ARE THEY CHANGED.
AND HERE YOU STAND, SEEKING MY WISDOM, HOPING TO COMPREHEND THAT WHICH IS BEYOND YOUR KEN.
YOU CAN'T. DON'T EVEN TRY.
BUT ASK NICELY, AND PERHAPS I'LL HELP YOU ALL THE SAME.

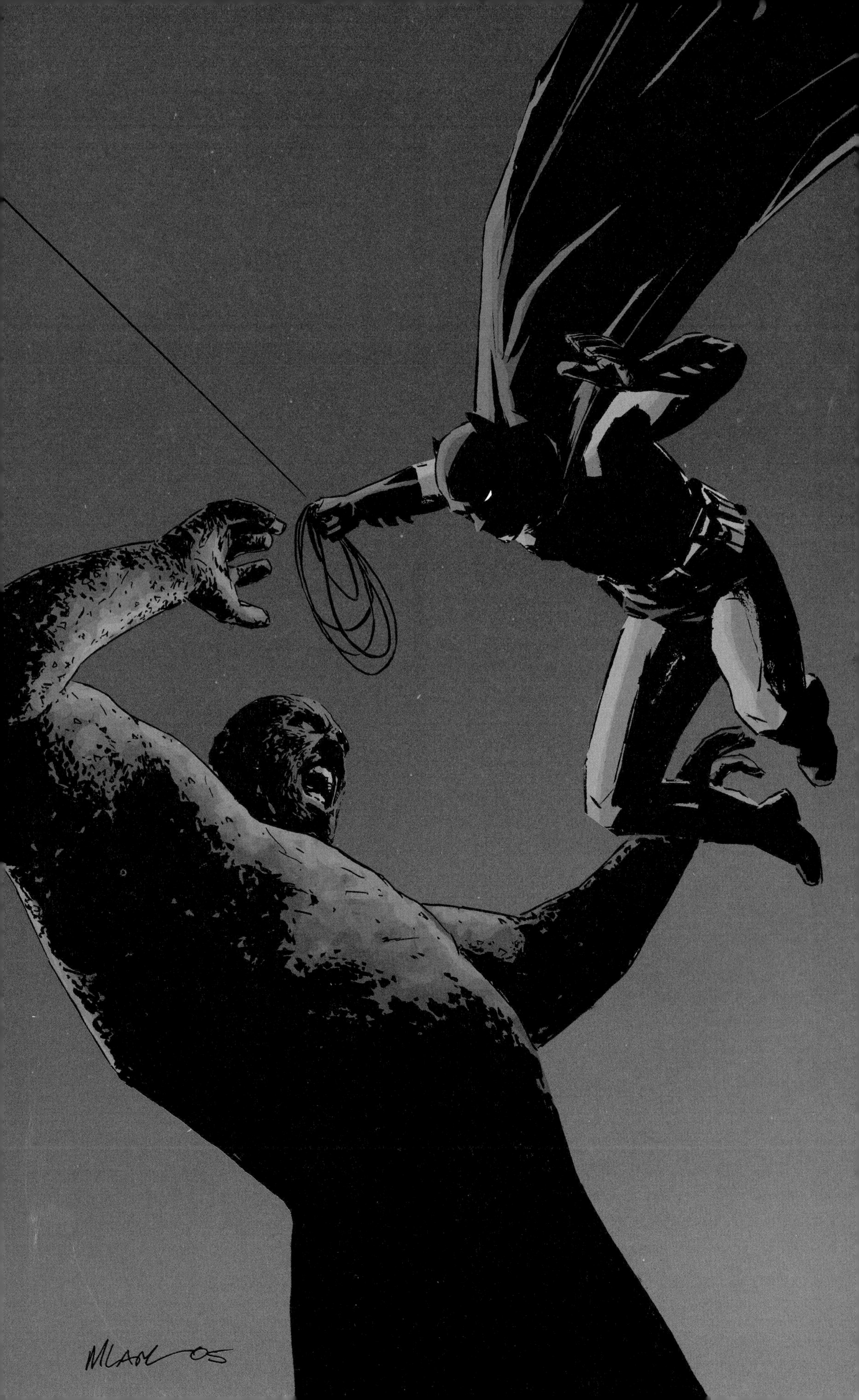

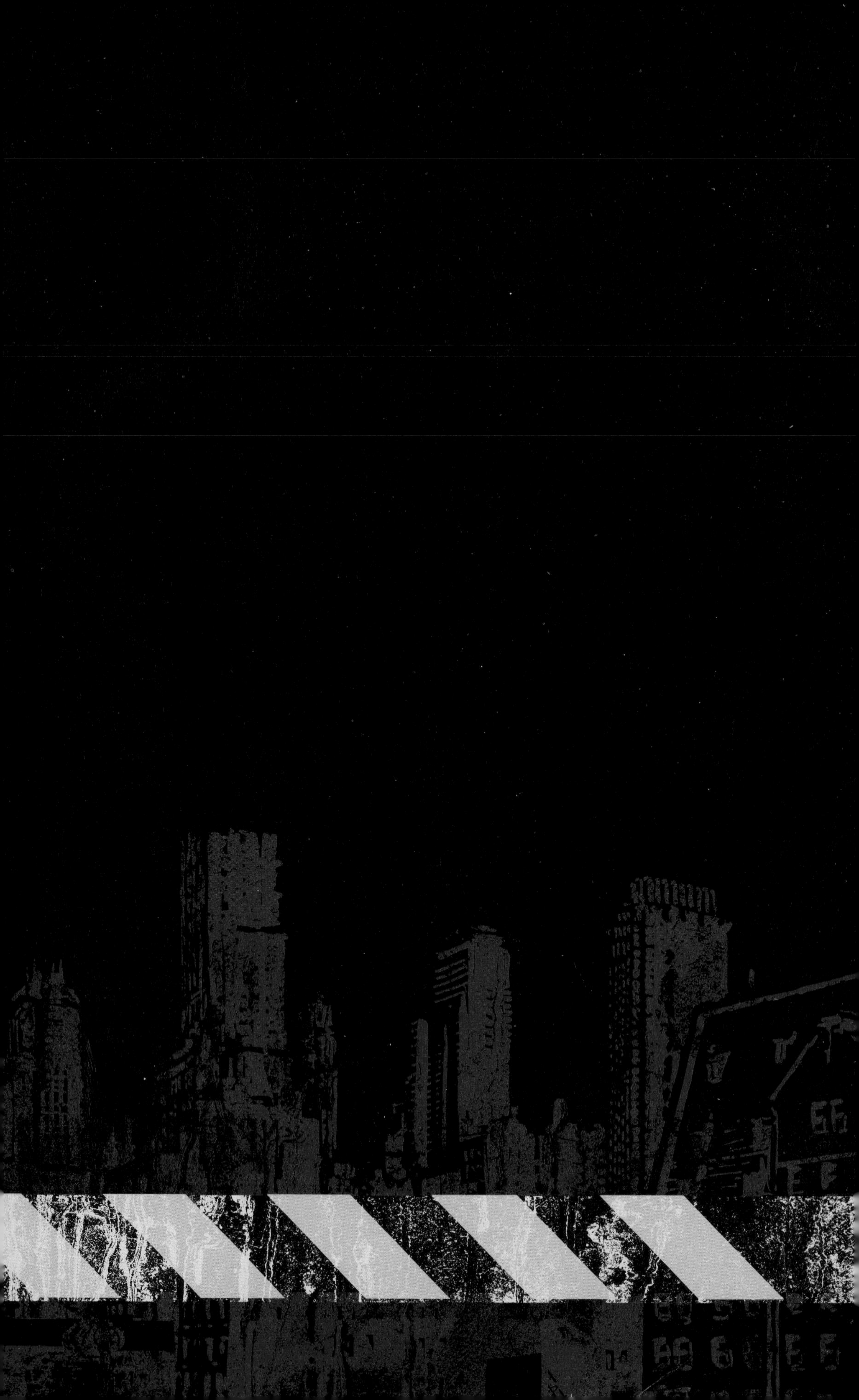

DOCTOR DESMOND, MY NAME'S DETECTIVE ALLEN. THIS IS MY *PARTNER* DETECTIVE MONTOYA.

THINK YOU CAN *ANSWER* A FEW *QUESTIONS* FOR US?

QUID PRO *QUO*, DETECTIVE ALLEN...

...OR FOR THOSE OF YOU *WEAK* WITH THE *LATIN*, "SOMETHING FOR SOMETHING."

TWO DETECTIVES COME *ALL* THE WAY FROM *GOTHAM* TO MINE MY *GRAY MATTER*, WHAT DO I GET IN *RETURN*?

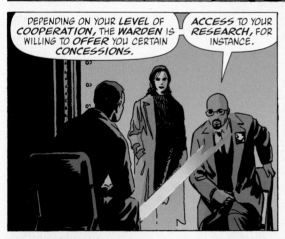

DEPENDING ON YOUR *LEVEL OF COOPERATION*, THE *WARDEN* IS WILLING TO *OFFER* YOU CERTAIN *CONCESSIONS*.

ACCESS TO YOUR *RESEARCH*, FOR INSTANCE.

VERY GOOD, DETECTIVE ALLEN. NO *HINT* OF *HESITATION*.

BUT WE *BOTH* KNOW THAT YOU'RE *LYING* TO ME. WARDEN WOLFE WOULD NEVER ALLOW FOR SUCH AN *ARRANGEMENT*.

TRY *AGAIN*.

LET'S *HEAR* WHAT YOU'VE *GOT*.

THEN WE'LL DECIDE WHAT IT'S *WORTH* TO US.

‹TSK TSK TSK›

DETECTIVE MONTOYA, *REALLY*. YOU KNOW HOW TO PLAY *BAD COP* BETTER THAN *THAT*.

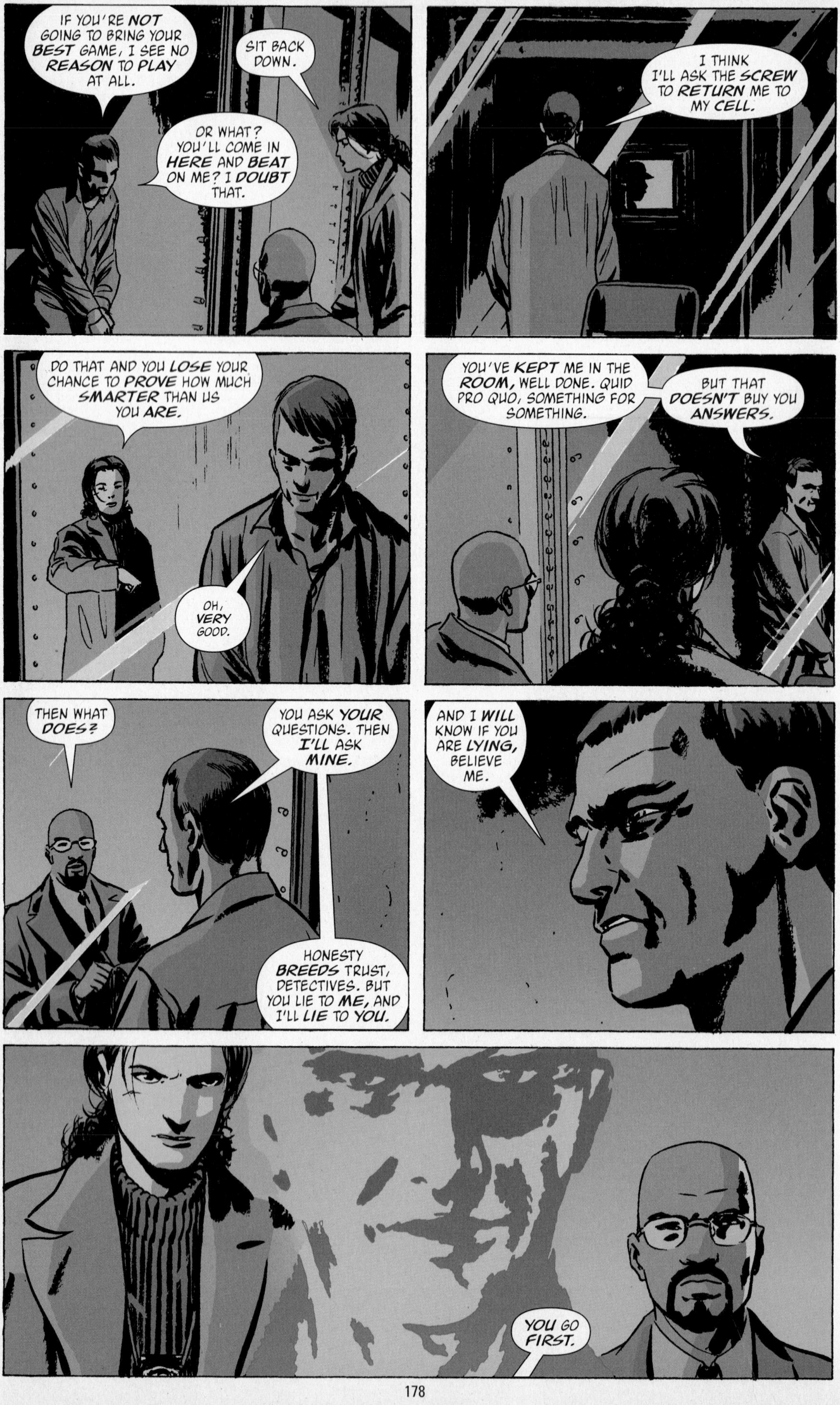
IF YOU'RE NOT GOING TO BRING YOUR BEST GAME, I SEE NO REASON TO PLAY AT ALL.
SIT BACK DOWN.
OR WHAT? YOU'LL COME IN HERE AND BEAT ON ME? I DOUBT THAT.
I THINK I'LL ASK THE SCREW TO RETURN ME TO MY CELL.
DO THAT AND YOU LOSE YOUR CHANCE TO PROVE HOW MUCH SMARTER THAN US YOU ARE.
OH, VERY GOOD.
YOU'VE KEPT ME IN THE ROOM, WELL DONE. QUID PRO QUO, SOMETHING FOR SOMETHING.
BUT THAT DOESN'T BUY YOU ANSWERS.
THEN WHAT DOES?
YOU ASK YOUR QUESTIONS. THEN I'LL ASK MINE.
HONESTY BREEDS TRUST, DETECTIVES. BUT YOU LIE TO ME, AND I'LL LIE TO YOU.
AND I WILL KNOW IF YOU ARE LYING, BELIEVE ME.
YOU GO FIRST.

...AS OF SIX HOURS AGO, THE *MUTATION* SEEMS TO HAVE *STABILIZED.*

GOTHAM CITY, ST. LUKE'S HOSPITAL.

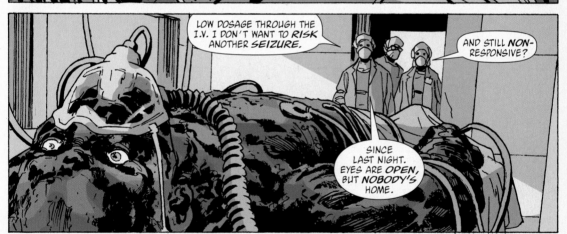

WHETHER THAT'S A *RESULT* OF MOVING OFFICER KELLY INTO THE *CLEAN ROOM* OR SOMETHING ELSE, WE CAN'T TELL.

HE'S STILL ON DIAZEPAM?

LOW DOSAGE THROUGH THE I.V. I DON'T WANT TO RISK ANOTHER *SEIZURE.*

AND STILL *NON-*RESPONSIVE?

SINCE LAST NIGHT. EYES ARE *OPEN,* BUT *NOBODY'S* HOME.

WHO'RE *THEY?* FAMILY?

SHE'S KELLY'S *GIRLFRIEND.* THE OTHER ONE IS HIS *PARTNER.*

THEY'RE *NOT* GOING TO WANT TO *WATCH* THIS.

CLOSE THE *BLINDS,* PLEASE.

YES, DOCTOR.

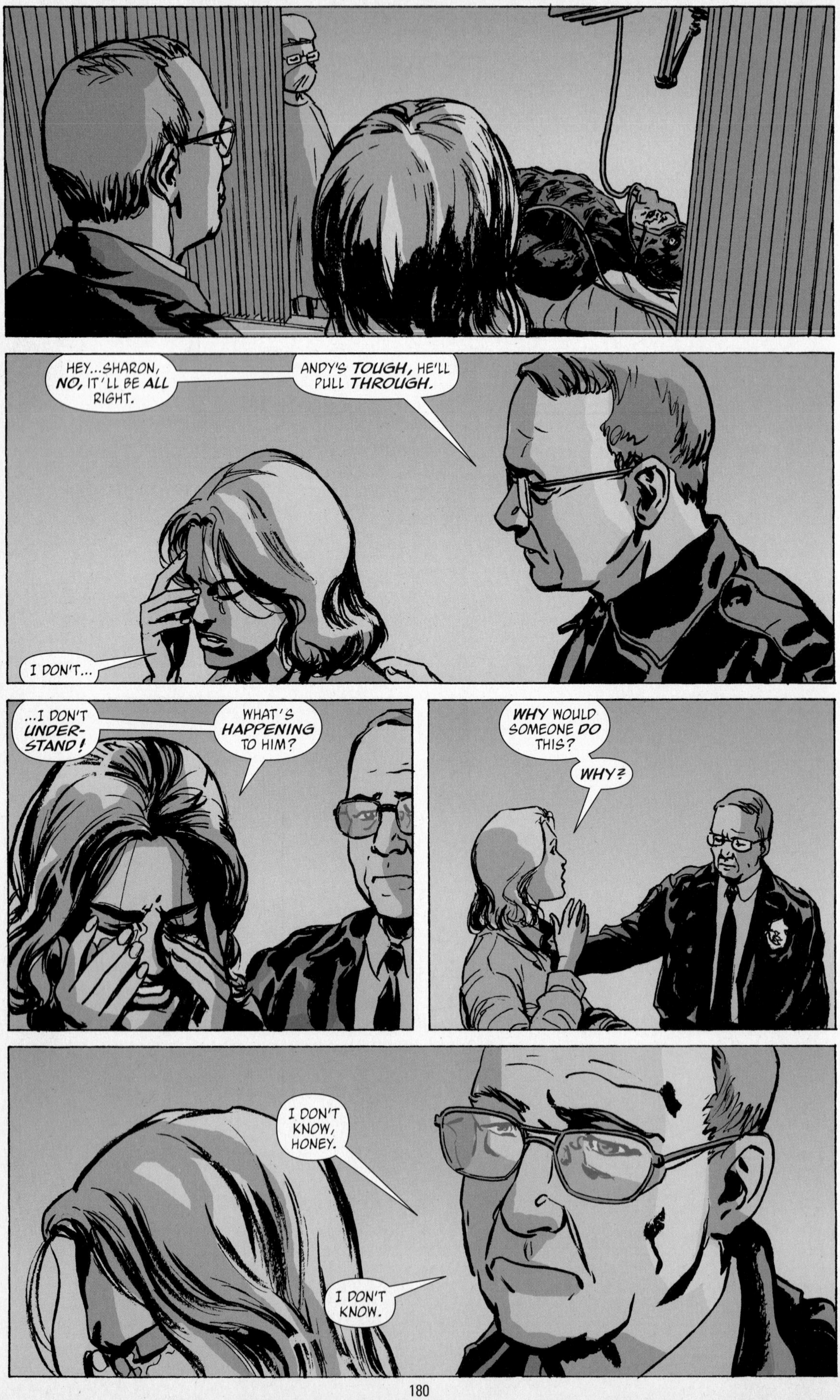
HEY...SHARON, NO, IT'LL BE ALL RIGHT.
ANDY'S TOUGH, HE'LL PULL THROUGH.
I DON'T...
...I DON'T UNDER-STAND!
WHAT'S HAPPENING TO HIM?
WHY WOULD SOMEONE DO THIS?
WHY?
I DON'T KNOW, HONEY.
I DON'T KNOW.

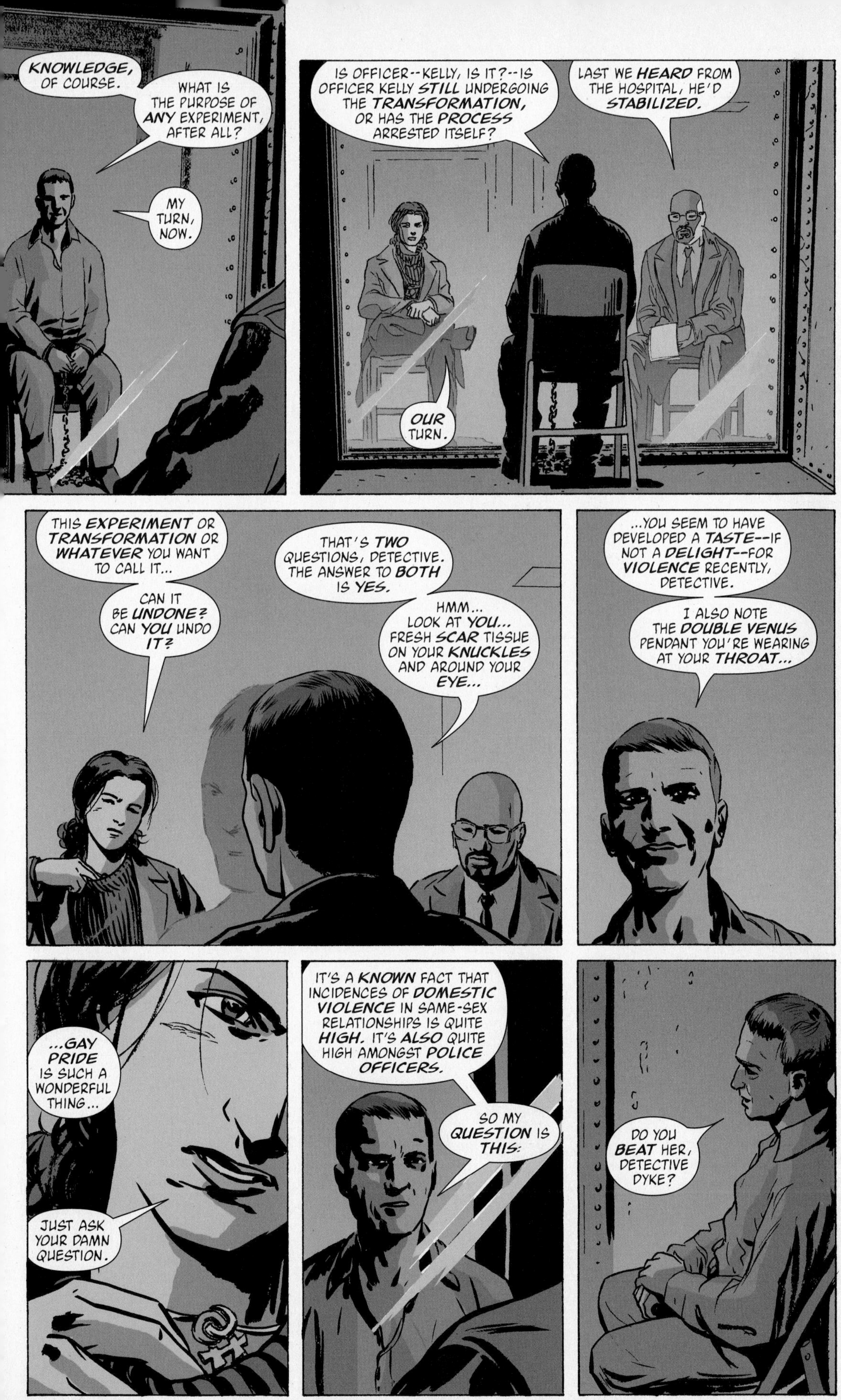
KNOWLEDGE, OF COURSE.
WHAT IS THE PURPOSE OF ANY EXPERIMENT, AFTER ALL?
MY TURN, NOW.
IS OFFICER--KELLY, IS IT?--IS OFFICER KELLY STILL UNDERGOING THE TRANSFORMATION, OR HAS THE PROCESS ARRESTED ITSELF?
LAST WE HEARD FROM THE HOSPITAL, HE'D STABILIZED.
OUR TURN.
THIS EXPERIMENT OR TRANSFORMATION OR WHATEVER YOU WANT TO CALL IT...
CAN IT BE UNDONE? CAN YOU UNDO IT?
THAT'S TWO QUESTIONS, DETECTIVE. THE ANSWER TO BOTH IS YES.
HMM... LOOK AT YOU... FRESH SCAR TISSUE ON YOUR KNUCKLES AND AROUND YOUR EYE...
...YOU SEEM TO HAVE DEVELOPED A TASTE--IF NOT A DELIGHT--FOR VIOLENCE RECENTLY, DETECTIVE.
I ALSO NOTE THE DOUBLE VENUS PENDANT YOU'RE WEARING AT YOUR THROAT...
...GAY PRIDE IS SUCH A WONDERFUL THING...
JUST ASK YOUR DAMN QUESTION.
IT'S A KNOWN FACT THAT INCIDENCES OF DOMESTIC VIOLENCE IN SAME-SEX RELATIONSHIPS IS QUITE HIGH. IT'S ALSO QUITE HIGH AMONGST POLICE OFFICERS.
SO MY QUESTION IS THIS:
DO YOU BEAT HER, DETECTIVE DYKE?

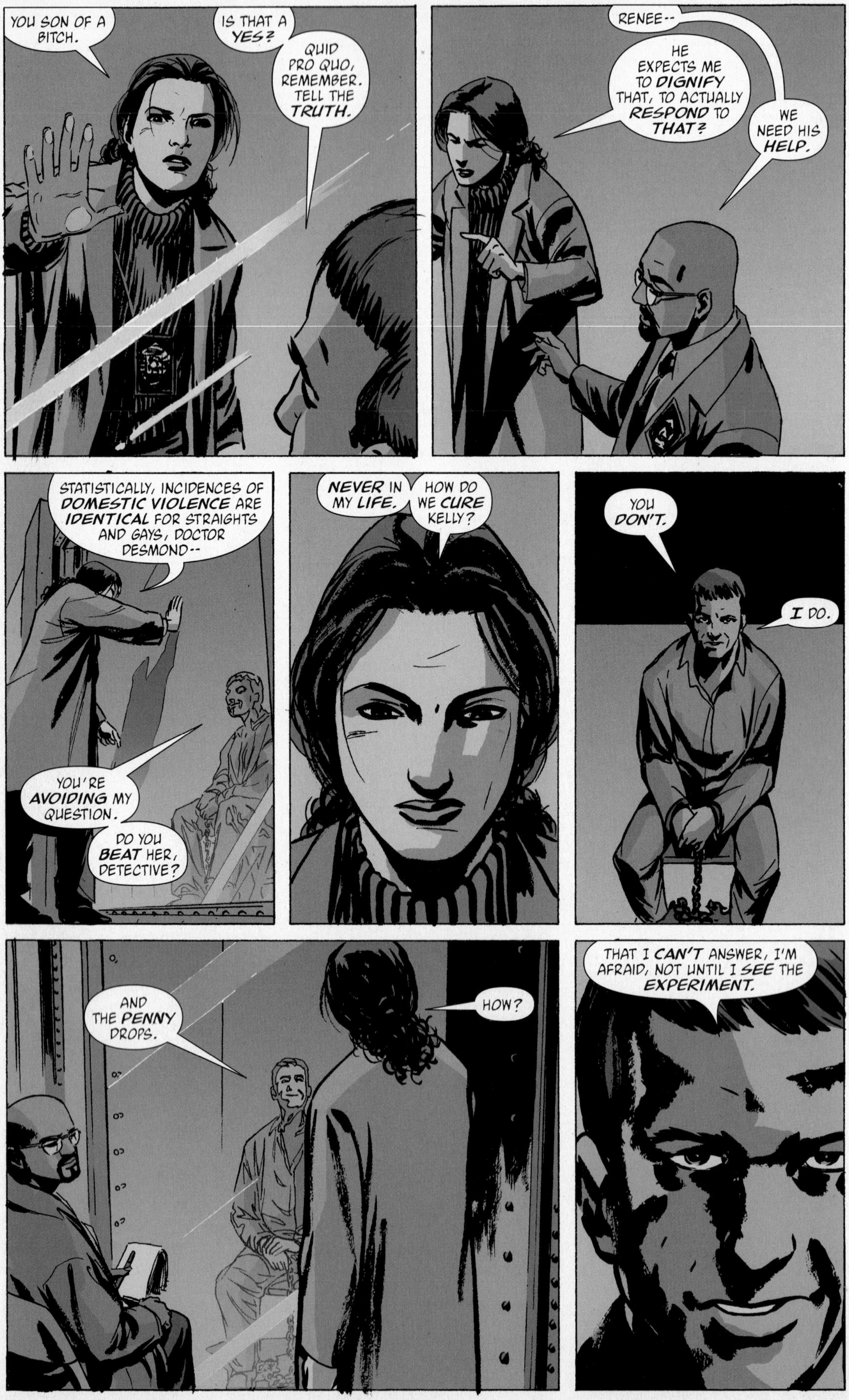
YOU SON OF A BITCH.
IS THAT A YES?
QUID PRO QUO, REMEMBER. TELL THE TRUTH.
RENEE--
HE EXPECTS ME TO DIGNIFY THAT, TO ACTUALLY RESPOND TO THAT?
WE NEED HIS HELP.
STATISTICALLY, INCIDENCES OF DOMESTIC VIOLENCE ARE IDENTICAL FOR STRAIGHTS AND GAYS, DOCTOR DESMOND--
YOU'RE AVOIDING MY QUESTION.
DO YOU BEAT HER, DETECTIVE?
NEVER IN MY LIFE.
HOW DO WE CURE KELLY?
YOU DON'T.
I DO.
AND THE PENNY DROPS.
HOW?
THAT I CAN'T ANSWER, I'M AFRAID, NOT UNTIL I SEE THE EXPERIMENT.

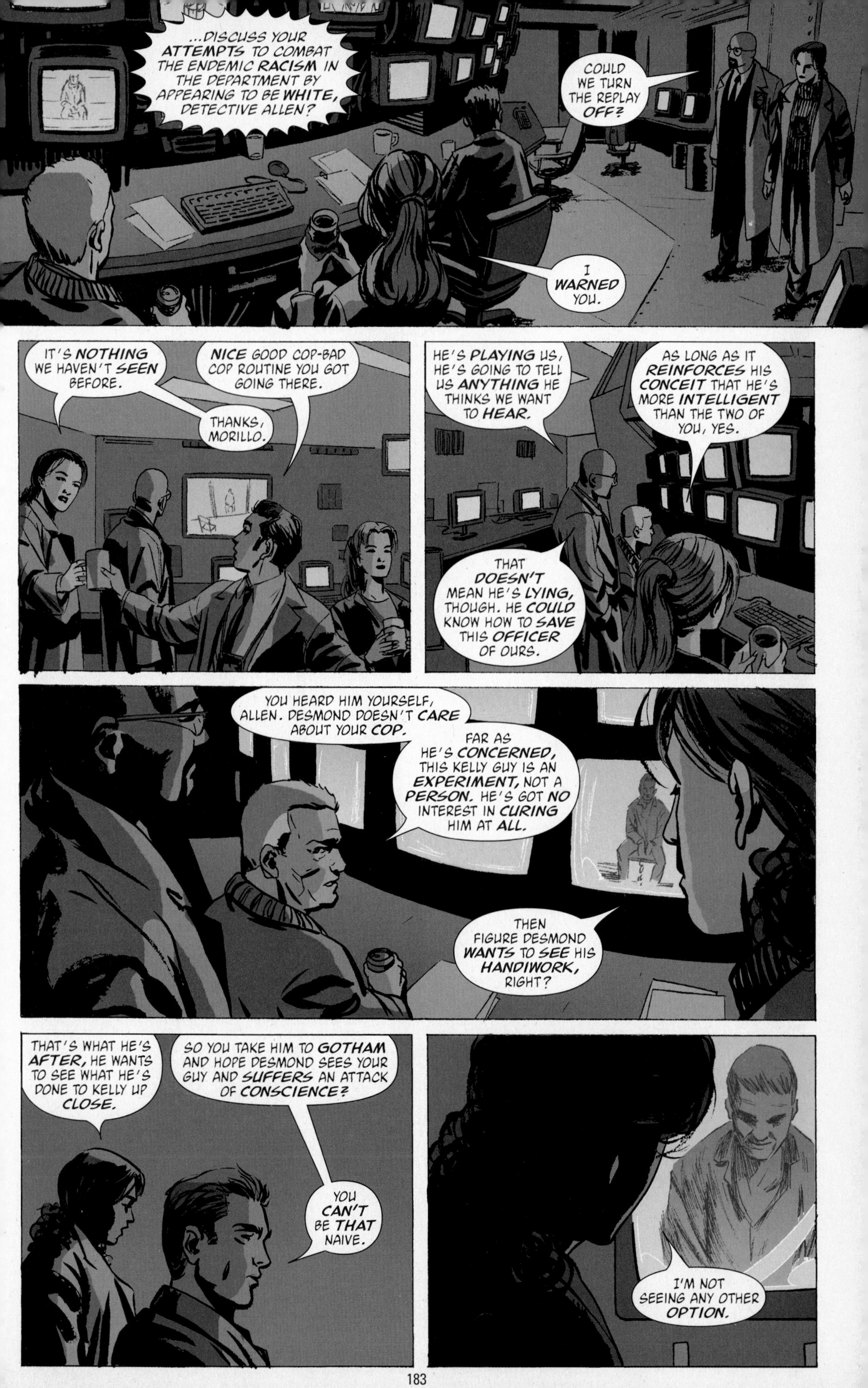
...DISCUSS YOUR ATTEMPTS TO COMBAT THE ENDEMIC RACISM IN THE DEPARTMENT BY APPEARING TO BE WHITE, DETECTIVE ALLEN?
COULD WE TURN THE REPLAY OFF?
I WARNED YOU.
IT'S NOTHING WE HAVEN'T SEEN BEFORE.
NICE GOOD COP-BAD COP ROUTINE YOU GOT GOING THERE.
THANKS, MORILLO.
HE'S PLAYING US, HE'S GOING TO TELL US ANYTHING HE THINKS WE WANT TO HEAR.
AS LONG AS IT REINFORCES HIS CONCEIT THAT HE'S MORE INTELLIGENT THAN THE TWO OF YOU, YES.
THAT DOESN'T MEAN HE'S LYING, THOUGH. HE COULD KNOW HOW TO SAVE THIS OFFICER OF OURS.
YOU HEARD HIM YOURSELF, ALLEN. DESMOND DOESN'T CARE ABOUT YOUR COP.
FAR AS HE'S CONCERNED, THIS KELLY GUY IS AN EXPERIMENT, NOT A PERSON. HE'S GOT NO INTEREST IN CURING HIM AT ALL.
THEN FIGURE DESMOND WANTS TO SEE HIS HANDIWORK, RIGHT?
THAT'S WHAT HE'S AFTER, HE WANTS TO SEE WHAT HE'S DONE TO KELLY UP CLOSE.
SO YOU TAKE HIM TO GOTHAM AND HOPE DESMOND SEES YOUR GUY AND SUFFERS AN ATTACK OF CONSCIENCE?
YOU CAN'T BE THAT NAIVE.
I'M NOT SEEING ANY OTHER OPTION.

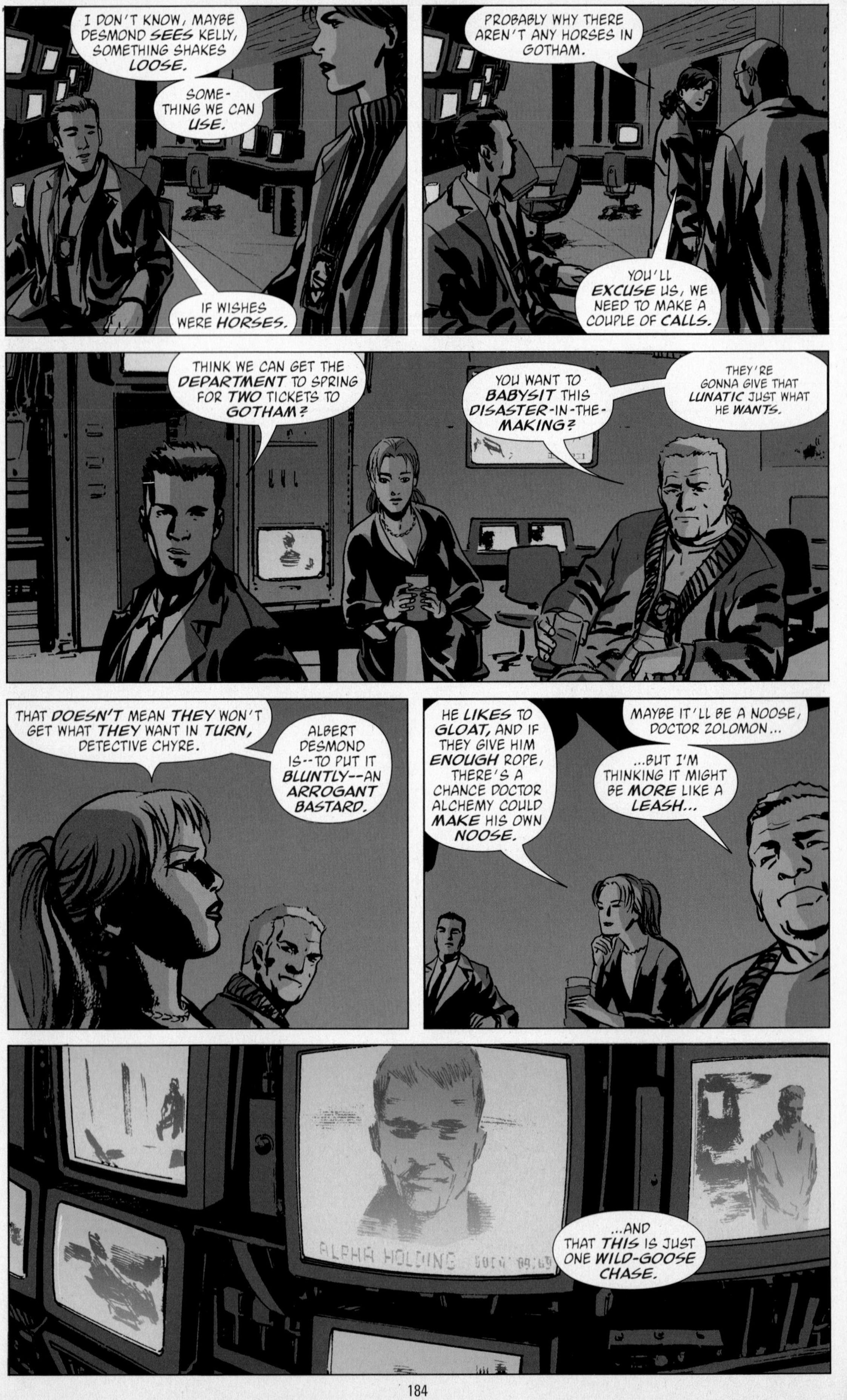
I DON'T KNOW, MAYBE DESMOND SEES KELLY, SOMETHING SHAKES LOOSE.
SOME-THING WE CAN USE.
IF WISHES WERE HORSES.
PROBABLY WHY THERE AREN'T ANY HORSES IN GOTHAM.
YOU'LL EXCUSE US, WE NEED TO MAKE A COUPLE OF CALLS.
THINK WE CAN GET THE DEPARTMENT TO SPRING FOR TWO TICKETS TO GOTHAM?
YOU WANT TO BABYSIT THIS DISASTER-IN-THE-MAKING?
THEY'RE GONNA GIVE THAT LUNATIC JUST WHAT HE WANTS.
THAT DOESN'T MEAN THEY WON'T GET WHAT THEY WANT IN TURN, DETECTIVE CHYRE.
ALBERT DESMOND IS--TO PUT IT BLUNTLY--AN ARROGANT BASTARD.
HE LIKES TO GLOAT, AND IF THEY GIVE HIM ENOUGH ROPE, THERE'S A CHANCE DOCTOR ALCHEMY COULD MAKE HIS OWN NOOSE.
MAYBE IT'LL BE A NOOSE, DOCTOR ZOLOMON...
...BUT I'M THINKING IT MIGHT BE MORE LIKE A LEASH...
ALPHA HOLDING
...AND THAT THIS IS JUST ONE WILD-GOOSE CHASE.

SIR? YOU HAVE A *MINUTE?*

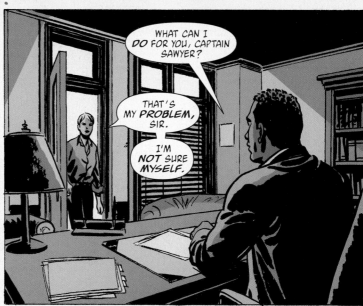

WHAT CAN I *DO* FOR YOU, CAPTAIN SAWYER?

THAT'S MY *PROBLEM,* SIR.

I'M *NOT* SURE MYSELF.

ALL RIGHT, I'M *INTRIGUED.*

EXPLAIN, MAGGIE.

IT'S ABOUT THE *THING* WITH OFFICER KELLY.

ALLEN AND MONTOYA ARE OUT IN *KEYSTONE,* THEY'VE BEEN TALKING TO DOCTOR ALCHEMY. THEY WANT TO *BRING* HIM *HERE.*

ALCHEMY HAS ADMITTED THAT HE'S *RESPONSIBLE* FOR KELLY'S CONDITION?

YES, SIR, COMMISSIONER.

THING IS, ALCHEMY'S *ALSO* CLAIMING HE CAN *CURE* KELLY.

BUT HE NEEDS TO *SEE* THE...*PATIENT*... FIRST.

OF COURSE HE DOES.

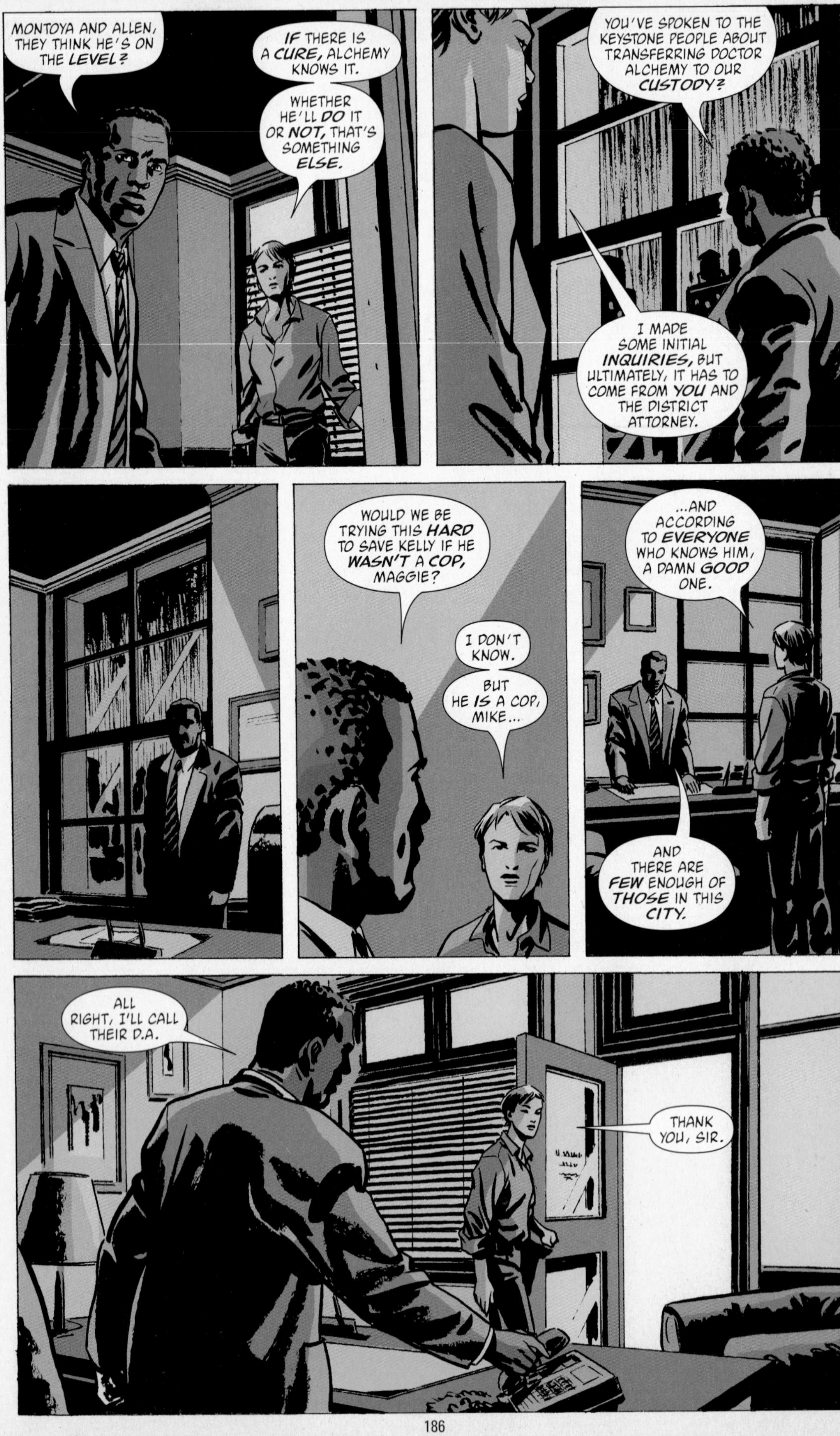
MONTOYA AND ALLEN, THEY THINK HE'S ON THE LEVEL?
IF THERE IS A CURE, ALCHEMY KNOWS IT.
WHETHER HE'LL DO IT OR NOT, THAT'S SOMETHING ELSE.
YOU'VE SPOKEN TO THE KEYSTONE PEOPLE ABOUT TRANSFERRING DOCTOR ALCHEMY TO OUR CUSTODY?
I MADE SOME INITIAL INQUIRIES, BUT ULTIMATELY, IT HAS TO COME FROM YOU AND THE DISTRICT ATTORNEY.
WOULD WE BE TRYING THIS HARD TO SAVE KELLY IF HE WASN'T A COP, MAGGIE?
I DON'T KNOW.
BUT HE IS A COP, MIKE...
...AND ACCORDING TO EVERYONE WHO KNOWS HIM, A DAMN GOOD ONE.
AND THERE ARE FEW ENOUGH OF THOSE IN THIS CITY.
ALL RIGHT, I'LL CALL THEIR D.A.
THANK YOU, SIR.

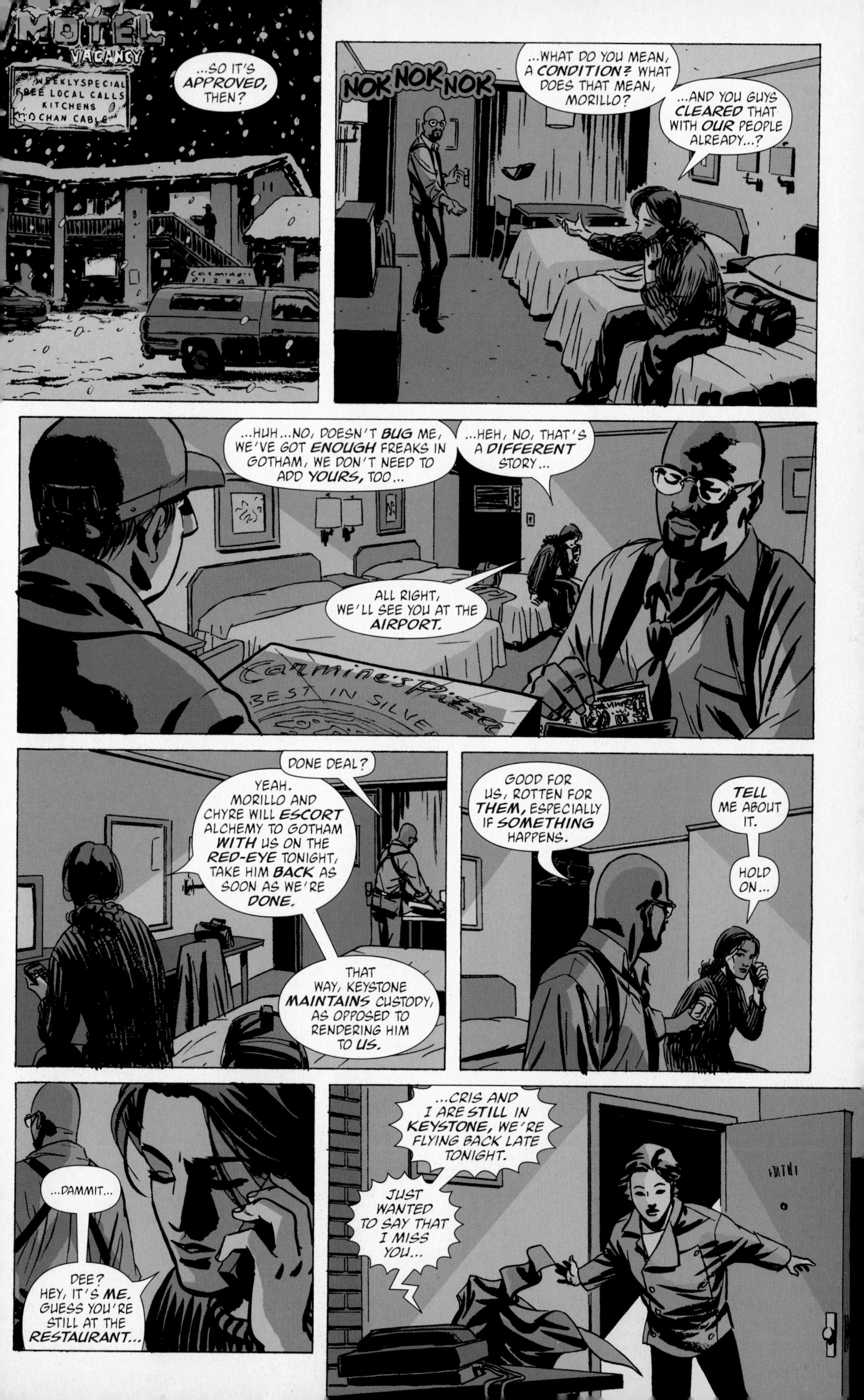
MOTEL
VACANCY
WEEKLY SPECIAL
FREE LOCAL CALLS
KITCHENS
...SO IT'S APPROVED, THEN?
NOK NOK NOK
...WHAT DO YOU MEAN, A CONDITION? WHAT DOES THAT MEAN, MORILLO?
...AND YOU GUYS CLEARED THAT WITH OUR PEOPLE ALREADY...?
...HUH...NO, DOESN'T BUG ME, WE'VE GOT ENOUGH FREAKS IN GOTHAM, WE DON'T NEED TO ADD YOURS, TOO...
...HEH, NO, THAT'S A DIFFERENT STORY...
ALL RIGHT, WE'LL SEE YOU AT THE AIRPORT.
Carmine's Pizza
DONE DEAL?
YEAH. MORILLO AND CHYRE WILL ESCORT ALCHEMY TO GOTHAM WITH US ON THE RED-EYE TONIGHT, TAKE HIM BACK AS SOON AS WE'RE DONE.
THAT WAY, KEYSTONE MAINTAINS CUSTODY, AS OPPOSED TO RENDERING HIM TO US.
GOOD FOR US, ROTTEN FOR THEM, ESPECIALLY IF SOMETHING HAPPENS.
TELL ME ABOUT IT.
HOLD ON...
...DAMMIT...
DEE? HEY, IT'S ME. GUESS YOU'RE STILL AT THE RESTAURANT...
...CRIS AND I ARE STILL IN KEYSTONE, WE'RE FLYING BACK LATE TONIGHT.
JUST WANTED TO SAY THAT I MISS YOU...

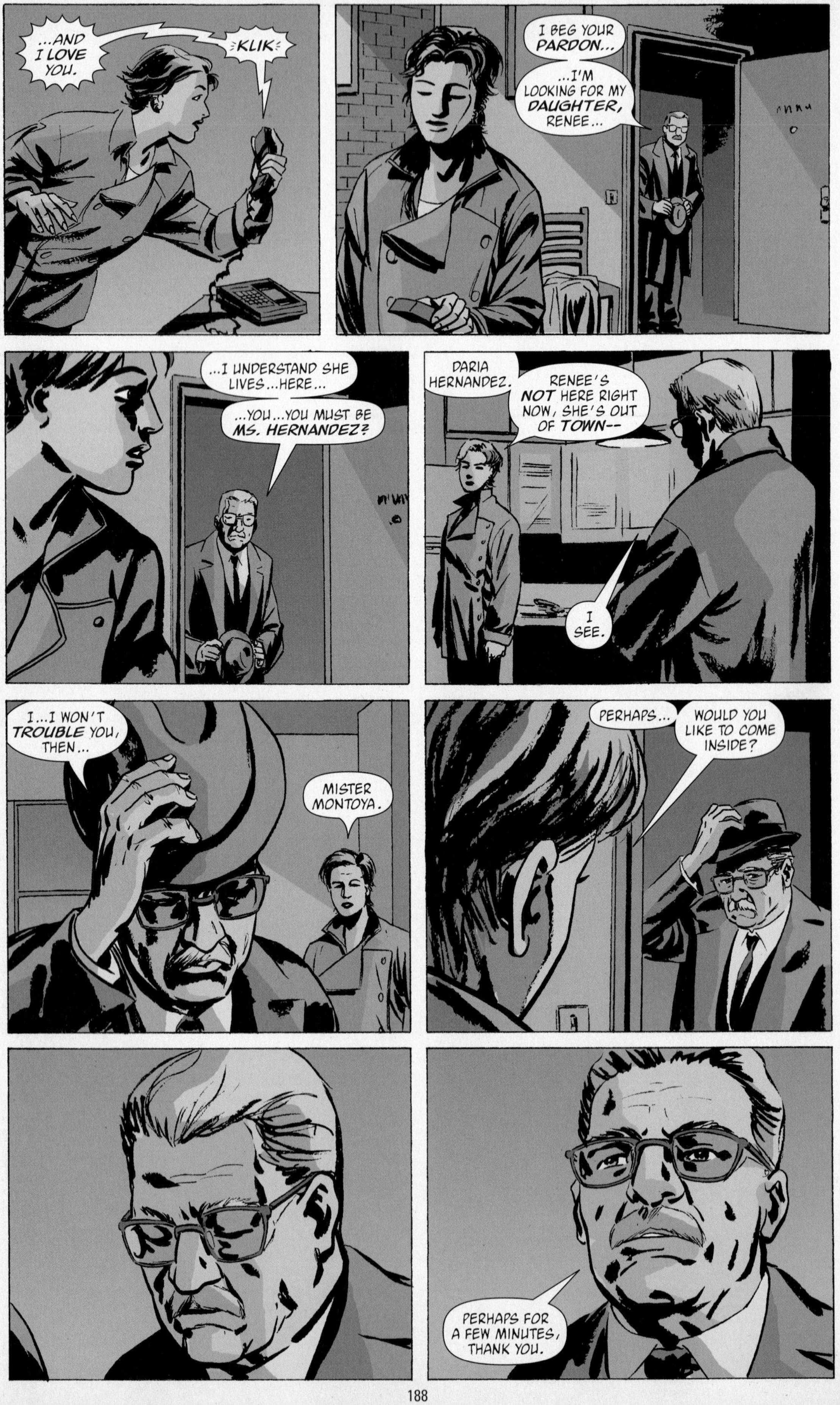
...AND I LOVE YOU.
KLIK
I BEG YOUR PARDON...
...I'M LOOKING FOR MY DAUGHTER, RENEE...
...I UNDERSTAND SHE LIVES...HERE...
...YOU...YOU MUST BE MS. HERNANDEZ?
DARIA HERNANDEZ.
RENEE'S NOT HERE RIGHT NOW, SHE'S OUT OF TOWN--
I SEE.
I...I WON'T TROUBLE YOU, THEN...
MISTER MONTOYA.
PERHAPS...
WOULD YOU LIKE TO COME INSIDE?
PERHAPS FOR A FEW MINUTES, THANK YOU.

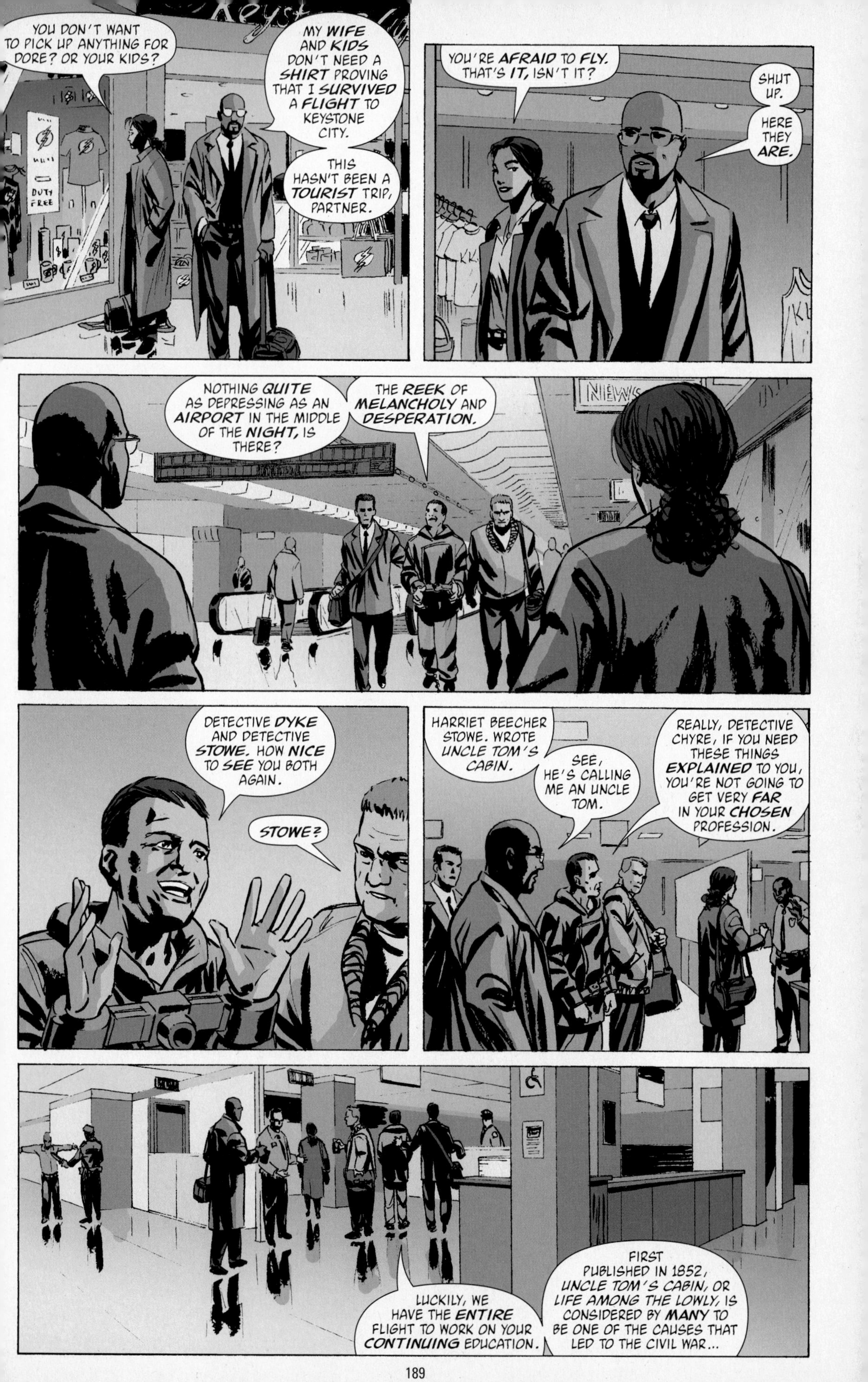
YOU DON'T WANT TO PICK UP ANYTHING FOR DORE? OR YOUR KIDS?
MY WIFE AND KIDS DON'T NEED A SHIRT PROVING THAT I SURVIVED A FLIGHT TO KEYSTONE CITY.
THIS HASN'T BEEN A TOURIST TRIP, PARTNER.
YOU'RE AFRAID TO FLY. THAT'S IT, ISN'T IT?
SHUT UP.
HERE THEY ARE.
NOTHING QUITE AS DEPRESSING AS AN AIRPORT IN THE MIDDLE OF THE NIGHT, IS THERE?
THE REEK OF MELANCHOLY AND DESPERATION.
NEWS
DETECTIVE DYKE AND DETECTIVE STOWE. HOW NICE TO SEE YOU BOTH AGAIN.
STOWE?
HARRIET BEECHER STOWE. WROTE UNCLE TOM'S CABIN.
SEE, HE'S CALLING ME AN UNCLE TOM.
REALLY, DETECTIVE CHYRE, IF YOU NEED THESE THINGS EXPLAINED TO YOU, YOU'RE NOT GOING TO GET VERY FAR IN YOUR CHOSEN PROFESSION.
LUCKILY, WE HAVE THE ENTIRE FLIGHT TO WORK ON YOUR CONTINUING EDUCATION.
FIRST PUBLISHED IN 1852, UNCLE TOM'S CABIN, OR LIFE AMONG THE LOWLY, IS CONSIDERED BY MANY TO BE ONE OF THE CAUSES THAT LED TO THE CIVIL WAR...

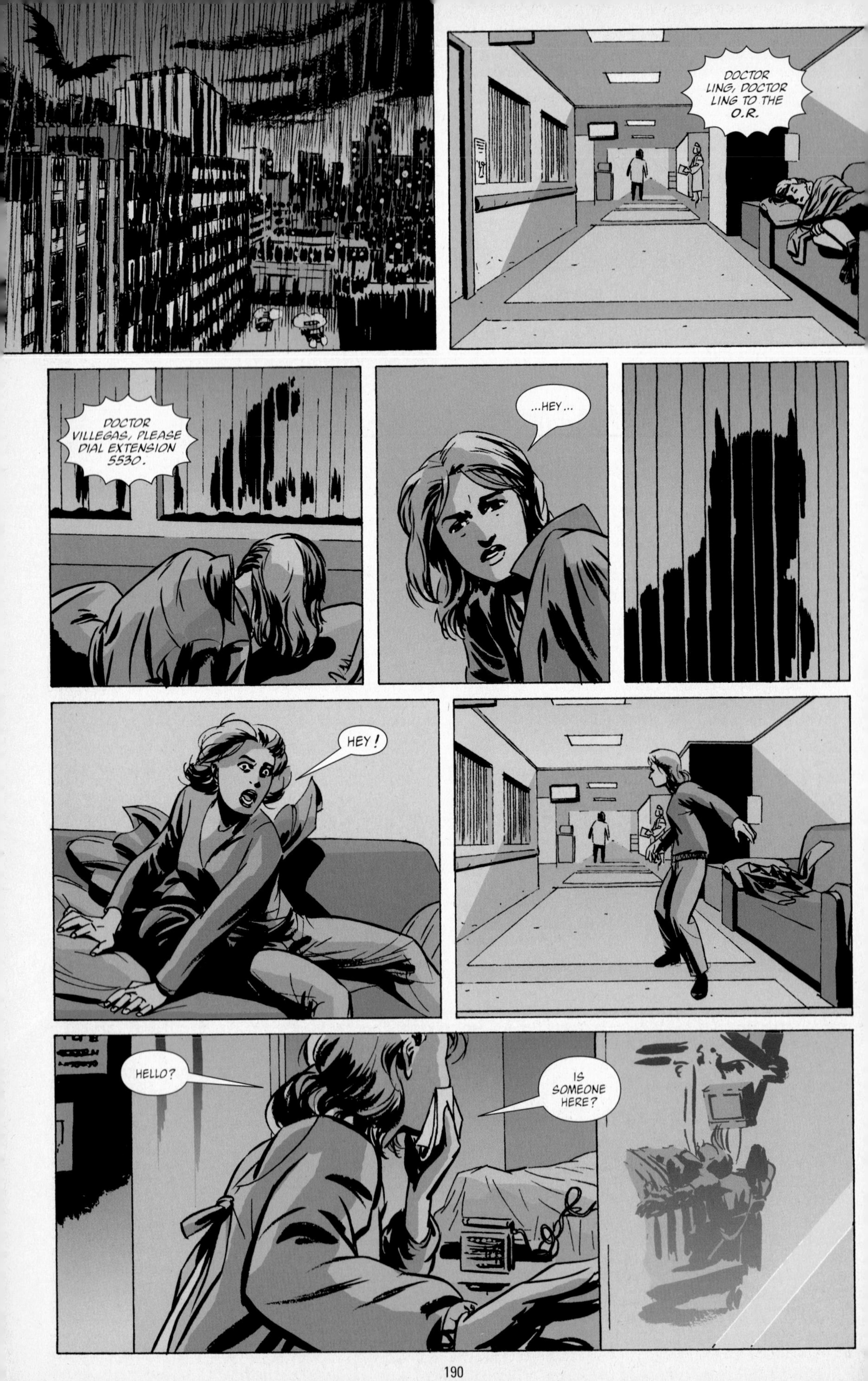
DOCTOR LING, DOCTOR LING TO THE O.R.
DOCTOR VILLEGAS, PLEASE DIAL EXTENSION 5530.
...HEY...
HEY!
HELLO?
IS SOMEONE HERE?

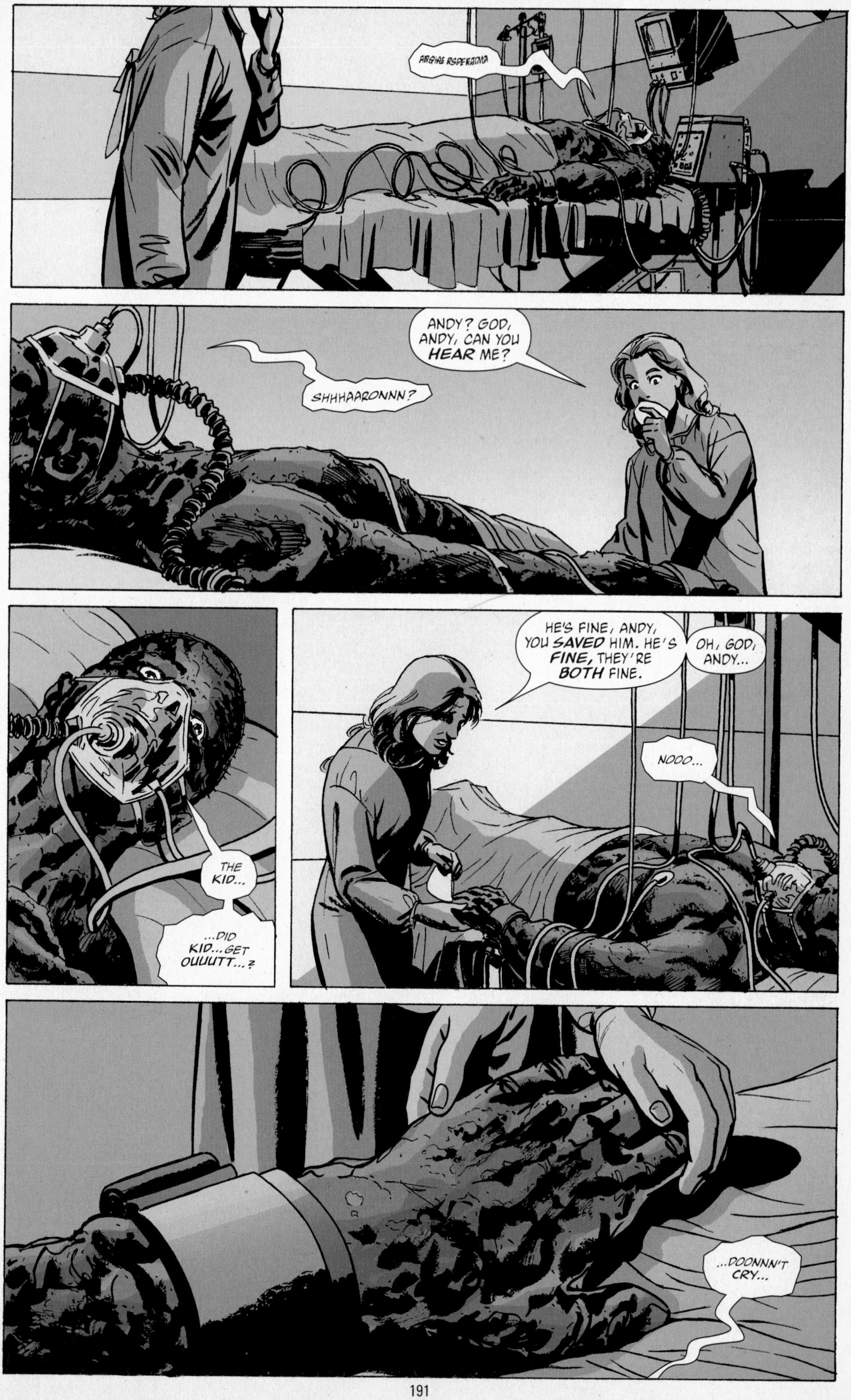
ANDY? GOD, ANDY, CAN YOU HEAR ME?
SHHHAARONNN?
THE KID...
...DID KID...GET OUUUTT...?
HE'S FINE, ANDY, YOU SAVED HIM. HE'S FINE, THEY'RE BOTH FINE.
OH, GOD, ANDY...
NOOO...
...DOONNN'T CRY...

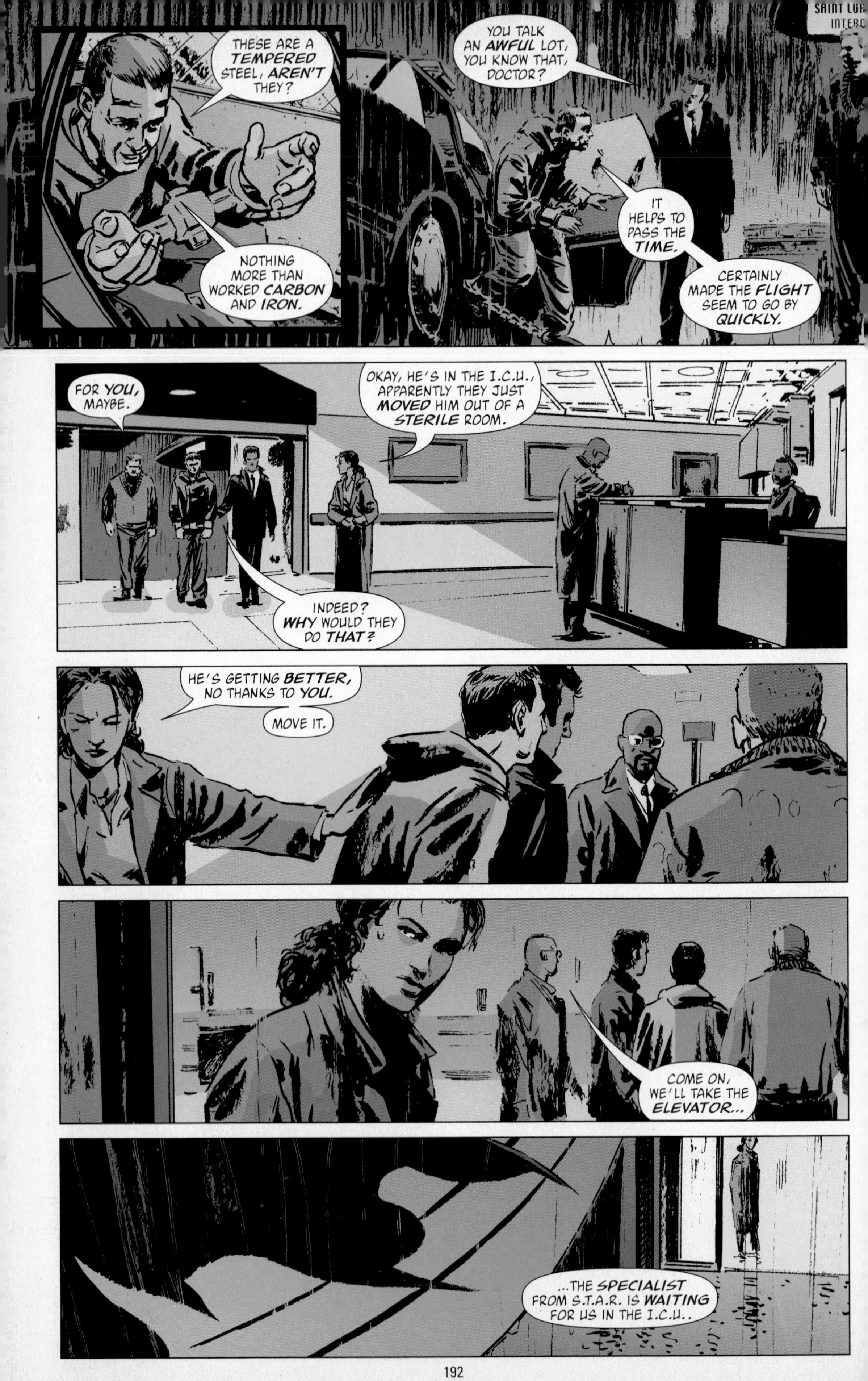

THESE ARE A TEMPERED STEEL, AREN'T THEY?
NOTHING MORE THAN WORKED CARBON AND IRON.
YOU TALK AN AWFUL LOT, YOU KNOW THAT, DOCTOR?
IT HELPS TO PASS THE TIME.
CERTAINLY MADE THE FLIGHT SEEM TO GO BY QUICKLY.
FOR YOU, MAYBE.
OKAY, HE'S IN THE I.C.U., APPARENTLY THEY JUST MOVED HIM OUT OF A STERILE ROOM.
INDEED? WHY WOULD THEY DO THAT?
HE'S GETTING BETTER, NO THANKS TO YOU.
MOVE IT.
COME ON, WE'LL TAKE THE ELEVATOR...
...THE SPECIALIST FROM S.T.A.R. IS WAITING FOR US IN THE I.C.U..

THAT WAS ROUGHLY *ONE* THIS MORNING.

HE'S BEEN *DRIFTING* IN AND OUT OF CONSCIOUSNESS EVER SINCE, BUT FOR THE TIME BEING, I'D SAY THAT OFFICER KELLY IS *STABLE.*

THEN YOU'RE AN *IDIOT.*

I BEG YOUR *PARDON?*

MONKEY WANT A 'NANA?

YOU'RE AN *IDIOT,* AN *IMBECILE,* A *MORON.*

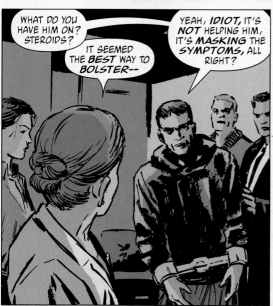

WHAT DO YOU HAVE HIM ON? STEROIDS?

IT SEEMED THE *BEST* WAY TO *BOLSTER*--

YEAH, *IDIOT,* IT'S *NOT* HELPING HIM, IT'S *MASKING* THE SYMPTOMS, ALL RIGHT?

AND WHEN HE *DECOMPENSATES*-- AND HE *WILL,* SWEET CHEEKS--HE'LL *DIE,* DO YOU UNDER- STAND?

I'LL USE *SMALL* WORDS:

YOU. ARE. KILLING. HIM.

YOU'RE THE *LUNATIC* WHO *DID* THIS TO HIM?

GUILTY AS CHARGED.

THEN WHY IN THE *WORLD* WOULD I *BELIEVE* YOU CARE ABOUT *CURING* HIM?

MY *EXPERIMENT* WAS TO *CHANGE* HIM, *NOT* MURDER HIM.

AND YOU, YOU'RE *MURDERING* HIM, *NOT* CURING HIM.

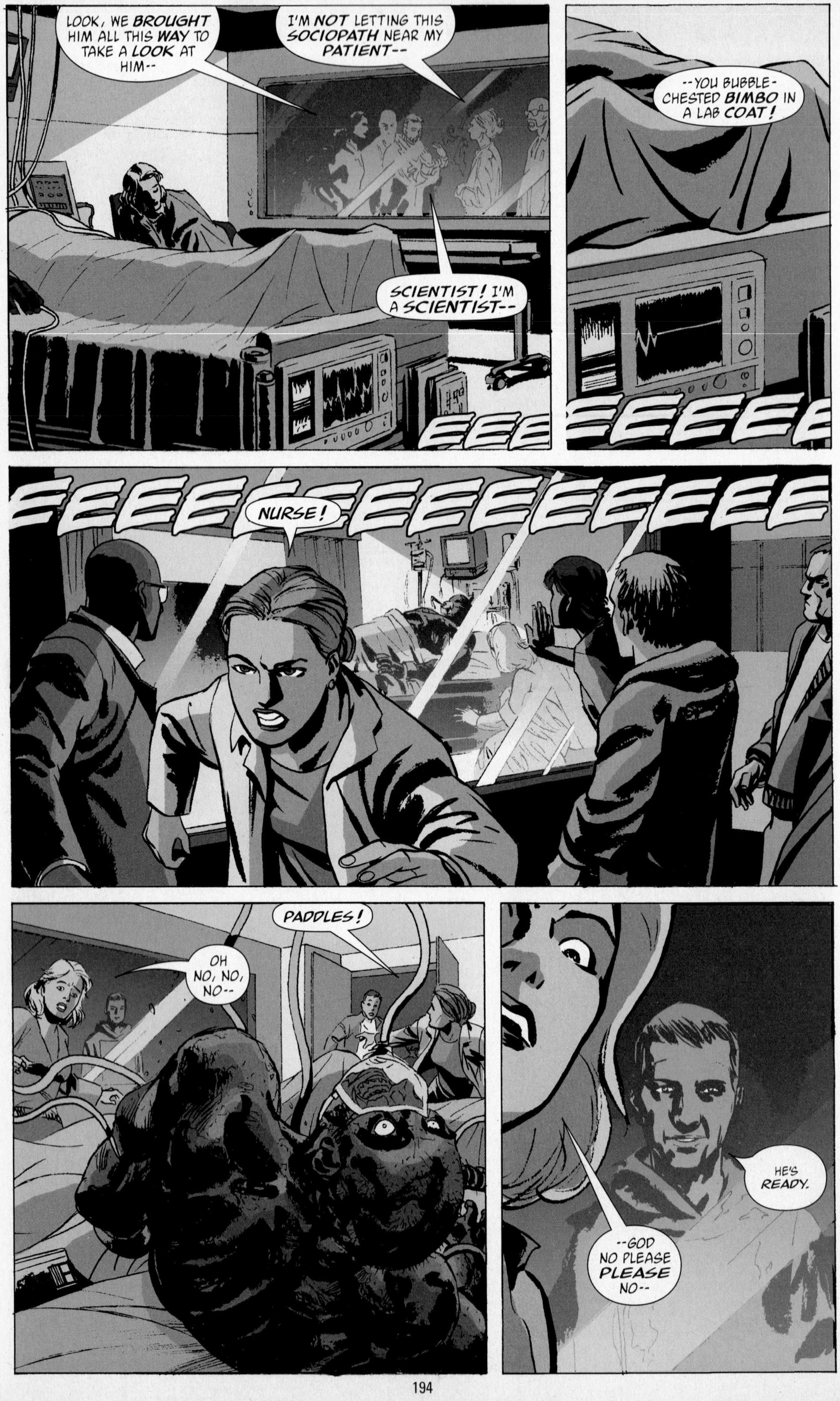
LOOK, WE BROUGHT HIM ALL THIS WAY TO TAKE A LOOK AT HIM--
I'M NOT LETTING THIS SOCIOPATH NEAR MY PATIENT--
SCIENTIST! I'M A SCIENTIST--
--YOU BUBBLE-CHESTED BIMBO IN A LAB COAT!
EEEEEEEEEE
EEEEEEEEEEEEEEEEEEEE
NURSE!
PADDLES!
OH NO, NO, NO--
HE'S READY.
--GOD NO PLEASE PLEASE NO--

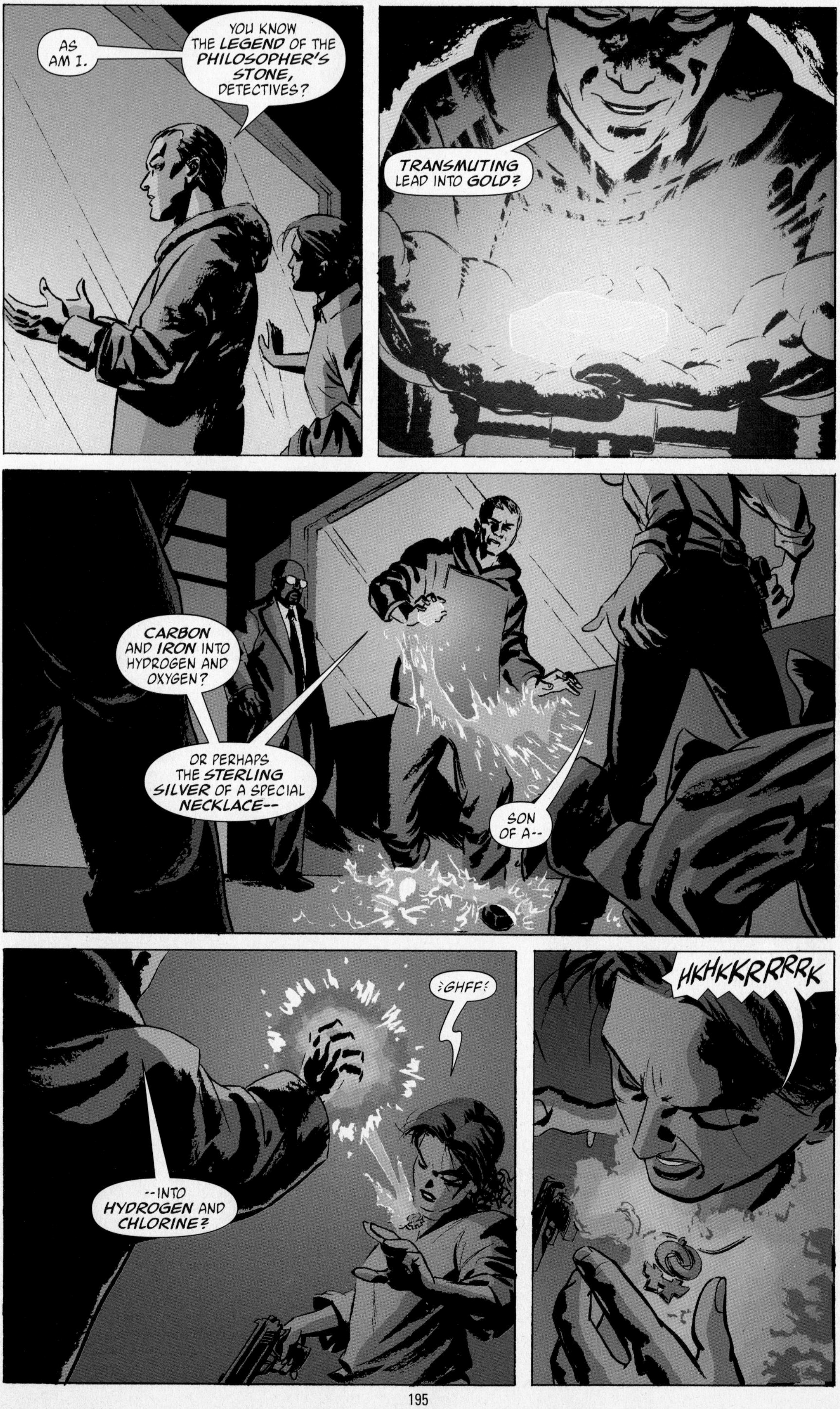
YOU KNOW THE LEGEND OF THE PHILOSOPHER'S STONE, DETECTIVES?
AS AM I.
TRANSMUTING LEAD INTO GOLD?
CARBON AND IRON INTO HYDROGEN AND OXYGEN?
OR PERHAPS THE STERLING SILVER OF A SPECIAL NECKLACE--
SON OF A--
GHFF
--INTO HYDROGEN AND CHLORINE?
HKHKKRRRRK

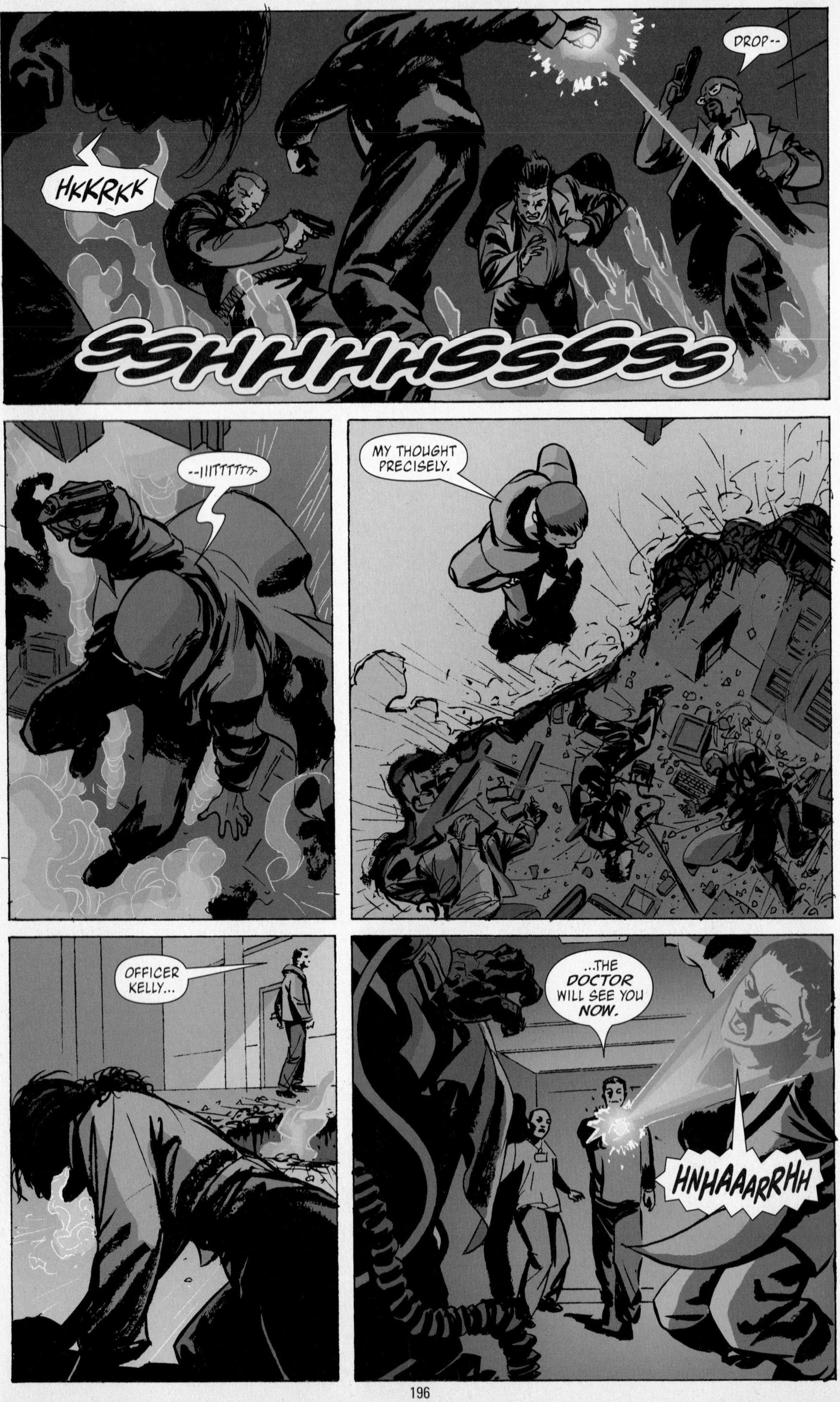

DROP--
HKKRKK
SSHHHHSSSSS
--IIITTTTTT
MY THOUGHT PRECISELY.
OFFICER KELLY...
...THE DOCTOR WILL SEE YOU NOW.
HNHAAARRHH

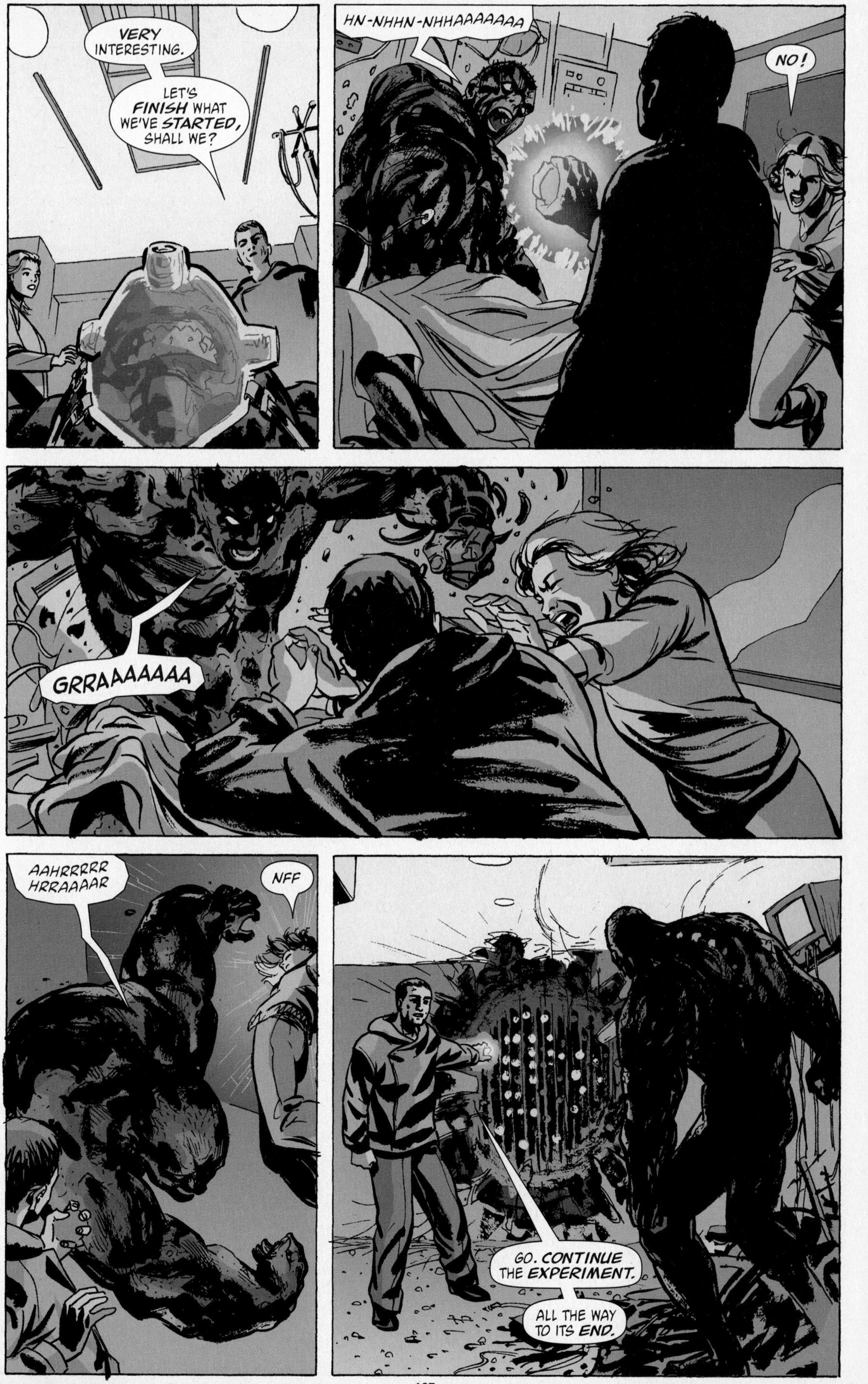
VERY INTERESTING.
LET'S FINISH WHAT WE'VE STARTED, SHALL WE?
HN-NHHN-NHHAAAAAAA
NO!
GRRAAAAAAA
AAHRRRRR HRRAAAAR
NFF
GO. CONTINUE THE EXPERIMENT.
ALL THE WAY TO ITS END.

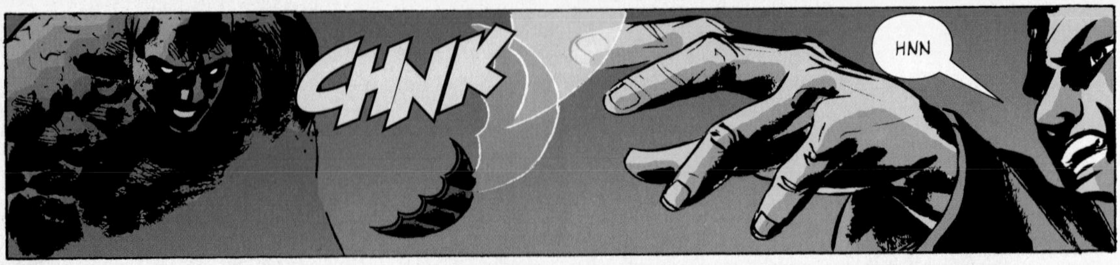
CHNK
HNN

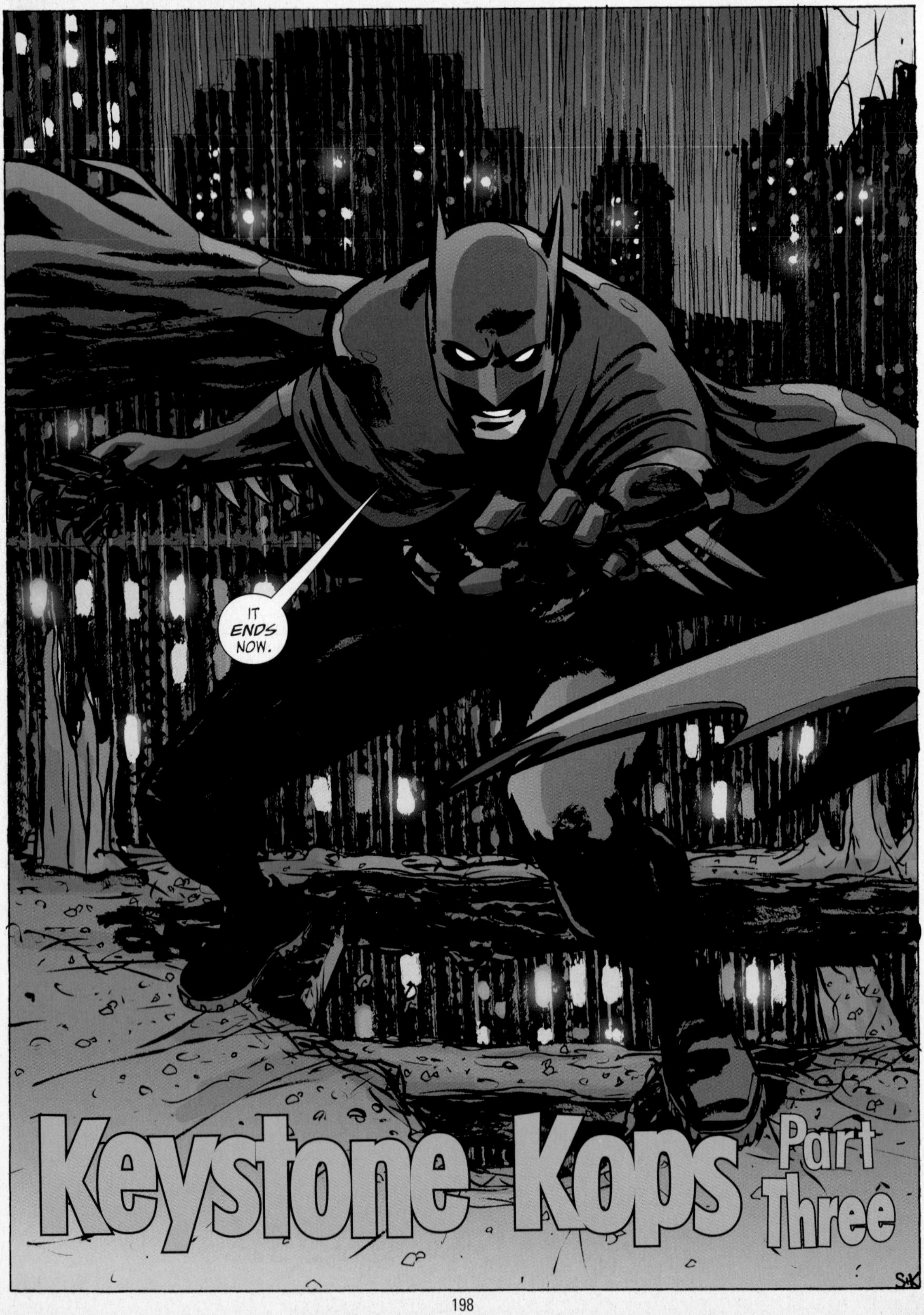
IT ENDS NOW.
Keystone Kops Part Three

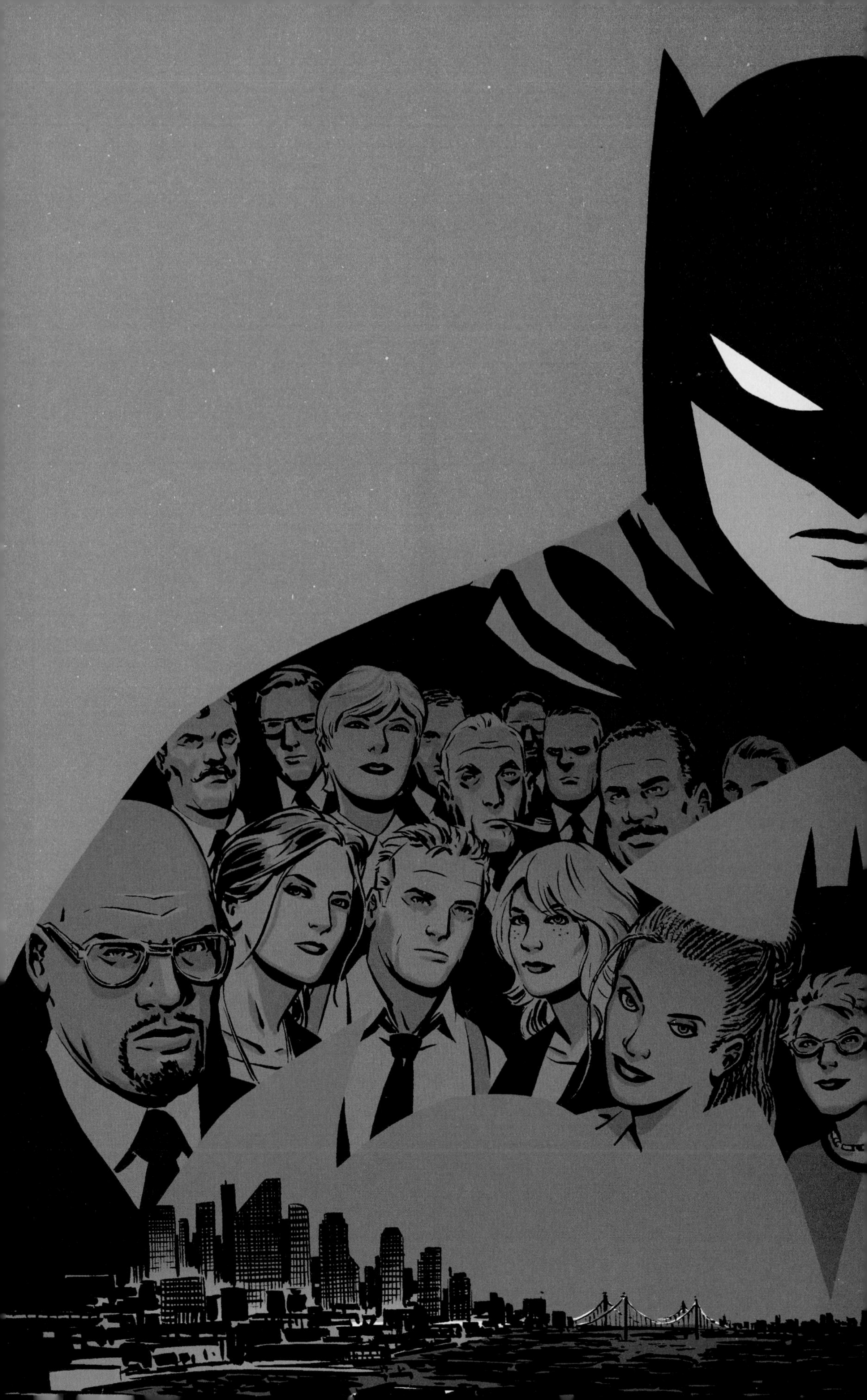

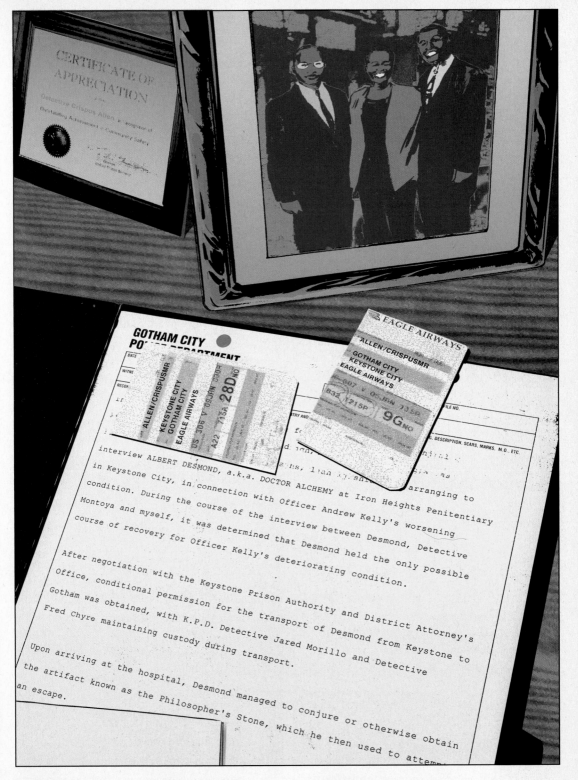

CERTIFICATE OF APPRECIATION
Detective Crispus Allen
GOTHAM CITY
EAGLE AIRWAYS
ALLEN/CRISPUSMR
GOTHAM CITY
KEYSTONE CITY
EAGLE AIRWAYS
9G
ALLEN/CRISPUSMR
KEYSTONE CITY
GOTHAM CITY
EAGLE AIRWAYS
28D
interview ALBERT DESMOND, a.k.a. DOCTOR ALCHEMY at Iron Heights Penitentiary in Keystone City, in connection with Officer Andrew Kelly's worsening condition. During the course of the interview between Desmond, Detective Montoya and myself, it was determined that Desmond held the only possible course of recovery for Officer Kelly's deteriorating condition.
After negotiation with the Keystone Prison Authority and District Attorney's Office, conditional permission for the transport of Desmond from Keystone to Gotham was obtained, with K.P.D. Detective Jared Morillo and Detective Fred Chyre maintaining custody during transport.
Upon arriving at the hospital, Desmond managed to conjure or otherwise obtain the artifact known as the Philosopher's Stone, which he then used to attempt an escape.

Keystone Kops Part Four

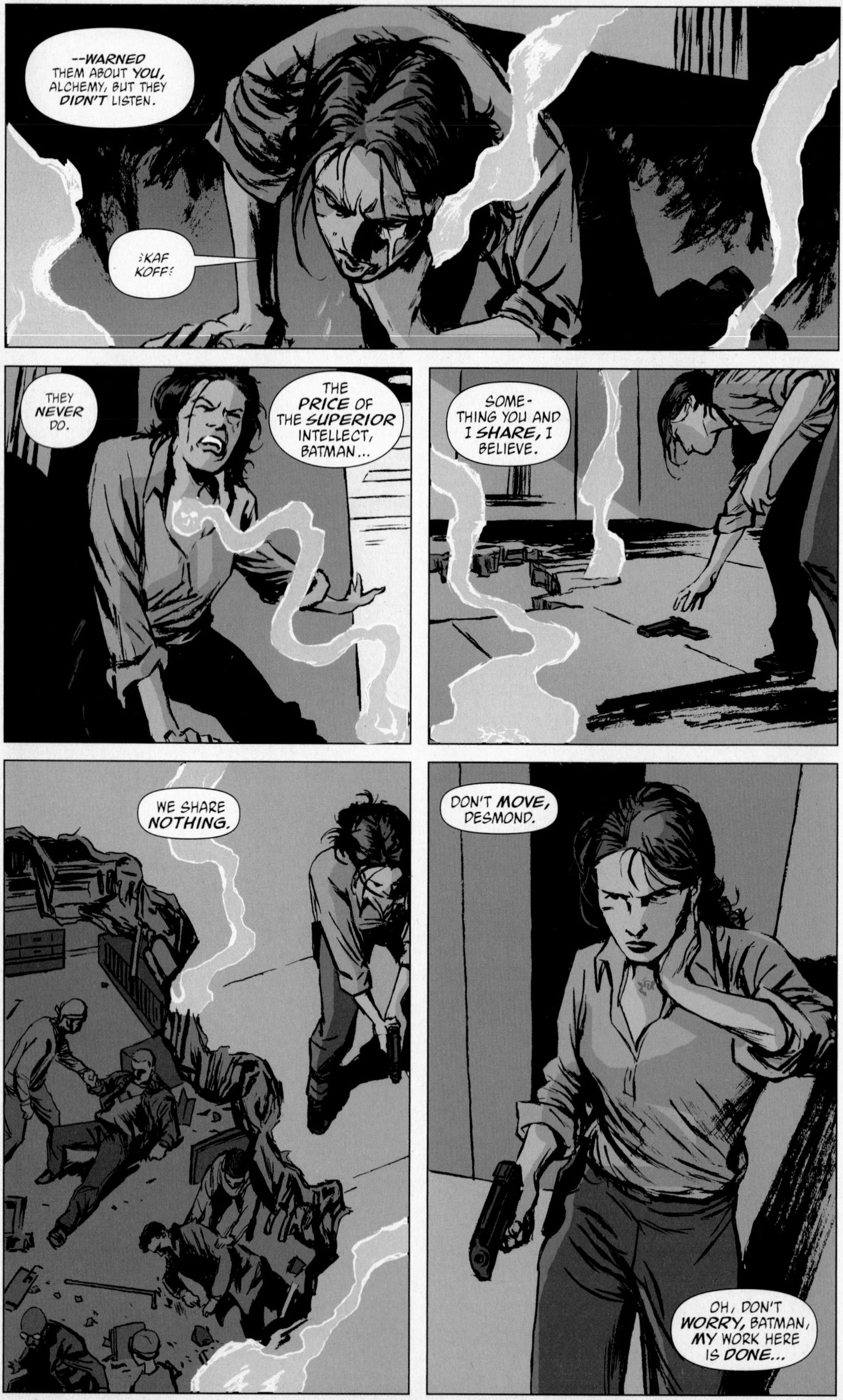
--WARNED THEM ABOUT YOU, ALCHEMY, BUT THEY DIDN'T LISTEN.
KAF KOFF
THEY NEVER DO.
THE PRICE OF THE SUPERIOR INTELLECT, BATMAN...
SOME-THING YOU AND I SHARE, I BELIEVE.
WE SHARE NOTHING.
DON'T MOVE, DESMOND.
OH, DON'T WORRY, BATMAN, MY WORK HERE IS DONE...

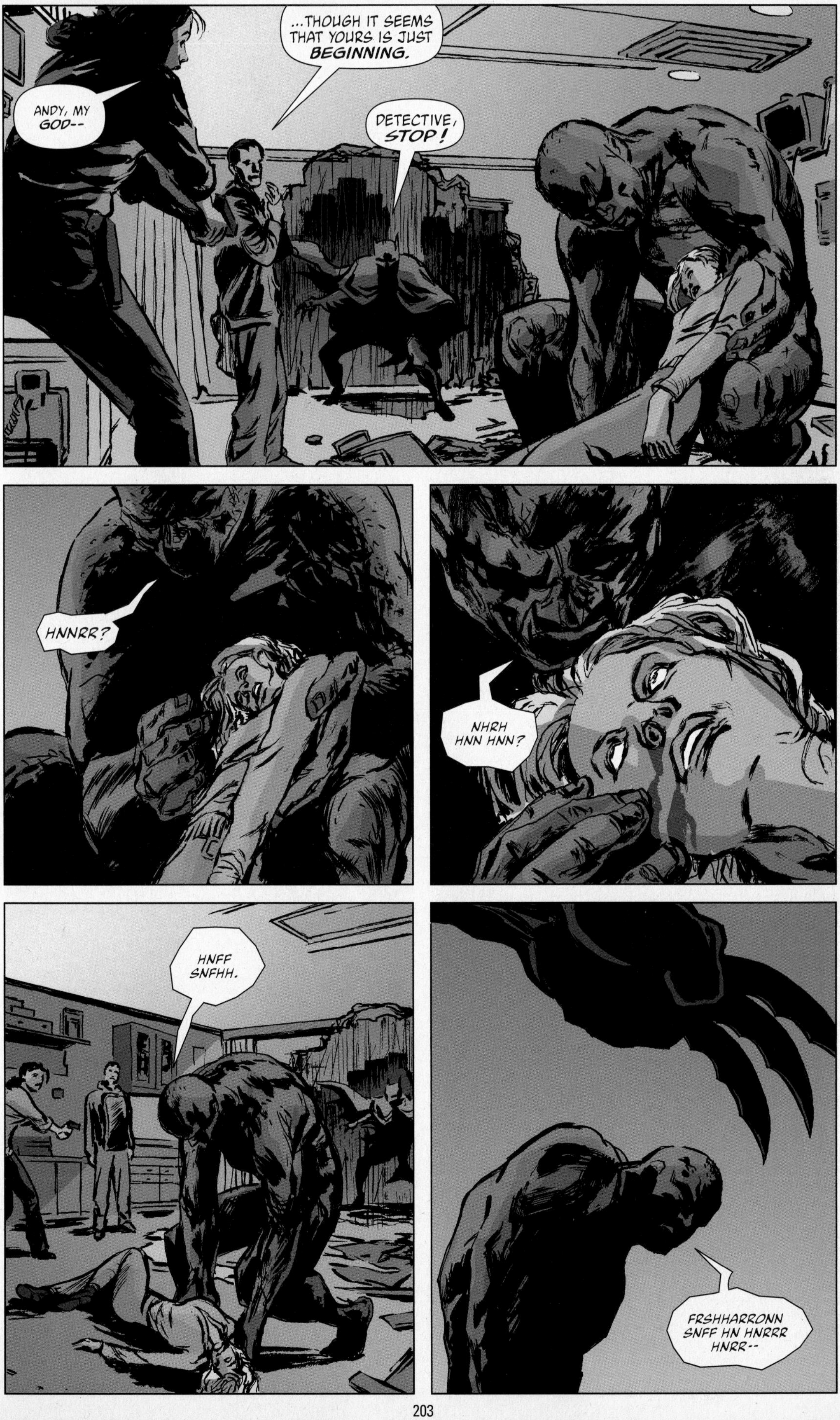
...THOUGH IT SEEMS THAT YOURS IS JUST BEGINNING.
ANDY, MY GOD--
DETECTIVE, STOP!
HNNRR?
NHRH HNN HNN?
HNFF SNFHH.
FRSHHARRONN SNFF HN HNRRR HNRR--

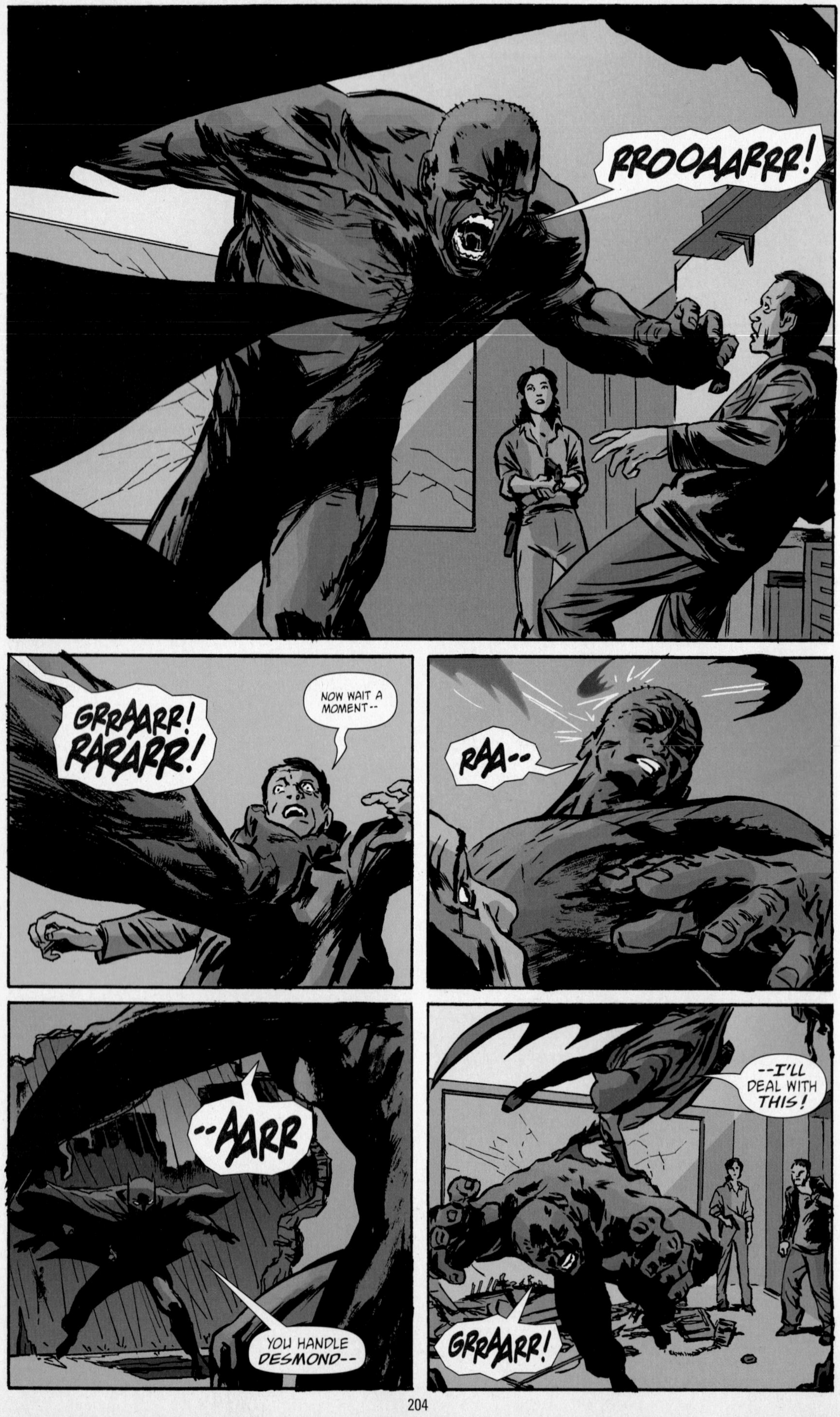
RROOAARRR!
GRRAARR! RARARR!
NOW WAIT A MOMENT--
RAA--
--AARR
YOU HANDLE DESMOND--
--I'LL DEAL WITH THIS!
GRRAARR!

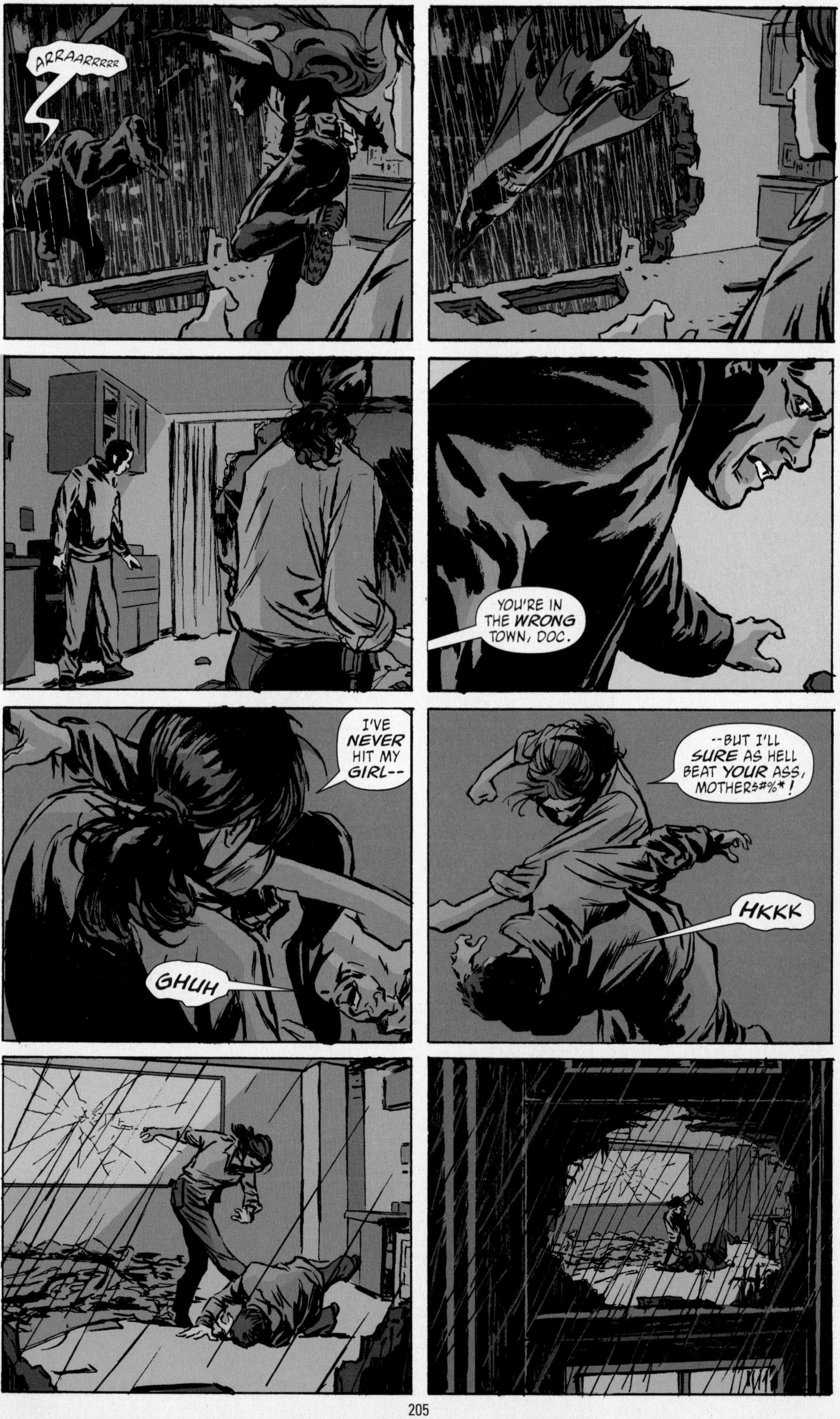
ARRAARRRRR
YOU'RE IN THE WRONG TOWN, DOC.
I'VE NEVER HIT MY GIRL--
--BUT I'LL SURE AS HELL BEAT YOUR ASS, MOTHER$#%*!
GHUH
HKKK

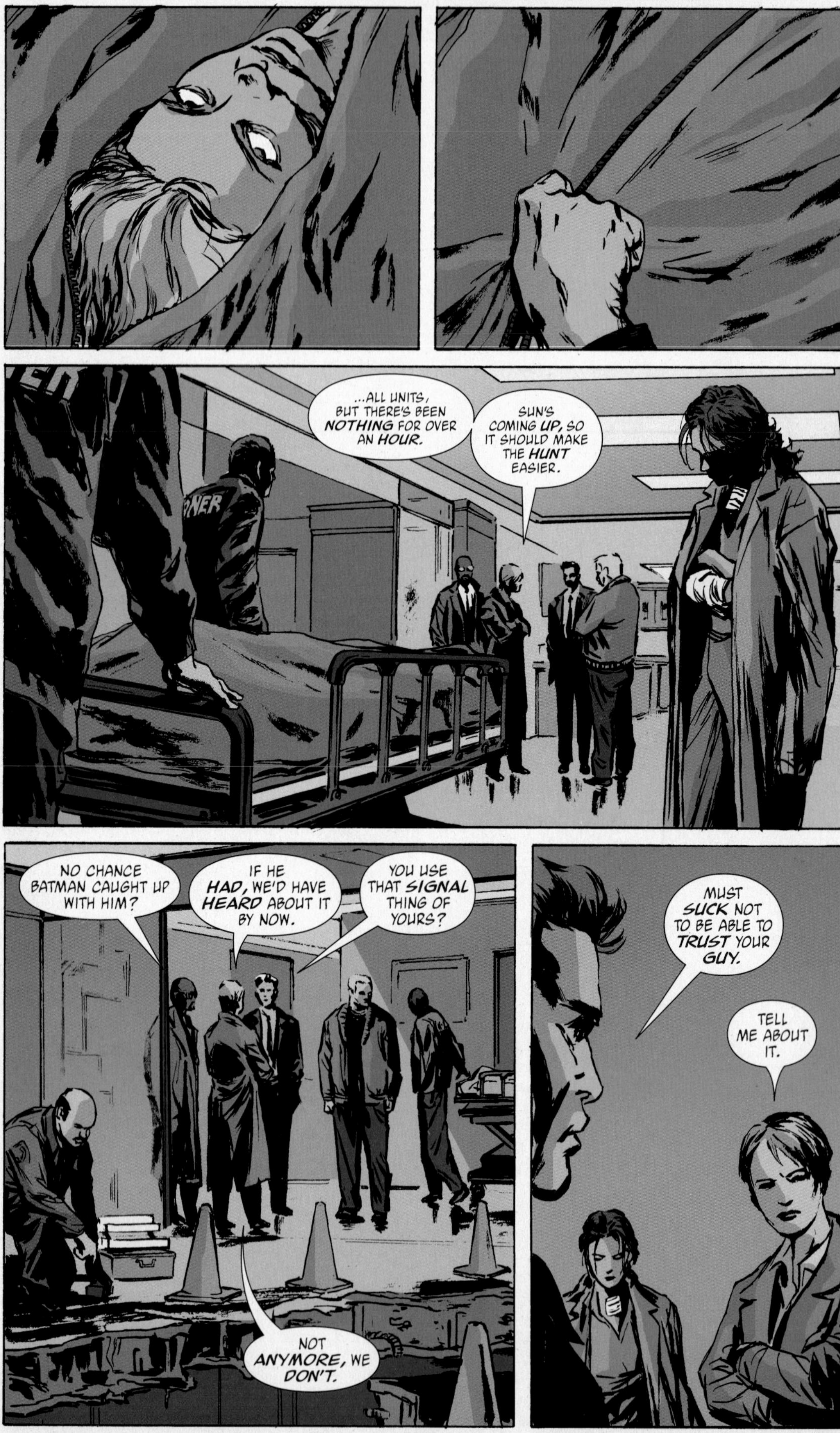
...ALL UNITS, BUT THERE'S BEEN NOTHING FOR OVER AN HOUR.
SUN'S COMING UP, SO IT SHOULD MAKE THE HUNT EASIER.
NO CHANCE BATMAN CAUGHT UP WITH HIM?
IF HE HAD, WE'D HAVE HEARD ABOUT IT BY NOW.
YOU USE THAT SIGNAL THING OF YOURS?
NOT ANYMORE, WE DON'T.
MUST SUCK NOT TO BE ABLE TO TRUST YOUR GUY.
TELL ME ABOUT IT.

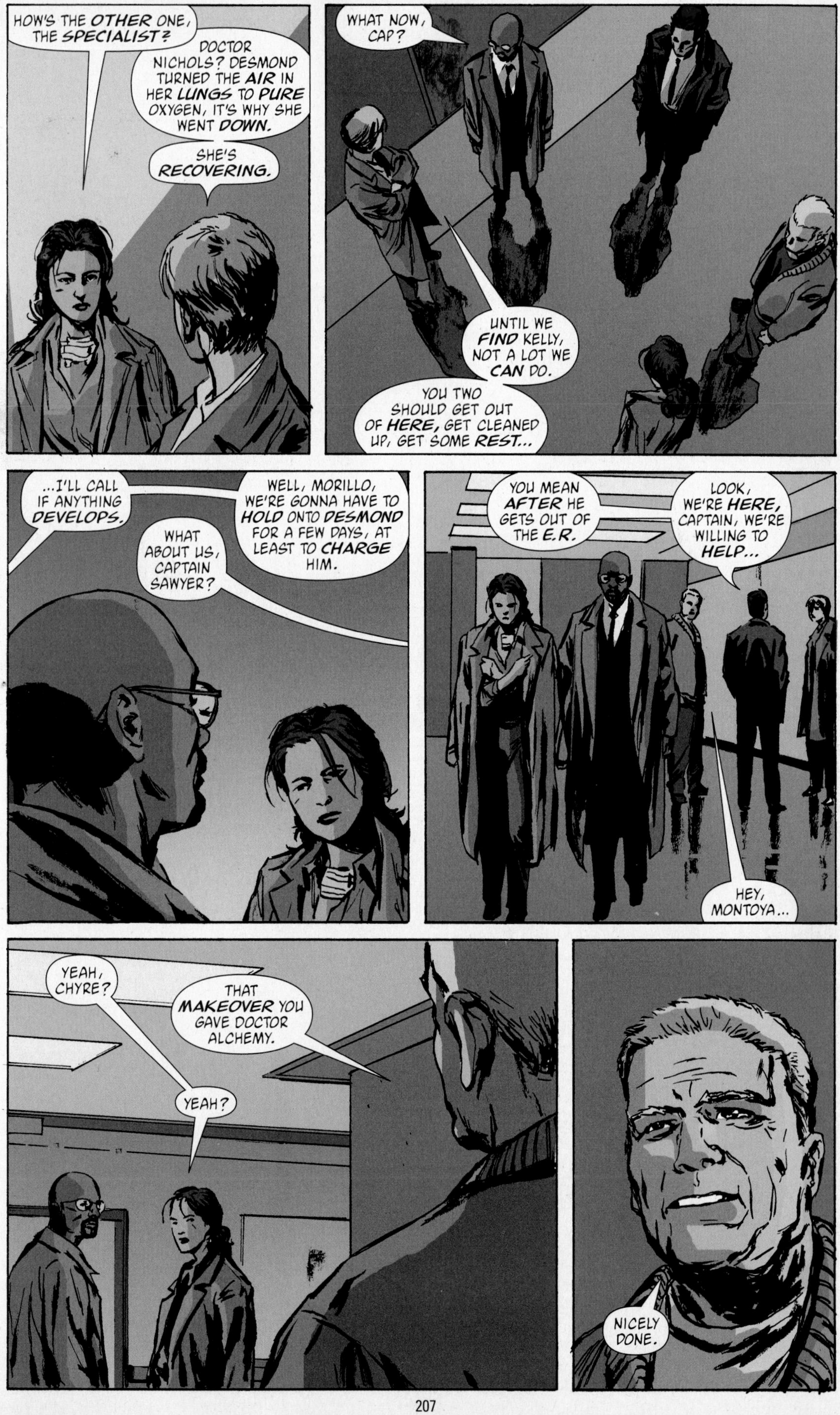
HOW'S THE OTHER ONE, THE SPECIALIST?
DOCTOR NICHOLS? DESMOND TURNED THE AIR IN HER LUNGS TO PURE OXYGEN, IT'S WHY SHE WENT DOWN.
SHE'S RECOVERING.
WHAT NOW, CAP?
UNTIL WE FIND KELLY, NOT A LOT WE CAN DO.
YOU TWO SHOULD GET OUT OF HERE, GET CLEANED UP, GET SOME REST...
...I'LL CALL IF ANYTHING DEVELOPS.
WHAT ABOUT US, CAPTAIN SAWYER?
WELL, MORILLO, WE'RE GONNA HAVE TO HOLD ONTO DESMOND FOR A FEW DAYS, AT LEAST TO CHARGE HIM.
YOU MEAN AFTER HE GETS OUT OF THE E.R.
LOOK, WE'RE HERE, CAPTAIN, WE'RE WILLING TO HELP...
HEY, MONTOYA...
YEAH, CHYRE?
THAT MAKEOVER YOU GAVE DOCTOR ALCHEMY.
YEAH?
NICELY DONE.

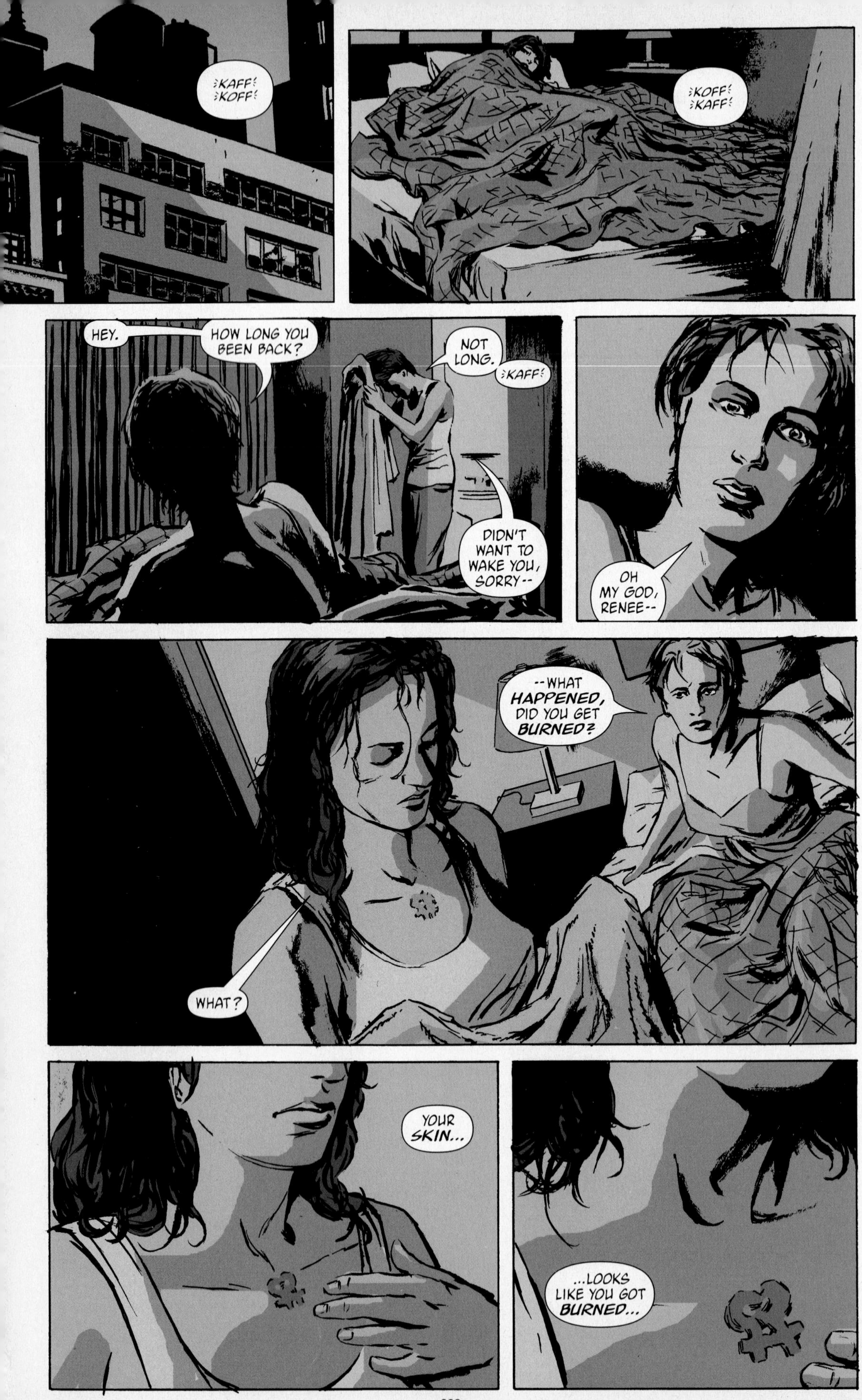

KAFF KOFF
KOFF KAFF
HEY.
HOW LONG YOU BEEN BACK?
NOT LONG.
KAFF
DIDN'T WANT TO WAKE YOU, SORRY--
OH MY GOD, RENEE--
--WHAT HAPPENED, DID YOU GET BURNED?
WHAT?
YOUR SKIN...
...LOOKS LIKE YOU GOT BURNED...

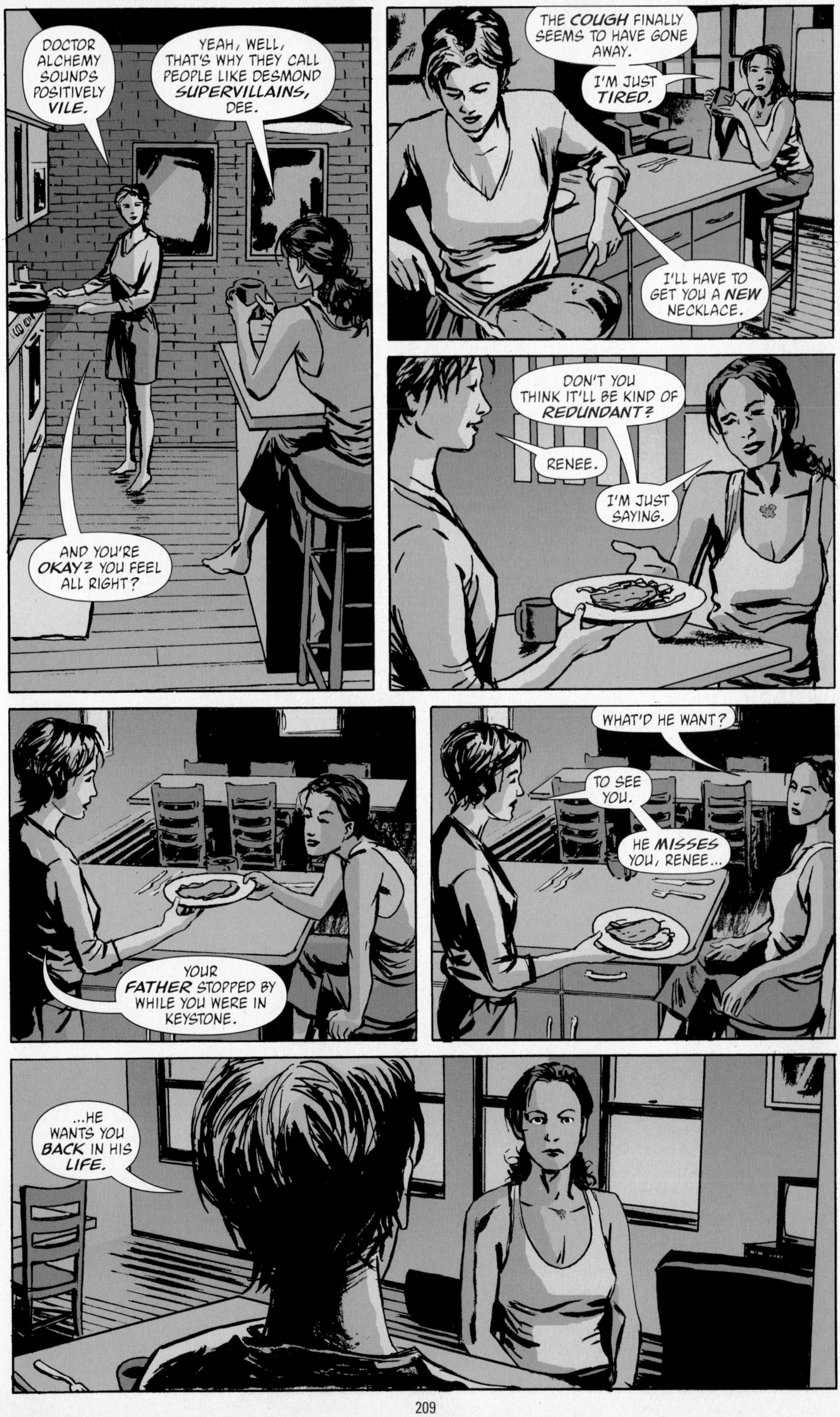
DOCTOR ALCHEMY SOUNDS POSITIVELY VILE.
YEAH, WELL, THAT'S WHY THEY CALL PEOPLE LIKE DESMOND SUPERVILLAINS, DEE.
AND YOU'RE OKAY? YOU FEEL ALL RIGHT?
THE COUGH FINALLY SEEMS TO HAVE GONE AWAY.
I'M JUST TIRED.
I'LL HAVE TO GET YOU A NEW NECKLACE.
DON'T YOU THINK IT'LL BE KIND OF REDUNDANT?
RENEE.
I'M JUST SAYING.
YOUR FATHER STOPPED BY WHILE YOU WERE IN KEYSTONE.
WHAT'D HE WANT?
TO SEE YOU.
HE MISSES YOU, RENEE...
...HE WANTS YOU BACK IN HIS LIFE.

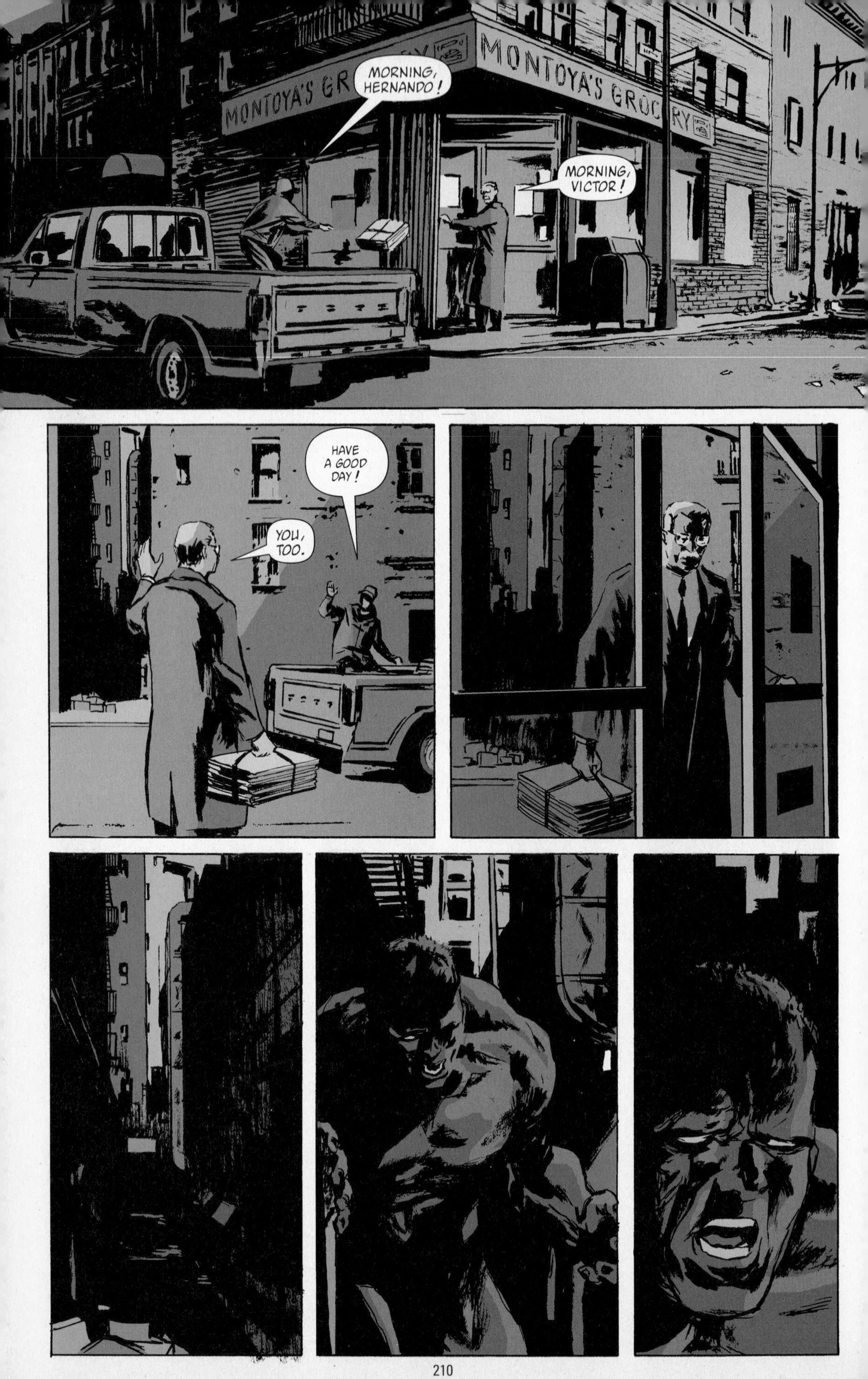
MONTOYA'S GROCERY
MONTOYA'S GROCERY
MORNING, HERNANDO!
MORNING, VICTOR!
HAVE A GOOD DAY!
YOU, TOO.

...COMPARED KELLY'S BLOOD BEFORE *AND* AFTER ALCHEMY *ZAPPED* HIM.

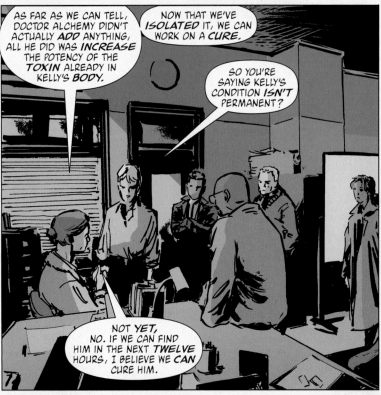

AS FAR AS WE CAN TELL, DOCTOR ALCHEMY DIDN'T ACTUALLY *ADD* ANYTHING, ALL HE DID WAS *INCREASE* THE POTENCY OF THE *TOXIN* ALREADY IN KELLY'S *BODY.*

NOW THAT WE'VE *ISOLATED* IT, WE CAN WORK ON A *CURE.*

SO YOU'RE SAYING KELLY'S CONDITION *ISN'T* PERMANENT?

NOT *YET,* NO. IF WE CAN FIND HIM IN THE NEXT *TWELVE* HOURS, I BELIEVE WE *CAN* CURE HIM.

WE'RE TALKING ABOUT KELLY?

DOCTOR NICHOLS THINKS THERE'S A WAY TO CHANGE HIM BACK--

⸢KAFF KOFFKOFF⸣

WHAT DO YOU *NEED* FROM US?

PARDON ME.

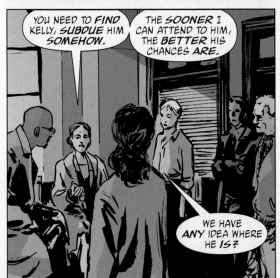

YOU NEED TO *FIND* KELLY, *SUBDUE* HIM SOMEHOW.

THE *SOONER* I CAN ATTEND TO HIM, THE *BETTER* HIS CHANCES *ARE.*

WE HAVE *ANY* IDEA WHERE HE *IS?*

NOTHING AT ALL.

DESMOND *MIGHT* KNOW.

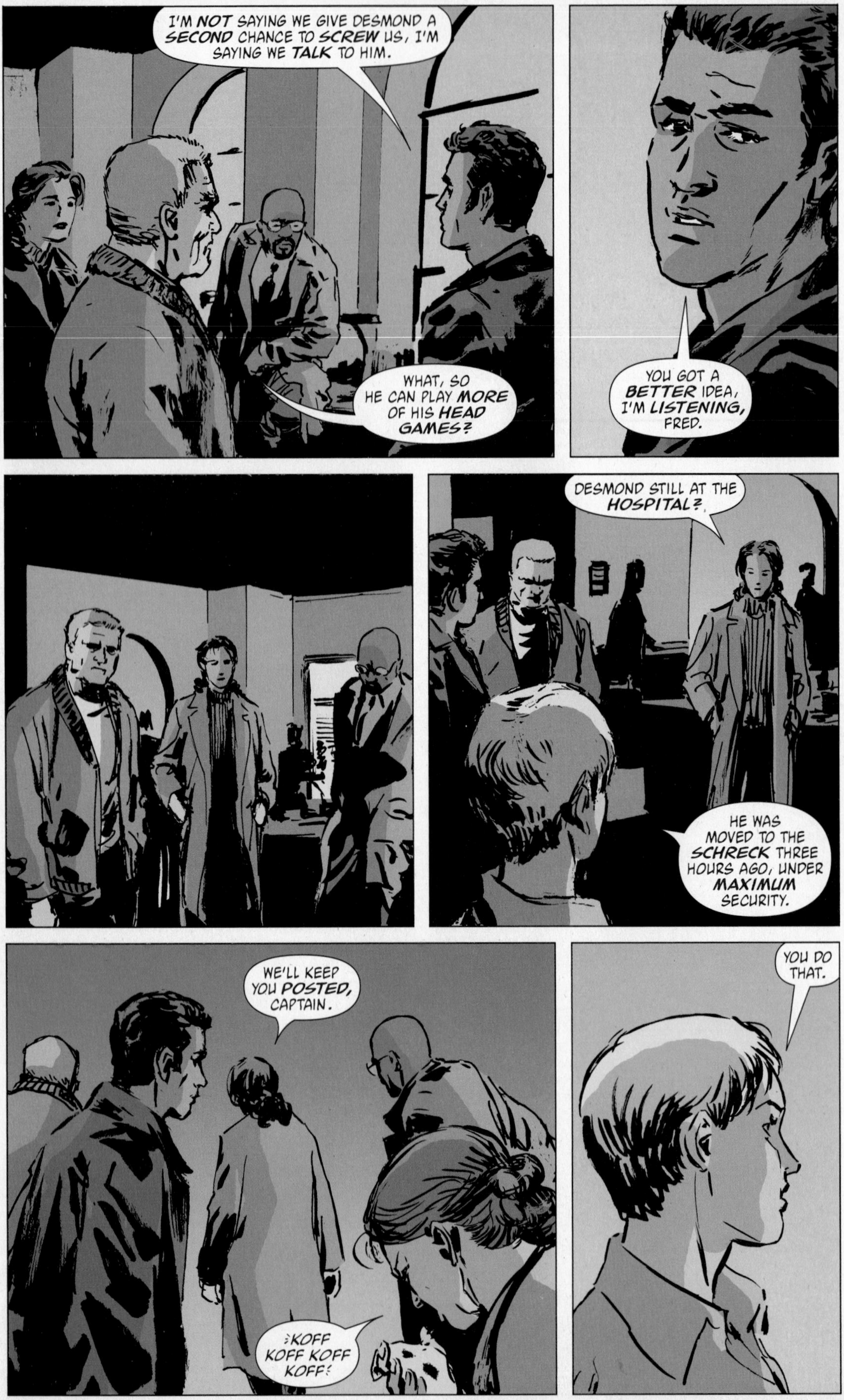
I'M NOT SAYING WE GIVE DESMOND A SECOND CHANCE TO SCREW US, I'M SAYING WE TALK TO HIM.
WHAT, SO HE CAN PLAY MORE OF HIS HEAD GAMES?
YOU GOT A BETTER IDEA, I'M LISTENING, FRED.
DESMOND STILL AT THE HOSPITAL?
HE WAS MOVED TO THE SCHRECK THREE HOURS AGO, UNDER MAXIMUM SECURITY.
WE'LL KEEP YOU POSTED, CAPTAIN.
KOFF KOFF KOFF KOFF
YOU DO THAT.

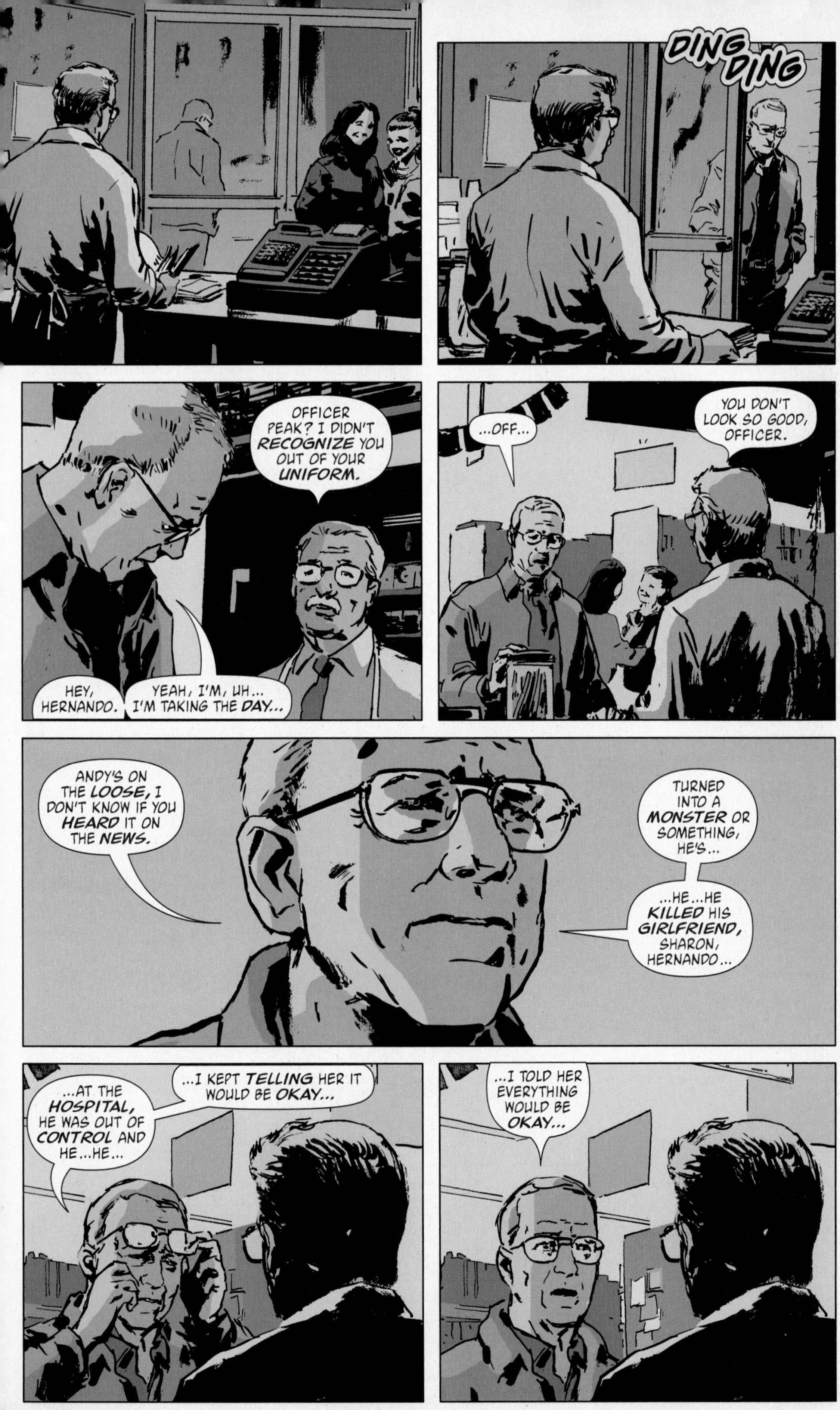
DING DING
HEY, HERNANDO.
YEAH, I'M, UH... I'M TAKING THE DAY...
OFFICER PEAK? I DIDN'T RECOGNIZE YOU OUT OF YOUR UNIFORM.
...OFF...
YOU DON'T LOOK SO GOOD, OFFICER.
ANDY'S ON THE LOOSE, I DON'T KNOW IF YOU HEARD IT ON THE NEWS.
TURNED INTO A MONSTER OR SOMETHING, HE'S...
...HE...HE KILLED HIS GIRLFRIEND, SHARON, HERNANDO...
...AT THE HOSPITAL, HE WAS OUT OF CONTROL AND HE...HE...
...I KEPT TELLING HER IT WOULD BE OKAY...
...I TOLD HER EVERYTHING WOULD BE OKAY...

YOU'LL GET *NO* HELP FROM *ME.*

IN FACT, THE *ONLY* THING YOU'LL BE GETTING FROM ME IS A *MASSIVE* SUIT FOR *DAMAGES,* FILED AGAINST DETECTIVE DYKE FOR *BRUTALITY.*

YOU WERE *RESISTING* ARREST.

SPTT

DAMNIT--

RENEE!

--GET OFF OF ME!

UH-OH, *LOOK OUT--*

--ANGRY LESBIAN, COMING *THROUGH!*

I'LL BE *OUTSIDE.*

NO, DON'T *LEAVE...*

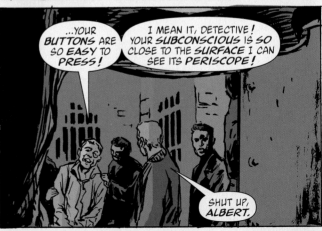

...YOUR *BUTTONS* ARE SO EASY TO *PRESS!*

I MEAN IT, DETECTIVE! YOUR *SUBCONSCIOUS* IS SO CLOSE TO THE *SURFACE* I CAN SEE ITS *PERISCOPE!*

SHUT UP, ALBERT.

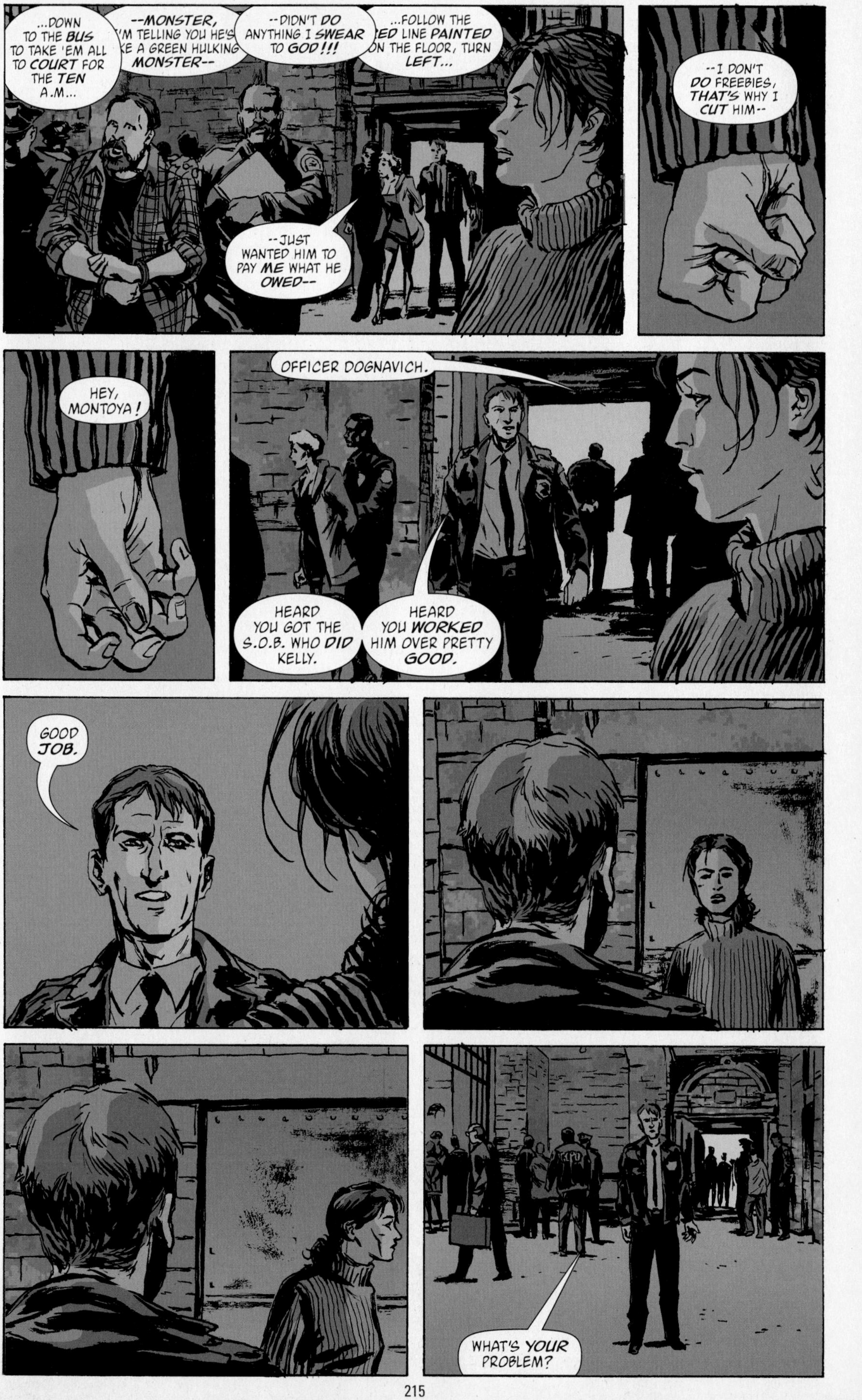
...DOWN TO THE BUS TO TAKE 'EM ALL TO COURT FOR THE TEN A.M...
--MONSTER, 'M TELLING YOU HE'S KE A GREEN HULKING MONSTER--
--DIDN'T DO ANYTHING I SWEAR TO GOD!!!
...FOLLOW THE ED LINE PAINTED ON THE FLOOR, TURN LEFT...
--JUST WANTED HIM TO PAY ME WHAT HE OWED--
--I DON'T DO FREEBIES, THAT'S WHY I CUT HIM--
HEY, MONTOYA!
OFFICER DOGNAVICH.
HEARD YOU GOT THE S.O.B. WHO DID KELLY.
HEARD YOU WORKED HIM OVER PRETTY GOOD.
GOOD JOB.
WHAT'S YOUR PROBLEM?

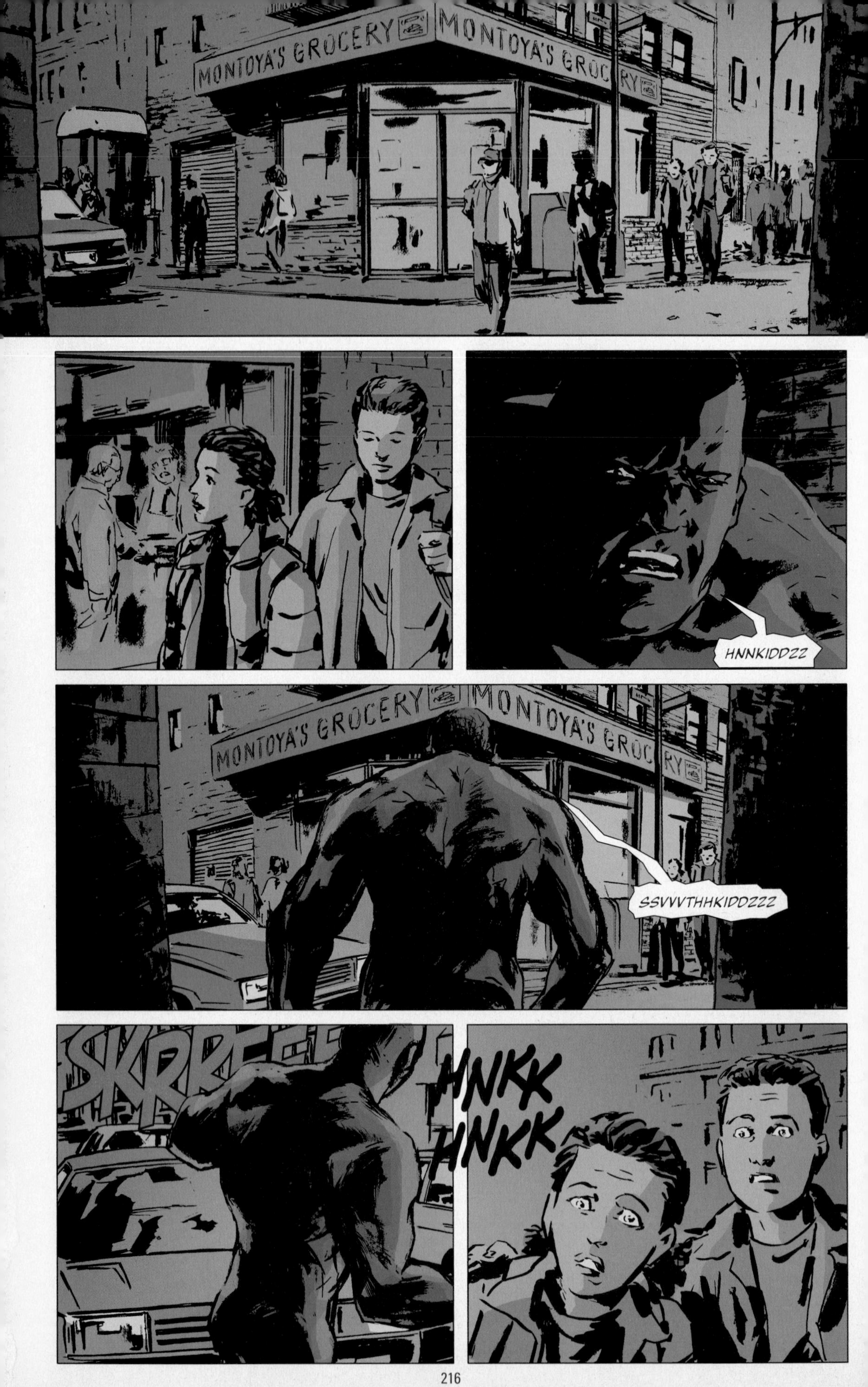
MONTOYA'S GROCERY
MONTOYA'S GROCERY
HNNKIDDZZ
MONTOYA'S GROCERY
MONTOYA'S GROCERY
SSVVVTHHKIDDZZZ
SKRREE
HNKK
HNKK

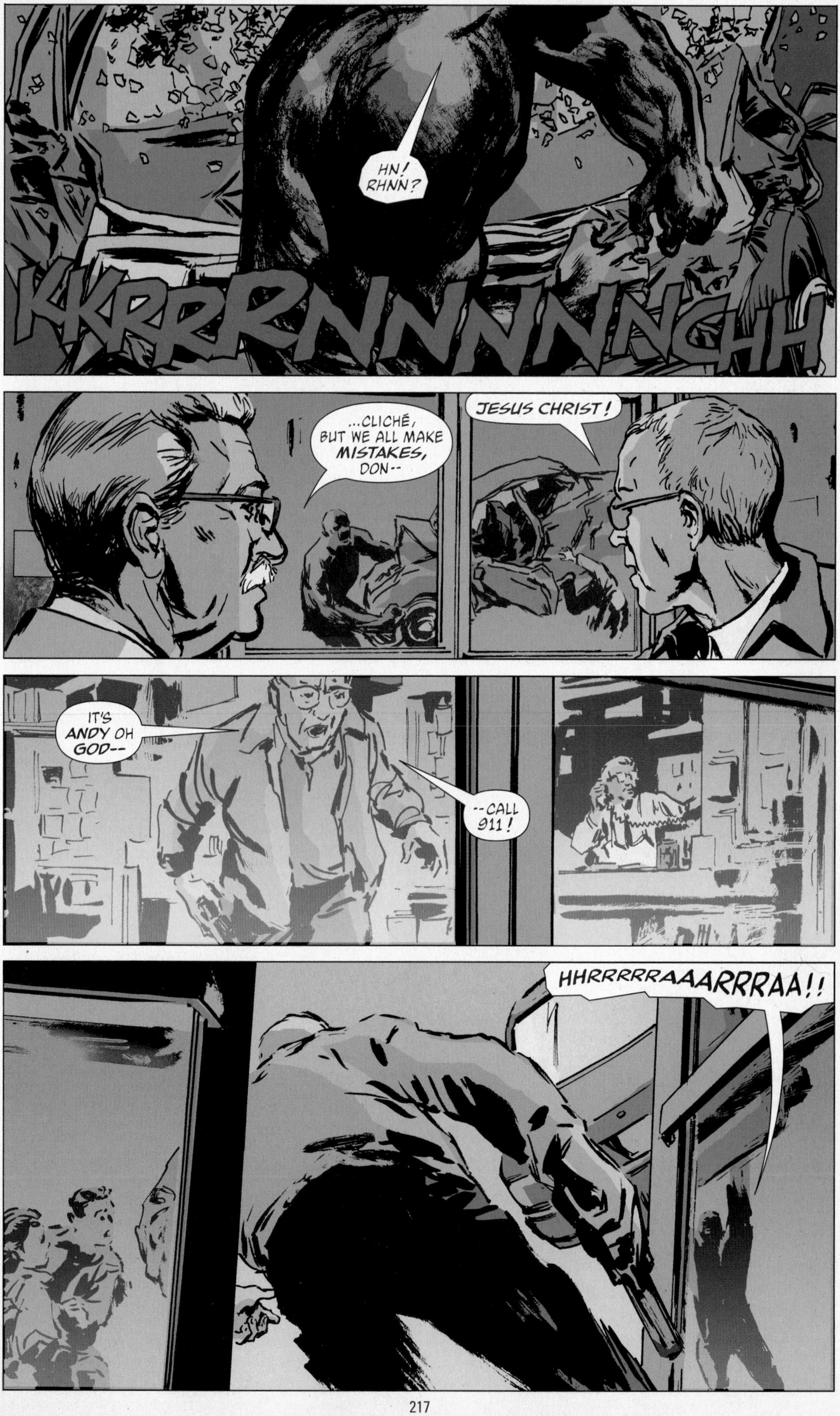
HN! RHNN?
KKRRRNNNNNCHH
...CLICHÉ, BUT WE ALL MAKE MISTAKES, DON--
JESUS CHRIST!
IT'S ANDY OH GOD--
--CALL 911!
HHRRRRRAAARRRAA!!

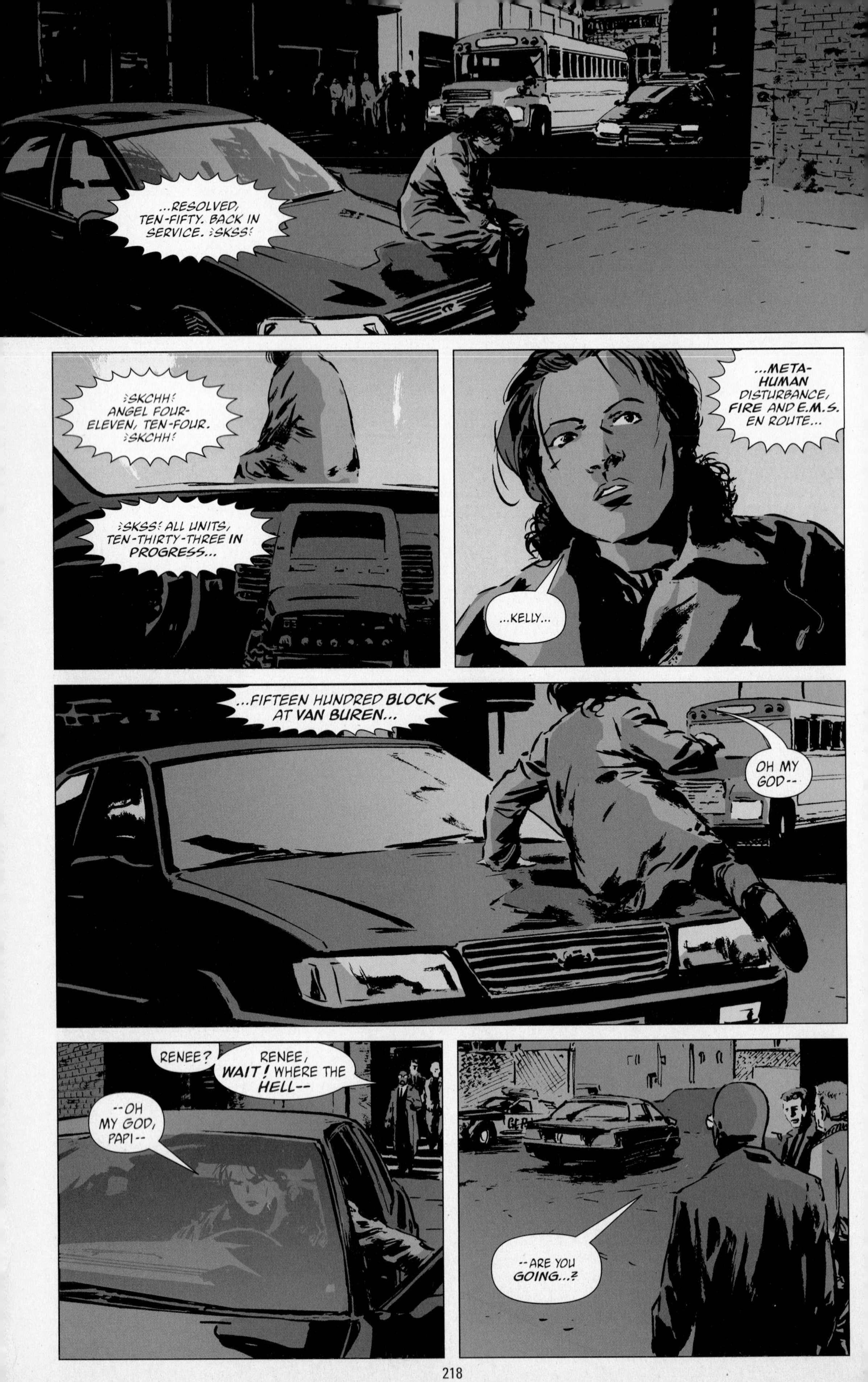
...RESOLVED, TEN-FIFTY. BACK IN SERVICE. ⸮SKSS⸮
⸮SKCHH⸮ ANGEL FOUR-ELEVEN, TEN-FOUR. ⸮SKCHH⸮
⸮SKSS⸮ ALL UNITS, TEN-THIRTY-THREE IN PROGRESS...
...META-HUMAN DISTURBANCE, FIRE AND E.M.S. EN ROUTE...
...KELLY...
...FIFTEEN HUNDRED BLOCK AT VAN BUREN...
OH MY GOD--
RENEE?
RENEE, WAIT! WHERE THE HELL--
--OH MY GOD, PAPI--
--ARE YOU GOING...?

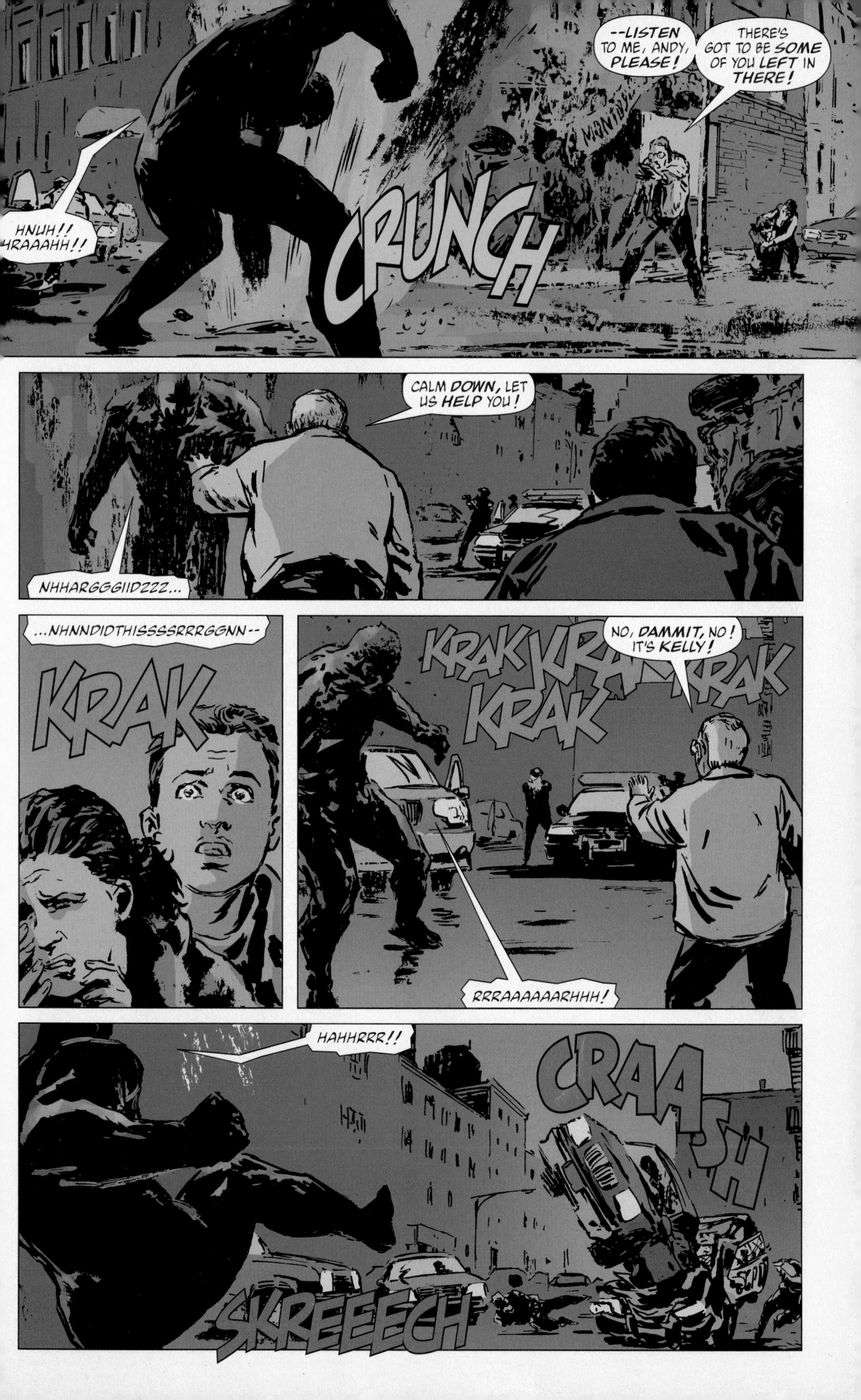
HNUH!! HRAAAHH!!
CRUNCH
--LISTEN TO ME, ANDY, PLEASE!
THERE'S GOT TO BE SOME OF YOU LEFT IN THERE!
CALM DOWN, LET US HELP YOU!
NHHARGGGIIDZZZ...
...NHNNDIDTHISSSSRRRGGNN--
KRAK
KRAK KRAK KRAK KRAK
NO, DAMMIT, NO! IT'S KELLY!
RRRAAAAAAARHHH!
HAHHRRR!!
CRAASH
SKREEEECH

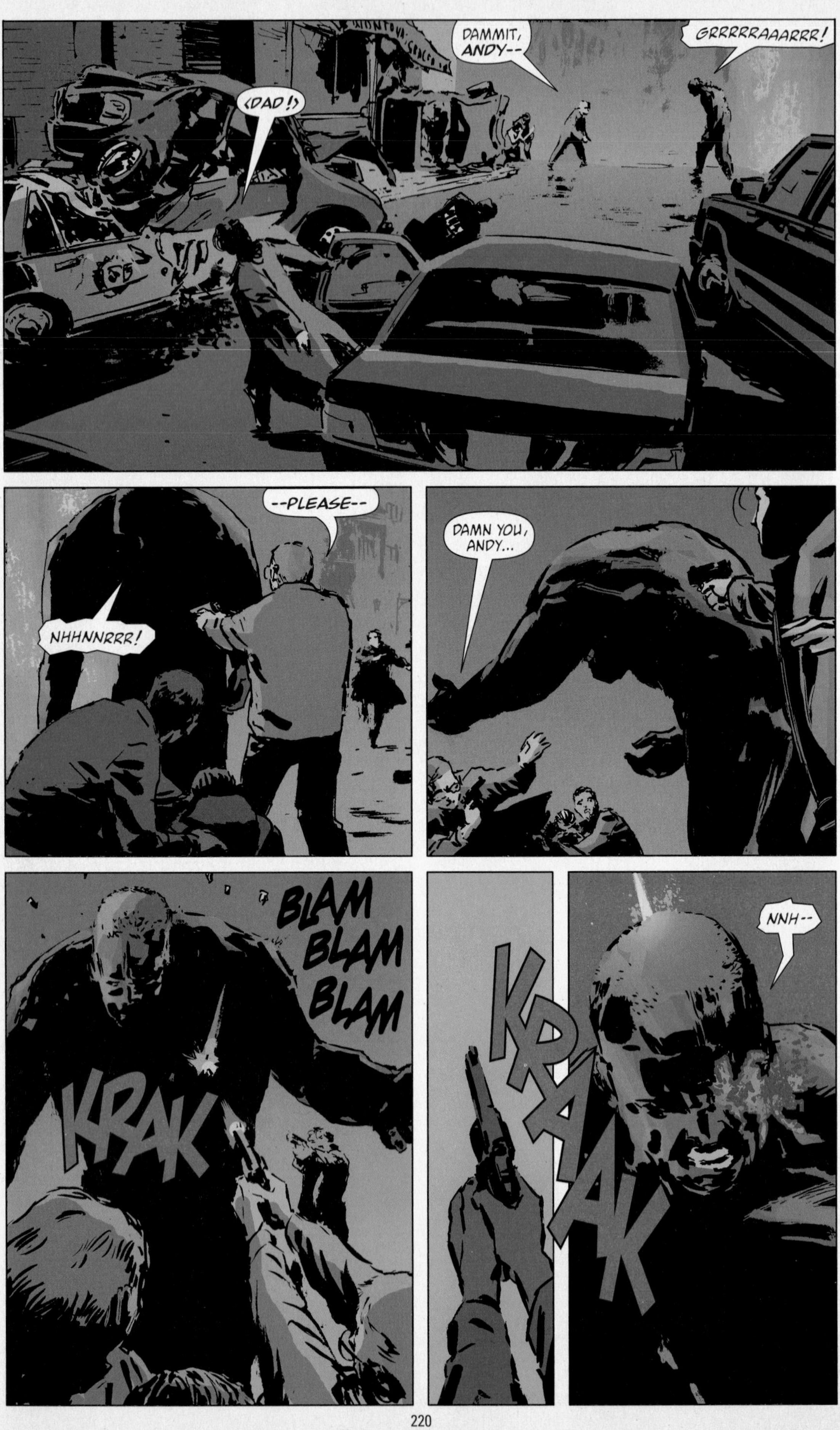
DAMMIT, ANDY--
GRRRRRAAARRR!
‹DAD!›
--PLEASE--
NHHNNRRR!
DAMN YOU, ANDY...
BLAM
BLAM
BLAM
KRAK
KRAAK
NNH--

--NNNN?

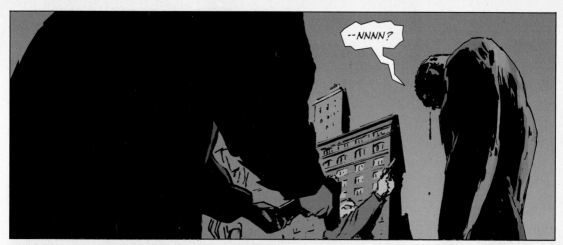

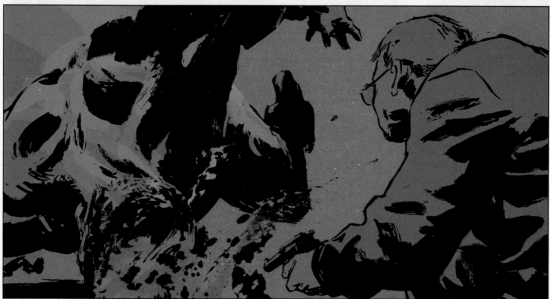

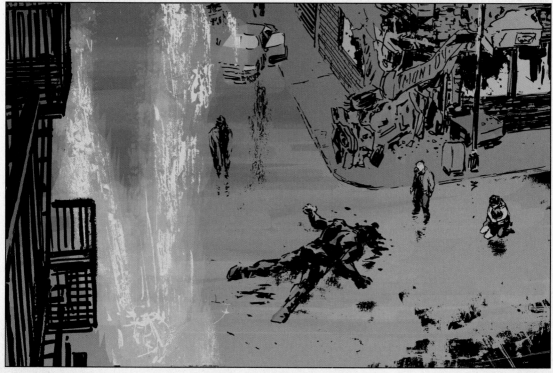

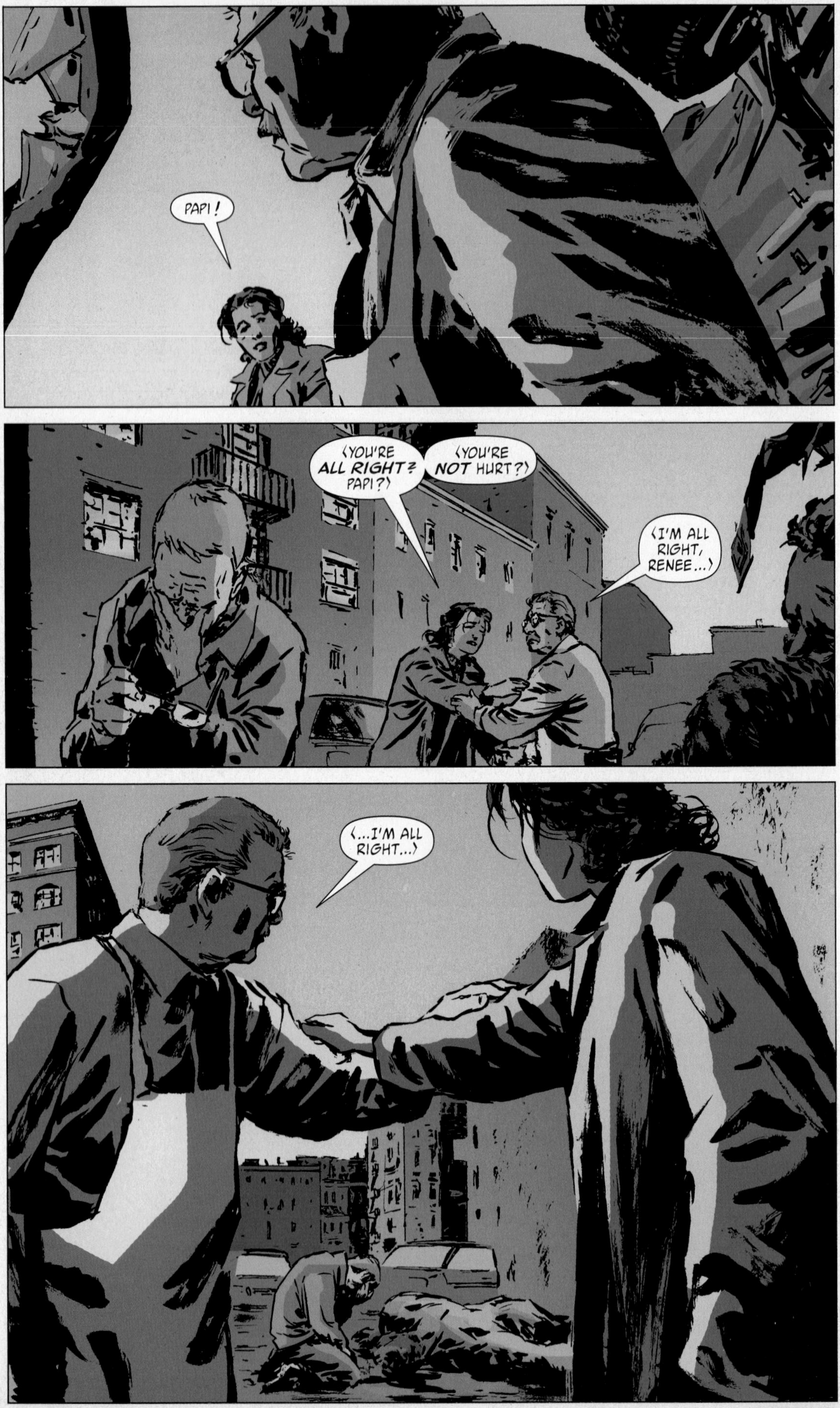
PAPI!
‹YOU'RE ALL RIGHT? PAPI?›
‹YOU'RE NOT HURT?›
‹I'M ALL RIGHT, RENEE...›
‹...I'M ALL RIGHT...›

THE END

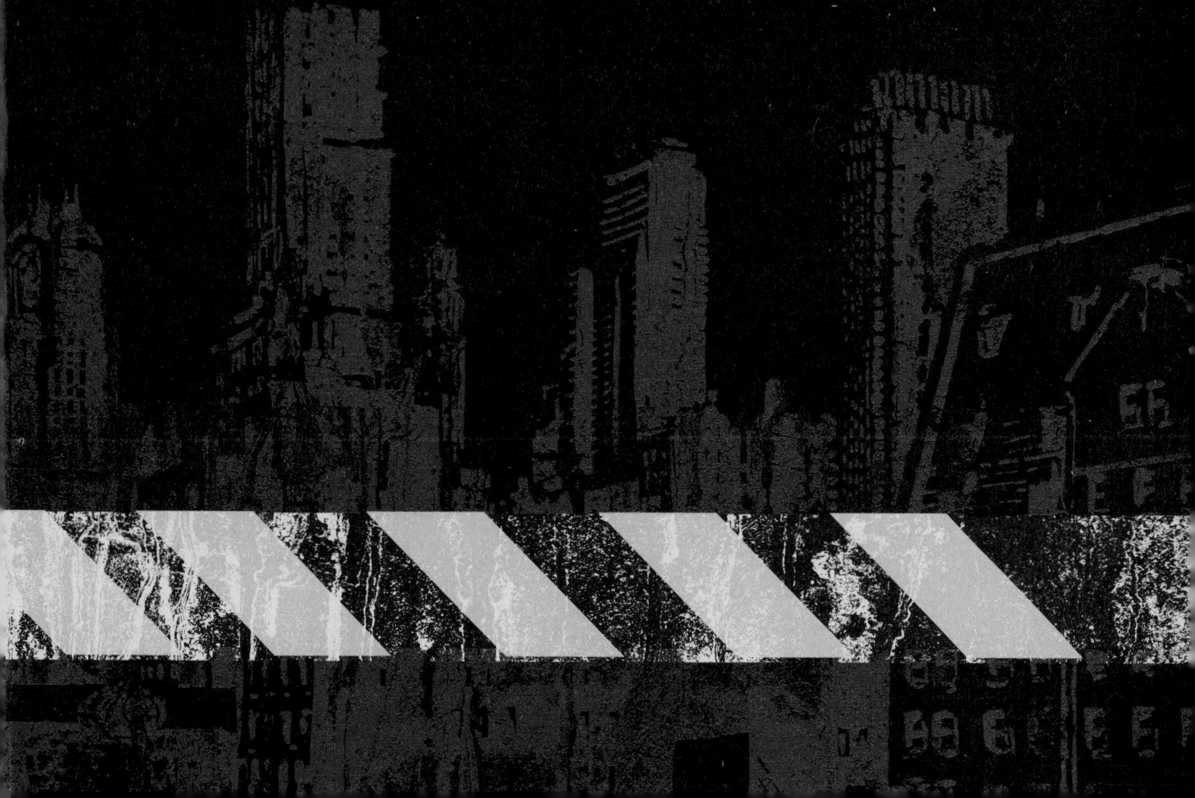

GREG RUCKA is the author of several novels, including *Finder, Keeper, Smoker, Shooting at Midnight, Critical Space,* and *Patriot Acts* (all of which feature the bodyguard character Atticus Kodiak), plus *Private Wars* and *A Gentleman's Game* (featuring the *Queen & Country* character Tara Chace), *A Fistful of Rain* and more.

In comics, he has written some of the most well known characters in the world, on titles such as BATMAN, WONDER WOMAN, *Wolverine,* and *Elektra.* Other work includes titles such as 52 (with Geoff Johns, Grant Morrison and Mark Waid), GOTHAM CENTRAL and *Daredevil* (with Ed Brubaker), CHECKMATE, and FINAL CRISIS: REVELATIONS. Currently he is writing DC's longest-running titles, ACTION COMICS and DETECTIVE COMICS.

His creator-owned comics include the award-winning *Queen & Country* and *Whiteout* (which is now a major motion picture starring Kate Beckinsale).

ED BRUBAKER is a one-time cartoonist whose early work in comics includes *Pajama Chronicles, Purgatory USA,* and *Lowlife.* He soon began predominantly writing comics, garnering attention for stories such as the Eisner Award-nominated "An Accidental Death," *The Fall,* and SCENE OF THE CRIME.

Brubaker began alternating his writing projects between DC's mainstream comics line, their mature-readers imprint Vertigo, and their WildStorm imprint. Some projects included BATMAN, DEADENDERS, SANDMAN PRESENTS: DEAD BOY DETECTIVES, CATWOMAN, SLEEPER, THE AUTHORITY, and GOTHAM CENTRAL (with Greg Rucka).

Currently, he is writing for Marvel Comics, including *Daredevil* and *Captain America* for their superhero line, and *Criminal* and *Incognito* for their Icon imprint.

MICHAEL LARK has been drawing his whole life, but his first published mainstream comics work was in 1994 — illustrating the Dean Motter-written TERMINAL CITY for Vertigo.

Since then, Lark's unique film noir style has been showcased in SCENE OF THE CRIME, LEGEND OF THE HAWKMAN, TERMINAL CITY: AERIAL GRAFFITI, SANDMAN MYSTERY THEATRE, SUPERMAN: WAR OF THE WORLDS, BATMAN: NINE LIVES, GOTHAM CENTRAL, *The Pulse,* and *Captain America.* Lark also has the honor of illustrating bestselling author Michael Chabon's first comics work, featured in JSA ALL STARS.

Currently, Lark is the artist on Marvel's *Daredevil* series, written by his GOTHAM CENTRAL comrade Ed Brubaker.

STEFANO GAUDIANO was born in Milan, Italy, and moved to the U.S. in the early '80s. Soon after, Gaudiano became a comic book artist and published the Eisner Award-nominated limited series *Kafka* (with Steven T. Seagle) while still in college. His art has since been featured in *Dark Horse Presents,* SANDMAN MYSTERY THEATRE, CATWOMAN, BATMAN: FAMILY, *Daredevil, The Pulse, Captain Marvel,* and many more books.

Gaudiano has also done art for other media, including storyboards for the likes of *Spider-Man Unlimited* and *Monster Mash,* as well as illustrations for roleplaying games like *HeroQuest.*